Gilchrist's Guide to Collectible Golf Book Prices

Roger E. Gilchrist

"Gilchrist's Guide to Collectible Golf Book Prices," by Roger E. Gilchrist. ISBN 978-1-949756-51-7 (softcover); 978-1-949756-92-0 (eBook).

Published 2019 by Virtualbookworm.com Publishing Inc., P.O. Box 9949, College Station, TX 77842, US. ©2019, Roger E. Gilchrist.

This book is dedicated to the memory of

MARK EMERSON

"The best friend a collector

could ever have."

I appreciate the many sources of the information included within

They include

PBA Galleries

Mullocks's Auction

Sports Pages

The Golf Auction

British Golf Collectors Society

Valuable Book Group

Irish Golf Archive

Artunderwraps

International Autograph Auctions

Golf Society of Australia

Pristine Auctions

Rare Book Hub

Amazon

Ausgolf

Berkelouw Books

Rare Book Cellar

Fine Golf Books

Pete Yagi Golf

Pure Golf Auction

Canadian Golf Hall of Fame

Alibris

Old Sports Auction

National Library of Ireland

Green Jacket Auction

Australian Golf Bibliography

Vintage Sports Authentics

Abe Books

eBay

British Columbia Golf House

Barter Books

World of Rare Books

Ash Rare Books

Foreword

The "Gilchrist's Price Guide to Golf Book Prices" is just that…. A Guide. The information contained herein was gleaned from a myriad of sources and depicted with the best of my ability. I have had to rely on the description of the original source as to the accuracy of the details. I have done my best to ascertain those details independently but was denied a second reference on many listings. The prices have been gathered over a ten-year period and some prices may have gone up while others have come down, but the prices notated are actual listed prices, either from auction or catalog prices. Edition numbers have been indicated where possible.

My focus was primarily on pre-1980 books with some specialized, or collectors' books in addition. The later may show the published price, but time, and the collector will determine the actual, demand price. The increase in demand for Club Histories did not go unnoticed and I have included as many as possible in this new volume.

Books as a category are not in as much demand as previously, although the rare, and the desirable, still command decent prices. Some authors are favored over others, and the prices of their books have remained higher than those of authors not favored by the collector.

Condition is everything and books with the correct dust jackets sell better than those without. I have thousands of books illustrated on my website and many are shown with, and without dust jackets to aid you in the identification of specific volumes.

Sellers have different pricing scales. Auction houses tend to receive books much desired and therefore selling prices are often higher than found elsewhere. Book prices are often inflated due to the demand of a collector wishing to add a prize book to his collection. The list of my sources shown on the next page may serve as a credible source for collectible books available at a wide difference in price.

The columns notate

Author – Title - Publication date – Approximate value

Should you have any suggestions, criticism, or information you wish to share do not hesitate to contact me at Roger@rogeregilchrist.com

AAA:
"Golf Courses of California" .... 1956 .... $15
A.B.:
"Told At The 19th Hole, Humorous St.
    Andrews Golfing Stories" .... 1928 .... $150
    Reprint.. 1975 .... $15
A.G.L:
"Golf Italia".. 1955 .... $45
A Keen Hand:
"The Golfer's Manual" .... 1857 ......$8,500
    Second Edition .... 1862 ......$4500
    Third Edition .... 1871 ......$2995
    Reprint (Darwin. 750 copies).............. 1947 .... $325
        50 cloth bound copies .... 1947 .... $900
    Reprint.. 1965 .... $95
A Member:
"The Duffers Golf Club Papers".................... 1891 .... $20,000
"St. Andrews to the Play" (300 Copies) .... 1994 .... $45
A Novice:
"On The Links...." .... 1889 ....$1250
"Shakespeare on Golf"............................... 1885 ....$2995
A Veteran:
"Golf for Occasional Players"....................... 1922 .... $125
B. R. Abbott:
"A Quiz Book Upon the USGA Rules of Golf".. 1914 .... $300
Aberdovey:
"Come to Aberdovey for Health and
    Recreation".................................... 1935 .... $100
Aberdovey G. C:
"Aberdovey Golf Club; A Round of 100 years"1986 .... $50
"Aberdovey Golf Club Centenary Brochure
    1892-1992" .... 1992 .... $25
Abersoch G. C:
"Abersoch Golf Club" .... 1966 .... $10
Aboyne G. C:
"Aboyne Golf Club 1893-1983" .... 1983 .... $25
Edward C. Acree:
"Golf Simplified" .... 1956 .... $25
David Adams:
"The Complete Golfer in Twelve Picture
    Lessons"... 1924 .... $375
Frederick U. Adams:
"John Henry Smith: A Golfing Romance" ..... 1905 .... $185

G. C. Adams:
"History of Barwon Heads Golf Club
    1907-1973" .... 1973 .... $75
Frederick U. Adams:
"John Henry Smith".................................. 1905 .... $60
Herbert Adams:
"The 19th Hole Mystery" .... 1939 .... $125
"The Body In The Bunker".......................... 1935 .... $18
"John Brand's Will".................................. 1933 .... $110
"Death Off The Fairway" .... 1936 .... $150
"Death On The First Tee" .... 1957 .... $200
"The Golf House Murder".......................... 1933 .... $200
"One To Play"... 1949 .... $150
"The Perfect Round: Tales of The Links" ...... 1927 .... $215
"The Secret of Bogey House" .... 1924 .... $230
John Adams:
"Huntercombe Golf Club 1900-1983" .... 1984 .... $35
"The Parks of Musselburgh" Leather Bound
    Presentation Copy Signed by Adams.... 1991 .... $450
    (125 copies)
    Limited Edition of 750 .... 1991 .... $150
Peter Adams:
"The Mayfield Country Club. 75th
    Anniversary 1911-1986".................... 1986 .... $50
Robert W. Adams:
"Timing Your Golf Swing" .... 1957 .... $25
"What Club Fits You?"............................... 1957 .... $10
Alistair B. Adamson:
"In The Winds Eye: North Berwick Golf Club" 1980 .... $350
"Millions of Mischiefs: Rabbits,
    Golf and St. Andrews" .... 1990 .... $30
    Ltd Ed of 500 signed .... 1990 .... $65
"Alan Robertson: His Life and Times" .... 1985 .... $95
    Leather Bound Review Edition of 12 ... 1985 .... $500
    Presentation Edition (55 Copies) .... 1985 .... $350
    Numbered Limited Edition of 1000 ..... 1985 .... $200
David Adamson:
"200 Years of Golf in Burntisland 1797-1997"1997 .... $45
Henry Adamson:
"The Muses Threnodie" .... 1774 ......$3500
Addington Palace G. C:
"Addington Palace Golf Club" .... 1934 .... $300
George Ade:
"Fables In Slang" .... 1900 .... $60

Aderley Edge G. C:
"Aderley Edge Golf Club"............................ 1960 .... $35
A Divotee:
"It's A Moral Beauty" .... 1923 .... $175
Ken Adwick:
"Alphabet of Golf" .... 1973 .... $10
"Dictionary of Golf" .... 1974 .... $10
"Golf"... 1975 .... $10
"X-Ray Way to Master Golf"........................ 1970 .... $20
F. G. Aflalo:
"The Sports of The World"........................... 1910 .... $95
Alfreton G. C:
"Allfreton Golf Club 1892-1992" .... 1992 .... $25
Agenda Club:
"The Rough and The Fairway"...................... 1922 ....$1495
George Aikman:
"Pen and Pencil Sketches on the Game of Golf" . 1888 .... $15,000
"A Round of The Links" .... 1893 .... $12,500
            Limited Edition Reprint .... 1980 .... $275
Air New Zealand:
"A Simpler Place in Time"........................... 1980 .... $25
Thomas S. Aitchison & George Lorimer:
"A Keen Hand: The Golfers Manual"............. 1857 ......$7,000
            Limited Edition of 750 reprint .... 1947 .... $450
            Reprint... 1965 .... $65
"Reminiscences of the Old Bruntsfield
            Links Golf Club 1866-1874"................ 1902 ....$1000
E. J. B. Akerman:
"The Leatherjackets Golfing Society
            1928-1949" .... 1949 .... $400
John Alanson:
"Ten Decades 1882-1982 The Australian
            Golf Club".. 1982 .... $75
Chuck Albury:
"Dunedin Country Club 1925-1970"............. 1970 .... $45
Amy Alcott:
"Golf Tips From Amy Alcott" .... 1983 .... $15
John Alenson:
"Ten Decades 1882-1982"........................... 1982 .... $65
Jules Alexander:
"The Hogan Mystique" .... 1994 .... $65
Peter Alfano:
"Grand Slam" .... 1973 .... $25

Helen Alfredson:
"A Good Swing Is Hard To Find" .... 1998 .... $15
Horatio Alger Jr:
"A Cousins Conspiracy" .... 1910 .... $35
"Andy Grant's Pluck" .... 1902 .... $45
"Harry Vane" .... 1911 .... $35
"The Telegraph Boy" .... 1911 .... $35
John C. Alicoate:
"Reference Year Book of Golf" .... 1971 .... $25
"Reference Year Book of Golf" .... 1972 .... $15
"Reference Year Book f Golf" .... 1973 .... $15
Allegheny C. C:
"Constitution, By Laws, and List of Members" 1919 .... $60
Frank K. Allen & Others:
"The Golfer's Bible" .... 1968 .... $10
Leslie Allen:
"Murder In The Rough" .... 1946 .... $75
Mark Allen:
"Royal Portrush Golf Club Coastal Erosion
          Appeal Fund" .... 1983 .... $10
Peter Allen:
"Famous Fairways" .... 1968 .... $150
"Play The Best Courses" .... 1973 .... $85
"The Sunley Book of Royal Golf" .... 1989 .... $45
Mark Allerton:
"The Girl on the Green" .... 1914 .... $225
"Golf Faults Remedied" .... 1911 .... $250
Mark Allerton & Robert Browning:
"Golf Made Easy" .... 1910 .... $150
Jane P. Alles:
"The History of the Philadelphia
          Country Club 1890-1965" .... 1965 .... $225
Benjamin R. Allison:
"The Rockaway Hunting Club" .... 1952 .... $100
Willie Allison:
"The First Golf Review" .... 1950 .... $50
Percy Alliss:
"Better Golf" .... 1926 .... $120
"Making Golf Easier" .... 1933 .... $85
Peter Alliss:
"Allis Through The Looking Glass" .... 1963 .... $35
"An Autobiography" .... 1981 .... $20
"Drive And Bunker Shot" .... 1955 .... $115
"The Duke" .... 1983 .... $50

Thousands of color book illustrations visible at
www.rogeregilchrist.com

"Golf - A Way of Life" .... 1989 .... $15
"The Golfer's Logbook" .... 1984 .... $15
"Lasting The Course" .... 1984 .... $35
"More Bedside Golf" .... 1982 .... $15
"Most Memorable Golf" .... 1986 .... $15
"The Open: The British Open
        Championship Since The War" .... 1984 .... $30
"Peter Alliss' Bedside Book" .... 1980 .... $30
"Peter Alliss's 100 Greatest Golfers" .... 1989 .... $20
"Play Golf With Peter Allis" .... 1977 .... $25
"The Best of Golf" .... 1989 .... $15
"The Supreme Champions of Golf"............... 1986 .... $20
"The Good Golf Guide"............................... 1986 .... $20
"The Shell Book of Golf"............................. 1981 .... $70
"The Who's Who of Golf"............................ 1983 .... $35
"Yet More Beside Golf"............................... 1985 .... $10
Peter Alliss & Alec Allis:
"The Parkstone Golf Club" .... 1965 .... $45
Peter Alliss & Bob Ferrier:
"The Best of Golf" .... 1989 .... $20
Alliss, Dobereiner, McCormack & Palmer:
"The Fifty Greatest Golfers"........................ 1985 .... $55
        Leather Bound edition .... 1985 .... $125
Peter Alliss & Paul Trevillion:
"Easier Golf"... 1969 .... $15
Peter Alliss & Michael Wade:
"The Lazy Golfer's Companion" .... 1995 .... $20
All Weather Golf:
"All Weather Golf Practices"........................ 1927 .... $75
Alpert, Mothner, & Schonberg:
"How To Play Double Bogey Golf" .... 1975 .... $15
Alston G. C:
"Alston Golf Club Yearbook 1900"............... 1900 .... $35
Amateur Golfers Association:
"Directory of Amateur Golfers, Volume 1
        Arizona, Nevada And Utah" .... 1976 .... $35
Amazing Golf Ball:
"The Amazing Golf Ball" .... 1978 .... $10
Charles Ambrose:
"The West Sussex Golf Club and Course"...... 1938 .... $65
American Annual:
"American Annual And Golf Guide
        and Year Book" .... 1916 .... $275

American Golf Foundation:
"Example Golf Club By-Laws"....................... 1947 .... $25
"A Golf Club Is A Business"......................... 1944 .... $40
"How To Secure More Members" .... 1946 .... $40
"Suggestions For Golf Club By-Laws" .... 1948 .... $30
"What Is The American Golf Foundation" ...... 1945 .... $40
American Golfer Magazine:
"Twelve Golf Lessons" .... 1929 .... $30
American Society Of Golf Course Architects:
"Master Planning: The Vital First Steps
    In Golf Course Construction" .... 1977 .... $25
"Planning The Municipal Golf Course".......... 1976 .... $30
"Planning The Real Estate Development
    Golf Course" .... 1977 .... $35
"Selecting Your Golf Course Architect" .... 1977 .... $25
William W. Amick:
"The Executive Golf Course" .... 1975 .... $10
John H. Amys:
"The Albany: A Celebration of the Centennial
    of the Albany Club of Toronto"............ 1981 .... $75
Carlyle E. Anderson:
"Glen View Club 1897-1982" .... 1982 .... $25
Harold A. Anderson & Others:
"Golf Club Construction: Design, Fitting, Repair"1968 ...... $10
Johnny M. Anderson:
"Better Golf -The Mental Approach to Winning"1980 .... $30
Robert Anderson:
"A Funny Thing Happened
    On The Way To The Clubhouse" .... 1971 .... $10
"Heard At The Nineteenth" .... 1966 .... $20
Willie Anderson:
"A Perfect Drive"....................................... 1910 .... $450
Thomas Anderson-Davis:
"The Ryder Cup Heritage" .... 1972 .... $35
Richard Andre:
"Colonel Bogey's Sketch Book" .... 1897 .... $750
"Golf Plays And Recitations" .... 1904 .....$2,000
Dale Andreason:
"Simplified Golf" .... 1960 .... $25
Gene Andrews:
"Scientific Analysis of The Plumb Bob
    Method of Reading Greens"................. 1968 .... $5
Andrews, Page & Sheehan:
"Ballycastle Golf Club 1890-1990" .... 1990 .... $20

50 Miles of Golf Around London

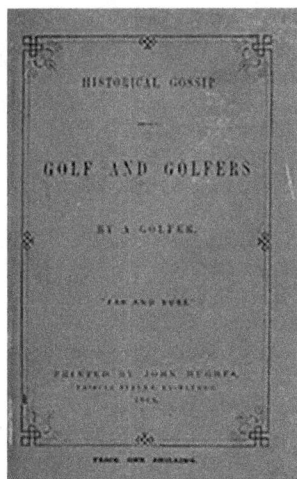

A Golfer – Historical Gossip
Golf and Golfers

A Keen Hand – The Golfers
Manual (1st Edition)

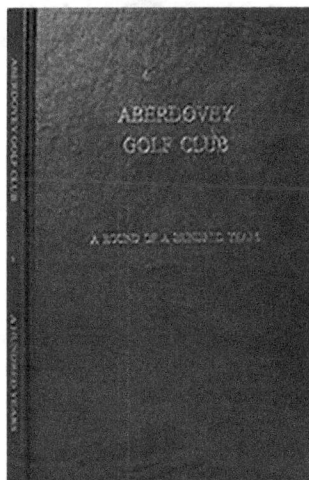

Aberdovey G. C. - A Round of
100 Years

Thousands of color book illustrations visible at
www.rogeregilchrist.com

Julia L. Andrews:
"Golf: A Play In Two Acts" .... 1902 .... $250
Major Angas:
"The Golf Swing In The Plural" .... 1962 .... $10
Anndandale G. C:
"Annandale Golf Club 75th Anniversary
1906-1981" .... 1981 .... $30
An Old Golfer:
"Golf On A Principle".................................. 1897 ......$1,125
Anonymous:
"Told At The 19ᵗʰ Hole" .... 1931 .... $135
Anstruther G. C:
"Anstruther Golf Club" .... 1953 .... $30
"Anstruther Golf Club 1890-1990" .... 1990 .... $45
Greg Anthony:
"Building Clubhead Speed, Leverage, and
Centrifugal Force in the Golf Swing" .... 1985 .... $10
Apawamis G. C:
"The Apawamis Tradition 1890-1965" .... 1965 .... $45
Audrey Apple:
"History of Richmond Country Club
1924-1978" .... 1978 .... $65
Des Appleton & Dave Hutton:
"Warrington Golf Club 1903-2003" .... 2003 .... $15
April In Augusta:
"Masters Week, April 1-7" .... 1963 .... $75
Arboath G. C:
"Arboath Golf Club".................................. 1920 .... $150
James Arbuckle:
"Glotta".. 1721 ......$8,000
Ardsley C. C:
"Ardsley Club 1929" .... 1929 .... $125
Angelo Argea:
"The Bear And I"....................................... 1979 .... $55
Ardglass G. C:
Ardglass Golf Club Centenary 1896-1996" .... 1996 .... $30
Reginald Arkell:
"Playing The Games" .... 1935 .... $55
Armed Forces G. C:
"Courtesy: The First Rule of Golf .... 1965 .... $35
J. C. Armitage:
"The 100th Open Championship Held at Royal
Birkdale Golf Club" (1000 Copies) .... 1971 .... $70

Richard Armour:
"Golf Bawls" .... 1946 .... $15
"Golf Is A Four Letter Word" .... 1962 .... $15
Tommy Armour:
"Tommy Armour Speaks" .... 1960 .... $15
"Tommy Armour Tells You How To
    Play Your Best Golf" .... 1956 .... $15
"Tommy Armour's ABC of Golf" .... 1967 .... $25
"How To Play Your Best Golf All The Time".... 1953 .... $55
    Reprint... 1985 .... $20
"Play Better Golf: The Drive" .... 1964 .... $15
"Play Better Golf: The Irons" .... 1963 .... $15
"A Round of Golf With Tommy Armour" .... 1959 .... $45
Army Navy C. C:
"Army Navy Country Club 1924-1989" .... 1989 .... $70
Henry Arnell:
"Royal Ashdown Forest Golf Club:
    1888-1988" .... 1988 .... $35
A. E. Arnold:
"Putting And Spared Shots" .... 1939 .... $65
John Arnold:
"Riversdale Golf Club: A History 1892-1977". 1977 .... $85
Arran Golf Guide:
"Arran Golf Guide" .... 1985 .... $10
Allan Arthur:
"The Country Club, Its First 75 Years
    1889-1964" .... 1964 .... $75
Jim Arthur:
"Practical Greenkeeping"............................ 1997 .... $35
Artists & Writers Golf Association:
"Artists And Writers Golf Association 1935"... 1935 .... $75
"Artists And Writers Golf Association 1948"... 1948 .... $95
Ashburnham G. C:
"Ashburnham Golf Club 1894-1969" .... 1969 .... $95
Ashford Manor C. C:
"History of The Ashford Manor Golf Club" ..... 1966 .... $65
M. J. Astle:
"The Principles of Golf" .... 1923 .... $75
"The PGA World Golf Hall of Fame Book" ...... 1991 .... $30
Ashton-On-Rible G. C:
"Rules of the Ashton-On-Ribble Golf Club" .... 1910 .... $65
J. Aspin:
"Ancient Customs, Sports and Pastimes,
    of the English..." .... 1835 .... $250

Thousands of color book illustrations visible at
www.rogeregilchrist.com

Anthony Atha:
"The World of Golf...................................... 1997 .... $20
Howie Atten:
"Chatten With Atten On Golf"...................... 1959 .... $15
Auchterarder G. C:
"Auchterarder Golf Club 1892-1992"........... 1992 .... $45
Audubon Society:
"Golf Clubs as Bird Sanctuaries"................. 1923 ......$2500
Augusta National G. C:
"By Laws" .... 1979 .... $50
"Records of the Masters Tournament
    1934-1947" .... 1848 .... $175
"The Masters: The First Forty-One Years" ..... 1978 .... $175
"Arnold Palmer's Scrapbook" .... 1964 .... $200
"Portraits: Early Members of the Augusta
    National Golf Club"........................... 1962 .... $325
Dick Aultman:
"101 Ways To Win" .... 1980 ....$5
"Better Golf In Six Swings"......................... 1982 .... $15
"Bob Toski's Guide To Better Golf"............... 1975 .... $20
"Golf Digest's Golf Primer"......................... 1977 .... $10
"Learn To Play Golf" .... 1969 .... $10
"The Square-To-Square Golf Swing" .... 1970 .... $15
Dick Aultman & Ken Bowden:
"Masters of Golf: Learning From
    Their Methods"................................. 1976 .... $25
"The Methods of the Golf Masters"............... 1975 .... $25
    Classics of Golf Reprint..................... 1987 .... $20
E. C. Austen-Leigh:
"Clubs in 1938" .... 1938 .... $80
Austin, Codyre & Morgan:
"Delgany Golf Club Centenary 2008"........... 2008 .... $25
Automobile Association:
"AA Guide To Golf In Great Britain" .... 1977 .... $10
Automobile Club of Southern California:
"Golf Courses of California and Nevada" .... 1962 .... $40
Automobile Green Book:
"New England States, Canada and
    Trunk Lines West and East"................ 1925 .... $100
"New England States, Canada and
    Trunk Lines West and South" .... 1928 .... $75
L. B. Ayton:
"How To Play Worthing Golf Course"............ 1951 .... $25

Ayton; Collett; Diegel; Farrell Etc:
"Golf As Champions Play It".......................... 1928 .... $95
Paul Azinger:
"A Champions Story".................................. 1995 .... $20
C. J. B. & P. S. W.:
"Horace On The Links".............................. 1903 .... $750
E. M. B. & G. R. T.:
"Humors And Emotions of Golf".................... 1905 .... $675
R. De C. B.:
"Golf Ballistics" .... 1941 .... $30
Sarah Baddiel:
"Beyond The Links" .... 1992 .... $40
"Golf The Golden Years"............................. 1989 .... $25
"Golfing Ephemera"................................... 1991 .... $30
"Millers Golf Memorabilia" .... 1994 .... $25
The Badminton Library:
"The Badminton Magazine of Sports &
    Pastimes" .... 1890 .... $450
Raymond Baert:
"Adventures Of Monsieur DuPont,
    Golf Champion" .... 1913 .... $850
Carlisle Bargeron:
"The Congressional Story"......................... 1957 .... $125
Baffy:
"Golf Problems" .... 1928 .... $125
Baguio C. C:
"The Baguio Country Club, Baguio Philippine
    Islands".. 1910 .... $175
George Bahto:
"The Evangelist of Golf" .... 2002 .... $450
George Bahato & Dane Bath:
"The Legend of The Knoll" .... 1993 .... $35
Baildon G. C:
"Baildon Golf Club 1896-1996".................... 1996 .... $20
Bill Bailey:
"Executive Golf: How To Win Big"................ 1985 .... $10
Charles W. Bailey:
"The Brain and Golf".................................. 1923 .... $350
    First American Edition .... 1924 .... $200
"The Professor on the Golf Links" .... 1925 .... $225
John W. Bailey:
"Enthusiastic Amateur Golfer Wanders
    The World" .... 1965 .... $45

Hugh Baillie:
"Golf at the Back of Beyond" .... 2000 .... $20
Archie Baird:
"Golf On Gullane Hill" .... 1982 .... $65
500 copies Signed .... 1982 .... $150
Frederick R. Baird:
"Crystal Downs Golf Club" .... 1981 .... $30
Baird, McIntosh & Koch:
"Westmount Golf and Country Club
1931-1981" .... 1981 .... $50
Arlene Baker And Elaine Lustig:
"Golf: To Play This Game You Gotta
Have Balls And Clubs And Trees" .... 1984 .... $10
Stephen Baker:
"How To Play Golf In The Low 120s" .... 1962 .... $25
Bald Peak C. C:
"Bald Peak Country Club" .... 1920 .... $750
J. Stuart Balfour:
"Spalding's Athletic Library: Golf" .... 1893 .... $3000
James Balfour:
"Reminiscences of Golf On St. Andrews
Links" .... 1887 .... $7000
Limited Edition Reprint of 300 .... 1982 .... $325
Classics of Golf reprint...................... 1987 .... $35
George Balharrie:
"A Centenary History of the Thornhill
Golf Club 1893-1993" .... 1993 .... $35
Brian Ball:
"Death of a Low Handicapped Man" .... 1978 .... $25
Ron Ball:
"Wagga Wagga Golf Club 100 Years of Golf
1895-1995" .... 1995 .... $45
T. A. Ball:
"Anleitung zum Golfspielen" .... 1928 .... $150
"Le Golf"... 1950 .... $95
R. E. Ballantine:
"How To Play Ganton Golf Course".............. 1952 .... $15
Eric H. Ballard:
"The Story of South Herts Golf Club" .... 1987 .... $45
Jimmy Ballard:
"How To Perfect Your Golf Swing"................ 1981 .... $35
Ballater G. C:
"Ballater Golf Club" .... 1980 .... $25

Severiano Ballesteros:
"Seve Tours: Golf Tours of Spain" .... 1982 .... $15
"Natural Golf" .... 1988 .... $25
"Trouble Shooting" .... 1994 .... $20
Severiano Ballesteros & Dudley Doust:
"Seve: The Young Champion" .... 1982 .... $20
Ballinasloe G.C:
Garbally to Rossgloss" .... 1994 .... $35
Michael Bamburger:
"The Green Road Home" .... 1986 .... $35
"To The Linksland" .... 1992 .... $35
Ian Bamford:
"Royal Portrush Golf Club A History
    1888-1988" .... 1988 .... $95
M. L. Bandeville:
"Le Parcours de Golf" .... 1928 .... $135
Ford Banes:
"Right Down The Fairway" .... 1947 .... $25
Banf G. C:
"The Book of The Banf Golf Club Bazaar" ...... 1895 .... $2000
John K. Bangs:
"The Enchanted Typewriter" .... 1899 .... $65
Colin C. Bannatyne:
"The Shiskine Golf & Tennis Club. A History
    1896-1996" .... 1996 .... $45
Miles Bantock:
"On Many Greens: A Book of Golf
    and Golfers" .... 1901 .... $500
Jerry Barber:
"The Art of Putting" .... 1967 .... $15
Miller Barber & Others:
"Top Tips From Senior Pros" .... 1990 .... $20
Ralph E. Barbour:
"The Half Back-A Story of School Football
    and Golf" .... 1907 .... $95
James Barclay:
"Golf In Canada" .... 1992 .... $45
R. Barclay:
"A Batch of Golfing Papers By Andrew Lang
    and Others" .... 1892 .... $375
John D Bardwell:
"A History of the Country Club at York,
    Maine" .... 1988 .... $75

Thousands of color book illustrations visible at
www.rogeregilchrist.com

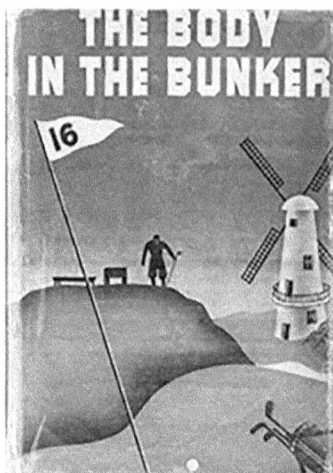

Adams – The Body in the
Bunker

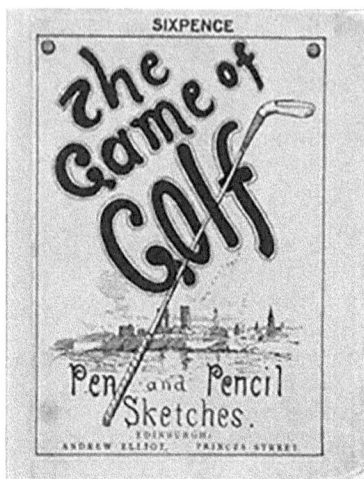

Aikman – The Game of Golf

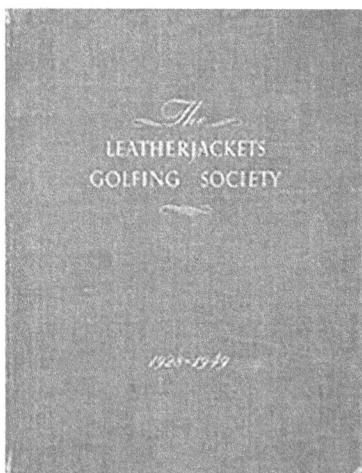

Akerman – The Leatherjackets
Golfing Society 1928-1949

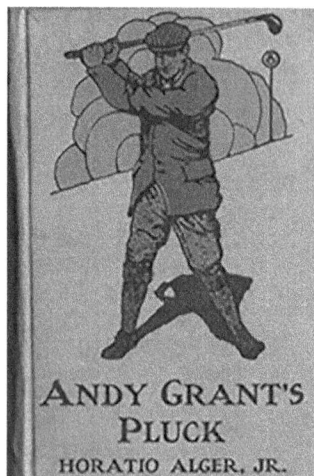

Alger – Andy Grant's Pluck

Reg Barker:
"Eighteen Forever" .... 1959 .... $10
Roland Barker:
"The Bass River Golf Club 1900-1974" .... 1974 .... $30
Al Barkow:
"Getting To The Dance Floor" .... 1986 .... $30
"Golf's Golden Grind: The History
    of The Tour" .... 1974 .... $30
"The History of The PGA Tour" .... 1989 .... $30
Al Barkow & David Barrett
"Golf Legends of All Time" .... 1998 .... $20
Al Barkow & Others:
"20th Century Golf Chronicle" .... 1993 .... $30
Raymond G. Barlow:
"Golf For The Beginner and Confused" .... 1954 .... $10
Jackson W. Barnaby:
"The History of The Sorrento Golf Club" .... 1974 .... $25
"The History of The Royal Melbourne
    Golf Club, 1941-1968" .... 1972 .... $80
"The History of The Canadian Open at
    Glenn Abby" .... 1984 .... $35
James M. Barnes:
"A Guide to Good Golf" .... 1925 .... $95
"Picture Analysis Of Golf Strokes" .... 1919 .... $250
Kamdene, Barnesburie & D'Alston:
"Tour In The North" .... 1894 .... $95
Frank H. Barnett:
"A Brief History of Claremont Country Club" .. 1960 .... $25
Ted Barnett:
"Golf Is Madness" .... 1977 .... $15
Howard Barney:
"The Country Club of Mobile: A History of
    the First Hundred Years" .... 1999 .... $35
Roy W. Barnhill:
"Golf in Bermuda" .... 1926 .... $650
Harry Baron:
"Golf Resorts of The U.S.A." .... 1967 .... $30
"NBC Sports Guide 1967" .... 1967 .... $5
Art Barr Jr:
"Foibles of The Links" .... 1999 .... $15
Michael Barratt:
"Golf With Tony Jacklin" .... 1978 .... $10
Les Barrett:
"From Tyne Green to the Spital 1892-1992... 1992 .... $50

Ted Barrett & Micheal Hobbs:
"The Ultimate Encyclopedia of Golf"............. 1995 .... $25
Wilfred Barrett:
"Links with the Past: The Story of the
        Harrogate Golf Club" .... 1991 .... $25
James Barrie:
"Historical Sketch of The Hawick Golf Club" .. 1898 .... $950
Smith Barrier:
"GCO: The First Forty-Four Years"............... 1982 .... $10
"GGO 50th Anniversary Book 1938-1988" ..... 1988 .... $25
John Barrington:
"The U.S. Golfer's Handbook" .... 1958 .... $45
Leonard Barron:
"Lawn Making" .... 1906 .... $175
"Lawn Making" .... 1923 .... $125
"Lawn Making... .... 1928 .... $75
Hugh C. Barry:
"Elanora, A History of Elanora Country Club". 1977 .... $20
Charles Bartlett:
"Chicago Golf Club Diamond Jubilee
        1892-1967" .... 1967 .... $25
"The New 1969 Golfer's Almanac" .... 1969 .... $10
James Bartlett:
"Death From The Ladies Tees" .... 1992 .... $20
"Death Is A Two Stroke Handicap"............... 1991 .... $20
"Golf Gurus"... 1996 .... $20
Michael Bartlett:
"Bartlett's World Golf Encyclopedia"............. 1973 .... $25
"The Golf Book" .... 1980 .... $25
"Celebrating One Hundred Years:
        Skokie Country Club 1897-1997" .... 1997 .... $85
Edmond P. Bartnett:
"Seventy Years of Wykagyl 1898-1968" .... 1968 .... $65
John Barton & Hunki Yun:
"Golf On The Web" .... 1997 .... $15
Pam Barton:
"A Stroke A Hole"..................................... 1938 .... $85
Charles T. Bassler & Nevin H. Gibson:
"You Can Play Par Golf" .... 1966 .... $15
E. A. Batchelor Jr.:
"In Good Company. A Centenial History of the
        Country Club of Detroit 1897-1979" .... 1978 .... $60
Gerald Batchelor:
"Golf Stories" .... 1914 .... $395

Graham Bateman:
"Selkirk Golf Club 1883-1983, A
    Century of Golf In Selkirk" .... 1983 .... $35
Henry M. Bateman:
"Adventures At Golf" .... 1923 .... $425
    Reprint... 1977 .... $20
"Brought Forward: A Further Collection of
    Drawings"... 1931 .... $350
Peter Bathurst & John Behrend:
"The Oxford & Cambridge Golf Society"
    (750 Copies) .... 1997 .... $250
    Limited Edition of 150 .... 1997 .... $675
Bath G. C:
"Bath Golf Club Centenary Festival
    1880-1980" .... 1980 .... $30
Jack Batten:
"Rosedale: The First 100 Years of the
    Rosedale Golf Club" .... 1993 .... $65
"The Toronto Golf Club 1876-1976"............. 1976 .... $85
C. Robertson Bauchope:
"The Golfing Annual" .... 1888 .... $800
Aleck Bauer:
"Hazards" .... 1913 ......$8,250
    Reprint (750 Copies) .... 1993 .... $250
    Reprint (100 Copies signed by 4) .... 1993 .... $375
Dave Bauer:
"Golf Techniques of The Bauer Sisters" .... 1951 .... $55
Ernest A. Baughman:
"How To Caddie"...................................... 1914 .... $700
John E. Baxter:
"Locker Room Ballads".............................. 1923 .... $145
Peter Baxter:
"Golf In Perth And Perthshire"..................... 1899 ......$4,500
Steven Baxter:
"Frilford Heath Golf Club 1908-2008 .... 2008 .... $45
Dan Bayless:
"Riviera's Fifty Golden Years"...................... 1976 .... $90
Dick Beach & Bob Ford:
"Golf: The Body, The Mind, The Game" .... 1992 .... $45
Reginald Beale:
"Lawns for Sport"..................................... 1924 .... $200
"The Practical Greenkeeper" .... 1914 ....$1975
    Fourth American Edition .... 1932 .... $900

S. G. Hulme Beaman:
  "The Adventures of Larry The Lamb" .... 1935 .... $175
Peter Beames:
  "Walk Thru To Par".................................... 1984 .... $5
Frank Beard:
  "Making The Turn" .... 1992 .... $15
  "Pro: Frank Beard On The Golf Tour" .... 1970 .... $15
  "Shaving Strokes"..................................... 1970 .... $15
Frank Beard, Harriet Beard, & David Martin:
  "Turfgrass Bibliography From 1672-1972" .... 1977 .... $45
Henry Beard:
  "The Official Exceptions To The Rules of Golf" 1992 .... $10
Henry Beard & Roy McKie:
  "Golfing: A Duffers Dictionary".................... 1987 .... $10
James B. Beard:
  "Turfgrass: Science and Culture"................. 1973 .... $150
James B. Beard & Harriet J. Beard:
  "Turfgrass Bibliography from 1672 to 1972" . 1977 .... $175
John B. Beardwood:
  "History of The Los Angeles Country Club
    1898-1973"..................................... 1973 .... $225
Chauncey H. Beasley:
  "Golf In Latin" .... 1954 .... $15
  "The Magnificent Golf Foursome"................. 1977 .... $125
  "The Most Difficult Golf Course In America" .. 1966 .... $10
James Beattie:
  "The Club Toter" .... 1929 .... $60
Alfred Beck:
  "Hints On Golf For Everyone"...................... 1925 .... $140
Fred Beck:
  "89 Years In A Sand Trap"......................... 1965 .... $20
  "To H*!! With Golf" .... 1956 .... $20
Fred Beck & O. K. Barnes:
  "73 Years In A Sand Trap"......................... 1949 .... $25
Myron Beck:
  "Golf Tales"... 1991 .... $20
Harland A. Becker:
  "The Knack of Golf" .... 1952 .... $75
    Limited Edition of 250 copies.............. 1952 ....$450
James Becker & Andrew Mayer:
  "Golf Courses You Will never Play"............... 1995 .... $15
Judy Beckton:
  "The History of Golf In Ripon 1891-1995"..... 1996 .... $15

J. P. Beckwith:
"The Golf Links Located In Florida
and Nassau" .... 1900 .... $3000
Lew Bedell:
"Every Golfer Should Have One" .... 1965 .... $10
Bedford And County G. C:
"The Bedford and County Golf Club" .... 1938 .... $150
"The Bedford Golf and Tennis 1891-1991" .... 1991 .... $100
Jane A. Beever:
"The History of Philadelphia Country
Club 1890-1990" .... 1990 .... $20
Harold Begbie:
"J. H. Taylor, Or, The Inside of a Week" .... 1925 .... $750
Anthony Begley:
"History of Bundoran Golf Club 1894-1994" .. 1994 .... $65
Max J. Behr:
"What Is Amateurism?" .... 1917 .... $50
John Behrend:
"John Ball of Hoylake -Champion Golfer"
Limited edition of 1800 .... 1989 .... $100
100 Presentation Copies .... 1989 .... $450
"St. Andrew's Night And Other Golfing Stories"
(900 Copies) .... 1992 .... $65
30 Presentation Copies .... 1992 .... $250
"Odes and Reminiscences" .... 2003 .... $100
"The Amateur: The Story of The Amateur
Golf Championship 1885-1995" .... 1995 .... $45
Limited Edition of 75 signed .... 1995 .... $325
John Behrend & John Graham:
"Golf At Hoylake, A Royal Liverpool Golf Club
Anthology" .... 1990 .... $75
Limited Edition of 125 signed .... 1990 .... $275
John Behrend & Peter N Lewis:
"Challenges And Champions The Royal And
Ancient Golf Club 1754-1883"
(275 Copies) .... 1998 .... $500
Limited Edition of 1750 .... 1998 .... $125
Behrend, Lewis & Mackie:
"Champions and Guardians 1884-1939"
(275 Copies) .... 2001 .... $500
Limited Edition of 1775 .... 2001 .... $125
Bel-Air C. C:
"Bel-Air Country Club; A Living Legend" .... 1993 .... $75

Thousands of color book illustrations visible at
www.rogeregilchrist.com

George W. Beldam:
"Golfing Illustrated".................................... 1908 .... $325
"Great Golfers: Their Methods At A Glance" .. 1904 .... $250
"The World's Champion Golfers"
    (11 Volumes).................................... 1924 .... $900
G. W. Beldam & J. H. Taylor:
"Golf Faults Illustrated"............................. 1905 .... $325
Joe Belfore:
"Golfing Aids" .... 1940 .... $30
The Belfry:
"The Making of A Dream" .... 1989 .... $25
Clarrie Bell:
"Eighty Golfing Years, A History of
    North Adelaide Golf Club 1905-1985" .. 1985 .... $40
Peggy Kirk Bell:
"A Woman's Way To Better Golf"................. 1966 .... $15
Belle Haven C. C:
"Belle Haven Country Club Roster of
    Membership"..................................... 1979 .... $50
Bellrive C. C:
"Bellrive Country Club" .... 1910 .... $100
Belleview:
"The Belleview: Belleair FLA" .... 1925 .... $300
Belton Park G. C:
"Belton Park Golf Club 1890-1990".............. 1990 .... $25
Belvedere Club:
The Belvedere Club Memoirs of Members
    1878-1968" .... 1969 .... $65
"The Belvedere Club Memoirs 1878-1990".... 1990 .... $45
Bend G. & C. C:
"Historical Review of The Bend Golf
    and Country Club" .... 1981 .... $20
Tom Bendelow:
"Golf Courses By The American
    Park Builders" .... 1926 .... $250
Josephine Bender:
"Kent Country Club, When Kent Was Young,
    An Early History and Reminiscences" ... 1980 .... $20
Tommy Bendert:
"Golf Is My Life"....................................... 1983 .... $10
David Benedictus:
"Guru And The Golf Club"........................... 1969 .... $5
L. W. Benham:
"Golftique: A Price Guide To Old Golf

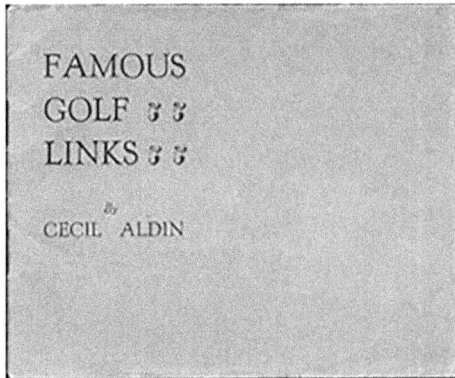

Aldin – Famous Golf Links

Allerton & Browning – Golf
Made Easy

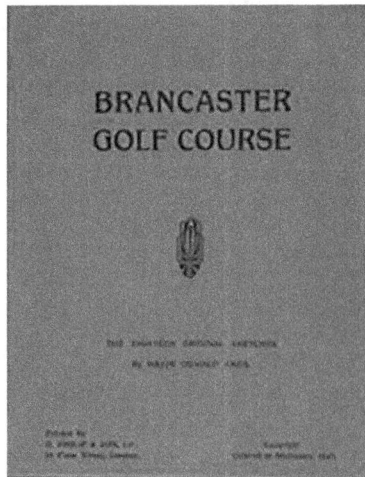

Ames – Brancaster Golf Course

Thousands of color book illustrations visible at
www.rogeregilchrist.com

Clubs and Other Golf Memorabilia" ...... 1977 .... $15

Andrew Bennett:
"The Book of St. Andrews Links"
(1000 copies).................................. 1898 ....$4000
Reprint (200 copies) .... 1984 .... $375
"St. Andrews Golf Club Centenary
1843-1943" .... 1943 .... $800

Arthur Bennett:
"Southern California Golf Directory"............. 1963 .... $25

Guy Bennett:
"Sunningdale Story" .... 1962 .... $30

Benson:
"Keeping An Eye On Your Balls" .... 1983 .... $10

E. F. Benson & E. H. Miles:
"A Book of Golf"...................................... 1903 .... $400

Frederick S. Benson:
"The History of Canoe Brook Country
Club From 1964 To 1976" .... 1976 .... $35

E. C. Bentley:
"Trents Last Case" .... 1930 .... $50
"Trents Own Case".................................. 1936 .... $50
"Trent Intervenes" .... 1938 .... $35

W. A. Bentley:
"History of the San Francisco Golf Club"
(1000 Copies) .... 1978 .... $495

Bruce Berdock & Michael Baier:
"Golf".. 1993 .... $35

Frank Beres:
"Building 18 Holes Miniature Golf" .... 1948 .... $30
"How To Build and The Forty Secrets
of a Golf Driving Range" .... 1948 .... $30

Patty Berg:
"Golf".. 1941 .... $40
"Inside Golf For Women"........................... 1977 .... $15

Patty Berg & Mark Cox:
"Golf Illustrated"..................................... 1950 .... $25

Patty Berg & Otis Dypwick:
"Golf".. 1941 .... $55

Bergstrom:
"History of Red Hill Country Club, Golden
Anniversary" .... 1971 .... $25

Berkhamsted G. C:
"Berkhamsted Golf Club"........................... 1972 .... $20

Earl of Berkeley:
"Sound Golf By Applying Principles
of Practice" .... 1936 .... $95
Berlinger:
"Old York Road Country Club: The First 75
Years" .... 1984 .... $25
Gus Bernardoni:
"Golf God's Way" .... 1978 .... $5
Bob Bernier:
"Pro-Golf Teaching Manual" .... 1964 .... $5
Edith Heal Berrien:
"Fiftieth Anniversary Women's
Metropolitan Golf Association" .... 1950 .... $35
Warner B. Berry:
"Scotsman's Dream" (1000 Copies) .... 2002 .... $450
Paul Bertholy:
"The Bertholy Bombshell" .... 1955 .... $10
C. H. Bertie:
"History of The Manly Golf Club" .... 1946 .... $50
Hugh Best:
"Thunderbird Country Club" .... 1988 .... $125
Bethesda C. C:
"Bethesda Country Club" .... 1985 .... $35
James Betinis:
"Hit The Nail On The Head" .... 1960 .... $5
BGSR Guide:
"BGSR Guide To British Golf Courses" .... 1985 .... $25
Chiberta Biarritz:
"Le Golf les Villas" .... 1929 .... $425
Michael Biddulph:
"The Golf Shot" .... 1980 .... $25
Dale L. Bidwell:
"A History of the Texas Association of Left
Handed Golfers" .... 1983 .... $35
Big Canyon C. C:
"Big Canyon Country Club 25th Anniversary" 1996 .... $50
Michael T. Biondo:
"The Club Pelican Bay. The First
Twenty Years" .... 2002 .... $25
Birdie:
"Golf The Game of A Lifetime" .... 1982 .... $5
Birdie Book:
"Pointers On Par" .... 1958 .... $5

Thousands of color book illustrations visible at
www.rogeregilchrist.com

Birkdale G. C:
"The Birkdale Golf Club"............................. 1952 .... $45
"Birkdale Golf Club Golden Jubilee
      1899-1939" .... 1939 .... $125
George Birtill:
"The Hall That Climbed the Hill: History
      of the Chorley Golf Club" .... 1990 .... $25
Furman Bisher:
"The Masters".. 1976 .... $55
"The Birth of A Legend: Arnold Palmer's
      Golden Year 1960"............................ 1972 .... $45
Louis F. Bishop:
"The Nine Hole Cure for heart Disease" .... 1934 .... $995
Schuyler Bishop:
"A Passion For Golf" .... 1998 .... $20
Bishopbriggs G. C:
"Bishopbriggs Golf Course Handbook" .... 1908 .... $450
H. A. Buz Bizell:
"Sunset Ridge Country Club: Our First
      Fifty Years 1923-1972"...................... 1973 .... $35
Andrew Black:
"The Golf Courses of Scotland" .... 1974 .... $25
Kevin Black:
"Five 9 Hole Perthshire Golf Courses".......... 1970 .... $20
"Six 9 Hole Perthshire Golf Courses" .... 1970 .... $20
William Black:
"Game at Golf" (Ltd Edition of 70) .... 1987 .... $550
Norman Blackburn:
"Lakeside Golf Club of Hollywood,
      50th Anniversary Book" (1150 Copies) 1974 .... $450
Blackie & Son:
"The Lucky Girls Budget"............................ 1920 .... $35
Peter Blackman:
"The Northwood Golf Club Centenary
      1891-1991" .... 1990 .... $40
Arthur Blackmur:
"In Old Diablo: A Social History" .... 1981 .... $45
Blackwood G. C:
"Blackwood Golf Club 1930-1980" .... 1979 .... $85
Blairgowrie G. C:
"Blairgowrie Golf Club 1889-1989" .... 1989 .... $35
Blake, McDowall, & Devlen:
"The 1978 Open Championship At St.
      Andrews: An Economic Impact Study" . 1979 .... $10

Mindy Blake:
"The Golf Swing of The Future" .... 1972 .... $25
"Golf: The Technique Barrier" .... 1978 .... $25
Jane Blalock:
"The Guts To Win" .... 1977 .... $10
Ken Blanchard:
"Playing The Great Game of Golf" .... 1992 .... $20
Jeff Blanchard:
"Tedesko Country Club 1903 to 2003" .... 2003 .... $25
William D. Blatch:
"The Law Relating To Golf Clubs" .... 1943 .... $185
Jane Blaylock:
"The Guts To Win" .... 1977 .... $25
Arthur Bligh:
"Crotchets And Foibles: Stories of Shooting
      Cricket And Golf" .... 1903 .... $150
Blue Mound G. & C. C:
"The Story of The Blue Mound Golf
      and Country Club" .... 1976 .... $75
Robert G. Bluth:
"Golf" .... 1979 .... $10
John A. Board:
"The Right Way To Become A Golfer" .... 1948 .... $55
Tommy Bolt:
"The Hole Truth: Inside Big-Time
      Money Golf" .... 1971 .... $30
"How To Keep Your Temper On The
      Golf Course" .... 1969 .... $5
G. L. Bond:
"The Dunstable Book" .... 1931 .... $40
John Bond:
"Frinton Golf Club" .... 1995 .... $35
Michael Bond:
"Paddington Hits Out" .... 1977 .... $5
"John Bonjenoor"
"Golf Books" (Ltd Edition of 15) .... 2008 .... $750
Barnett Bookatz:
"Oakwood Club, 75th Anniversary" .... 1980 .... $50
Percy Boomer:
"On Learning Golf" .... 1942 .... $95
      Limited Edition of 500 .... 1942 .... $150
      Classics of Golf Edition .... 1988 .... $30
Alan Booth & Michael Hobbs:
"The Sackville Illustrated Dictionary of Golf" . 1987 .... $20

Thousands of color book illustrations visible at
www.rogeregilchrist.com

Border Golfers' Assoc:
"Border Golfers' Association 1893-1993" ...... 1993 .... $25
Michael Borissow:
"The Naked Fairways".............................. 1984 .... $5
Julius Boros:
"The 3 Tenets For Better Golf" .... 1956 .... $10
"How To Play Golf With An Effortless Swing" . 1964 .... $10
"How To Play Par Golf"............................. 1953 .... $35
"How To Win At Weekend Golf".................... 1965 .... $10
"Swing Easy Hit Hard" .... 1965 .... $20
Tony Bortolin:
"Golf's Greatest Lessons" .... 1994 .... $20
Larry Bortstein:
"Who's Who In Golf"................................. 1972 .... $15
Les Bostad & Others:
"Golf"... 1964 .... $15
Charles Boswell:
"Now I See" .... 1969 .... $15
James W. Boswell:
"Golf: From Another Angle" .... 1983 .... $5
Thomas Boswell:
"Strokes of Genius"................................. 1987 .... $20
George McDonald Bottome:
"Golf For The Middle Aged and Others"......... 1946 .... $25
"Modern Golf".. 1949 .... $20
Roger J. Bounds:
"Municipal Golf Courses" .... 1930 .... $265
Kevin Bourke:
"Cobram-Barooga Golf Club Jubilee History
    1928-1978" .... 1978 .... $45
John L. Bovis:
"The It if Golf"....................................... 1927 .... $60
C. Mal Bowden:
"Golfer's Diary, Where He Keeps Scores
    I Can't Forget, Or Lies Lies Lies" .... 1962 .... $5
Ken Bowden:
"The Golf Gazetter"................................. 1968 .... $10
Bob Bowen & B. J. Clemence:
"Golf Everyone"..................................... 1984 .... $5
Maurine Bowling:
"Tested Ways of Teaching Golf Classes" .... 1964 .... $5
Brian Bowness:
"The Golf Courses of Newbury and
    Crookham 1873-1995" (750 Copies) ... 1996 .... $50

Auguste Boyer:
"Le Golf".. 1920 .... $150
Sydney Box:
"Alibi In The Rough" .... 1977 .... $15
Angelo V. Boy:
"Psychological Dimensions of Golf" .... 1980 .... $5
Andrew R. H. Boyd:
"Twenty Five Years of St Andrews
        September 1865 to September 1890".. 1892 .... $125
Mickey Boyle:
"Ninety Years of Golf"............................... 1987 .... $20
Henry W. Boynton:
"The Golfer's Rubaiyat"............................. 1901 .... $725
Richard Bradbeer & Ian Morrison:
"100 Golfing Tips".................................... 1990 .... $10
"The Ultimate Golfer" .... 1993 .... $20
Leland P. Bradford & Robert A. Hunt:
"The Tin Whistles 1904-1979"..................... 1979 .... $35
Bettie Bradley:
"The Mississauga Golf & Country Club
        1906-1981" .... 1981 .... $75
James Braid:
"Advanced Golf"....................................... 1908 .... $275
"Golf Guide and How To Play Golf".............. 1906 .... $120
"Ladies' Field Golf Book" .... 1908 .... $750
Braid, Bramston & Hutchinson:
"A Book of Golf"....................................... 1903 .... $675
James Braid & Harry Vardon:
"How To Play Golf".................................... 1907 .... $150
Bramshaw G. C:
"Bramshaw Golf Club" .... 1946 .... $25
Brand Hall G. C:
"Brand Hall Golf Club" .... 1938 .... $55
Alan Brandie:
"Peterhead Golf Club 150 Years 1841-1991". 1991 .... $15
Joy Branson:
"Taupo Golf Club 1928-1985" .... 1985 .... $45
V. M. Branson:
"Kooyonga 1923-1983 The Story of
        A Golf Club" (1500 Copies) .... 1983 .... $30
Brantford G & C. C:
"Branford Golf And Country Club
        1879-1979" .... 1979 .... $30

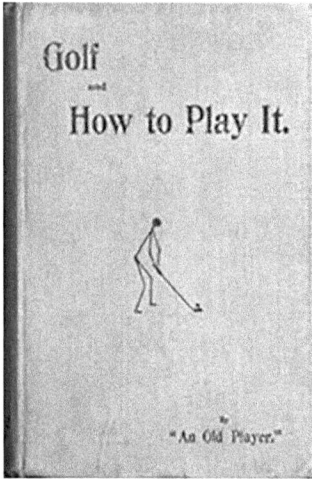

An Old Player – Golf and How
To Play It

Andre – Golf Plays and
Recitations

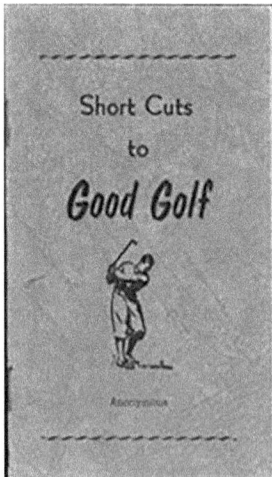

Anonymous – Short Cuts
To Good Golf

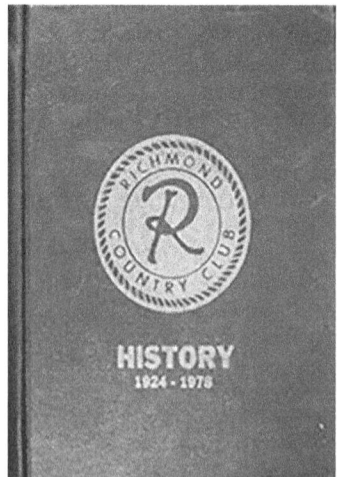

Apple – Richmond Country Club
History 1924 - 1978

Bray G. C:
"Bray Golf Club" .... 1952 .... $25
George Brelsford:
"Palmetto Golf Club: The First 100 Years"..... 1992 .... $35
Marshall Breeden:
"Us Golfers and Our California Links" .... 1923 .... $325
Tom Brennand:
"Richmond Country Club, A Centennial
     History 1891-1991" .... 1990 .... $35
"Dulwich and Sydenham Hill"...................... 1994 .... $35
Frank Brett:
"Cutten Club 1931-1981" .... 1981 .... $20
Gay Brewer:
"Gay Brewer Shows You How To Score
     Better Than You Swing"..................... 1968 .... $20
"Gay Brewer's Golf Guidebook" .... 1968 .... $10
Sid Brews:
"Golf In A Nutshell" .... 1937 .... $65
Brigadier E. Brickman:
"A Brief Introduction to the Club and
     St. Andrews Courses"........................ 1969 .... $35
"The Royal and Ancient Golf Club
     of St. Andrews" .... 1984 .... $35
Claire Briggs:
"Golf: The Book of A Thousand Chuckles"..... 1916 .... $400
"The Selected Drawings of Claire Briggs"...... 1930 .... $250
Alan Brinton:
"Mr. And Mrs. Golfer Cut Their Handicaps".... 1954 .... $10
British Masters:
"How To Improve Your Golf: Lessons
     By British Masters" .... 1925 .... $75
British Travel Association:
"Golf The Great Greens of Britain" .... 1966 .... $25
R. T. Brittenden:
"Golf In New Zealand" .... 1979 .... $20
W. F. Broadbent:
"Golf: Fundamental Instructions" .... 1938 .... $45
Broadstone G. C:
"The Broadstone Golf Club" .... 1966 .... $25
Catherine & Loren Broadus Jr.:
"From Loneliness To Intimacy".................... 1976 .... $10
Howard W. Brod:
"By Golf Possessed" .... 1972 .... $5

Sidney S. Brody:
"How To Break 90 Before You Reach It" .... 1967 .... $15
Brokenhurst Manor G. C:
"Brokenhurst Manor Golf Club" .... 1972 .... $25
"Brokenhurst Manor Golf Club" .... 1981 .... $20
Bromborough G. C:
"Bromborough Golf Club 1904-1979" .... 1979 .... $15
Nelson Bromley:
"Work And Sport" .... 1934 .... $35
Brooklawn Country Club:
"A Brief History of Golf At The Brooklawn
        Country Club" .... 1974 .... $20
Brookmans Park G.C:
"Brookmans Park Golf Club 1930-1980" .... 1980 .... $25
Brooks Brothers:
"The Links Book" .... 1900 .... $200
Dick Brooks:
"The Offensive Golfer" .... 1963 .... $20
James H. Brookuure:
"Notes On Golf Pertaining to the Art of Putting
        And The Short Approach Shots" .... 1935 .... $45
J. E. Broome:
"Keep Your Eye On The Ball" .... 1936 .... $125
Brora G. C:
"Brora Golf Club 1891-1991" .... 1991 .... $35
James Brosnan:
"Kenmare Golf Club. An Illustrated Centenary
        History 1903-2003 " .... 2003 .... $25
Broughty G. C:
"Broughty Golf Club" .... 1953 .... $45
A. C. Brown:
"Victor Harbour Golf Club 1925-1985" .... 1986 .... $45
Cal Brown:
"Butler National Golf Club: The First
        Twenty Five Years 1972-1997" .... 1997 .... $75
"Masters Memories" .... 1998 .... $15
        Limited Edition of 25 Copies .... 1998 .... $50
"The Vintage Club" .... 1991 .... $150
E. G. Brown:
"Isles of Scilly Golf Club" .... 1985 .... $10
Eric C. Brown:
"Knave of Clubs" .... 1961 .... $30
"Out of The Bag" .... 1964 .... $30

Gene Brown:
"The Complete Book of Golf........................ 1980 .... $30
George S. Brown:
"First Steps To Golf"................................ 1913 .... $125
Horace Brown:
"Murder In The Rough" .... 1948 .... $175
Innis Brown:
"About Golf at White Sulphur".................... 1930 .... $950
"Getting Out of Trouble" .... 1934 .... $50
"How To Play Golf"................................... 1930 .... $75
"How To Putt Better" .... 1933 .... $75
"Digest of the USGA Rules of Golf" .... 1940 .... $100
J. Lewis Brown:
"Golf At Glens Falls Country Club" .... 1923 .... $195
"The American Annual Golf Guide"............... 1926 .... $250
James Brown:
"Songs of Golf"....................................... 1902 ......$3,750
John A. Brown:
"Short History of Pine Valley".................... 1963 .... $150
            Later Edition .... 1968 .... $100
            Later Edition .... 1974 .... $95
Kenneth Brown:
"Putter Perkins"....................................... 1923 .... $125
"The Medchester Club" (950 Copies)............ 1938 .... $225
M. Gillette Brown:
"Fell's Teen Age Guide To Winning Golf"....... 1963 .... $10
Thomas Brown:
"Golfiana Or A Day At Gullane" .... 1869 .... $20,000
Virginia P. Brown:
"Grand Old Days Of Birmingham Golf
            1899-1930" .... 1984 .... $25
William Garrott Brown:
"Golf"... 1902 .... $750
Liam Browne:
"The Royal Dublin Golf Club 1885-1985" ...... 1985 .... $150
Thomas Browne:
"The Game of Golf" .... 1902 .... $245
Robert H. K. Browning:
"Aberdare Golf Club" .... 1946 .... $45
"Aberdovey Golf Club" .... 1947 .... $110
"The Aberystwyth Golf Club"...................... 1934 .... $55
"Addington Golf Club"............................... 1946 .... $60
"The Alloa Golf Club" .... 1948 .... $30
"The Alnmouth Golf Club"......................... 1948 .... $45

"The Appleby Golf Club"............................. 1946 .... $150
"The Ardeer Golf Club"............................... 1948 .... $30
"The Arkley Golf Club" .... 1955 .... $15
"The Ashford Manor Golf Club".................... 1947 .... $50
"The Aspley Guise & Woburn Sands
      Golf Club"....................................... 1947 .... $40
"Axe Cliff Golf Club" .... 1939 .... $40
"The Ayr Corporation Golf Courses" .... 1928 .... $200
"Ballater Golf Club" .... 1947 .... $45
"Banchory Golf Club".................................. 1938 .... $35
"Banstead Downs Golf Club"....................... 1951 .... $30
"The Barrow Golf Club" .... 1948 .... $35
"Bath Golf Club" .... 1931 .... $60
"Bedfordshire Golf Club" .... 1947 .... $40
"Beeston Fields Golf Club".......................... 1947 .... $30
"The Betchworth Park Golf Club" .... 1947 .... $40
"Bexhill Golf And Sports Club".................... 1938 .... $35
"Bexley Heath Golf Club"............................ 1947 .... $45
"Bigbury-on-Sea and Burgh Island Golf Club" 1936 225
"Bin Down Golf Club"................................. 1939 .... $40
"The Birkdale Golf Club"............................. 1934 .... $95
"The Bishop Auckland Golf Club" .... 1947 .... $40
"The Blackburn Golf Club" .... 1947 .... $45
"The Blackmoor Golf Club" .... 1947 .... $40
"The Blackpool Golf Club"........................... 1939 .... $55
"The Blackpool North Shore Golf Club" .... 1947 .... $40
"Bolton Golf Club" .... 1947 .... $40
"The Borth & Ynslas Golf Club".................... 1934 .... $40
"The Bramley Golf Club" .... 1950 .... $25
"Brampton Golf Club" .... 1952 .... $25
"The Bramshaw Golf Club" .... 1947 .... $40
"Branford Golf Club".................................. 1938 .... $35
"The Brighton & Hove Golf Club" .... 1947 .... $50
"The Bristol & Clifton Golf Club" .... 1948 .... $35
"The Brocton Hall Golf Club"....................... 1948 .... $35
"The Brokenhurst Manor Golf Club" .... 1939 .... $50
"The Brookmans Park Golf Club" .... 1938 .... $40
"Bude And North Cornwall Golf Club" .... 1932 .... $40
"Burhill Club" .... 1949 .... $30
"The Burnham Beeches Golf Club"................ 1938 .... $40
"Burton-On-Trent Golf Club"....................... 1953 .... $30
"The Bury Golf Club" .... 1947 .... $40
"The Bush Hill Park Golf Club"..................... 1951 .... $30
"The Bushey Hall Golf Club"........................ 1951 .... $20

"Caernarvonshire Golf Club" .... 1947 .... $45
"Caerphilly Golf Club" .... (nd) $45
"The Calcot Golf Club" .... 1952 .... $30
"Callander Golf Club" .... 1939 .... $45
"The Calthorpe Golf Club" .... 1947 .... $40
"The Camberley Heath Golf Club" .... 1947 .... $45
"The Carlisle City Golf Club" .... 1947 .... $40
"Carmarthen Golf Club" .... 1939 .... $45
"The Castletown Golf Club" .... 1947 .... $40
"Cathcart Castle Golf Club" .... 1937 .... $225
"The Cavendish Golf Club" .... 1939 .... $40
"The Chester Golf Club" .... 1947 .... $40
"The Chesterfield Golf Club" .... 1947 .... $40
"Chigwell Golf Club" .... 1951 .... $30
"The Childwall Golf Club" .... 1950 .... $20
"The Chipstead Golf Club" .... 1938 .... $35
"Church Stretton Golf Club" .... 1936 .... $225
"Churston Golf Club" .... 1939 .... $50
"Churston Golf Club" .... 1961 .... $40
"The Cirencester Golf Club" .... 1949 .... $25
"The City of Newcastle Golf Club" .... 1952 .... $30
"The Clacton-On-Sea Golf Club" .... 1938 .... $225
"Clevedon Golf Club" .... 1947 .... $45
"The Cleveleys Hydro Golf Club" .... 1947 .... $35
"The Colchester Gold Club" .... 1948 .... $30
"The Cooden Beach Golf Club" .... 1950 .... $75
"Coventry Golf Club" .... 1947 .... $40
"Crews Hill Golf Club" .... 1948 .... $45
"Crichel Park Golf Club" .... 1938 .... $35
"Crieff Golf Club" .... 1938 .... $55
"The Croham Hurst Golf Club" .... 1955 .... $25
"Cuddington Golf Club" .... 1934 .... $45
"Dalmahoy Golf Club" .... 1938 .... $65
"Dartford Golf Club" .... 1948 .... $35
"The Deepdale Golf Club" .... 1947 .... $35
"The Deeside Golf Club" .... 1938 .... $45
"The Dewsbury District Golf Club" .... 1948 .... $30
"The Didsbury Golf Club" .... 1948 .... $35
"The Didsley Golf Club" .... 1948 .... $35
"The Dinas Powis Golf Club" .... 1947 .... $35
"The Doncaster Golf Club" .... 1950 .... $25
"Duddington Golf Club" .... 1948 .... $40
"The Dulwich And Sydenham Hill Golf Club".. 1952 .... $75
"Dumfries And County Golf Club" .... 1938 .... $45

Thousands of color book illustrations visible at
www.rogeregilchrist.com

"The Dunscar Golf Club"............................. 1948 .... $30
"The Dunstable Downs Golf Club"................ 1948 .... $40
"The Eaglescliffe & District Golf Club".......... 1938 .... $35
"Ealing Golf Club" .... 1950 .... $20
"East Berks Golf Club" .... 1947 .... $50
"East Brighton Golf Club" .... 1947 .... $45
"East Herts Golf Club"................................ 1947 .... $40
"East Renfrewshire Golf Club" .... 1939 .... $40
"The Eastbourne Downs Club"...................... 1949 .... $25
"Edgbaston Golf Club" .... 1939 .... $55
"Effingham Golf Club"................................ 1947 .... $40
"Elgin Golf Club" .... 1947 .... $95
"Enfield Municipal Golf Course" .... 1932 .... $195
"Enfield Golf Club".................................... 1948 .... $35
"Epsom Golf Club"..................................... 1947 .... $40
"The Exmouth Golf Club"............................ 1931 .... $55
"The Fairhaven Golf Club" .... 1939 .... $40
"The Farnham Golf Club"............................ 1955 .... $225
"The Filey Golf Club" .... 1936 .... $45
"The Finchley Golf Club"............................. 1938 .... $35
"The Firbeck Hall Golf Club"........................ 1938 .... $35
"The Flackwell Heath Golf Club" .... 1952 .... $20
"The Fleetwood Club" .... 1938 .... $75
"The Folkstone Golf Club"........................... 1932 .... $50
"The Formby Ladies Golf Club"..................... 1953 .... $20
"The Freshwater Bay Golf Club" .... 1948 .... $30
"The Frinton Golf Club" .... 1938 .... $75
"Fulford (York) Golf Club"........................... 1937 .... $225
"The Fulford Golf Club" .... 1948 .... $30
"Fulford Heath Golf Club" .... 1951 .... $25
"Fulneck Golf Club" .... 1948 .... $35
"Ganton Golf Club".................................... 1939 .... $95
"The Ganton Golf Club".............................. 1955 .... $75
"The Gerrards Cross Golf Club" .... 1947 .... $35
"The Glamorganshire Golf Club".................... 1955 .... $15
"The Glen Gorse Golf Club"......................... 1953 .... $20
"Gog-Magog Golf Club" .... (nd) $45
"Golf In Cornwall" .... 1952 .... $60
"Golf In Devon" .... 1952 .... $50
"Golf In Devon And Cornwall" .... 1970 .... $15
"Golf In Essex" .... 1952 .... $55
"Golf In Gloustershire"............................... 1954 .... $30
"Golf In Hants & Dorset" .... 1955 .... $50
"Golf In Kent".. 1952 .... $55

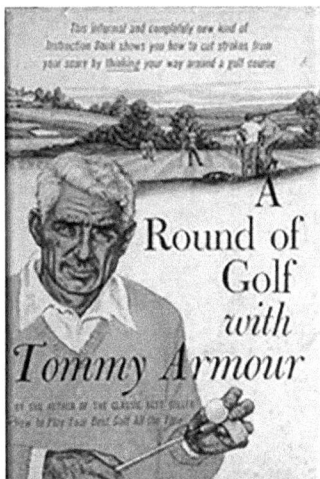

Armour – A Round of Golf
With Tommy Armour

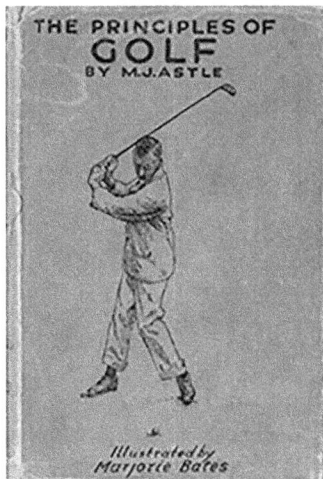

Astle – The Principles of Golf

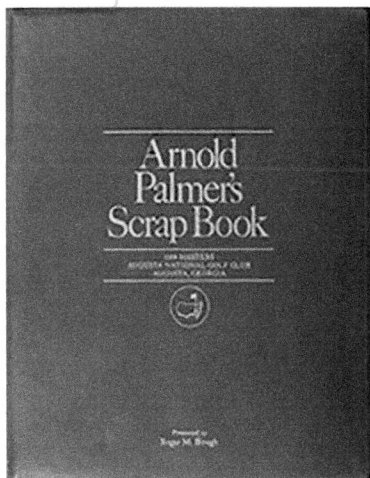

Augusta National G. C. – Arnold
Palmer's Scrapbook

Bailey – The Brain and Golf

Thousands of color book illustrations visible at
www.rogeregilchrist.com

"Golf In Somerset" .... 1952 .... $60
"Golf In Somerset and Gloucestershire" .... 1975 .... $15
"Golf In Surrey" .... 1957 .... $30
"Golf In Sussex" .... 1959 .... $40
"Golf In The Channel Islands" .... 1953 .... $40
"Golf In The Isle of Man" .... 1955 .... $20
"Golf On The Lancs Coast" .... 1957 .... $40
"Golf With Seven Clubs" .... 1950 .... $100
"Golfing Hints When You are off Your Game". 1929 .... $295
"Golfing In Southern England And On The
        Continent" .... 1931 .... $400
"The Golfer's Catechism" .... 1935 .... $185
"Goodwood Golf Club" .... 1939 .... $65
"Gosforth Golf Club" .... 1947 .... $40
"The Gosport And Stokes Bay Golf Club" ...... 1948 .... $35
"The Grand Marine Hotel And Barton-On-Sea
        Golf Club" .... 1950 .... $30
"The Grange Park Golf Club" .... 1948 .... $35
"The Greenway Hall Golf Club" .... 1948 .... $30
"The Guildford Golf Club" .... 1948 .... $30
"The Hadley Wood Golf Club" .... 1948 .... $30
"Halifax Bradley Hall Golf Club" .... 1948 .... $40
"Hallamshire Golf Club" .... 1947 .... $45
"Handsworth Golf Club" .... (nd) $35
"Harpenden Golf Club" .... 1946 .... $40
"The Harrogate Golf Club" .... 1947 .... $55
"The Hastings Golf Club" .... 1934 .... $40
"The Hawick Golf Club" .... 1947 .... $55
"The Hayling Golf Club" .... 1931 .... $45
"The Haywards Heath Golf Club" .... 1955 .... $30
"Helensburgh Golf Club" .... 1938 .... $75
"The Hendon Golf Club" .... 1950 .... $25
"Henley Golf Club" .... 1938 .... $40
"The Herne Bay Golf Club" .... 1948 .... $65
"The Hesketh Golf Club" .... 1947 .... $45
"The Hessle Golf Club" .... 1948 .... $25
"Highgate Golf Club" .... 1936 .... $50
"The Highwoods Bexhill-On-Sea Golf Club" ... 1949 .... $35
"The Hillsborough Golf Club" .... 1952 .... $30
"The Hindhead Golf Club" .... 1938 .... $75
"A History of Golf, The Royal and
        Ancient Game" .... 1955 .... $300
        Classics of Golf Edition .... 1985 .... $30
"Hockley Golf Club" .... 1949 .... $35

"Holyhead Golf Club" .... 1947 .... $45
"The Honiton Golf Club" .... 1939 .... $40
"Hornsea Golf Club" .... 1947 .... $50
"The Huddersfield Golf Club" .... 1947 .... $60
"The Hull Golf Club" .... 1947 .... $35
"Hunstanton Golf Club" .... 1950 .... $40
"The Huntercombe Golf Club" .... 1952 .... $25
"Ilford Golf Club" .... 1952 .... $25
"The Ilkley Golf Club" .... 1939 .... $75
"The Inverness Golf Club" .... 1947 .... $60
"The Irvine Golf Club" .... 1947 .... $40
"The Keighley Golf Club" .... 1946 .... $40
"The Kettering Golf Club" .... 1948 .... $30
"The King's Lynn Golf Club" .... 1949 .... $20
"Kingsthorpe Golf Club" .... 1946 .... $40
"Kingswood Golf Club" .... 1938 .... $45
"The Kington Golf Club" .... 1950 .... $30
"Kirby Muxloe Golf Club" .... 1949 .... $20
"The Knaresborough Golf Club" .... (nd) $150
"Knock Golf Club" .... (nd) $35
"Knole Park Golf Club" .... 1951 .... $25
"The Knott End & Fleetwood Golf Club" .... 1949 .... $25
"Langland Bay Golf Club" .... 1955 .... $20
"Lansdown Golf Club" .... 1932 .... $45
"The Leatherhead Golf Club" .... 1939 .... $75
"Lee-On-The-Solent Golf Club" .... 1931 .... $55
"Leek Golf Club" .... 1947 .... $40
"The Leighton Buzzard Golf Club" .... 1948 .... $25
"The Lewes Golf Club" .... 1948 .... $30
"The Lindrick Golf Club" .... 1955 .... $25
"The Littlehampton Golf Club" .... 1938 .... $50
"The Llandrindod Wells Golf Club" .... 1951 .... $25
"The Llandudno Golf Club" .... 1937 .... $75
"Long Ashton Golf Club" .... 1948 .... $35
"Lothianburn Golf Club" .... 1948 .... $35
"The Ludlow Golf Club" .... 1947 .... $40
"The Lundin Golf Club" .... 1947 .... $50
"The Lytham Golf Club" .... 1948 .... $40
"Malden Golf Club" .... (nd) $35
"Maidenhead Golf Club" .... 1937 .... $65
"The Manchester Golf Club" .... 1953 .... $25
"The Mannings Heath Golf Club" .... 1938 .... $35
"Mere Golf Club And Country Club" .... 1938 .... $35
"Mersea Island Golf Club" .... 1938 .... $50

Thousands of color book illustrations visible at
www.rogeregilchrist.com

"Minehead And West Somerset Golf Club" .... 1946 .... $55
"Moments With Golfing Masters" .... 1932 .... $150
"The Moray Golf Club" .... 1947 .... $50
"The Morecambe Golf Club" .... 1934 .... $40
"The Morpeth Golf Club" .... 1948 .... $35
"The Mortonhall Golf Club" .... 1952 .... $20
"The Mullion Golf Club" .... 1949 .... $30
"Murcar Golf Club" .... 1938 .... $40
"The Muswell Hill Golf Club" .... 1951 .... $30
"The Naze Golf Club" .... 1939 .... $40
"Nevin & District Golf Club" .... 1947 .... $40
"The New Golf Club, St. Andrews" .... 1946 .... $85
"The New Highwood Golf Club" .... 1947 .... $35
"The Newbattle Golf Club" .... 1947 .... $40
"The Newbury And Crookham Golf Club" ...... 1952 .... $20
"Newbury District Golf Club" .... 1933 .... $35
"Newport Golf Club" .... 1953 .... $20
"The Newquay Golf Club" .... 1937 .... $225
"The Newton Abbot Golf Club" .... 1932 .... $40
"The North Manchester Golf Club" .... 1953 .... $35
"The North Shore Golf Club" .... 1938 .... $40
"North Wales Golf Club" .... (nd) $35
"Northcliff Golf Club" .... 1948 .... $35
"The Oakdale Golf Club" .... 1947 .... $55
"The Old Colwyn Golf Club" .... 1952 .... $35
"The Old Links Golf Club" .... 1948 .... $30
"Olton Golf Club" .... 1948 .... $55
"Ormskirk Golf Club" .... 1938 .... $45
"Oxley Park Golf Club" .... 1947 .... $45
"The Pannal Golf Club" .... 1946 .... $55
"The Panure Golf Club" .... 1949 .... $45
"The Parkstone Golf Club" .... 1928 .... $60
"The Peebles Municipal Golf Course" .... 1947 .... $30
"The Penmaenmawr Golf Club" .... 1955 .... $25
"The Penwortham Golf Club" .... 1949 .... $30
"The Perranporth Golf Club" .... 1938 .... $40
"The Piltdown Golf Club" .... 1947 .... $40
"Ponteland Golf Club" .... 1939 .... $40
"The Prenton Golf Club" .... 1949 .... $30
"The Preston Golf Club" .... 1947 .... $30
"Prestonfield Golf Club" .... 1948 .... $35
"Prestwick St. Nicholas Golf Club" .... 1939 .... $95
"Purley Downs Golf Club" .... 1948 .... $55
"The Pwlheli Golf Club" .... 1947 .... $45

"The Queen's Park Golf Club"...................... 1949 .... $55
"The Ramsey Golf Club"............................. 1948 .... $50
"The Reading Golf Club"............................ 1953 .... $30
"The Rhondda Golf Club"........................... 1948 .... $35
"The Rhyl Golf Club"................................. 1940 .... $40
"The Ringway Golf Club" .... 1949 .... $30
"Robin Hood Golf Club"............................. 1938 .... $40
"The Rochelle Golf Club" .... 1948 .... $30
"The Roehampton Club"............................. 1955 .... $35
"The Romford Golf Club" .... 1947 .... $40
"Rothley Park Golf Club" .... 1949 .... $30
"Rowlands Castle Golf Club" .... 1948 .... $35
"The Royal Aberdeen Golf Club" .... 1940 .... $150
"Royal Ashdown Forest Golf Club" .... 1948 .... $65
"The Royal County Down Golf Club"............. 1951 .... $125
"The Royal Cromer Golf Club" .... 1938 .... $145
"The Royal Isle of Wight Golf Club".............. 1947 .... $115
"The Royal Jersey Golf Club"....................... 1939 .... $150
"Royal Musselborough Golf Club".................. (nd) $95
"The Royal Norwich Golf Club" .... 1949 .... $75
"The Royal Porthcawl Golf Club" .... 1951 .... $80
"The Royal Portrush Golf Club"..................... 1949 .... $110
"The Royal Portrush Golf Club"..................... 1954 .... $75
"Royal Winchester Golf Club" .... 1934 .... $125
"The Rushcliffe Golf Club" .... 1953 .... $30
"The Rushmere Golf Club"........................... 1948 .... $30
"The Ryde Golf Club".................................. 1949 .... $25
"The Salisbury And South Wilts Golf Club" .... 1928 .... $135
"The Sand Moor Golf Club" .... 1948 .... $55
"Sandiway Golf Club"................................. 1939 .... $40
"The Scarborough South Cliff Golf Club" .... 1939 .... $90
"The Seacroft Golf Club" .... 1939 .... $40
"The Seaford Golf Club" .... 1938 .... $55
"Shaw Hill Golf Club" .... 1948 .... $55
"The Sherringham Golf Club" .... 1938 .... $50
"The Sherwood Forest Golf Club".................. 1948 .... $30
"The Sidmouth Golf Club"........................... 1947 .... $45
"Shifnal Golf Club" .... 1948 .... $35
"Shipley Golf Club".................................... 1948 .... $40
"Shrewsbury Golf Club" .... 1939 .... $40
"Sickleholme Golf Club" .... 1938 .... $40
"Sitwell Park Golf Club".............................. 1948 .... $35
"The Sonning Golf Club".............................. 1938 .... $40
"The South Herts Golf Club" .... 1932 .... $75

"The South Shields Golf Club" .... 1948 .... $30
"The Southport & Ainsdale Golf Club" .... 1946 .... $75
"The Spalding Golf Club" .... 1951 .... $20
"The St. Annes Old Links Golf Club" .... 1946 .... $60
"St. Enodoc Golf Club" .... 1934 .... $250
"St. Georges Hill Golf Club" .... 1955 .... $35
"The St. Ives Golf Club" .... 1949 .... $30
"St. Leonard's Golf Club" .... 1938 .... $45
"The Stanley Park Golf Course" .... 1949 .... $50
"The Stanmore Golf Club" .... 1955 .... $25
"The Stinchcombe Hill Golf Club" .... 1948 .... $35
"The Stoneham Golf Club" .... 1947 .... $40
"The Strathpeffer Spa Golf Club" .... 1947 .... $35
"The Strawberry Hill Golf Club" .... 1951 .... $20
"The Stymie" .... 1910 ...... $1650
"The Sunningdale Golf Club" .... 1950 .... $95
          Reprint .... 1995 .... $25
"Super Golf" .... 1919 .... $125
"Sutton Coldfield Golf Club" .... 1948 .... $75
"The Swanage & Studland Golf Club" .... 1939 .... $45
"The Swansea Bay Golf Club" .... 1948 .... $35
"The Swindon Golf Club" .... 1938 .... $225
"The Tavistock Golf Club" .... 1938 .... $45
"The Teignmouth Golf Club" .... 1948 .... $45
"The Tenby Golf Club" .... 1947 .... $95
"Thorndon Park Golf Club" .... 1948 .... $55
"Thorpeness C.C. .... 1932 .... $50
"The Thrope Hall Golf Club" .... 1949 .... $20
"Thurlestone Golf Club" .... 1939 .... $50
"The Tiverton Golf Club" .... 1947 .... $35
"Torbay Country Club" .... 1947 .... $35
"The Trentham Golf Club" .... 1938 .... $40
"Trevose Golf Club" .... 1934 .... $55
"Troon Golf Club" .... 1951 .... $95
"The Truro Golf Club" .... 1947 .... $35
"Tyneside Golf Club" .... 1948 .... $40
"Tyrrells Wood Golf Club" .... 1939 .... $40
"The Ulverston Golf Club" .... 1939 .... $70
"The Vale of Leven Golf Club" .... 1947 .... $45
"The Wakefield Golf Club" .... 1949 .... $25
"Walsall Golf Club" .... 1956 .... $45
"The Wanstead Golf Club" .... 1947 .... $40
"The Warren Golf Club" .... 1947 .... $35
"The Waterlooville Golf Club" .... 1948 .... $30

Thousands of color book illustrations visible at
www.rogeregilchrist.com

"The Wentworth Golf Club, Virginia Water" ... 1953 .... $65
"The Wentworth Golf Club".......................... 1953 .... $60
"The West Byfleet Golf Club" .... 1950 .... $25
"The West Herts Golf Club"......................... 1952 .... $35
"West Hove Golf Club" .... 1939 .... $45
"The West Kent Golf Club"........................... 1939 .... $45
"The Westgate-On-Sea and Birchington
     Golf Club".. 1929 .... $95
"The Weston-Super-Mare Golf Club" .... 1949 .... $40
"West Surrey Golf Club"............................... (nd) $35
"The Whitley Bay Golf Club" .... 1939 .... $60
"The Whitsand Bay Golf Club" .... 1948 .... $25
"The Windwhistle Golf Club" .... 1948 .... $25
"The Winterfield Golf Club"......................... 1938 .... $45
"The Withington Golf Club"......................... 1948 .... $30
"Wolstanton Golf Club" .... (nd) $35
"Woodbridge Gold Club"............................. 1948 .... $50
"The Woodcote Park Golf Club" .... 1952 .... $25
"The Woolton Golf Club"............................. 1948 .... $25
"The Worcestershire Golf Club" .... 1939 .... $40
"The Workington Golf And Country Club"...... 1949 .... $55
"The Worlebury Golf Club".......................... 1938 .... $40
"The Worthing Golf Club" 1938 $55
"The Wrekin Golf Club" .... 1938 .... $75
     Later Edition .... 1947 .... $60
"The Yelverton Golf Club"........................... 1951 .... $25
"York Golf Club".. 1951 .... $25
R.C. Brownlee:
"Dunbar Golf Club, A Short History
     1794-1980" .... 1980 .... $75
Bruce & Evelyn Davies:
"Beginning Golf" .... 1962 .... $10
George Bruce:
"Destiny And Other Poems" .... 1876 .... $165
Jeremy Bruce-Watt:
"Gleneagles Hotel Diamond Jubilee
     Souvenir Book 1924-1984" .... 1984 .... $10
Nancy Bruff:
"The Country Club" .... 1969 .... $45
Dorothy & Marguerite Bryan:
"Michael and Patsy On The Golf Links" .... 1933 .... $125
Mike Bryan:
"Dogleg Madness".................................... 1988 .... $15

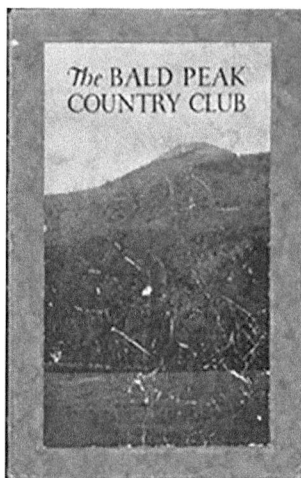

Bald Peak C. C. – The Bald
Peal Country Club

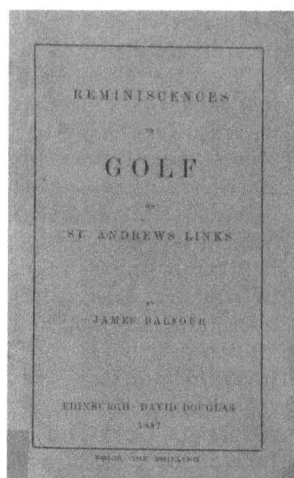

Balfour – Reminiscences
of Golf

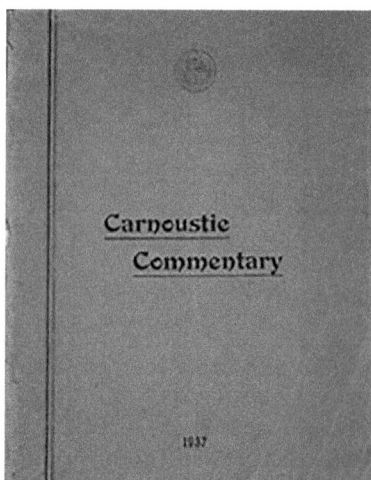

Ballantine, Chapman & Alexander
- Carnoustie Commentary

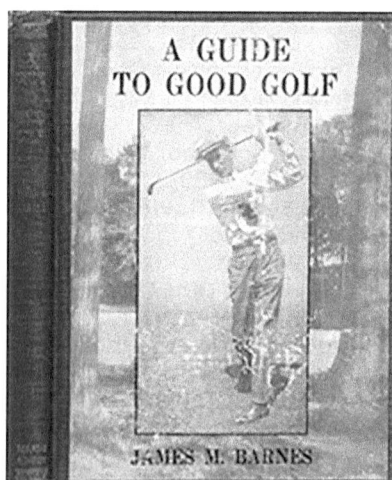

Barnes – A Guide to Good Golf

Thousands of color book illustrations visible at
www.rogeregilchrist.com

James C Bryant:
"Druid Hills Golf Club in Atlanta" .... 1998 .... $175
R. I. Bryden and D. T. Hood:
"The Kittansett Club A Brief History
     1922-1968" .... 1968 .... $150
Walter C. Brzoza:
"Putting Secrets of the Old Masters" .... 1968 .... $20
Bob Bubka & Tom Clavin:
"The Ryder Cup" .... 1999 .... $20
Judy Buckton:
"The History of Golf In Ripon 1895-1995"..... 1996 .... $15
Tom Buggy:
"Lady of The Hudson: A Centennial History
     Of Dutchess Golf and Country Club" .... 1998 .... $50
Kate Buford:
"From Hudson to Hillside: Time, Change
     and the Ardsley Country Club"........... 1997 .... $95
Bulawayo G. C:
"The Bulawayo Golf Club 1895-1970" .... 1970 .... $25
W. W. Bulger:
"Echos from the Links"............................. 1924 .... $250
William P. Bull:
"From Ratlesnake Hunts To Hockey: The
     History of Sports In Canada and of
     The Sportsmen of Peel, 1798-1934"
     (1000 Copies) .... 1934 .... $225
Linda K. Bunker & De De Owens:
"Golf: Better Practice For Better Play" .... 1984 .... $5
H. C. Bunner:
"The Suburban Sage" .... 1896 .... $80
Terry Bunton:
"The History of The Heritage" .... 1989 .... $35
Ron Burd:
"Ron Burd's Basic Principles of Golf" .... 1966 .... $5
E. A. R. Burden:
"A History of St. Enodoc Golf Club".............. 1965 .... $20
J. Howard Burgess:
"Fore!" .... 1913 .... $100
Burke Golf Company:
"Golf".. 1929 .... $75
"Golf As She Ought To Be Played" .... 1929 .... $70
"Making The Clubhead Work"...................... 1931 .... $40
Jack Burke:
"The Natural Way To Better Golf" .... 1954 .... $30

Thousands of color book illustrations visible at
www.rogeregilchrist.com

"Ten Lessons In Golf" .... 1923 .... $55
Jack Burke Jr.:
"The Three Dimensions of Golf"................... 1966 .... $5
Jack Burke Jr. & Others:
"How To Solve Your Golf Problems" .... 1963 .... $5
James Francis Burke:
"Guard The Game of Golf Against The Danger
    Of Becoming A Humdrum, Haphazard,
    Meaningless Pastime"........................ 1925 .... $125
John Burke:
"Southwald Golf Club 1884-1984" .... 1984 .... $25
Burles & Piper:
"Bernard Darwin and Aberdovey"
    (650 Copies)................................... 1996 .... $75
    Limited edition of 125 .... 1996 .... $350
Burly:
"The Early History of Rolling Green"............. 1988 .... $20
Stan Burdy:
"The Augusta National Golf Club" .... 2005 .... $35
Bobby Burnet:
"An Anecdotal History of The Royal and Ancient"1995 ...... $20
Bobby Burnette:
"The St. Andrews Opens" .... 1990 .... $45
Jim Burnette:
"Tee Times" .... 1997 .... $20
Burnham & Barrow G. C:
The Burnham & Barrow Golf Club
    1890-1990" .... 1989 .... $20
Burnham Ladies G C:
"Burnham Ladies Golf Club"........................ 1947 .... $45
Burning Tree Club:
"Burning Tree Club" .... 1932 .... $150
"Burning Tree Club, A History 1922-1962".... 1962 .... $200
"Burning Tree Club, The Fifth Decade
    1963-1972" .... 1972 .... $90
"The Story of Burning Tree"....................... 1993 .... $75
Ralph F. Burns:
"Historical Review of LaGrange Country Club
    1899-1949" .... 1949 .... $45
Miles Burton:
"Tragedy At The Thirteenth Hole"................ 1933 .... $350
Percy Burton:
"To Sweden & Denmark & Back" .... 1947 .... $25

Richard Burton:
"Length With Discretion".............................. 1940 .... $30
James M Burway:
"Picture Analysis of Golf Strokes" .... 1919 .... $175
Scott M. Bushnell & Andrew Hancock:
"A Century of Graciousness"........................ 2011 .... $35
Business Man's G. C:
"Business Man's Golf Course" Six Volumes.... 1924 .... $200
Buston & High Peak G. C:
"The Buston & High Peak Golf Club"............. 1948 .... $30
William M. Butler:
"The Golfers Manual"................................. 1907 .... $250
"The Golfer's Guide".................................. 1907 .... $300
W. Meredith Butler & W. R. Foster:
"Ilfracombe Golf Club" .... 1926 .... $225
Butte C. C:
"Observing 30 Years With The Present Butte
 CountryClub House".......................... 1945 .... $30
Butterfield C. C:
"Butterfield Country Club 50th
 Anniversary 1920-1970".................... 1970 .... $35
Mrs. Howard P. Buttress:
"The History of Women's Golf In Southern
 California" .... 1959 .... $25
Byrne:
"Interesting Facts For Every Golfer"............. 1926 .... $75
Mike Byrne:
"South Shields Golf Club 1893-1993".......... 1993 .... $25
D. B. C:
"Golf at Filey with Six Views of the
 Golf Course" .... 1911 .... $400
W. K. C.:
"The History of the Warrender Golf Club" ..... 1906 .... $65
Caddie Coloring Book:
"Caddie Coloring Book"............................... 1950 .... $15
Caddie Manual:
"Caddie Manual" .... 1948 .... $75
David Cadney:
"The Story of Olton Golf Club" (1000 Copies) 1991 .... $30
Michael Cady:
"AA 1986 Guide To Golf Courses In Britain" .. 1985 .... $10
Caernarvonshire G. C:
"Caernarvonshire Golf Club" .... 1937 .... $45

William Caesar:
"Carnoustie Golf Links Bazaar"................... 1892 .... $500
Howard Cain:
"Briarwood Country Club 1958-1983" .... 1983 .... $25
Sylvia Potter Cain:
"Instruction For Elementary Golfers"............ 1939 .... $30
Patrick Cake:
"The Pro-Am Murders" .... 1979 .... $35
Mrs. Guy T. Calafato:
"Deal Golf and Country Club 1898-1973"...... 1973 .... $30
Calcutta Ladies G. C:
Ladies Golf Club Calcutta – Rules" .... 1932 ....$150
John W Caldwell:
"Mountain Lake: A History" .... 1984 .... $25
Calgary Golf & C. C:
"Calgary Golf And Country Club
        1897-1972 75th Anniversary"............. 1972 .... $30
Leighton Calkins:
"A System For Club Handicapping" .... 1905 .... $75
Tom Callahan & Dave Kindred:
"Around The World In 18 Holes".................. 1994 .... $20
Lionel F. Callaway:
"New And Improved System of Simplified
        Handicapping For Golfers".................. 1952 .... $10
Came Down G. C:
"The Came Down Golf Club" .... 1933 .... $55
"Came Down Golf Club 1896-1996" .... 1996 .... $20
Dave Camerer:
"Golf With The Masters"............................ 1955 .... $30
"Improve Your Game" .... 1958 .... $20
Scotty Cameron:
"The Art of Putting Book 2" .... 2001 .... $125
Keith Camp:
"Leighton Buzzard Golf Club
        Diamond Jubilee 1925-1985".............. 1985 .... $25
Walter Camp:
"The Book of Sports And Games" .... 1923 .... $50
Walter Camp & Lillian Brooks:
"Drives And Putts" .... 1899 .... $250
Alexander Campbell:
"A Journey From Edinburgh Through
        Parts of North Britain" .... 1802 .... $395
Bailey Campbell:
"Golf Lessons From Sam Snead" .... 1964 .... $20

Thousands of color book illustrations visible at
www.rogeregilchrist.com

Duncan C. Campbell:
"The Royal Montreal Golf Club 1873-1973" ... 1973 .... $125
Guy Colin Campbell:
"Golf For Beginners" .... 1922 .... $95
"Golf At Prince's And Deal" .... 1950 .... $350
John Campbell:
"Greenkeeping" .... 1982 .... $15
Malcolm Campbell:
"European Golf Courses" .... 1994 .... $45
"The Random House International Golf
    Encyclopedia" .... 1991 .... $40
"The Scottish Golf Book" .... 1999 .... $40
Patrick Campbell:
"Patrick Campbell's Golfing Book" .... 1972 .... $10
"How To Become A Scratch Golfer" .... 1963 .... $40
"Round Ireland With A Golf Bag" .... 1937 .... $145
Shepherd Campbell & Peter Landau:
"Presidential Lies" .... 1996 .... $15
Campbell, Collard & Walsh:
"The Royal Montreal Golf Club 1873-2000 .... 2001 .... $65
Canada Pacific Hotels:
Banff Springs Hotel Golf Course" .... 1938 .... $175
James Campbell Irons:
"Leith And Its Antiquities" .... 1897 .... $500
F. C. Canausa:
"How To Win At Golf" .... 1956 .... $5
George C. Caner Jr:
"History of the Essex Country Club
    1893-1993" .... 1995 .... $75
Peter Canham:
"Introduction To Golf" .... 1975 .... $5
Kiki Canniff:
"Northwest Golfer" .... 1987 .... $10
Victor Canning:
"The Limbo Line" .... 1977 .... $30
Cannington Park G. C:
"Cannington Park Golf Club" .... 1935 .... $35
Dave Cannon:
"Severiano Ballesteros" .... 1986 .... $15
Capilano G. & C. C:
"Capilano Golf & Country Club Limited" .... 1939 .... $350
Capper & Capper:
"Motor Guide To Golf Links About Chicago" ... 1918 .... $100

Elmer O. Cappers:
"Centennial History of the Country Club
1882-1982" .... 1981 .... $75
Howard Capps:
"Take The Wrists Out, A Life In Golf" .... 1985 .... $5
Phil Carradice:
"Southerdown Golf Club, 1905-2005" .... 2005 .... $50
Henry M. Carl:
"Analytical Physical Culture Golf"................. 1928 .... $250
Alexander Carlyle:
"Autobiography of The Rev.Dr. Alexander
Carlyle, Minister of Inversek"............. 1860 .... $250
Robert D. Carlisle:
"The Montclair Golf Club,
A Way of Life 1893-1983" .... 1984 .... $75
Carmina:
"Carminum Rariorum Marcaronicorum
Delectus".. 1813 ....$1900
George F. Carnegie:
"Golfiana" .... 1842 .... $39,995
Later Edition .... 1883 ..$12,000
Carnoustie
"The Open Golf Championship Carnoustie".... 1931 ....$4000
"Carnoustie: Three Private Citizens" .... 1933 ......$1000
"Carnoustie And Its Golf Courses" .... 1937 ......$1000
"British Open Golf Championship July 1937
Plan in Color of the Carnoustie Course" 1937 .... $300
Later Edtion .... 1957 .... $100
"Carnoustie Commentary" .... 1937 .... $950
"Carnoustie Commentary, Championship
Supplement"................................... 1937 .... $900
"Carnoustie Golf Course" .... 1933 .... $975
"Carnoustie The New Championship
Golf Course" .... 1931 .... $750
Ashley Carpenter:
"In The Rough"....................................... 1984 .... $10
Edward Carpenter:
"Subjective Golf Strategy"......................... 1979 .... $5
Joseph Carpenter:
"Only Golfers Know The Feeling" .... 1983 .... $5
Dick Carr:
"You Too Can Golf In The Eighties".............. 1977 .... $5
Steven Carr & Sally Strugnell:
"The Complete Book of Golf" .... 1992 .... $20

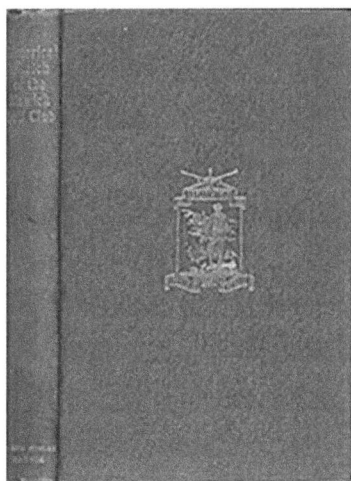

Barrie – Historical Sketch of
The Hawick Golf Club

Batchelor – Golf Stories

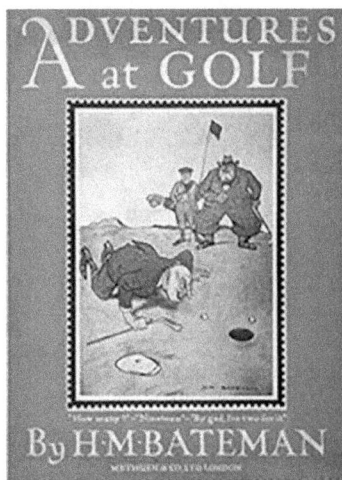

Bateman – Adventures at Golf
(1923 Dust Jacket)

Bauchope – The Golfing Annual

Thousands of color book illustrations visible at
www.rogeregilchrist.com

Michael Carrick:
"Caddie Sense".. 1999 .... $10
John Carrido:
"The Fitness Approach To Power Golf".......... 1997 .... $10
Major C. J. Lloyd Carson:
"Leamington And County Golf Club"............. 1914 .... $95
Eric Carter:
"The First 100 Years: The Story of The
　　　Tunbridge Wells Golf Club"................. 1989 .... $30
James Carter & Co:
"Golf Courses, Tennis Courts, Lawns etc" ..... 1920 .... $125
Louis G Cashera Jr:
"Strictly Golf Balls".................................. 1994 .... $10
Dennis Casley:
"Mullion Golf Club 1895-1995, The History
　　　of Golf on Gwills Towans"................... 1994 .... $35
Charles Cason:
"Some Golf Prizes" .... 1929 ....$1250
Billy Casper:
"295 Golf Lessons".................................... 1973 .... $15
"Chipping And Putting: Golf Around
　　　The Greens"..................................... 1961 .... $20
"Golf Shotmaking With Billy Casper"........... 1966 .... $20
"The Good Sense of Golf".......................... 1980 .... $20
"My Million Dollar Shots"........................... 1970 .... $20
"Saving Strokes Around The Green" .... 1973 .... $20
Castle G.C:
History of the Castle Golf Club 1913-1963"... 1963 .... $95
Nesbit H. Caughman:
"Indian Hill Country Club 1899-1999" .... 1999 .... $25
James O. Causey;
"Killer Take All" .... 1957 .... $75
Cavalcade of Golf:
"Cavalcade of Golf: From
　　　King James To King Jones"................. 1935 .... $60
"Cavalcade of Golf: From
　　　King James To Silver King"................. 1938 .... $65
Walter Cavanaugh:
"The Art of Golf" .... 1927 .... $375
Lewis Cave:
"Caves Guide To Turf Culture" .... 1972 .... $45
Paul Cave:
"Guide To Golf In Hampshire Bournemouth
　　　and The Isle of Wright...................... 1977 .... $20

William Caw:
"King James VI Golf Club, Record
    and Records" .... 1912 .... $550
Caxanga G. & C.C:
"Estatutos" .... 1945 .... $75
Susan E. Cayleff:
"Babe - The Life and Legend of Babe
    Didrikson Zaharias"........................... 1990 .... $20
Thelma Cazalet-Keir:
"Homage to P.G. Wodehouse"..................... 1973 .... $35
Teresa Celsi:
"Golf: The Lore of The Links" .... 1992 .... $10
Philip & Florence Chabody:
"The 86 Proof Pro" .... 1974 .... $5
H. H. Chadwick:
"Golf In Vermont: A Directory of Courses" .... 1946 .... $45
Alan Challen:
"Seaford Head Golf Course Centenary
    Handbook 1887-1987" .... 1987 .... $10
Chalmers, Nichols, Crombie, Pedersen & Thompson:
"Royal Canberra Golf Club Jubilee History
    1926-1976" (2000 Copies)................. 1977 .... $125
Faustina E. Chamberlain:
"Charley Emery, Pro: Biography of a Maine
    Golf Pro" .... 1982 .... $5
Peter Chamberlain:
"Good Golf".. 1985 .... $10
"Winning Golf".. 1985 .... $10
Charles E. S. Prsactical :
"Early Golf At Bruntsfield And Leith" .... 1932 ......$1,250
"Golfing, A Handbook To The Royal and
    Ancient Game With A List of Clubs,
    Rules, & Also Golfing Sketches
    And Poems"................................... 1887 ......$1,500
    2nd Edition .... 1891 .... $325
Marcia Chambers:
"The Unplayable Lie" .... 1995 .... $20
Robert Chambers:
"A Few Rambling Remarks On Golf With
    The Rules As Laid Down By The Royal
    And Ancient Club of St. Andrews."...... 1862 .... $10,500
    USGA Reprint................................... 1983 .... $75
"Gymnastics, Golf and Curling" .... 1866 ......$2,750
"Golfing: A Handbook of The Royal and

Ancient Game" .... 1887 ...... $2,750
Revised 2nd edition......................... 1891 ..... $1,995
"Traditions of Edinburgh" .... 1825 .... $400
Robert & William Chambers:
"The Gazetteer of Scotland" .... 1832 .... $400
Hotel Champlain:
"The Hotel Champlain and its Golf Course" ... 1920 .... $400
Leonard R. Chandler:
"A History of Essex Golf and Country
Club 1902-1983" .... 1983 .... $75
Eric Channon:
"Lewes Golf Club" .... 1952 .... $20
T. Chape & W. Ogilvie:
"Newbiggin Golf Country Centenary
1884-1984" .... 1984 .... $25
Gary P. Chapin & T. Liam MacDonald:
"Sun Tzu's Ancient Art of Golf".................... 1992 .... $15
H. J. Chapman:
"The Story of The Dalhousie Golf Club
1868-1968" .... 1968 .... $30
Hay Chapman:
"Law of the Links: Rules, Principles and
Ettiquette of Golf"............................. 1922 .... $200
Kenneth G. Chapman:
"The Rules of The Green" .... 1997 .... $25
Richard Chapman & Ledyard Sands:
"Golf As I Play It" .... 1940 .... $65
Bob Charles:
"The Bob Charles Left Handers Golf Book" .... 1985 .... $20
"Golf For Seniors" .... 1994 .... $15
"Left Handed Golf" .... 1965 .... $20
"Left Hander From New Zealand" .... 1965 .... $35
Charles River C. C:
"Life at the Charles River Country Club
1921-1947" .... 1946 .... $125
"75th Anniversary Charles River Country
Club 1921-1996" .... 1996 .... $45
Chattanooga G. & C. C:
"At The End of The Trolley: A History of the
Chattanooga Golf and Country Club
1896-1961" .... 1962 .... $50
C. C. Chattell:
"The Golfers Guide 1908".......................... 1908 .... $595
"The Golfers Guide 1909".......................... 1909 .... $475

Billye Ann Cheatum:
"Golf".. 1969 .... $5
John Cheever:
"The Brigadier And The Golf Widow" .... 1964 .... $95
Ike Cheeves:
"Play Better Golf"..................................... 1966 .... $5
Edward Cheney:
"An Eightsome of Golfing Badgers" .... 1945 .... $15
George Cherellia:
"All About Hitting The Sweet Spot" .... 1975 .... $5
"Tempo: The Heart of a Golf Swing" .... 1971 .... $20
Cherry Hills C. C:
"Cherry Hills Country Club" .... 1978 .... $40
Cherry Valley Club:
"Cherry Valley Club: Club House and Links".. 1929 .... $200
Chevy Chase Club:
"The Chevy Chase Club 1918" .... 1918 .... $75
Chevin G. C:
"Chevin Golf Club Official Handbook" .... 1933 .... $75
"Chevin Golf Club" .... 1958 .... $40
Robert Z. Chew & David D. Pavoni:
"Golf In Hollywood" .... 1998 .... $30
Chicago Daily Fee Golf Association:
"Let's Play Golf".. 1933 .... $450
Chicago District Golf Association:
"Chicago District Golf Association Year Book" 1937 .... $75
"Method of Rating Golf Courses and Official
        Handicaps" .... 1940 .... $150
Chicago G. C:
"Chicago Golf Club, Wheaton, Illinois 1909".. 1909 ....$1250
"Chicago Golf Club 1892-1992"
        (1000 copies)................................... 1991 .... $700
Bob Chieger & Pat Sullivan:
"Inside Golf: Quotations on the Royal and
        Ancient Game" .... 1985 .... $10
Frank Chinnock:
"How To Break 90 Consistently".................. 1976 .... $15
Chislehurst G. C:
"Chislehurst Golf Club" .... 1928 .... $60
"Chislehurst Golf Club 1894-1994" .... 1994 .... $20
        Limited Edition of 10 Publisher Copies.. 1994 .... $45
Maureen Chodosh & Maggie Weiss:
"The Golfer's Cookbook: Recipes Collected
        At Pebble Beach" .... 1984 .... $20

Thousands of color book illustrations visible at
www.rogeregilchrist.com

H. Roy Chopping:
"100 Years of Golf: Taunton & Pickeridge
    Golf Club 1892-1992"......................... 1992 .... $55
Agatha Christie:
"The Murder on The Links" .... 1923 ......$1,950
    1st American Edition .... 1923 .... $925
"Towards Zero" .... 1944 .... $375
G. Fyffe Christie:
"Golf of All Kinds" .... 1937 .... $175
Frank Christian:
"The Masters" (200 Copies) .... 1993 ......$1500
"Augusta National And The Masters"
    (150 Copies).................................... 1996 .... $150
Joe Chronicles:
"Uncle Jed, Caddie Master"......................... 1934 .... $700
Edward Chui:
"Golf".. 1969 .... $5
Churston G. C:
"Churston Golf Club Official Handbook" .... 1990 .... $20
Cincinnati C. C:
"Cincinnati Country Club 1903-1975".......... 1975 .... $35
"The Cincinnati Country Club. A History" ...... 1991 .... $45
Bob Cisco:
"The Ultimate Game of Golf"....................... 1993 .... $15
C. B. Clapcott:
"The History of Handicapping" .... 1924 ......$7,500
    Reprint (Limited Edition of 150) .... 2002 .... $325
"The Early Days of the Honourable Company
    of Edinburgh Golfers 1744-1764" .... 1938 .... $22,500
"The Effect of Change To The Golf Ball"........ 1935 ....$5000
    Reprint (Limited Edition of 75)............ 2002 .... $750
"The Honourable Company of Edinburgh
    Golfers Its Titles in the Past
    1744-1948" .... 1948 .... $25,000
"The Honourable Company of Edinburgh
    Golfers on Leith Links"...................... 1939 ....$4000
"The Oldest Golf Club" .... 1939 ....$2500
"The Match Dinners of The Honourable
    Company of Edinburgh Golfers
    1744-1932 .... 1940 ....$2500
"The Rules of Golf of the Ten Oldest
    Clubs From 1754 To 1848 Together
    With The Rules of Golf of The Royal
    & Ancient Golf Club of St. Andrews For

The Years 1858, 1875, 1888"
(500 Copies) .... 1935 .... $2000
John R. Claridge:
"Kahkwa Club: The First Hundred Years" ...... 1993 .... $45
Bill Clark:
"Helen's Bay Golf Club" .... 1996 .... $45
Charles E. Clark:
"The New Haven Country Club, The First
Fifty Years 1898-1948" .... 1949 .... $50
Eric D Clark:
"A History of The St Andrews Golf Club
The 150 Years 1843 to 1993" .... 1993 .... $30
Robert Clark:
"Golf, A Royal & Ancient Game"
First Edition of 200 .... 1875 ..... $2,500
First Trade Edition .... 1875 .... $1250
Large Paper Edition .... 1875 .... $6000
(Limted Edition of 50) 1875 12,500
Second Edition .... 1893 .... $1750
Third Edition .... 1899 .... $495
Reprint .... 1975 .... $175
Reprint .... 1984 .... $25
"Poems On Golf" .... 1867 ..... $3,450
Subscribers Edition .... 1867 .... $2995
Mrs. A. B. Clarke:
"History of Elie Golf House Club Jubilee" .... 1925 .... $150
Charles Clarke & Mottram Gilbert:
"Common-Sense Golf" .... 1914 .... $95
E. A. S. Clarke:
"Metropolitan Club, Bridge Dinner Club:
Minutes and Records, 1906-1931" .... 1931 .... $150
Fred C. Clarke Jr.:
"The Woodstock Country Club 1895-1959" ... 1959 .... $50
R. N. Clarke:
"A Sudbrook Chronicle, Being a History of
Richmond Golf Club 1891-1932" .... 1976 .... $25
Richard W. Clarke:
"The Bedford Golf and Tennis Club
1890-1965" .... 1965 .... $35
Cleckheaton & District G. C:
"Cleckheaton & District Golf Club" .... 1957 .... $25
Joe Clement:
"Classic Golf Clubs: A Pictorial Guide" .... 1980 .... $145

Bauer – Hazzards

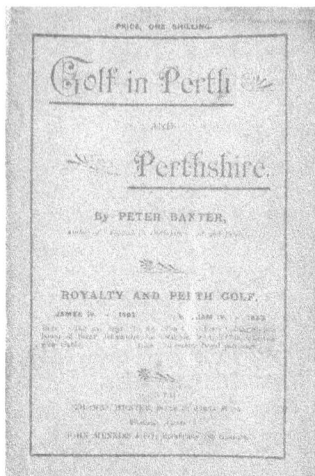

Baxter – Golf in Perth and Perthshire (1st Edition)

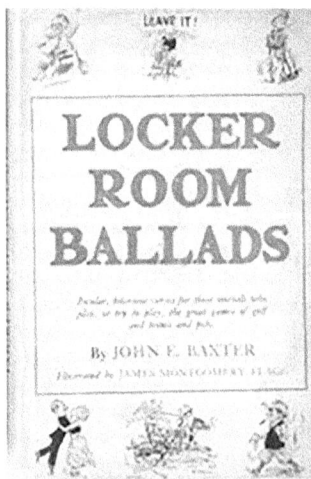

Baxter – Locker Room Ballads (1st Edition Dust Jacket)

Beale – Lawns for Sports (1st Edition Dust Jacket)

Thousands of color book illustrations visible at
www.rogeregilchrist.com

Cleveland G. C:
"Cleveland Golf Club 1887-1987" .... 1987 .... $25
Charles Blair Cleveland:
"Approaching And Putting" .... 1953 .... $40
Harold J. Cliffer:
"Planning The Golf Club House"................... 1956 .... $125
           National Golf Foundation Reprint........ 1967 .... $45
Ben Clingain:
"The International Golf Almanac" .... 1995 .... $15
Clitheroe G.C:
"Clitheroe Golf Club. 50th Anniverserary
     Commemoration of the Occupancy of
     the Barrow Gardens Site. 1932-1982" . 1982 .... $35
Reginald Clough:
"The Black Hall Club .... 1988 .... $35
T. R. Clougher:
"Golf Clubs of the Empire A Golfing Annual".. 1926 .... $550
"Golf Clubs of the Empire A Golfing Annual".. 1927 .... $350
"Golf Clubs of the Empire A Golfing Annual".. 1928 .... $300
"Golf Clubs of the Empire A Golfing Annual".. 1929 .... $250
"Golf Clubs of the Empire A Golfing Annual".. 1930 .... $175
"Golf Clubs of the Empire A Golfing Annual".. 1931 .... $125
"Golf Clubs of the Empire A Golfing Annual".. 1932 .... $125
Clovelly C. C:
"Clovelly Country Club 1932-1982
     50th Anniversary"............................. 1982 .... $20
William E. Clow Jr.:
"Good Golf".. 1942 .... $15
Coale & Gower:
"Agawam Hunt: The First Hundred Years
     1897-1997" .... 1997 .... $65
Albert Cobe:
"Great Spirit" .... 1970 .... $5
Cockermouth G. C:
"The Cockermouth Golf Club" .... 1961 .... $25
Alistair Cochran & John Stobbs:
"The Search For The Perfect Swing"............. 1968 .... $95
A. S. Cockfield & Herb McNally:
"Mount Bruno Country Club 1918-1978"....... 1978 .... $45
"The Pro Golf Teacher" .... 1980 .... $10
Martin E. Coffey:
"Golfing In Ireland" .... 1953 .... $135
Jean P. Colby:
"The Greatest Golf Tournament of Them All". 1988 .... $25

Colchester G. C:
"Colchester Golf Club" .... 1938 .... $80
Coldstream C. C:
"Coldstream Country Club 25th Anniversary
1959-1984" .... 1984 .... $20
Douglas Cole:
"A Brief History of the Vernon Golf And
Country Club 1913-1988" .... 1988 .... $35
Albert Colebank:
"A History of Red Hill Country Club"............. 1972 .... $40
Vernon Coleman:
"The Man Who Inherited a Golf Course" .... 1993 .... $30
John K. Coleridge:
"1892-1992: The Royal West Norfolk Golf
Club a Celebration of a Way of Golf".... 1991 .... $35
Neil Coles:
"Neil Coles On Golf" .... 1965 .... $15
Ben Coll:
"I Love Golf" .... 1950 .... $150
"The Country Club" .... 1961 .... $25
W. G. P. Colledge:
"Mortonhall Golf Club 1892-1992" .... 1992 .... $45
Glenna Collett:
"Golf for Young Players"............................. 1926 .... $195
Reprint.................................... 1984 .... $25
"Ladies in The Rough" .... 1928 .... $450
Second Edition .... 1929 .... $175
Basil Collier:
"Local Thunder"....................................... 1936 .... $10
Sargent F. Collier:
"Green Grows Bar Harbour, Reflections
From Kebo Valley" .... 1964 .... $75
500 Numbered & Signed Copies. .... 1964 .... $175
Valerie Collins:
"100 Years at Notts Golf Club 1887-1987" .... 1989 .... $25
David R. Collins:
"Super Champ! The Story of Babe
Didrikson Zaharias"........................... 1982 .... $20
William J. Collins:
"Lawns, Golf & Sport Turf..." .... 1925 .... $150
Albert W. K. Colmer & Ivor D. Ray:
"Ardglass Golf Club: From Castle
to Clubhouse" .... 1982 .... $20

Reggie Colomb:
"Rutland Country Club" .... 1985 .... $40
The Colonel:
"Golfing By the Numbers" .... 1927 .... $95
Harry S. Colt & C. H. Alison:
"Some Essays on Golf Course Architecture" .. 1920 ...... $4,000
      Reprint (100 copies) .... 1990 .... $500
      Reprint (600 copies) .... 1990 .... $200
      Reprint (1000 Copies) .... 1993 .... $125
J. Arthur Colver:
"A History of Lindrick Golf Club 1891-1979". 1980 .... $30
George M. Colville:
"Five Open Champions and the Musselburgh
      Golf Story" .... 1980 .... $95
      Signed edition (100 Copies) .... 1980 .... $250
James Colville:
"The Glasgow Golf Club 1787-1907" .... 1907 .... $650
Colwyn Bay G. C:
"Colwyn Bay Golf Club" .... 1934 .... $75
John L. Comer:
"Putting: A New Approach" .... 1962 .... $100
Archie Compston:
"Golfing In Scotland at 100 Holiday Resorts". 1936 .... $90
Archie Compston & Stanley Anderson:
"Love on The Fairway: A Romance of
      the Open Championship" .... 1936 .... $225
Archie Compston & Henry Longhurst:
"Go Golfing" .... 1937 .... $100
C. H. Compton:
"The Antiquity of Golf" .... 1881 ...... $2,750
Comrie, Dakers, & Wright:
"Liberton Golf Club 1920-1980" .... 1980 .... $55
Timothy F. Cornstock:
"The Sutter Club. One Hundred Years" .... 1989 .... $65
Dale Concannon:
"Golfing Bygonnes" .... 1989 .... $20
"Golf The Early Days" .... 1995 .... $30
Harvey Conley:
"Golf Made Easy The H.A.R.D. Way" .... 1965 .... $10
Conaught Club:
"Connaught Club" .... 1930 .... $75
"Connaught Club" .... 1932 .... $50
Connecticut State Seniors Golf Association:
" Connecticut State Seniors Golf Association" 1940 .... $125

James Connelly:
"A Temple of Golf: A History of Woking Golf
Club 1893-1993" .... 1992 .... $35
Joseph Connolly:
"P. G. Wodehouse".................................... 1979 .... $15
Robert Connolly:
"How To Become A Golfer And Have No
One To Blame But Yourself" .... 1955 .... $5
"Carnaby Threep's Golf Class".................... 1970 .... $5
Brandon Conron:
"The London Hunt and Country Club".......... 1985 .... $25
William Conroy:
"Fifty Years of Apawamis" .... 1940 .... $400
Conservative Club:
"Rules And Bye-Laws of the
Conservative Club" .... 1929 .... $75
"Rules And Bye-Laws of the
Conservative Club" .... 1932 .... $50
A. D. Converse:
"Toy Town Golf Course" .... 1926 ....$1200
Bernard Cooke:
"Newnes All Color Golf Guide"..................... 1984 .... $20
"Golf The Professional Approach" .... 1987 .... $10
Cyrus G. Cooke:
"Boys' Outdoor Sports" .... 1895 ....$1000
Richard Coop:
"Mind Over Golf"...................................... 1993 .... $15
David Cooper:
"Golfing Resorts On The Glasgow and
South-Western Railway" .... 1907 ....$3750
"Far & Sure Notes on the Golfing Resorts on
The Glasgow & South Western
Railway".. 1912 ....$4500
Jim Cooper:
"A.G. Spalding & Bros., Pre-1930 Clubs,
Trademarks, Sub-Marks And Etc. And
Other Spalding Collectibles" .... 1985 .... $10
Samuel W. Cooper:
"The Nineteenth Hole And Other Lyrics
of the Links" .... 1921 .... $375
Winston Copper:
"Links with a past - A history of the
St Clair Golf Club .... 2004 .... $20

Edwin J. Coopman:
"The History of the San Francisco Golf Club". 1978 .... $300
Copt Heath Golf Club:
"Copt Heath Golf Club 1907-1977" .... 1977 .... $20
"Copt Heath Golf Club 1910-1985" .... 1985 .... $20
Coquillard G & C. C:
"Coqullard Golf Club .... 1926 .... $150
Jim Corbett & Chris Aoki:
"The Golf Book For Kids" .... 2000 .... $15
Ronnie Corbett:
"Ronnie Corbett's Armchair Golf" .... 1986 .... $10
Fred Corcoran:
"The Official Golf Guide With The Official
    USGA Rules" .... 1949 .... $65
"Unplayable Lies" .... 1965 .... $65
Michael Corcoran:
"The Golf Dictionary" .... 1997 .... $15
Corrigan & Reynolds:
"The Glamorganshire Golf Club: A Centenary
    History 1890-1990" .... 1990 .... $45
Barry Cork:
"Dead Ball" .... 1989 .... $25
"Laid Dead" .... 1990 .... $25
"Unnatural Hazard" .... 1990 .... $25
"Winter Rules" .... 1991 .... $20
Peter Corley-Smith:
"Victoria Golf Club 1893-1993" .... 1992 .... $75
    100 Copies Signed .... 1992 .... $300
Geoffrey S. Cornish:
"Eighteen Stakes on a Sunday Afternoon" .... 2002 .... $125
    Ltd Ed of 75 Fiddlers Green Edition...... 2002 .... $475
Cornish & Hurdzan:
"Golf Course Design" (700 Copies) .... 2006 .... $150
    Ltd Edition of 75 Copies..................... 2006 .... $425
Geoffrey S. Cornish & William G. Robinson:
"Golf Course Design, An Introduction".......... 1972 .... $95
Geoffrey S. Cornish & Ronald W. Whitten:
"The Golf Course" .... 1981 .... $75
    200 Copies Signed .... 1981 .... $195
    Revised Edition.............................. 1988 .... $40
"The Architects of Golf"............................. 1981 .... $95
    Revised Edition.............................. 1993 .... $75
David Cornwell:
"Hanover Country Club at Dartmouth

College 1899-1999" .... 1999 .... $25
Corral de Tierra C. C:
"Corral de Tierra Country Club
25th Anniversary"............................. 1984 .... $30
Royal Cortissoz:
"Nine Holes of Golf".................................. 1922 .... $250
"The Ekwanok Country Club" .... 1937 .... $600
Roaslynde Cossey:
"Golfing Ladies: Five Centuries of Golf in
Great Britain And Ireland"................. 1984 .... $50
Con Costello:
"100 Years on The Short Grass" .... 1996 .... $50
Ralph Costello:
"The First Fifty Years." .... 1987 .... $45
A. J. Costelloe:
"Faversham Golf Club 1902-1983".............. 1983 .... $20
Geoffrey Cotterell:
"Go Said The Bird" .... 1966 .... $65
C. K. Cotton:
"Porters Park Golf Club" .... 1971 .... $10
Henry Cotton:
"Henry Cotton Says..."............................. 1962 .... $35
"Henry Cotton's Guide To Golf In
The British Isles" .... 1969 .... $40
"This Game of Golf"................................. 1948 .... $250
Memorial Tournament reprint
(200 Copies) .... 1989 .... $175
"Golf: Being A Short Treatise For the Use of
Young People Who Aspire to Proficiency
in The Royal and Ancient Game" .... 1931 .... $225
"Golf: A Pictorial History" .... 1975 .... $40
"Hints on Playing With Steel Shafts" .... 1933 .... $300
"A History of Golf Illustrated"..................... 1975 .... $60
"My Golfing Album" .... 1959 .... $75
"My Swing" .... 1952 .... $35
"The Picture Story of The Golf Game" .... 1965 .... $45
"Play Better Golf"..................................... 1973 .... $35
"Some Golfing Ifs" .... 1948 .... $175
"Study The Golf Game With Henry Cotton" ... 1964 .... $45
"Thanks For The Game" .... 1980 .... $75
William Coull:
"Golf In Montrose" .... 1993 .... $20
Country Club of Asheville:
"One Hundred Years: The History of the

Beardwood – History of the
Los Angeles Country Club

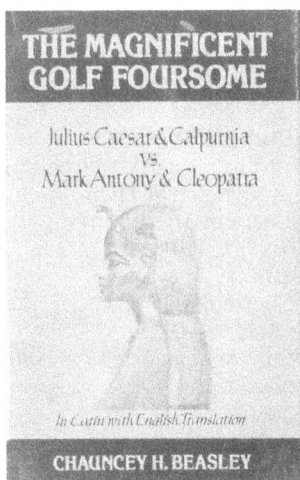

Beasley – The Magnificent
Golf Foursome

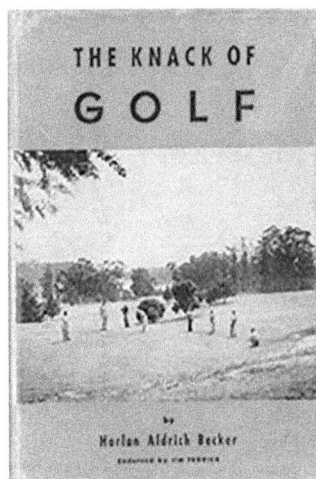

Becker – The Knack of Golf
(Dust Jacket (250 Copies)

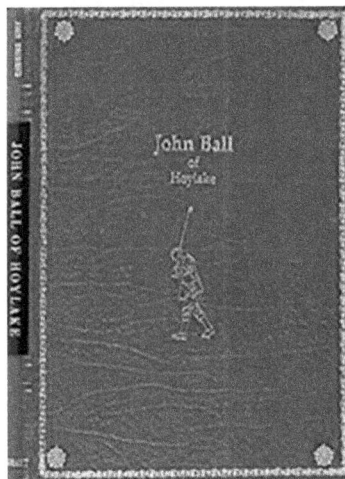

Behrend – John Ball of Hoylake
(100 Copies)

Thousands of color book illustrations visible at
www.rogeregilchrist.com

Country Club of Asheville Inc" .... 1994 .... $45
Country Club of Fairfield:
"The Country Club of Fairfield
1914-1966" .... 1966 .... $75
Country Club of York:
"Country Club of York Yearbook In Which
The History of The Club Is Reviewed" .. 1929 .... $250
"The History of The Country Club of York
1899-1975" .... 1975 .... $125
Fred Couples:
"Total Shotmaking" .... 1994 .... $15
Cowdray Park G. C:
"Cowdray Park Golf Club Official Handbook".. 1975 .... $25
Geoffrey Cousins:
"Golf In Britain" .... 1975 .... $55
"Golfers At Law" .... 1958 .... $135
"The Handbook of Golf" .... 1969 .... $30
"Lords of the Links" .... 1977 .... $65
"Manor House Hotel Golf Course" .... 1965 .... $15
Geoffrey Cousins & Bill Cox:
"The State Express: The Book of Golf" .... 1962 .... $20
Geoffrey Cousins & Don Pottinger:
"An Atlas of Golf" .... 1974 .... $25
Geoffrey Cousins & Tom Scott:
"A Century of Opens" .... 1961 .... $75
Coventry Hearsall G. C:
"Coventry Hearsall Golf Club" .... 1937 .... $75
"The History of Coventry Hearsall Golf
Club 1894-1994 .... 1994 .... $25
A. T. Cowell:
"Kinderminster Golf Club" .... 1971 .... $25
James J. Cowen:
"Hacienda Golf Club. A History".................. 1995 .... $35
A. Bertran Cox:
"A History of the Mount Osmond Golf Club" .. 1977 .... $90
"Out of The Rough, A History of The
Mount Lofty Golf Club 1925-1975" ...... 1975 .... $75
Charles S. Cox:
"Spalding's Official Golf Guide"(3rd Edition) ... 1897 ....$1550
Fifth Edition .... 1900 .... $175
Paul Cox & Jim Koger:
"The City That Broke Par" .... 1971 ....$5
Wiffy Cox:
"The Wiffy Cox Story"................................ 1970 .... $150

"How To Cut Strokes Off Your Score" .... 1960 .... $35
William J. Cox:
"Can I Help You? The Guide To Better Golf" .. 1954 .... $55
"W. J. Cox And Golf" .... 1936 .... $25
"Improve Your Game" .... 1963 .... $15
"Play Better Golf" .... 1952 .... $20
William J. Cox & Nicholas Tremayne:
"Bill Cox's Golf Companion" .... 1969 .... $15
Barry Coyne:
""The West Lancaster Golf Club; A History
of Golf at Blundellsands .... 1992 .... $50
John Coyne:
"Better Golf" .... 1972 .... $25
"Golf For Women" .... 1975 .... $10
"Playing With The Pros" .... 1990 .... $20
"The New Golf For Women" .... 1973 .... $20
Linda Craft & Penny Zavichas:
"The Craft-Zavichas Golfer's Cookbook" .... 1979 .... $5
"The Craft-Zavichas Golfer's Cookbook II" .... 1983 .... $5
Brian Crafter:
"Winning Golf" .... 1983 .... $5
John C. Craigie:
"Golf Match Club: Record of Matches
1897 to 1938" .... 1938 .... $175
Robert A. Crampsey:
"The History of Cathkin Braes Golf
Club 1888-1988" .... 1988 .... $35
"Ranfurly Castle Golf Club" .... 1989 .... $30
"St Mungo's Gowfers: The History of
Glasgow Golf Club 1787-1987 .... 1987 .... $45
"The Breezy Links o'Troon" .... 2000 .... $35
Charles E. Crane:
"Brattleboro Country Club" .... 1926 .... $50
Leo Crane:
"California Golf Directory" .... 1953 .... $35
"Putting: The Name of The Game" .... 1966 .... $10
Peter G. Cranford:
"The Winning Touch In Golf" .... 1961 .... $20
Frank Craven:
"The 19th Hole, A Comedy In Three Acts" ..... 1928 .... $150
Crawford, MacGregor, & Canby:
"Golf Score Book" .... 1899 .... $225
"How Boys Can Enjoy Golf" .... 1920 .... $95
"The Influence of Golf In Industry" .... 1921 .... $150

Thousands of color book illustrations visible at
www.rogeregilchrist.com

"Stepping Stones To A Golf Course".............. 1921 .... $110
"Golf: The Game of Games"........................ 1922 .... $150
"Municipal Golf Courses" .... 1925 .... $125
"Inside Information On Golf Clubs .... 1928 .... $125
"Rule & Scorebook" .... 1930 .... $95
Iain Crawford:
"The Open Guide To Royal St. George's
    And Sandwich".................................. 1981 .... $25
"The Open Guide To Royal Troon And Kyle" .. 1982 .... $25
"Scottish Brewers Open Guide To The
    Old Course & St. Andrews"................. 1982 .... $20
"The Open Guide To Royal Lytham
    & St Anne's" .... 1988 .... $20
Leonard Crawley:
"Playfair Golf Annual 1950" .... 1950 .... $25
"Playfair Golf Annual 1951" .... 1951 .... $25
"Playfair Golf Annual 1952" .... 1952 .... $35
"Playfair Golf Annual 1953" .... 1953 .... $35
"The Golfing Year 1954"............................. 1954 .... $15
"The Golfing Year 1960"............................. 1960 .... $15
John Creagh:
"Golden Years of Australian Golf" .... 1977 .... $20
William Crehan:
"Who's Who In Golf"................................... 1971 .... $10
Eric Cremin:
"Par Golf" .... 1952 .... $10
D. D. Crews & J. G. Germuga:
"Caddie Handbook" .... 1946 .... $50
T. M. Cribbin:
"The Wilmslow Golf Club".......................... 1950 .... $35
Thomas Cribbin:
"Correct Caddy Conduct" .... 1920 .... $95
Criccieth G. C:
"Criccieth Golf Club"................................. 1952 .... $65
Martha O. Crisp & Ruth A. Leffer:
"Women's Long Island Golf Association,
    The First Fifty Years 1930-1980"........ 1980 .... $20
Bruce Critchley:
"Golf And All Its Glory" .... 1993 .... $25
Claude Crockford:
"The Complete Golf Course" (1000 Copies)... 1993 .... $175
Corrine Crogen:
"Golf Fundamentals".................................. 1964 .... $5
"Golf Fundamentals For Students

And Teachers"................................... 1960 ....$5
Charles Crombie:
  "Par For The Course"................................ 1964 .... $45
  "Some Rules of Golf"................................ 1966 .... $125
  "The Rules of Golf Illustrated"..................... 1905 .....$2,400
  "The Rules of Golf Album Two".................... 1910 ....$2000
      Reprint.. 1966 .... $150
      Reprint.. 1993 .... $20
Cromer G. C:
  "Cromer Golf Club History - Golden Jubilee
      1929-1979" .... 1979 .... $45
Robert A. Cromie:
  "Golf For Boys And Girls" .... 1965 .... $10
  "New Angles On Putting And Chipping"......... 1960 .... $15
  "Par For The Course: A Golfer's Anthology"... 1964 .... $25
Tim Cronin:
  "A Century of Golf -Western Golf Association
      1899-1999" .... 1999 .... $35
  "The Spirit of Medinah"............................. 2001 .... $125
A. C. M. Croome:
  "The Camberley Heath Golf Club"................ 1913 .... $150
Povan Crosbie:
  "Fairways And Foul" .... 1964 .... $65
Crosby, Lockwood & Co:
  "The Boy's Own Book" .... 1886 .... $45
Charles Cross:
  "Golfers Foot"... 1916 .... $75
William H. Crouch:
  "Guide To The Analysis of Golf Clubs
      And Country Clubs"........................... 1968 .... $50
Thomas Y. Crowell:
  "How to Play Golf.................................... 1907 .... $125
F. Crucelli:
  "Mistura Curiosa"..................................... 1869 .... $200
Cruden Bay G.C:
  "A Century of Golf at Cruden Bay
      1899-1999" .... 1998 .... $50
Stewart Cruden:
  "Bruntsfield Links Golfing Society".............. 1992 .... $45
Charles Cruickshank:
  "The History of Royal Wimbledon
      1865-1986" .... 1987 .... $95
  "The Tang Murders" .... 1976 .... $35

Frederick D. Cruickshank:
"The History of The Weston Golf and
Country Club" (1000 Copies) .... 1980 .... $65
George A. Crump:
"Monument to Golf".................................. 1948 ....$1100
Leon Crump & John Stravinsky:
"Drive For Show, Putt For Dough" .... 1997 .... $15
John Cubbage:
"Chronicle of the Islay Golf Club And
The Machrie Links"............................ 1996 .... $95
Cubbon & Markuson:
"Soil Management for Greenkeepers"........... 1933 .... $750
Cumberland & Westmoreland:
"Cumberland and Westmoreland Union
of Golf Clubs".................................. 1936 .... $650
T. E. Cumings:
"Golf Simplified Through the Inductive
Method" .... 1927 .... $350
George L. Cummings:
"It Goes Where You Hit It" .... 1948 .... $120
James Cundell:
"Rules of The Thistle Golf Club".................. 1824 .... $20,000
Golf House Reprint (1900 Copies) .... 1983 .... $145
Tom Cunneff:
"Hollywood On The Links" .... 1998 .... $10
Andrew S. Cunningham:
"The Golf Clubs Round Largo Bay".............. 1909 .....$2,750
"Inverkeithing, North Queens Ferry,
Limekilns, Charlestown, The Ferryhills" 1899 ....$1075
"Lundin Links, Upper And Lower
Largo And Leven" .... 1913 .... $950
Carl Cunningham:
"Down The Middle"................................... 1952 .... $15
George Cunningham:
"Roscrea Golf Club 1892-1992 .... 1992 .... $25
J. P. Cunningham:
"Stirling Golf Club Centenary 1869-1969"..... 1969 .... $45
A. Curely & R. Perrier:
"Le Golf".. 1923 .... $250
Calamo Currente:
"Half Hours With An Old Golfer" .... 1895 .... $750
Frederick H. Curtiss & John Heard:
"The Country Club 1882-1932" .... 1932 .... $400

Norman Dabell:
"How We Won The Ryder Cup"..................... 1997 .... $15
Muriel D'Agostino:
"Yahnundasis Golf Club A Century of
    Tradition 1897-1997" .... 1997 .... $75
Dalbeattie G. C:
"The Book of Dalbeattie Golf Club" .... 1912 ....$1250
Paul Daley:
"Golf Links the Inside Story) (100 Copies).... 2000 .... $150
"Golf Architecture A World Wide
    Perspective" (Six Volumes) .... 2002-2014 .... $400
    (100 Leather Bound Copies)....... 2002-2014 .... $900
J. More Dall:
Guide to Elie & Earlsferry Golf Course" .... 1899 .... $900
W. Dalrymple:
"Golfer's Guide To The Game And Greens of
    Scotland" .... 1894 ....$2995
"The Golfer's Referee" .... 1897 .... $745
"Handbook of Golf" .... 1895 .... $700
Conor Daly:
"Buried Lies" .... 1996 .... $10
Fred Daly:
"Golf As I See It" .... 1951 .... $35
"Golfing In Northern Ireland"..................... 1971 .... $35
John Daly:
"Grip It And Rip It"................................... 1992 .... $15
Marshall Dann:
"Golfdom's Greatest Tournaments".............. 1952 .... $10
T. C. Danskin:
"Whitley Bay Golf Club 1890-1990" .... 1990 .... $25
James Dante & Leo Diegel:
"The Nine Bad Shots In Golf And What To
    Do About Them" .... 1947 .... $95
    1st UK edition .... 1948 .... $45
James Dante & Len Elliott:
"Four Magic Moves To Winning Golf" .... 1962 .... $40
"Stop That Slice" .... 1953 .... $40
"What's Wrong With Your Golf?"................. 1978 .... $10
Michael D'Antonio:
"Tin Cup Dreams" .... 2000 .... $15
Allison Danzig & Peter Brandwein:
"Sport's Golden Age"................................ 1948 .... $20
L. Claughton Darbyshire:
"Go Golfing In Britain A Hole By Hole Survey

Thousands of color book illustrations visible at
www.rogeregilchrist.com

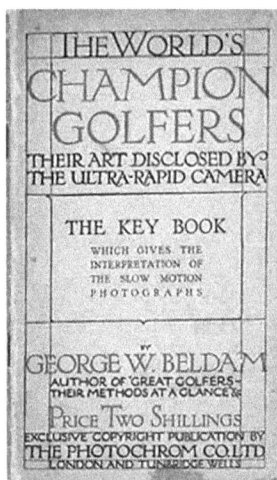

Beldham – Champion Golfers

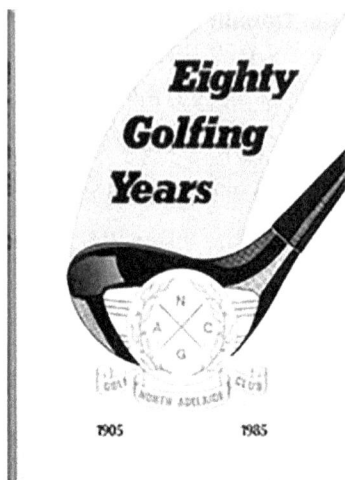

Bell – Eighty Golfing Years

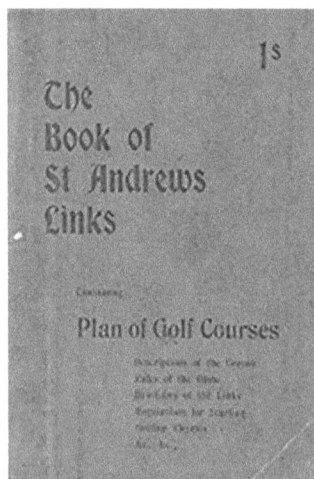

Bennett – The Book of St Andrews Links

Black – Game of Golf (70 Copies)

of 25 Famous Seaside Courses" .... 1961 .... $65
Dee Darden:
"Inside The Ropes".................................... 1994 .... $35
Robert Darden & P. J. Richardson:
"The Way of An Eagle"............................... 1996 .... $15
Richard Darlington:
"Aberdovey Golf Club: A Round of
    A Hundred Years 1886-1986" .... 1986 .... $45
August F. Daro:
"The Inside Swing. Key To Better Golf" .... 1972 .... $15
Darsie L. Darsie:
"My Greatest Day In Golf" .... 1950 .... $45
Bernard Darwin:
"Aberdovey Golf Club" .... 1952 .... $175
"Aberdovey Golf Club" .... 1966 .... $175
"About These New Rules" .... 1954 .... $200
"Aldeburgh Golf Club"................................ 1939 .... $395
"Ashridge Golf Club"................................. 1938 .... $200
"At Odd Moments" .... 1941 .... $95
"The Beaconsfield Golf Club"....................... 1947 .... $250
"Berkhamsted Golf Club"............................ 1946 .... $110
"The Bogner Golf Club" .... 1938 .... $195
"James Braid"... 1952 .... $195
    Reprint (200 Copies) .... 1981 .... $60
"Brancepeth Castle Golf Club"..................... 1954 .... $100
"British Clubs" .... 1933 .... $50
"British Golf" .... 1946 .... $175
"British Sport And Games" .... 1940 .... $235
"Burhill Club" .... 1939 .... $175
"The Burnham & Berrow Golf Club".............. 1938 .... $200
"The Carlisle & Silloth Golf Club" .... 1946 .... $95
"Come To Britain for Golf" .... 1946 .... $400
"The Cooden Beach Golf Club Bexhill-on Sea. 1936 .... $595
"The Crowsborough Beacon Golf Club" .... 1934 .... $195
"Darwin On The Green"............................... 1986 .... $40
"A Day's Golf At Leeds Castle May 15th 1934"1934........ $875
"Dorset Golf Club"..................................... 1932 .... $500
"The Downe Golf Club" .... 1947 .... $75
"The East Devon Golf Club" .... 1947 .... $275
"Every Idle Dream" .... 1948 .... $65
"The Farnham Golf Club"............................ 1938 .... $350
"Fifty Years Of "Country Life"...................... 1947 .... $150
"The Formby Golf Club" .... 1934 .... $300
"A Friendly Round".................................... 1922 .... $900

With Dust Jacket .... 1922 ...... $4500
"The Frilford Heath Golf Club" .... 1938 .... $175
"The Game's Afoot!: An Anthology
     of Sports Games and the Open Air" ..... 1926 .... $450
     Reprint .... 1999 .... $35
"Golf Between Two Wars" .... 1944 .... $175
     Reprint .... 1985 .... $20
"The Golf Courses of The British Isles" .... 1910 ...... $1500
     Reprint .... 1925 .... $375
     Classics of Golf Reprint .... 1988 .... $75
"The Golf Courses Of Great Britain" .... 1925 ...... $1250
     2nd Edition .... 1925 .... $750
"Golf From The Times" .... 1912 ..... $1,750
"Golf In Great Britain And Ireland" .... 1930 .... $575
"Golf, Pleasures of Life Series" .... 1954 .... $275
"Golf: Some Hints And Suggestions" .... 1920 ..... $2,500
     2nd Edition .... 1920 ..... $1,500
     Reprint .... 1999 .... $45
"A Golfer's Gallery of Old Masters" .... 1920 ..... $2,100
"Golfing By-Paths" .... 1946 .... $200
"W. G. Grace" .... 1934 .... $65
"Green Memories" .... 1928 .... $495
     Limited Edition Reprint .... 1998 .... $50
"John Gully and His Times" .... 1935 .... $75
"The Happy Golfer - The American
     Golfer Magazine 1922-1936" .... 1997 .... $35
"Harewood Downs Golf Club" .... 1948 .... $60
"The Hayling Golf Club" .... 1947 .... $75
"Hints On Golf" .... 1912 ..... $2,550
"Huntstanton Golf Club" .... 1928 .... $350
"Knole Park Golf Club" .... 1926 .... $350
"The Ilfield Golf And Country Club" .... 1947 .... $375
"The Ilkley Golf Club" .... 1931 .... $300
"Langley Park Golf Club" .... 1938 .... $450
"Life Is Sweet Brother" .... 1940 .... $225
"The Liphook Golf Club" .... 1947 .... $60
"The Lucifer Golfing Society" .... 1942 .... $125
"The Lure of London" .... 1930 .... $200
"Mr Tootleloo One & Two" .... 1932 .... $275
"The New Golf Club St. Andrews" .... 1924 ...... $1250
"North Foreland Golf Club" .... 1939 .... $250
"North Hants G. C. Official Handbook" .... 1938 .... $525
"North Hants Golf Club" .... 1949 .... $110
"Out of The Rough" .... 1932 .... $175

Leather Bound Edition .... 1932 .... $500
"The Oxhey Golf Club" .... 1934 .... $400
"Pack Clouds Away" .... 1941 .... $150
"Playing The Like" .... 1934 .... $595
Leather Bound Edition .... 1934 .... $500
Reprint .... 2001 .... $35
"Prince's Golf Club" .... 1938 .... $375
"Robinsons of Bristol 1844-1944" .... 1945 .... $150
"The Rochester And Cobham Park Golf Club". 1938 .... $300
"A Round of Golf" .... 1937 .... $500
"A Round of Golf On The L. & N.E.R." .... 1925 .... $550
Reprint .... 1937 .... $300
"The Royal And Ancient Golf Club of
St. Andrews Report For 1948" .... 1948 .... $750
"The Royal Ashdown Forest Golf Club" .... 1938 .... $350
"The Royal Blackheath Golf Club" .... 1938 .... $400
"The Royal Cinque Ports Golf Club" .... 1935 .... $300
"The Royal Liverpool Golf Club" .... 1922 .... $3000
"The Royal Liverpool Golf Club" .... 1924 .... $2500
"The Royal North Devon Golf Club" .... 1921 .... $475
"The Royal North Devon Golf Club
Westward Ho!' .... 1946 .... $200
"The Royal West Norfolk Golf Club" .... 1923 .... $375
"The Royal Wimbleton Golf Club" .... 1922 .... $450
"Rubs of The Green" .... 1936 .... $725
"The Rye Golf Club" .... 1939 .... $550
"The Saunton Golf Club" .... 1926 .... $350
"Second Shots: Casual Talks About Golf" ...... 1930 .... $295
"Six Golfing Shots by Six Famous Players" .... 1927 .... $375
"St. Enodoc Golf Club" .... 1947 .... $300
"St. Enodoc Golf Club" .... 1957 .... $250
"St. Enodoc Golf Club" .... 1970 .... $200
"The St Georges Hill Golf Club" .... 1934 .... $350
"The Sundridge Park Golf Club" .... 1946 .... $50
"The Tandridge Golf Club" .... 1925 .... $350
"The Tale of Mr Tottleloo" .... 1925 .... $275
"Tee Shots And Others" .... 1911 .... $475
USGA Reprint (1500 Copies) .... 1984 .... $165
"The Teignmouth Golf Club" .... 1925 .... $350
"The Walton Heath Golf Club" .... 1937 .... $425
"Walton Heath Golf Club" .... 1975 .... $95
"Welshpool Golf Club Ltd" .... 1958 .... $125
"West Hill Golf Club" .... 1946 .... $250
"West Kent Golf Club" .... 1951 .... $45

Thousands of color book illustrations visible at
www.rogeregilchrist.com

"The West Lancashire Golf Club" .... 1934 .... $265
"The West Surrey Golf Club" .... 1938 .... $265
"The West Sussex Golf Club" .... 1935 .... $275
"The Willingdon Golf Club" .... 1947 .... $55
"The Woking Golf Club" .... 1949 .... $40
"Worchester Golf Club Malvern" .... 1927 .... $400
"The World That Fred Made" .... 1955 .... $150
"The Worplesdon Golf Club" .... 1946 .... $90
Bernard Darwin & Others:
"A History of Golf In Britain" .... 1952 .... $175
    Classics of Golf Reprint .... 1990 .... $35
Keith Davey & Norman Griffiths:
"Cannoch Chase & Brocton Hall Golf Clubs
    1894-1994" .... 1994 .... $45
John Davidson:
"Wilshire Golf Club Centenary 1890-1990" .... 1990 .... $10
R. E. Davidson:
"Golfing At Yokine" .... 1967 .... $10
Dalton R. Daves:
"Putters of Distinction" .... 1996 .... $40
David & Patricia Davies:
"Golf: The Major Championships 1987" .... 1987 .... $30
Donald Davies:
" The History of Cardigan Golf Club" .... 1991 .... $45
D. J. Davies:
"Pontypool Golf Club, Jubilee 1903-1953" ..... 1954 .... $150
E. J. Davies & G. W. Brown:
"The Royal North Devon Golf Club
    1864-1989" Deluxe Ed (100 Copies) .... 1989 .... $250
        Regular Edition (500 Copies) ..... 1989 .... $125
John Davies:
"Yardley Country Club A Casual History
    1928-1978" .... 1978 .... $20
Peter Davies:
"Davies' Dictionary of Golf Terms" .... 1980 .... $25
"Historical Dictionary of Golfing Terms" .... 1992 .... $25
Bob Davis:
"The Way of A Caddie With A Man" .... 1926 .... $125
Evangeline McLennon Davis:
"The Lure of the Highlands" (750 Copies) ..... 1981 .... $175
Joe G. Davis:
"Blue Book of Chicago Golfers" .... 1925 .... $250
"Blue Book of Chicago Golfers, 1925-26" ...... 1926 .... $165
"Blue Book of Chicago Golfers" .... 1928 .... $150

Thousands of color book illustrations visible at
www.rogeregilchrist.com

"Major Golf Trophies" .... 1928 .... $165

Martin Davis:
"The Legend of Bobby Jones"...................... 1996 .... $30
"Byron Nelson" .... 1996 .... $50

Robert H. Davis:
"Do You Know How A Golf Ball Is Made" .... 1928 .... $65
"The Way of A Caddie With A Man".............. 1926 .... $150

William H. Davis:
"100 Great Golf Courses–And Then Some".... 1982 .... $30
"Great Golf Courses of The World"............... 1974 .... $35
"The Punch Book of Golf" .... 1973 .... $35
"The Worlds Best Golf" .... 1991 .... $20

Davyhulme Park G. C:
"Davyhulme Park Golf Club 75th Anniversary"1985.......... $15

George Dawkins:
"Keys To The Golf Swing"............................ 1976 .... $15

R. B. Dawson:
"Practical Lawn Craft" .... 1939 .... $125

Dayton C. C:
"History of the Dayton Country Club
  1896-1976" .... 1976 .... $45

Deal Golf & C. C:
"Deal Golf And Country Club, Club House
  And Grounds, Deal, New Jersey"......... 1911 .... $50
"Deal Golf Club, Incorporated June 13th
  1899, Deal, New Jersey".................... 1917 .... $50
"Deal Golf And Country Club 1898-1973" ..... 1973 .... $35

W. DeAula:
"St. Andrews: Ancient and Modern"............. 1870 .... $850

Betty Debenham:
"Bournemouth Golf Club" .... 1951 .... $20
"Carlisle And Silloth Golf Club".................... 1950 .... $20
"Chestfield Golf Club" .... 1950 .... $20
"Delamere Forest Golf Club" .... 1950 .... $20
"Epsom Golf Club"..................................... 1950 .... $20
"Goring & Streatley Golf Club" .... 1950 .... $20
"Hallowes Golf Club".................................. 1950 .... $20
"Luffenham Heath Golf Club" .... 1950 .... $20
"Northampton Golf Club"............................. 1950 .... $20
"Painswick Golf Club".................................. 1950 .... $20
"Peterborough Golf Club" .... 1950 .... $20
"Royal Epping Forest Golf Club" .... 1950 .... $20
"Scarcroft Golf Club" .... 1950 .... $20
"South Staffordshire Golf Club" .... 1950 .... $20

"Thorpe Hall Golf Club" .... 1950 .... $20
"Worsely Golf Club" .... 1950 .... $20
"Wyke Green Golf Club" .... 1950 .... $20
Robert Debenham:
 "The Metropolitan Golf Club 1908-1929" ...... 1929 .... $1350
Paul Deegan:
 "Jack Nicklaus: The Golden Bear" .... 1974 .... $15
Deeside G. C:
 "Deeside Golf Club 1903-1953" .... 1953 .... $95
John DeGarmo & Ray Ellis:
 "The Road to Ballybunion" .... 1997 .... $35
Louis DeGarmo:
 "Play Golf And Enjoy It" .... 1954 .... $10
Elisabeth De Gramont:
 "Le Golf" .... 1930 .... $100
Christian DeGuerre & Patrick Failliott:
 "Europe's Golf Guide" .... 1982 .... $15
Brian J. Delacey:
 "Battlefield of The Best" (200 Copies) .... 1999 .... $225
John Delery:
 "The Golfers Companion" .... 1992 .... $25
John Delery & Angus Garber:
 "100 Years of The US Open" .... 1993 .... $20
Delaware & Hudson Railroad:
 "Golf: A Directory of Courses In The Summer
      Paradise On The Delaware and
      Hudson Line" .... 1916 .... $145
G. Delgado:
 "Golf of All Kinds" .... 1935 .... $225
Delgany G. C:
 "Delgany Golf Club 75th Anniversary
      1908-1983" .... 1983 .... $15
Ralph Dellor:
 "British Golf Courses: A Guide To
      Courses In The British Isles" .... 1974 .... $20
Deming Co:
 "Deming Water Supply Installations in Golf
      and Country Clubs, Private Estates
      and Summer Homes" .... 1930 .... $150
John Delaforce:
 "A Short History of the Oporto Golf Club" ..... 1960 .... $125
Del Paso C. C:
 "Del Paso Country Club Seventy Five Years
      1916-1991" .... 1991 .... $90

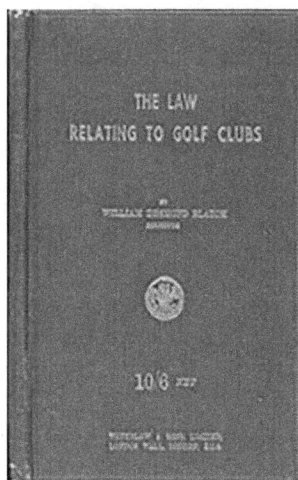

Blatch – The Law Relating to
Golf Clubs

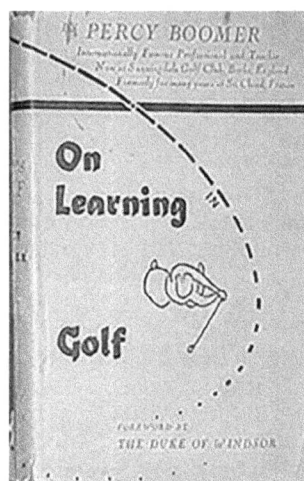

Boomer – On Learning Golf

Bowman – Westchester Biltmore
Country Club

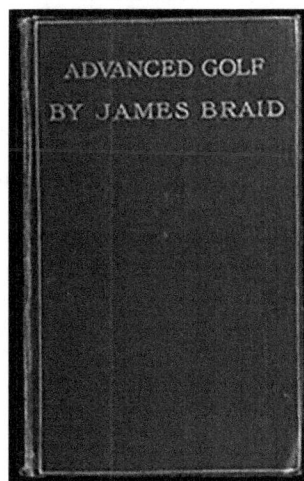

Braid – Advanced Golf

Thousands of color book illustrations visible at
www.rogeregilchrist.com

Del Monte G & C. C:
"Golf At Del Monte California" .... 1903 ...... $2400
"Golf Links at Del Monte" .... 1903 ...... $2750
"Golf And Other Sports At Del Monte" .... 1913 .... $300
James Demaret:
"My Partner Ben Hogan" .... 1954 .... $195
John DeMonte:
"A Collection And Portfolio of Golf Humor" .... 1983 .... $10
"The Kings James' Version of The
    Game of Golfe"................................. 1980 .... $15
"The Kings James' Version of The
    Game of Golfe Book II"...................... 1982 .... $15
Frank T. Denis & Reginald E Knight:
"The Kanawaki Golf Club 50th
    Anniversary Book" .... 1964 .... $125
Tom Dentino:
"The Basic Golf Swing" .... 1970 .... $10
George Bernhard Depping:
"Evenings Entertainments"   2 Volumes........ 1811 .... $175
Lord Desborough:
"Fifty Years of Sport at Oxford, Cambridge
    and the Great Public Schools"
    (Three Volumes)............................. 1913 .... $195
Thure De Thulstrup:
"Outdoor Pictures" .... 1899 .... $300
Blaine R. Detrick:
"Golf And The Gospel: How To Improve Your
    Score In The Game of Life" .... 1985 .... $10
Detroit C. C:
"Facts About The Links of The Detroit
    Country Club" .... 1916 .... $195
Detroit G. C:
"Detroit Golf Club A Chronicle of Forty Years
    of Substantial Achievement
    1899-1939" (1000 copies) .... 1939 .... $295
"Detroit Golf Club. 100 Years"..................... 1998 .... $45
Dominic Devine:
"Three Green Bottles"................................ 1972 .... $10
Barry Devlin:
"The Golf Widow"..................................... 1953 .... $45
Bruce Devlin:
"Australia's Bruce Devlin Championship Golf" 1970 .... $20
"Bruce Devlin Flip Book Instructions,
    Drive And Wedge" .... 1971 .... $20

Thousands of color book illustrations visible at
www.rogeregilchrist.com

"Play Like The Devil" .... 1967 .... $25
Duke Of Devonshire:
"The Buxton & High Peak Golf Club;
    The First 100 Years"......................... 1987 .... $25
William O. DeWitt:
"DeWitt's Golf Year Book" .... 1953 .... $70
E. R. Ted Dexter:
"My Golf".. 1982 .... $15
E. R. Ted Dexter & Clifford Makins:
"Deadly Putter"....................................... 1979 .... $50
E. R. Ted Dexter & Michael McDonnell:
"The World of Golf" .... 1970 .... $10
Joseph C. Dey Jr:
"Golf"... 1977 .... $20
"Golf Rules In Pictures" .... 1964 .... $20
M. E. Deyo:
"The Easy Way To Stay In Shape For Golf" ... 1971 .... $10
Carrol Diaz:
"Golf: A Beginners Guide" .... 1974 .... $5
Diaz & Hartough:
"Hallowed Ground"................................... 1999 .... $50
Thomas F. Dibdin:
"A Bibliographical Antiqarian And
    Picturesque Tour" (Two Volumes)...... 1838 .... $450
Ethel Dickie:
"Ladies Panmure Golf Club Bazaar"............. 1908 .... $700
Bill & Meredith Dickinson:
"A History of Enfield Golf Club" .... 1993 .... $40
Gardner Dickinson:
"Let Er Rip!"... 1994 .... $30
Patric Dickinson:
"The Good Minute: An Autobiographical
    Study" .... 1965 .... $75
"A Round of Golf Courses: A Selection
    of The Best Eighteen"....................... 1951 .... $165
William C. Dickinson:
"Two Students At St Andrews 1711-1716".... 1952 .... $45
Pat Dickson:
"Short History of The Covelly Country Club".. 1974 .... $15
Paul Dickson:
"The Official Rules For Golfers" .... 1997 .... $10
Kettering
"Didsbury Golf Club 1891-1991" .... 1991 .... $25

Thousands of color book illustrations visible at
www.rogeregilchrist.com

Digby Diehl:
"San Gabriel Country Club. One Hundred
Years of History and Tradition".................... 2004 .... $75
Robert W. Diehl & Tom Vardon:
"The Diehl-Vardon Manual"......................... 1927 .... $140
Joseph B Dietz Jr:
"The History of Wilmington Country Club" .... 2001 .... $45
Paula DiPerna & Vikki Keller:
"Oakhurst: The Birth and Rebirth of
America's First Golf Club .... 2002 .... $25
Direlton Castle G. C:
"Direlton Castle Golf Club, 1854-1954
First Centenary" .... 1954 .... $30
Harold Dix:
"A Handbook on The Rules of Golf"............. 1927 .... $45
H. MacNeile Dixon:
"Golf-and How".. 1949 .... $35
Nancy Dixon:
"Heskeith Ladies"..................................... 1989 .... $25
Tom Doak:
"The Anatomy of A Golf Course".................. 1992 .... $45
"The Confidential Guide To Golf Courses"
(40 Copies).................................... 1988 ....$2000
1000 Copies.................................... 1994 .... $950
Revised edition............................... 1996 .... $50
Doak, Scott & Haddock:
"The Life and Work of Dr. Alister MacKenzie" 2001 .... $300
Tom Dobbin:
"Durham City Golf Centenary Year" .... 1980 .... $20
David L. Dobby:
Royal Cinque Ports Golf Club Deal" .... 1992 .... $395
Peter Dobereiner:
"The Book of Golf Disasters"...................... 1983 .... $35
"Down The Nineteenth Fairway;
A Golfing Anthology" .... 1982 .... $25
"For The Love of Golf: The Best
of Dobereiner"................................ 1981 .... $25
"The Game With A Hole In It" .... 1970 .... $55
"The Glorious World of Golf" .... 1973 .... $75
"Golf a' la Cart" .... 1991 .... $30
"Golf Explained: How To Take
Advantage Of The Rules". .... 1977 .... $35
"Prefered Lies About Golf".......................... 1987 .... $30
"The Golfers - The Inside Story".................. 1982 .... $35

"Stroke, Hole Or Match"............................. 1976 .... $50
"The World of Golf: The Best of Peter
    Dobereiner" .... 1981 .... $20
Marcus Dods:
    "The Bunker At The Fifth"........................ 1927 .... $125
James Dodson:
    "Final Rounds"....................................... 1996 .... $15
Randy Dodson & Joe Watts:
    "100 Years of the Utah State Amateur" .... 1998 .... $20
James Doh:
    "Bluff Point Golf and Country Club
        1890-1990" .... 1990 .... $65
Mike Doherty:
    "Golf Classics Price And Identification Guide" 1978 .... $45
Anne R. Dolan:
    "Congressional Country Club 1924-1984" ..... 1984 .... $80
Lawrence Donegan:
    "Maybe It Should Have Been A Three Iron"... 1998 .... $10
Charles Donohue & Paul Care:
    "Guide To Golf In Hampshire" .... 1977 .... $15
Richard E. Donovan & Rand Jerris:
    The Game of Golf and the Printed Word
        1566-2005" .... 2006 .... $650
Richard E. Donovan & Joseph E. Murdoch:
    "The Game of Golf And The Printed Word
        1566-1985" .... 1988 .... $125
        Presentation Copy (20 Copies)............ 1988 .... $800
Robert Donovan:
    "GHO '84 - The New Era" .... 1985 .... $10
Dooks:
    "Dooks: A Hundred Years of Golf" .... 1989 .... $35
Tarpell Dorling:
    "The Hurlingham Golf Club 1869-1953"........ 1953 .... $25
Dorwood:
    "Torwoodlee Golf Club 1895-1995 .... 1995 .... $45
Dale Douglas:
    "Lays of The Links" .... 1895 .... $325
George A. Douglas:
    "Our Little Golf Club in Maine, Cape Arundel" 2001 .... $35
George Douglas & Dalhouse Ramsey:
    "The Panmure Papers..." (2 Vols) .... 1918 .... $65
J. H. Douglas & E. R. Wastnedge:
    "The History of Carlisle Golf Club" .... 1985 .... $25

Thousands of color book illustrations visible at
www.rogeregilchrist.com

Dudley Doust:
  "Seve".. 1986 .... $15
Derek A. Dow:
  "Far and Sure: The Auckland Golf Club
      1894-1994"...................................... 1994 .... $45
James Gordon Dow:
  "The Crail Golfing Society 1786-1936" .... 1936 ....$1995
Dow & MacDonald:
  "The Crail Golfing Society 1936-1986"
      (2 Vols) .... 1986 .... $225
John C. Downie:
  "The First 100 Years of Golf at Newtonmore" 1993 .... $45
Colin Downie:
  "J. R. McKay" .... 1997 .... $15
Rick Doyle:
  "How To Cheat At Golf"............................. 1985 .... $5
Doyon & Kedl:
  Le Club de Golf Royal Quebec,
      125 ans d'histoire, 1874-1999 .... 1999 .... $75
Drives And Puts:
  "Drives And Puts : A Book of Golf Stories" .... 1899 .... $500
Tom Drury:
  "Blackwell Golf Club, Worcestershire
      A History"... 1953 .... $15
W. A. S. Dryden:
  "The History of the Panmure Golf Club
      1845-1995"...................................... 1996 .... $150
Alasdair M. Drysdale:
  "The Golf House Club, Elie: A Centenary
      History".. 1975 .... $60
Abel Dubb:
  "Why Golf"... 1921 .... $45
Dudley G. C:
  "Dudley Golf Club 1893-1993" .... 1993 .... $25
Joe Duffer:
  "The Power Swing".................................. 1949 .... $25
Charles L Dufor:
  "Seventy-Five Years: New Orleans Country
      Club 1913-1988" .... 1988 .... $95
Will Duke:
  "Fair Prey" .... 1958 .... $10
Thomas Dulack:
  "Pork, Or The Day I Lost The Masters" .... 1968 .... $35

Dumfries & Callaway G. C:
"Dumfries And Callaway Golf Club
    1880-1980" .... 1980 .... $30
Dun Laoghair G. C:
"Dun Laoghair Golf Club 1910-1985" .... 1985 .... $35
Dunany C. C:
"The Story of The Dunany Country Club"...... 1967 .... $25
Mike Dunaway & John Andrisani:
"Hit It Hard".. 1992 .... $20
Dunbar G. C:
"Dunbar Golf Club"..................................... 1955 .... $45
"Dunbar Golf Club 1794-1980".................... 1980 .... $35
Dunblane:
"Dunblane: The Official Guide".................... 1925 .... $30
David Scott Duncan:
"The Golfing Annual 1887-88 Vol 1 .... 1888 ....$1250
"The Golfing Annual 1888-1889" Vol 2 .... 1889 .... $750
"The Golfing Annual 1889-1890" Vol 3 .... 1890 .... $725
"The Golfing Annual 1890-1891" .... 1891 .... $725
"The Golfing Annual 1892-1893" .... 1893 .... $645
"The Golfing Annual 1893-1894" .... 1894 .... $600
"The Golfing Annual 1897-1898" .... 1898 .... $575
George Duncan:
"Golf At The Gallop" .... 1951 .... $150
"Golf For Women" .... 1912 .... $200
George Duncan & Bernard Darwin:
"Present Day Golf" .... 1921 .... $150
Dundas Valley Golf And Curling Club:
"Dundas Valley Golf And Curling Club
    1929-1979 50th Anniversary"............. 1979 .... $20
Caddie Dunlop:
"Leaves From My Diary"............................. 1919 .... $495
Dunlop:
"The Dunlop Book the Motorist's Guide" .... 1920 .... $225
Dunlop Rubber:
"The Making of a Maxfli" .... 1924 .... $60
Dunlop Tire:
"Golf Penalties".. 1920 .... $225
"Golf Penalties".. 1922 .... $125
"Golf Penalties".. 1931 .... $95
"Golf Penalties".. 1932 .... $30
"Golf Penalties".. 1933 .... $20
Noel Dunlop-Hill:
"History of The Scottish Ladies Golfing

Thousands of color book illustrations visible at
www.rogeregilchrist.com

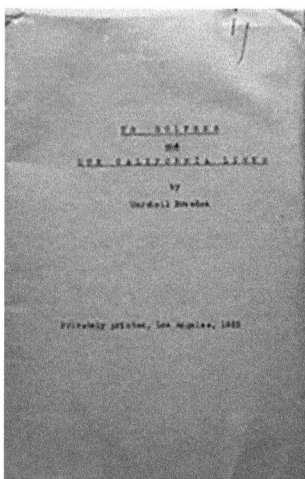

Breeden – Us Golfers and Our California Links (DJ)

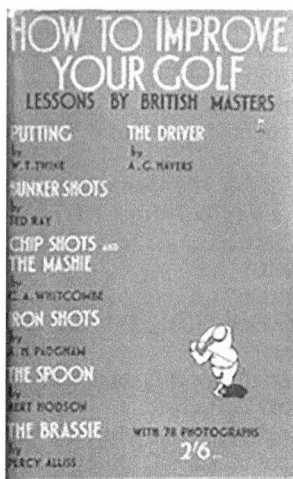

British Masters – How to Improve your Golf (DJ)

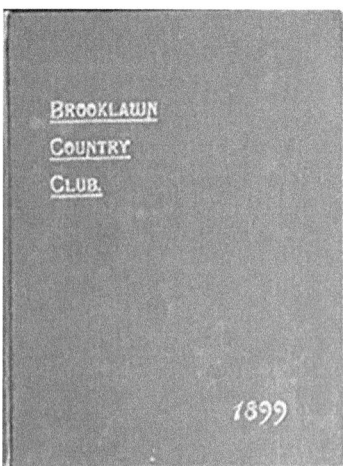

Brooklawn C.C. – Club Corporation Bridgeport Conn.

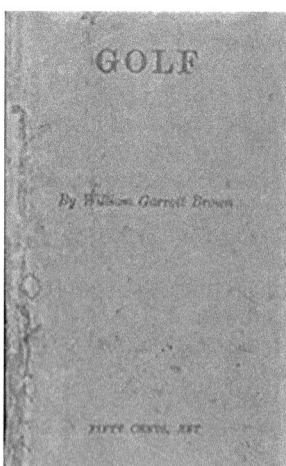

Brown – Golf (Dust Jacket)

Association 1903-1928"..................... 1929 .... $950

Sandy Dunlop:
"The Golfing Bodymind" .... 1980 .... $10

Edward T. Dunn:
"The Park Club of Buffalo 1903-1978" .... 1978 .... $35

J. Dunn:
"Golf From Rabbit To Tiger" .... 1955 .... $30

John D. Dunn:
"A-B-C Of Golf".. 1916 .... $125
Later Edition .... 1921 .... $75
"Elements of The Golf Swing" .... 1930 .... $60
"Golf"... 1941 .... $70
"Golf – Elementary Instruction"................... 1900 .... $400
"How To Drive-How To Approach–
How To Putt" (3 Vols)....................... 1922 .... $475
"Intimate Golf Talks" .... 1920 .... $175
"Natural Golf"... 1931 .... $195

John D. Dunn & Elon Jessup:
"Intimate Golf Talks" .... 1920 .... $100

Seymour Dunn:
"The Complete Golf Joke Book".................... 1953 .... $65
"Golf Fundamentals"................................. 1922 .... $295
Reprint .... 1977 .... $20
"Standardized Golf Instructions" .... 1934 .... $150

Cyril Dunne:
"A History of Golf in Bray"......................... 1997 .... $45

Don Dunne:
"The First Five Rounds of Golf at the
Australian Golf Club" .... 1992 .... $55

Dorothy Dunnett:
"Match For A Murderer" .... 1971 .... $50

Bob Dunning:
"Green Construction"................................ 1960 .... $15

Colin Dunsmore:
"In Celebration of The Golden Anniversary
of the New South Wales Golf Club
1928-1978" .... 1978 .... $25

Dunwoodie G. C:
"The Book of The Dunwoodie Golf Club,
Yonkers, New York" .... 1911 .... $50

Durham City G. C:
"Durham City Golf Club Centenary" .... 1987 .... $15

John Durant & Otto Bettmann:
"Pictorial History of American Sports" .... 1952 .... $25

Thousands of color book illustrations visible at
www.rogeregilchrist.com

Ted Durien:
"The First Fifty Years, 1925-1975;
        Monterey Penninsula Country Club"... 1975 .... $300
Duties of A Caddie:
"The Duties of A Caddie"............................ 1932 .... $60
Olin Dutra:
"All You Need To Know To Start Golf".......... 1941 .... $60
"Golf Doctor".. 1948 .... $50
Olin Dutra & Others:
"Your Guide To Golf In Southern California".. 1940 .... $45
James Dwight:
"Golf: A Handbook For Beginners" .... 1895 ....$2875
D. H. Dwyer:
"Killara Golf Club A History"........................ 1966 .... $35
Pete Dye:
"Bury Me In A Pot Bunker" .... 1995 .... $20
James Dyet:
"Out of The Rough" .... 1996 .... $15
Thomas Dykes:
"Sporting Scotland"................................... 1902 .... $75
Duncan Eales:
"Croydon Golf Club 1925-1975" .... 1975 .... $45
East Devon G. C:
"Official Handbook" .... 1991 .... $35
East London G. C:
"East London Golf Club 1893-1968"............. 1968 .... $25
East Lothian Golf:
"East Lothian Golf".................................... 1983 .... $20
Charlie Earp:
"Life Under Par".. 1990 .... $10
East Devon G. L:
"Mate's Illustrated Budleigh Salterton"......... 1902 150
J. Victor East:
"Better Golf In 5 Minutes" .... 1956 .... $35
Wayne Eastep:
"Last Blast At Wethersfield"........................ 1983 .... $55
L. F. Easterbrook:
"Ipswich Golf Club" .... 1965 .... $35
Herbert H. Easterley:
"Detroit Golf Club 1899-1939" (1000 Copies) 1939 .... $295
Eastern Airlines:
"Eastern's Guide To Great Golf Courses"....... 1966 .... $10
Eastman Kodak:
"Championship Golf by Bobby Jones"........... 1934 .... $400

Eatwood Ho C. C:
"History of the Eastwood Ho Country Club"... 1973 .... $45
Eaton G. C:
"Eaton Golf Club" .... 1948 .... $50
Harry Eaton:
"Dunmurray Golf Club 75th Anniversary
    1905-1980" .... 1980 .... $20
George Eberl:
"Golf Is A Good Walk Spoiled"..................... 1992 .... $10
Bill Ebert:
"The Invitation" .... 1983 .... $20
Echo Lake C. C:
"Echo Lake Country Club: Ninety Years In
    The Forefront of New Jersey Golf" .... 1988 .... $25
Jackie Eddy:
"The Second Slice: Over 250 Delicious, Time
    Saving Recipes For Golfers And People
    On The Go"...................................... 1985 .... $10
"Slicing, Hooking And Cooking".................... 1987 .... $10
Arthur C. Eden:
"Tees: New And Old" 1987 250
J. Douglas Edgar:
"The Gate To Golf" .... 1920 .... $100
    Reprint UK....................................... 1982 .... $25
    Reprint.. 1983 .... $20
    (100 Copies signed by Grandson)....... 1983 .... $25
Edinburgh Burgess Golfing Society:
"History of The Edinburgh Burgess Golfing
    Society" .... 1906 ....$7500
    Reprint... 1984 .... $125
"Rules and Bye-Laws"............................... 1911 .... $450
Jolee Edmondson:
"The Woman Golfer's Catalogue"................. 1980 .... $15
C. G. Edmonstone:
"A Study of Golf From its Mechanical Aspect" 1954 .... $250
Edmondstown G. C:
"Edmondstown Golf Club Golden Jubilee
    Year 1944-1994" .... 1994 .... $45
Nick Edmund:
"Benson & Hedges Golf Year"...................... 1990 .... $10
"Classic Courses of Great Britain
    & Ireland"....................................... 1997 .... $35
"Following The Fairways 1987".................... 1987 .... $20
"Following The Fairway 1989" .... 1989 .... $20

"Heineken World of Golf 95" .... 1995 .... $10
"Ping Women's Golf Year" .... 1994 .... $15
"The European Masters".............................. 1990 .... $25
Brian Edwards & Jack Bull:
"A Centenary of Golf On Outney Common " .. 1989 .... $35
Ian Edwards:
"The Royal Aberdeen Golfers" .... 2005 .... $95
Leslie Edwards:
"Golf On Merseyside And District"................ 1954 .... $30
"The Royal Liverpool Golf Club
        1869-1969; A Short History of
        The Club and of Championships
        Played Over The Holyoake Links" .... 1969 .... $150
"A Short History of The Royal Liverpool
        Golf Club and of Championships
        Played Over The Links"...................... 1983 .... $95
"The Game That Was Golf" .... 1992 .... $25
"Wallasey Golf Club".................................. 1960 .... $45
"The West Lancashire Golf Club
        Centenary 1873-1973" .... 1973 .... $30
Edwards & Brocklehurst:
"Historic Hoylake" .... 1983 .... $35
"Royal Liverpool Golf Club"......................... 1983 .... $125
R. Stanford Edwards:
"Wee Burn Country Club"........................... 1949 .... $45
Russ Edwards:
"The Golpher: His Origin And His Finish" ...... 1929 .... $75
John Egan:
"Castlebar Golf Club 1910-1985"................. 1985 .... $15
Armand Eisen:
"Life On The Links"................................... 1997 .... $10
Lee Eisenberg:
"Breaking 80"... 1997 .... $15
Elanora C. C.
"Elanora NSW" .... 1977 .... $100
El Caballero C. C:
"El Caballero Country Club, Silver
        Anniversary 1957-1982".................... 1982 .... $35
Rose Elder:
"The Golfer's Cookbook" .... 1977 .... $25
Eldorado C. C:
"Eldorado Country Club 1957-1985" .... 1985 .... $35
Patricia Eldred:
"Kathy Whitworth" .... 1975 .... $10

Thousands of color book illustrations visible at
www.rogeregilchrist.com

Ashton G. Eldridge:
"A History of the Huntington Country
Club 1910-1980" .... 1981 .... $50
Elements of Golf Course Layout:
"Elements of Golf Course Layout And
Design" .... 1968 .... $25
T. E. Elias & G. A. Philpot:
"British Sports And Sportsmen"
(1000 Copies) .... 1933 .... $550
Steve Elkington:
"Five Fundementals" .... 1998 .... $10
Charlotte & Aaron Elkins:
"A Wicked Slice" .... 1989 .... $25
"Rotten Lies" .... 1995 .... $15
Ellangowan:
"Outdoor Sports In Scotland"...................... 1889 .... $275
Ellesborough G. C:
"Ellesborough Golf Club" .... 1963 .... $25
Allan Elliott & John A May:
"Golf Monthly Illustrated History of Golf" ...... 1990 .... $20
Bill Elliott:
"This Sporting Life. Golf"............................ 1998 .... $25
Charles Elliott:
"East Lake Country Club History,
Home Course of Bobby Jones" .... 1984 .... $75
Len Elliott & Barbara Kelly:
"Who's Who In Golf"................................. 1976 .... $40
A. D. Ellis:
"History of the Royal Melbourne
Golf Club. Vol. 1 1891-1941".............. 1941 .... $200
Ray Ellis & Ben Wright:
"The Spirit of Golf" .... 1992 .... $75
Soft Cover Edition............................. 1996 .... $25
Wes Ellis Jr.:
"All Weather Golf" .... 1967 .... $20
James Ellroy:
"Brown's Requiem" .... 1981 .... $10
Elm Park G. & S. C:
"Elm Park 1925-1993" .... 1993 .... $35
Elmira C. C:
"Elmira Country Club Celebrates 100 Years
of Comoradarie 1897-1997".............. 1997 .... $25
Ernie Els:
"How To Build A Classic Golf Swing" .... 1996 .... $20

Thousands of color book illustrations visible at
www.rogeregilchrist.com

"The Complete Short Game"........................ 1998 .... $15
"Ernie Els' Guide To Golf Fitness" .... 2000 .... $15
El Sereno C. C:
"El Sereno Plan of Organization of El Sereno" 1926 .... $400
Neil Elsey:
"Golf"... 1980 .... $10
Bill Elston:
"Golf History of Spokane Washington".......... 1999 .... $45
E. L. Tourist Board:
"Golf In East Lothian" .... 1976 .... $35
David Emery:
"The Ryder Cup '85".................................. 1985 .... $30
"Who's Who In International Golf" .... 1983 .... $30
Fred Emery:
"Colonel Bogey's Coloring Book For Golfer's". 1981 .... $15
Howard R. Endersby:
"Lessons From Great Golfers" .... 1924 .... $95
Enfield G. C:
"Enfield Golf Club Official Handbook" .... 1975 .... $25
Paul Engleman:
"Murder In-Law" .... 1987 .... $20
English Golf Union:
"Golfing Year 1961"................................... 1961 .... $15
Kjell Enhager:
"Quantum Golf" .... 1991 .... $15
Epsom G. C:
"Epsom Golf Club: A Reflection of The First
        100 Years"...................................... 1989 .... $20
Dr. Bee Epstein-Shepherd:
"Mental Mangement For Great Golf"............. 1996 .... $20
Erewash Valley G. C:
"The Erewash Valley Golf Club
        75th Aniversary 1905-1980" .... 1980 .... $25
Erskine Park G. C:
"Erskine Park Golf Club Silver
        Anniversary 1925-1950".................... 1950 .... $25
J. R. Escritt:
"ABC of Turf Culture"................................ 1978 .... $35
Richard Esquinas:
"Michael And Me"..................................... 1993 .... $15
Esquire Magazine:
"The Name of The Game Is Golf"................. 1968 .... $35
Essex C. C:
"Essex County Club, Incorporated

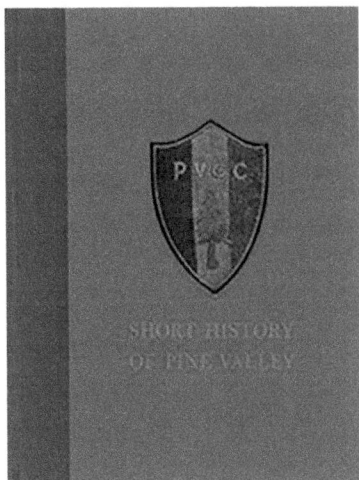

Brown – Short History of Pine Valley

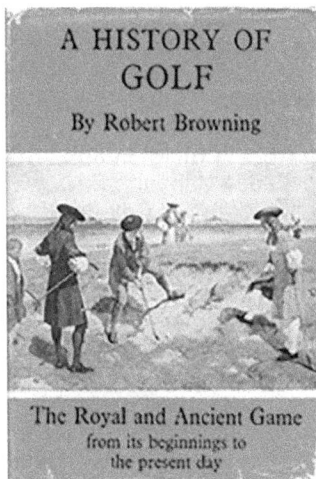

Browning – A History of Golf

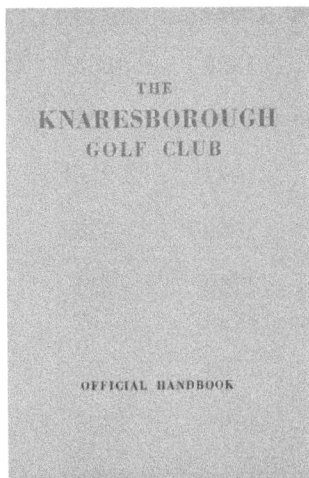

Browning – The Knaresborough Golf Club

Browning – Enfield Municipal Golf Course

January 5, 1893" .... 1911 .... $95
Steve Eubanks:
"Augusta: Home of The Masters" .... 1997 .... $25
Eurogolf:
"Eurogolf 1972" .... 1972 .... $10
Charles "Chick" Evans Jr.:
"Caddy Manual" .... 1928 .... $425
"Chick Evans Golf Book" .... 1921 .... $200
    Signed Subscription Edition
    (999 Copies) .... 1921 ..... $1,250
    Reprint .... 1969 .... $45
    Memorial Tournament Edition
    (425 Copies) .... 1985 .... $150
"Chick Evans Golf Book, The Story of The
    Sporting Battles of The Greatest
    of All Amateur Golfers" .... 1924 .... $500
    Signed Limited Edition .... 1924 ...... $1500
    Reprint .... 1978 .... $35
"Chick Evans Guide To Better Golf" .... 1924 .... $695
"Golf For Boys And Girls" .... 1954 .... $100
"How to Improve Your Golf" .... 1925 ...... $3250
"Chick" Evans Jr. & Barrie Payne:
"Ida Broke..." .... 1929 .... $125
Chick Evans & Others:
"The Grip In Golf" .... 1922 .... $350
David Evans:
The History of Worsley Golf Club 1894-1994" 1994 .... $30
Webster Evans:
"Encyclopedia of Golf" .... 1971 .... $20
"Rub of The Green: Golf's Triumphs and
    Tragedies" .... 1969 .... $25
Webster Evans & Tom Scott:
"In Praise of Golf" .... 1950 .... $35
    Reprint .... 1991 .... $10
Brian Evens:
"One Hundred Years Without a Course" .... 1994 .... $50
H. S. C. Everard:
"Golf In Theory and Practice" .... 1896 .... $300
    Reprint .... 1910 .... $125
"Haver With Tom Morris" .... 1895 .... $595
"A History of The Royal And Ancient Golf
    Club, St. Andrews From 1754-1900" ... 1907 ...... $4,500
Helen Exley:
"Golf" .... 1993 .... $15

"Golf Quotations" .... 1991 .... $15
Exmoor C. C:
"The Book of the Exmoor Country Club " ...... 1898 .... $350
"Exmoor Country Club, Highland Park, Ill" .... 1911 .... $75
"Exmoor Country Club Semi-Centennial
    Year 1896-1946" .... 1946 .... $60
"Exmoor Country Club Seventy-Fifth
    Anniversary, 1896-1971" .... 1972 .... $40
Fable of The Lost Golf Ball:
"The Fable of The Lost Golf Ball" .... 1940 .... $50
Walter Fairbanks:
"Some Hints On Learning Golf" .... 1900 .... $275
H. L Fairclough:
"Grange Park Golf Club 1891-1991" .... 1991 .... $65
Gerard Fairlie:
"Men for Counters" .... 1933 .... $40
"Mr Malcolm Presents" .... 1934 .... $30
Jack Fairlie:
"Chicagoland Golf Course Guide" .... 1974 .... $15
Walter E. Fairlie:
"The Old Course At St. Andrews" .... 1908 .... $850
"The Old Course At St. Andrews" .... 1920 .... $200
Fairview C. C:
"Fairview Country Club Twenty-Fifth
    Anniversary 1904-1929" .... 1929 .... $125
Fairways:
"Fairways; A Detailed Graphic Description
    Of All Los Angeles City And County
    Operated Golf Courses" .... 1967 .... $25
Fakenham G .C:
"Fakenham Golf Club 1888-1989" .... 1989 .... $25
Nick Faldo:
"Enjoying Golf With Nick Faldo" .... 1985 .... $20
"Faldo A Swing For Life" .... 1995 .... $20
"Golf: The Winning Formula" .... 1989 .... $20
"On Course For The Open" .... 1987 .... $30
"The Rough With The Smooth" .... 1980 .... $20
Robert G. Fall:
"Golfing In South Africa: Edition 1958" .... 1958 .... $75
"Golf Courses of Natal" .... 1965 .... $95
"Golf Courses of The O.F.S. And
    Northern Cape" .... 1964 .... $125
"Golf Courses of The Western Cape" .... 1964 .... $125
"Golf Courses of The Southern Cape" .... 1964 .... $125

Thousands of color book illustrations visible at
www.rogeregilchrist.com

"Golf Courses of The Transvaal" .... 1965 .... $125
"History f Golf At The Cape" .... 1918 ....$1100
"Ladies Golf In South Africa from
      1897-1965" .... 1965 .... $125
"A Short History of The Mowbray Golf Club".. 1939 .... $85
"Southern Africa Golf Annual 1967-68" .... 1968 .... $35
Fall River C. C:
    The History of Fall River Country Club"......... 1990 .... $45
Gertrude A. Farley:
    "Golf Course Common Sense"..................... 1931 .... $450
Farmington C. C:
    "Farmington Country Club"......................... 1932 .... $65
    "News Letter".. 1985 .... $25
Guy B. Farrar:
    "The Royal Liverpool Golf Club".................. 1947 .... $200
    "The Royal Liverpool Golf Club" (handbook).. 1955 .... $125
    The Royal Liverpool Golf Club" (handbook) ... 1965 .... $40
    "The Royal Liverpool Golf Club, A History
        1869-1932" .... 1933 .... $900
        Reprint.. 2006 .... $125
Guy B Farrar & Joe Pinnington:
    "Mighty Champions: The Official History
        of The Royal Liverpool Golf Club" .... 2006 .... $75
    "The Fascination of Golf"........................... 1918 .... $75
Johnny Farrell:
    "Golf Score Record Book .... 1929 .... $125
    "Golf Sportsmanship" .... 1928 .... $125
    "How to Play "Your" Golf Course" .... 1929 .... $125
    "Putting to Win"..................................... 1929 .... $125
Major Farrell:
    "Golf".. 1930 .... $35
Max Faulkner:
    "Golf-Right From the Start". .... 1965 .... $35
    "Play Championship Golf All Your Life" .... 1972 .... $25
Neal Faulkner & John T. Thatcher:
    "The Garden City Golf Club" (1000 Copies) ... 1974 .... $400
W. H. Faust:
    "The Hectic Game of Golf"......................... 1930 .... $65
Dike Faxon:
    "History of Echo Lake Country Club
        1899-1956" .... 1956 .... $85
Michael Fay:
    "Golf As It Was Meant To Be Played"........... 2000 .... $30

Michael Faye & Michael Murphy:
"Images" .... 1994 .... $75
Tom Fazio:
"Golf Course Designs by Fazio" .... 1984 .... $65
"Golf Course Designs" .... 2000 .... $95
Max Feldman:
"Our First Fifty Years, Elm Ridge Country
    Club 1924-1974 .... 1974 .... $50
Felix:
"Philadelphia Country Club Charter History" .. 1961 .... $65
H. B. Fenn:
"A Box of Matches" .... 1922 .... $850
Ronnie Fenton:
"The Easy Road To Good Golf" .... 1962 .... $10
Len Fereday:
"The Burbage Common Golf Club" .... 1951 .... $25
Charles B. Ferguson:
"Sixty Seven Years of the Fishers Island
    Golf Club Links 1926-1993"
    (2000 Copies) .... 1993 .... $325
Charles Ferguson & Pierce Rafferty:
"The Fishers Island Club and its Golf Links
    The First Seventy Five Years 1926-2001
    400 Copies .... 2002 .... $250
    100 Copies Signed .... 2002 .... $325
Douglas M. Ferguson:
"Dunfermline Golf Club 1887-1987" .... 1987 .... $50
Marvin H. Ferguson:
"Building Golf Holes for Good Turf
    Management" .... 1968 .... $95
Pam Fernando & Gun Pieris:
"Nuwara Elyia Golf Club 100 Years
    1889-1989" .... 1989 .... $125
Fernando, Kadirgamar, & Candappo:
"Royal Columbo Golf Club 100 Years
    1879-1979" .... 1979 .... $65
Ferndown G. C:
"Ferndown Golf Club" .... 1939 .... $75
Bob Ferrier:
"The World Atlas of Golf Courses" .... 1990 .... $20
Bob Ferrier & Graham Hart:
"The Johnnie Walker Encyclopedia of Golf" .... 1994 .... $35
James Ferrier:
"Golf Shots" .... 1940 .... $55

"Low Score Golf"....................................... 1948 .... $45
Roland Fiddy:
    "The Fanatics Guide To Golf" .... 1989 .... $10
Field:
    "The Country Club of Fairfield A History
        1914-1989" .... 1989 .... $50
Fife Golfing Association:
    "A History of Golf Clubs In Fife" .... 1989 .... $20
    "A History of Golf Clubs In Fife" (12 Vols)..... 1991 .... $95
50 Miles of Golf:
    "50 Miles of Golf Round London" .... 1937 .... $50
    "50 Miles of Golf Round London" .... 1938 .... $35
    "50 Miles of Golf Round London" .... 1939 .... $25
Benjamin & Howard Fine:
    "The Fine Method of Golf" .... 1958 .... $30
James W. Finegan:
    "Blasted Heaths and Blessed Greens"........... 1996 .... $20
    "The Great Links In Ireland" .... 1977 .... $20
    "Emerald Fairways And Foam-Flecked Seas" . 1996 .... $25
    "Pine Valley Golf Club"............................... 2000 .... $200
Joseph S. Finger:
    "The Business End of Building or
        Rebuilding a Golf Course" .... 1972 .... $25
Dow Finsterwald:
    "Fundamentals of Golf".............................. 1961 .... $40
    "The Wedges, Pitching And Sand"................ 1965 .... $65
Morris Fishbein:
    "To Golf Or Not To Golf"............................. 1943 .... $50
Anne Kinsman Fisher:
    "The Masters of The Spirit"......................... 1997 .... $15
    "The Legend of Tommy Morris" .... 1996 .... $20
Garth Fisher & John Geertsen Jr:
    "Golf - Your Turn For Success".................... 1992 .... $10
Mark Fisher:
    "The Golfer And The Millionaire".................. 1998 .... $20
Richard Fisher:
    "A Centenary History of the Royal
        St David's Golf Club"......................... 1994 .... $95
Lew Fishman:
    "Golf Magazine's Short Cuts To Better Golf" .. 1979 .... $20
George Fitch:
    "Golf For The Beginner" .... 1908 .... $200
Robert S. Fittis:
    "Illustrations of the History and Antiquities

of Perthshire"..................................... 1874 .... $350
"Sports And Pastimes of Scotland" .... 1891 .... $300
Hugh Louis Fitz Patrick:
"Golf Don'ts" .... 1900 .... $395
Five Secrets of Winning Golf:
"Five Secrets of Winning Golf" .... 1945 .... $20
Thomas Flaherty:
"The Masters: The Story of Golf's
    Greatest Tournament"....................... 1961 .... $75
"The U.S. Open 1895-1965" .... 1966 .... $45
Jerome Flannery:
"The American Cricket Annual And
    Golf Guide"...................................... 1898 .... $750
H. A. Fleager:
"History of the Seattle Golf Club" .... 1959 .... $350
Alvin Fleishman:
"Compend of Golf Supplemented By Atomic
    Gold Aids" .... 1946 .... $35
David Hay Fleming:
"Historical Notes & Extracts Concerning the
    Links of St. Andrews 1552-1893"........ 1893 ..$12,500
"Hay Fleming's Guide To St Andrews
    And Neigbourhood"........................... 1897 .... $195
"Hand-Book of St Andrews"........................ 1910 .... $750
    Later edition .... 1927 .... $200
Ian Fleming:
"Goldfinger" (1st UK Edition) .... 1957 ....$1195
Charles Fletcher:
"How To Play Bad Golf"............................. 1935 .... $175
Robert F. Fletcher:
"Sutton Coldfield Golf Club 1889-1989"........ 1988 .... $40
Jim Flick:
"Square To Square Golf In Pictures" .... 1974 .... $20
"Jim Flick On Golf" .... 1997 .... $20
Violet Flint:
"A Golfing Idyll Or The Skippers Round With
    The Devil On The Links At St. Andrews"1892 ......$7,500
    Reprint (250 Copies) .... 1978 .... $65
Mrs. Harrison F. Flippin:
"Golf Is Fun" .... 1956 .... $10
Flossmoor C. C:
"Flossmoor Country Club Fiftieth Anniversary
    1898-1948 .... 1948 .... $225
"Flossmoor Country Club, 1899-1979

Thousands of color book illustrations visible at
www.rogeregilchrist.com

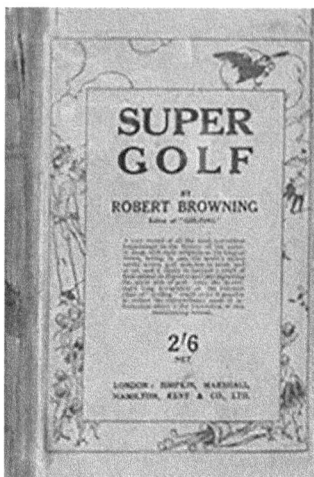

Browning – Super Golf
(Dust Jacket)

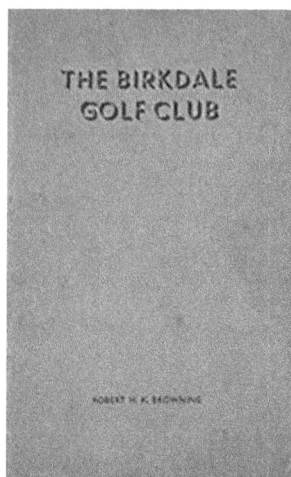

Browning – The Birkdale
Golf Club

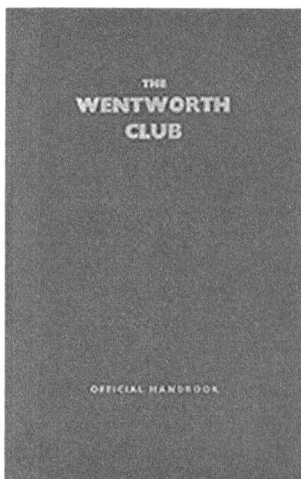

Browning – The Wentworth
Club

Browning – Troon Golf Club

Thousands of color book illustrations visible at
www.rogeregilchrist.com

80th Anniversary"............................. 1979 .... $35
Channing Floyd:
"The Little Golf Teacher" .... 1925 .... $65
Frank Harris Floyd:
"The Mechanics of The Golf Swing And The
    Techniques of The Contestants At
    Oakmont, Pittsburgh Open
    Tournament 1927"............................ 1927 .... $145
Raymond Floyd:
"The Elements of Scoring"........................ 1998 .... $15
"From 60 Yards In" .... 1989 .... $20
Brendon Flynn:
"Wicklow Golf Club 1904 to 2004" .... 2004 .... $45
J. M. Flynn:
"Terror Tournament" .... 1959 .... $95
Colleen Fogarty:
"The Powelton Club The First Hundred Years
    1882-1982" .... 1982 .... $20
Follow Through:
"The Essence of Golf" .... 1954 .... $30
Edwin B. Foote:
"Oakmont Country Club: The First Seventy
    Five Years" .... 1980 .... $125
John D. Forbes:
"The Mt. Anthony Country Club".................. 1944 .... $60
Doug Ford:
"The Brainy Way To Better Golf" .... 1961 .... $15
"Getting Started In Golf"............................ 1964 .... $15
"Golf".. 1960 .... $10
"How I Play Inside Golf"............................. 1960 .... $10
"Start Golf Young"..................................... 1955 .... $30
"The Wedge Book" .... 1963 .... $25
Jason Foreman:
"The Country Club - A Short History.
    Steubenville Country Club 1908-1999" 1999 .... $60
Forest Lake Club:
"Forest Lake Club From its Beginning
    Through 1964"................................. 1965 .... $55
Forfar G. C:
"Forfar Golf Club"...................................... 1923 .... $90
"Forfar Golf Club 1871-1971" .... 1971 .... $25
Robert Forgan:
"The Golfers Handbook"............................. 1881 ......$5,000
    Fourth Edition .... 1890 ....$1750

Thousands of color book illustrations visible at
www.rogeregilchrist.com

"The Golfers Manual"................................. 1897 ......$3,250
  Reprint... 1973 .... $225
James Forrest:
 "The Basis of The Golf Swing"..................... 1925 .... $250
 "Golf Made Easy" .... 1933 .... $75
 "The Golf Stroke"...................................... 1930 .... $45
 "A Natural Golfer: Hand Action in Games" ... 1938 .... $175
Fred Forrester:
 "The Guilford Golf Club A Centenary
  1886-1985" .... 1985 .... $25
Forster, Sayle, Watterson & Felton:
 "A Century at the Congary: The History of
  the Peel Golf Club, 1895-1995"........... 1994 .... $45
Les Forsyth & David Innes:
 "History of Cromer Golf Club 1926-1991" ..... 1991 .... $35
Fortrose & Rosemarkie G. C:
 "Fortrose And Rosemarkie Golf Club" .... 1948 .... $75
Fort Washington G. & C. C:
 "Fort Washington Golf & Country Club
  1923-1998" .... 1998 .... $50
Fort Wayne C. C:
 "Fort Wayne Country Club Diamond
  Jubilee 1908-1983"........................... 1983 .... $25
Bruce Fossum & Mary Dagraedt:
 "Golf"... 1969 .... $10
Cy Foster:
 "Golf Is Easy".. 1950 .... $30
David Foster:
 "Thinking Golf" .... 1979 .... $15
Harry Foster:
 "Annals of the Hesketh Golf Club
  1885-2000" (750 Copies) .... 2001 .... $45
N. R. Foster:
 "History of The Royal Wimbledon Golf
  Club 1865-1929" .... 1929 .... $575
W. Foulsham:
 "200 Funny Golf Stories As Told At The 19th" 1932 .... $175
Peter Fowlie:
 "The Science of Golf"................................. 1922 .... $85
 "The Technique of The Golf Swing".............. 1934 .... $65
Fowler, Abercrombie, Simpson & Groome:
 "Golf Architects, Scale of Fees. Examples
  of Our Work"..................................... 1933 .... $850

G. D. Fox:
"The Golfer's Pocket Tip Book" .... 1911 .... $135
"The 6 Handicap Golfer's Companion" .... 1909 .... $250
Peter Fox:
"Natural Golf" .... 1996 .... $15
W. F. Fox Jr.:
"Golf's Guardian Angels" .... 1954 .... $10
William P. Fox:
"Doctor Golf" .... 1963 .... $30
Gladys L. Foxley:
"A History of Bexley Heath Golf Club 1907-1977"1977 ..... $25
Oscar Fraley:
"Golf In Action" .... 1952 .... $45
C. Edwin Francis:
"Waverley Country Club 1896-1987" .... 1987 .... $25
"Waverley Country Club 1886-1996" .... 1996 .... $45
Joseph Francis:
"Dutch Open Champion 1959 'Papwa'
    Sewsunker Sewgoolum" .... 1959 .... $25
Richard S. Francis:
"Golf: Its Rules and Decisions" .... 1937 .... $110
            US Edition. .... 1939 .... $50
"Rules of Golf With Interpretations" .... 1937 .... $95
James A. Frank:
"The Golfer's Companion" .... 1992 .... $15
"Golf Magazine's Private Lessons" .... 1990 .... $15
H. Xavier M. Frankenberg:
"Golf Made Easy" .... 1948 .... $20
Franklin Hills C. C:
The 60th Anniversary of The Franklin Hills
        Country Club 1927-1987" .... 1987 .... $35
"The 'Royal & Ancient' Beginnings of The
        Franklin Hills Country Club" .... 1987 .... $30
George Fraser
"Fraser's Golf Directory and Year Book 1923" 1923 .... $220
"Fraser's International Year Book 1924" .... 1924 .... $125
"Fraser's International Year Book 1925-26" .. 1925 .... $100
"Fraser's International Year Book 1926-27" .. 1926 .... $95
"Fraser's International Year Book 1927" .... 1927 .... $95
"Fraser's International Year Book 1928" .... 1928 .... $95
"Fraser's International Year Book 1929" .... 1929 .... $95
"Fraser's International Year Book 1930" .... 1930 .... $250
"Fraser's International Year Book 1931" .... 1931 .... $75
"Fraser's International Year Book 1932" .... 1932 .... $75

Thousands of color book illustrations visible at
www.rogeregilchrist.com

"Fraser's International Year Book 1933" .... 1933 .... $75
"Fraser's International Year Book 1934" .... 1934 .... $75
"Fraser's International Year Book 1935" .... 1935 .... $75
"Fraser's International Year Book 1936" .... 1936 .... $75
"Fraser's International Year Book 1937" .... 1937 .... $75

George M. Fraser;
"McAuslan In The Rough" .... 1974 .... $10

George Fraser & James Mearns:
"Royal Aberdeen Golf Club" .... 1981 .... $35

Fraserburgh G. C:
"The Fraserburgh Golf Club" .... 1947 .... $50

Chick Frasier:
"Pictorial Golf" 4 Vols................................ 1922 .... $125

Oliver Frawley & Others:
"Greystones Golf Club Centenary
      1895-1995" .... 1995 .... $55

George M. Frazier:
"Records And Statistics, Firestone
      Country Club" .... 1975 .... $25

Adrian Frederick:
"The 1984 South African PGA Golf Annual" ... 1984 .... $15

Victor Fredericks:
"For Golfers Only" .... 1964 .... $15

James L. Freeborn:
"The Edgewood Club 1884-1937" .... 1937 .... $60

Jane Freeburg:
"The Valley Club of Montecito 1928-1998" .... 1998 .... $50

John Freeman:
"Crieff Golf Club 1891-1991" .... 1991 .... $35

Adrian French:
"World Senior Golf International Team
      Matches And World Senior
      Championships A History" .... 1977 .... $15

Ford Frick:
"This Is St. Andrews 1888-1973" .... 1973 .... $40

Friendly Fairways:
"Friendly Fairways of Michigan; A Directory
      of Public, Municipal And Semi Private
      Golf Courses Located Within The
      State of Michigan" .... 1979 .... $15

David Frome:
"The Murder On The Sixth Hole"................. 1931 .... $150
"The Strange Death Of Martin Green" .... 1931 .... $75

A. B. Frost:
"A Book of Drawings" .... 1904 .... $175
James A. Frost:
"The Country Club of Farmington
    1892-1995" .... 1996 .... $50
John G. Frothingham:
"The Country Club of New Canaan
    1893-1968" .... 1968 .... $30
John P Fruit:
"The XVIII Hole" .... 1933 .... $25
Peter Fry:
"Samuel Ryder The Man Behind the
    Ryder Cup" (500 Copies) .... 2000 .... $95
    Limited edition of 50 .... 2000 .... $350
"Verulam Golf Club 1905-2005 – The Home
    of the Ryder Cup .... 2006 .... $45
"The Whitcombes"..................................... 1994 .... $30
    Limited Edition of 70 signed .... 1994 .... $450
Robert Fukushima:
"Kagero Golf Club Fiftieth Anniversary
    1925-1975" .... 1975 .... $25
Harry Fulford:
"Golf's Little Ironies" .... 1919 .... $175
"Potted Golf" .... 1910 .... $95
Neal Fulkerson & John T. Thatcher:
"The Garden City Golf Club, Seventy-Fifth
    Anniversary 1899-1974"
    (1000 copies)................................. 1974 .... $450
J. R. Fullarton:
"Instructions For Caddies".......................... 1938 .... $75
Barbara Fuller:
"Sharing A Vison" .... 1992 .... $55
George Fuller:
"Hawaii Golf"... 1991 .... $10
Timothy Fuller:
"Reunion With Murder" .... 1941 .... $145
Bobby Furber:
"The Royal St Georges Golf Club 1887-1987" 1988 .... $35
F. R. Furber:
"A Course for Heroes: A History of the Royal
    St George's Golf Club"....................... 1996 .... $75
Nicola Furlong:
"Teed Off"... 1996 .... $20

Furness G. C:
"Furness Golf Club, A Centenary Story
1872-1972" .... 1972 .... $75
Leather Bound Edition of 250 signed ... 1975 .... $125
J. G. Fyfe:
"The Historie of the Lyff of James Melvill" ..... 1948 .... $55
Hector Farini Fynn:
"El Hoyo 19: Commentarios Sobre Casos
y Cosas del Golf" .... 1940 .... $50
Charlie Gaal & Nate Collier:
"Your Golf".. 1948 .... $25
Jonothan Gair:
"The Australian Masters 1972-1982"............ 1983 .... $35
William Galbraith:
"Prestwick St. Nicholas Golf Club" .... 1950 .... $295
Barbara J. Gale:
"The History of the Sunningdale Ladies
Golf Club The First Hundred Years
(Ltd Ed of 450)................................ 2002 .... $100
Saul Galin:
"Golf In Europe: A Traveler's Guide To 200
of Europe's Best Golf Courses".......... 1967 .... $15
Bernard Gallacher:
"Captain At Kiawah" .... 1991. .... $20
Diane Caylor Galloway:
"Dallas Country Club. The First 100 Years" ... 1996 .... $50
Paul Gallico:
"Farewell to Sport".................................... 1941 .... $40
"Golf is a Friendly Game" .... 1942 .... $45
Don Gallup:
"Golf Courses of Colorado" .... 1984 .... $15
W. Timothy Gallwey:
"The Inner Game of Golf"........................... 1981 .... $25
Phil Galvano:
"The Gentle Arts of Chipping and Putting"..... 1959 .... $30
"Seagram's Guide To Strategic Golf"............ 1960 .... $30
"Secrets of Accurate Putting And Chipping"... 1957 .... $25
"The Secrets of The Perfect Golf Swing" .... 1961 .... $30
Joe Gambatese:
"Golf Guide 1963" .... 1963 .... $10
"Pro Am Guide To Golf"............................... 1981 .... $5
Game of Golf:
"The Game of Golf" .... 1900 .... $325

Thousands of color book illustrations visible at
www.rogeregilchrist.com

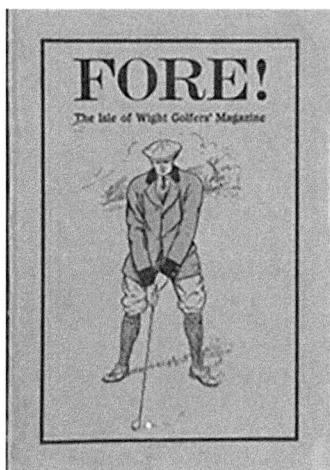

Burgess & Brannon – Fore!

Burntisland G.C.–1797-1997

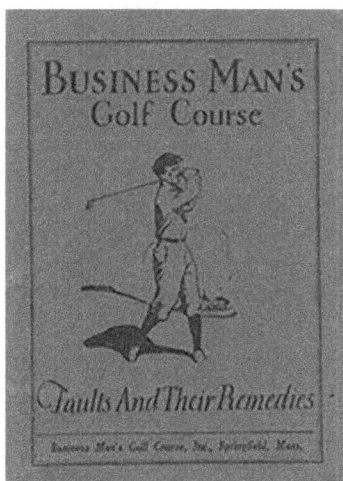

Business Mans Golf Course -
Faults and Their Remedies

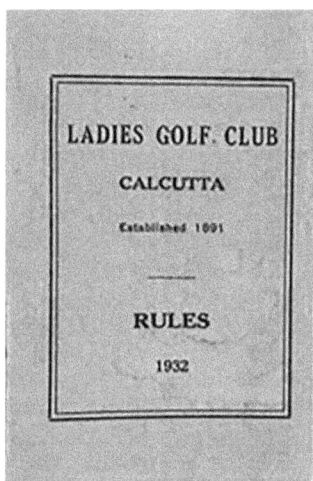

Calcutta Ladies Golf Club -
Rules

Thousands of color book illustrations visible at
www.rogeregilchrist.com

Peter Gammond:
   "Bluff Your Way In Golf"............................ 1985 .... $10
Angus Garber:
   "Golf Legends: Players, Holes, Life on the
         PGA Tour".. 1988 .... $25
   "Golf Legends".. 1993 .... $20
John L. B. Garcia:
   "Harold Hilton, His Golfing Life And Times" ... 1992 .... $30
         Limited Edition of 750 signed .... 1992 .... $150
Garden Golf:
   "A Golf Course in Your Garden".................... 1932 .... $225
Garden City G. C:
   "Facts About The Course At Garden City" ..... 1913 .... $275
   "The Garden City golf Club, Club House
         And Links" (500 Copies) .... 1909 .... $250
Don Gardner:
   "Don Gardners's Golf Book: Three
         Point Method" .... 1947 .... $45
Howard R. Garris:
   "Uncle Butter and Uncle Wiggley Play Golf"... 1924 .... $95
J. T. Garrity:
   "Golfer's Guide To Florida Courses".............. 1973 .... $25
John Garrity:
   "Golf"... 1996 .... $15
   "Putting"... 1991 .... $10
Bud Gaskill:
   "Golf At A Glance".................................... 1958 .... $15
John B. Gates:
   "The First Seventy-Five Years of The
         United States Seniors Golf Association
         1905-1980" .... 1980 .... $15
   "Round Hill Golf Club 1972-1979"
         (600 Copies) .... 1979 .... $ 40
Anthony Gatrell:
   "The History of Cirencester Golf Club
         1893-1993" (1000 Copies)................. 1993 .... $25
J. W. Gaudin:
   "Method In Golf"...................................... 1929 .... $75
William C. Gault:
   "The Long Green" .... 1965 .... $15
W. K. Gault:
   "Practical Golf Greenkeeping" .... 1911 ....$1650
Michael Gedye:
   "Golf In Portugal".................................... 1975 .... $10

"Golf In The Sun 1974-75" .... 1975 .... $10
"Holiday Golf In Spain & Portugal" .... 1970 .... $20
John Gee:
"Stratford-On-Avon Golf Club "
    (1000 Copies) .... 1994 .... $30
Geelong G. C:
"Geelong Golf Club 100th Anniversary" .... 1992 .... $25
Al Geiberger:
"Tempo: Golf's Master Key" .... 1980 .... $15
Archibald Geike:
"Scottish Reminiscences" .... 1905 .... $75
Lou Gellos:
"Seattle Golf Club 1900-2000" .... 2000 .... $150
Robin Gems:
"The Story of Malden Golf Club" .... 1990 .... $20
The General:
"Golf And How To Play It" .... 1912 .... $145
Pete Georgiady:
"Collecting Antique Golf Clubs" .... 1995 .... $25
"North American Club Makers" .... 1998 .... $45
"Pete Georgiady's Wood Shafted Golf Club
    Value Guide" .... 1997 .... $35
"Views And Reviews" .... 1996 .... $35
P. Georgiady & Leo M Kelly:
"Quick Reference Guide To Antique
    Golf Club Names" .... 1993 .... $15
German Railways:
"Golf In Germany" .... 1927 .... $325
Paul H. Gerrits:
"The Golfer's Guide" .... 1947 .... $15
Walt Gerzin:
"Eclectic Golf: Featuring The AWH Takeaway"1976 .... $10
Averille Dayton Geus:
"The Second Fifty Years 1941-1991" .... 1991 .... $100
Hal Gevertz & Mark Oman:
"World's Greatest Golf Excuses" .... 1989 .... $10
James Gibbins:
"Sudden Death" .... 1983 .... $25
Nevin H. Gibson:
"The Encyclopaedia of Golf" .... 1958 .... $75
"Great Moments In Golf" .... 1973 .... $35
"A Pictorial History of Golf" .... 1968 .... $55
Nevin H. Gibson & Tom Kouzmentoff:
"Golf's Greatest Shots By The World's

Greatest Golfers" .... 1981 .... $15
William H. Gibson:
"A Century of Golf at Carlow – From Gotham
    To Deer Park 1899-1999" .... 1999 .... $25
"Curragh Golf Club Centenary 1883-1983" ... 1983 .... $20
"Early Irish Golf"....................................... 1988 .... $35
James Gilbert:
"Boyce Hill Golf Club" .... 1938 .... $60
Reg Gilchrist:
"The Knott End Story, History of A
    Golf Club"... 1983 .... $10
Roger E. Gilchrist & Mark Emerson:
"Gilchrist's Guide to Golf Collectibles" .... 1997 .... $95
"Gilchrist's Guide To Golf Collectibles".......... 2004 .... $25
"Gilchrist's Who's Who In Golf" .... 2000 .... $15
A. C. Giles:
"The Golf Society of Great Britain"............... 1955 .... $25
Gill & MacLaren:
"A History of Ponteland Golf Club " .... 1988 .... $25
Howard Gill:
"Fun In The Rough From Golf Digest".......... 1957 .... $20
Dermot Gilleece:
"Co. Sligo Golf Club: The First 100 Years
    1894-1994" .... 1994 .... $75
"Malahide Golf Club 1892-1992 a History" .... 1992 .... $25
"Touching Greatness: Memorable Encounters
With Golfing Legends" .... 2008 .... $25
Dermot Gilleece & John Redmond:
"Irish Ladies Golf Union: An Illustrated
    Centenary History 1893-1993" .... 1993 .... $125
"Killiney Golf Club an Illustrated Centenary
    History 1903-2003" .... 2003 .... $35
Dermot Gilleece & Michael O'Rourke:
"Malahide Golf Club, A History. 1892-1992".. 1992 .... $65
Donald J. Gillen:
"A History of Wolforts Roost Country Club" ... 1985 .... $10
Norman Giller:
"The Book of Golf Lists" .... 1985 .... $10
Percy J. Gillespie:
"Putting"... 1957 .... $95
Stair A. Gillon:
"The Honorable Company of Edinburgh
    Golfers At Muirfield 1891-1914".......... 1946 .... $675

Thousands of color book illustrations visible at
www.rogeregilchrist.com

John Gillum:
"The Sacred Nine"...................................... 1993 .... $50
"110 Golf Matches Oxford v Cambridge
    1878-1999" .... 1999 .... $30
John R Gillum:
"Oxford Versus Cambridge Golf Matches" ..... 1978 .... $75
C. J. L. Gilson:
"Golf".. 1928 .... $95
"Golf".. 1930 .... $75
J. D. Gilruth:
"Arbroath Golf Course" .... 1909 .... $795
Geoffrey Gimcrack:
"Gimcrackiana, Or Fugitive Pieces On
    Manchester Man And Manners Ten
    Years Ago"...................................... 1833 .... $950
Bernard Glacier:
"Captain At Kiawah" .... 1991 .... $25
Irving A. Gladstone:
"Confessions of A Golf Duffer"..................... 1977 .... $20
Glamorganshire G. C:
"Short History of The Glamorganshire
    Golf Club 1890-1950"......................... 1950 .... $45
Dan Gleason:
"The Great, The Grand And The Also-Ran:
    Rabbits and Champions On The Pro
    Golf Tour"....................................... 1976 .... $40
John F. Gleason Jr.:
"A Brief History of The Shaker Heights
    Country Club" .... 1978 .... $15
Peter Glenn:
"The Golfers Guidebook: A Guide To The
    PGA Winter Spring Tour".................... 1965 .... $20
Rhonda Glenn:
"The Illustrated History of Women's Golf" ..... 1991 .... $45
"Brook Hollow Golf Club: The first 75 Years" . 1995 .... $95
Rhonda Glenn and Robert McCord:
"The Whole Golf Catalog" .... 1990 .... $25
Glen View Club:
"Glen View Club 1897-1972" .... 1972 .... $35
"The First One Hundred Years".................... 1997 .... $65
Gloucester G. C:
"Gloucester Golf Club" .... 1938 .... $65
Thomas Glover:
"Ladies Open Golf Championship May 1902" . 1902 .... $125

Webster Glynes:
"The Maiden: A Golfing Epic" .... 1893 .... $11,500
Edna Glynn:
"A Century of Golf At Lahinch 1892-1992" .... 1991 .... $50
Ray Goates:
"Los Angeles City Bicentennial Honor of
       Champions" .... 1981 .... $20
David Goddard:
"The Maidstone Links" .... 1997 .... $125
Doug Godlington:
"The Un-Golfer" .... 1974 .... $15
Austin Goetz:
"The Golf Champ" .... 1934 .... $55
Golf:
"Golf" .... 1973 .... $20
"Golf" .... 1983 .... $15
Golf At A Glance:
"Golf at a Glance" .... 1933 .... $395
       Second Edition .... 1934 .... $195
Golf & Club Magazine:
"Great Golf Cartoons From Golf & Club
       Magazine"....................................... 1971 .... $15
Golf & Ping Pong:
"Golf And Ping Pong" .... 1903 .... $65
Golf Association of Philadelphia:
"Golfers' Record 1903, Sanctioned And
       Endorsed By The Golf Association of
       Philadelphia and The Womens' Golf
       Association of Philadelphia" .... 1903 .... $300
Golf Canada:
"Golf Canada"... 1984 .... $25
Golf Clubs of Devon:
"The Golf Clubs of Devon" .... 1935 .... $60
Golf Clubs of Fife:
"The Golf Clubs of Fife"............................. 1933 .... $65
Golf Course Superintendents:
"History Of The Northern Ohio Chapter of
       The Golf Course Superintendents
       AssociationOf America 1923-1976"...... 1976 .... $15
Golf Courses California And Nevada:
"Golf Courses California And Nevada" .... 1970 .... $15
Golf Courses In New York State:
"Golf Courses In New York State"................ 1968 .... $15

Golf Courses In Switzerland:
"Golf Courses In Switzerland" .... 1928 .... $75
Golf Courses Of Victoria:
"Golf Courses Of Victoria, A Listing of Over
    300 Golf Courses In The State of
    Victoria, Australia" .... 1980 .... $15
Golf Courses On the G.W.R.:
"Golf Courses On The G.W.R" .... 1923 .... $275
"Golf Courses Served By The G.W.R. and
    Where To Stay" .... 1934 .... $150
"Golf Courses Served By The G.W.R. and
    Where To Stay" .... 1937 .... $150
"Golf Courses Served By The G.W.R. and
    Where To Stay" .... 1939 .... $125
Golf Digest Almanac:
"The Golf Digest Almanac 1984" .... 1984 .... $15
"The Golf Digest Almanac 1985" .... 1985 .... $10
Golf Digest Magazine:
"15 Point Annual Check Up" .... 1983 .... $5
"80 5-Minute Golf Lessons" .... 1968 .... $15
"All About Putting" .... 1973 .... $20
"The Art of Putting" .... 1976 .... $10
"The Best of Golf Digest: The First 25 Years" 1975 .... $25
"Better Golf For Boys" .... 1965 .... $5
"Better Golf" .... 1974 .... $10
"Golf Digest's 20 Ways To Hit It Farther" ...... 1982 .... $10
"Golf Digest's Pocket Golf Tips" .... 1977 .... $10
"Golf: A Golden Pocket Guide" .... 1968 .... $10
"How To Break 90 At Golf" .... 1967 .... $5
"How To Solve Your Golf Problems" .... 1963 .... $20
"Instant Golf Lessons" .... 1978 .... $10
"Gene Littler Presents 38 Checkpoints To
    Improve Your Swing" .... 1962 .... $15
"Arnold Palmer" .... 1967 .... $25
"Rand McNally Golf Course Guide" .... 1966 .... $25
"The Golfers Trillogy" .... 1965 .... $85
"Three Pillars Of Power" .... 1965 .... $10
"Tips From The Tour" .... 1985 .... $5
"Travelers Guide To Golf" .... 1976 .... $20
Golf Fitness Instruction Course:
"Golf Fitness Instruction Course" .... 1984 .... $10
Golf Foundation:
"Making Room For Golf" .... 1963 .... $5
"Golf Guidebook" .... 1965 .... $10

Thousands of color book illustrations visible at
www.rogeregilchrist.com

Camp & Brooks – Drives And Puts
(1st Edition)

Campbell – Golf for
Beginners

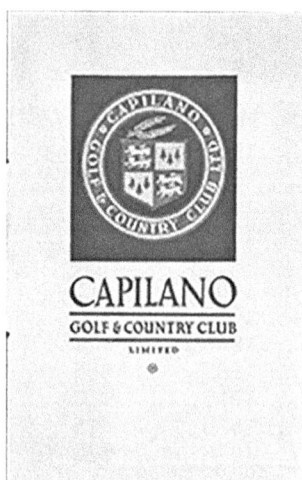

Capilano G&CC – Capilano
Golf & Country Club

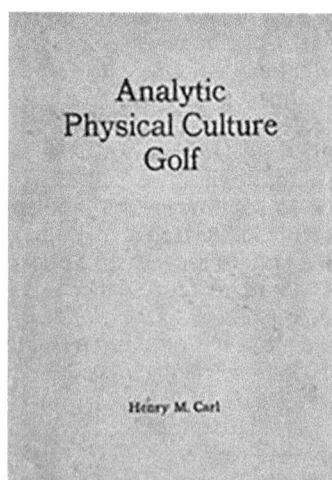

Carl – Analytic Physical
Culture Golf

Thousands of color book illustrations visible at
www.rogeregilchrist.com

Golf Illustrated Magazine:
"Fore! Golf Illustrated Annual" .... 1912 .... $275
Golf In Bermuda:
"Golf In Bermuda"..................................... 1957 .... $35
Golf In Britain:
"Golf In Britain" .... 1959 .... $20
Golf In California:
"Golf In California" .... 1900 .... $550
Golf In Italy:
"Golf In Italy"... 1935 .... $175
Golf In Maine:
"Golf In Maine Annual Guide"...................... 1930 .... $125
"Golf In Maine for 1945" .... 1945 .... $60
"Golf In Maine for 1949" .... 1949 .... $45
Golf In Scandinavia:
"Golf In Scandinavia" .... 1972 .... $15
Golf In Schools:
"Golf In Schools" .... 1939 .... $75
Golf In Scotland:
"Golf In Scotland" .... 1939 .... $250
Golf In Spain:
"Golf In Spain" .... 1971 .... $25
Golf In The Sun:
"Golf In The Sun"..................................... 1963 .... $25
Golf In Town and Country:
"The Golf Courses in Angus and Kincardine".. 1932 .... $65
Golf In Ulster:
"Golf In Ulster"....................................... 1949 .... $45
Golf In Yorkshire:
"Golf In Yorkshire" .... 1934 .... $225
Golf It Up:
"Golf It Up! Tips For Juniors" .... 1983 .... $10
Golf Know How:
"An Amazing Encyclopedia of Golf Tips"........ 1957 .... $15
Golf Links Of France:
"The Golf Links of France" .... 1930 .... $275
Golf Links On The Grand Rapids
  & Indiana Railroad:
"Golf Links On The Grand Rapids &
      Indiana Railroad"............................. 1900 .... $200
Golf Made Easy:
"Golf Made Easy Through Scotch Secrets" .... 1936 .... $75
Golf Magazine:
"America's Golf Book"................................ 1970 .... $35

Thousands of color book illustrations visible at
www.rogeregilchrist.com

"Encyclopedia of Golf" .... 1970 .... $25
    1979 Revised Edition.................................. .... $15
"Georgia Guide To Golf"............................ 1970 .... $10
"Handbook of Putting" .... 1973 .... $15
"Pro Pointers And Stroke Savers" .... 1964 .... $15
"Tips From The Teaching Pros".................... 1969 .... $20
"Winning Pointers From The Pros" .... 1965 .... $15
"Your Long Game" .... 1964 .... $20
"Your Short Game".................................... 1962 .... $15
"The Greenbriar's Sam Snead Teaches
    Golf"... 1966 .... $10
"Handbook of Golf Strategy"....................... 1971 .... $20
"Kwik Pro" .... 1963 .... $10
"Short Cuts To Better Golf" .... 1979 .... $15
"The World of Golf 1973" .... 1973 .... $25

Golf Masters:
    "A Sure Way To Play Better Golf" .... 1940 .... $55

Golf Match Club:
    "Record of Matches 1897-1908".................. 1909 .... $200

Golf Mind Vs. Business Mind:
    "The Neutro-Mental System For the Golfer" .. 1924 .... $120

Golf Par Excellence:
    "Golf Par Excellence 1980" .... 1980 .... $10

Golf Professional's Handbook:
    "Golf Professional's Handbook of Business" ... 1932 .... $90

Golf Rules:
    "Golf Rules" .... 1900 .... $750

Golf Quotes:
    "Golf Quotes" .... 1984 .... $10

Golf Service Book:
    "Golf Service Book For Caddies and
    Members".. 1922 .... $155

Golf Slang:
    "Golf Slang" .... 1978 .... $10

Golf Society Of The US:
    "A Season of Greatness" .... 1998 .... $20

Golf Technique And Guide:
    "Golf Technique And Guide of Southern
    California" .... 1940 .... $75

Golf Twaddle:
    "Golf Twaddle, Containing A Few Hints To
    Duffers" .... 1897 .... $625

Golf Union:
    "The Schemes For Standard Scratch Scores

and Uniform Handicapping" .... 1925 .... $95
Golf Where To Play And Where To Stay:
"Encyclopedia of Golf" .... 1970 .... $25
Revision .... 1979 .... $15
"Golf: Where To Play And Where To Stay" .... 1983 .... $15
Golf World Magazine:
"Golf In Scotland And Ireland" .... 1987 .... $25
"The Picadilly World of Golf 1972" .... 1972 .... $20
"The Picadilly World of Golf 1973-1974" .... 1973 .... $20
"Turf Mirth Compiled From The Pages
of Golf World" .... 1962 .... $10
"The World of Golf 1973" .... 1973 .... $35
"The World of Golf 1974" .... 1974 .... $25
"The World of Golf 1975" .... 1975 .... $20
"The World of Golf 1976" .... 1976 .... $20
Golfer's Digest:
"Golfer's Digest Volume I" .... 1966 .... $25
"Golfer's Digest Volume II" .... 1967 .... $20
"Golfer's Digest Volume III" .... 1968 .... $15
"Golfer's Digest Volume IV" .... 1969 .... $15
"Golfer's Digest Volume V" .... 1970 .... $15
"Golfer's Digest Volume VI" .... 1971 .... $15
"Golfer's Digest Volume VII" .... 1972 .... $15
Golfers' Guide:
"Golfers' Guide And Handbook" .... 1931 .... $90
"The Golfers' Guide And Official
Handbook For Scotland" .... 1901 .... $975
"Golfers' Guide For The United Kingdom" ...... 1895 ......$1,300
"Golfer's Guide Annual Vol 5" .... 1898 .... $600
"Golfers' Guide To Georgia 1980" .... 1980 .... $15
"Golfers' Guide To Happy Holidays" .... 1924 .... $60
"Golfers' Guide To The Counties of
Kent, Surrey, Sussex" .... 1967 .... $20
"Golfers' Guide To The Game And
Greens of Scotland" .... 1894 ......$1,950
Golfer's Handbook:
"Golfer's Handbook" First published .... 1899 .... $600
Golfers Magazine:
"The Grip In Golf" .... 1923 .... $250
Golfers' Record:
"Golfers' Record 1903" .... 1903 .... $350
Golfer's Trilogy:
"The Golfer's Trilogy: The Driver Book;
The Putter Book; The Wedge Book" ..... 1965 .... $85

Thousands of color book illustrations visible at
www.rogeregilchrist.com

Golfers Vade Mecum:
"The Golfer's Vade Mecum" .... 1909 .... $300
Golfers Yearbook:
"Golfers Yearbook 1938" .... 1938 .... $95
"Golfers Yearbook 1939" .... 1939 .... $65
Golfing Annual:
"Golfing Annual" First published .... 1888 .... $875
Golfing In Scotland:
"Golfing In Scotland In 100 Holiday Resorts" 1936 .... $450
Golfing On Long Island:
"Golfing On Long Island" .... 1902 .... $375
Golfing Year Book:
"Golfing Year Book" .... 1923 .... $95
Golfmasters:
"Fourteen Champions Write A book" .... 1940 .... $75
Allen Gofton:
"Wollaton Park Golf Club"(750 Copies) .... 2000 .... $35
Bob Considine & Fred Jarvis:
"A Portrait of the NYAC" .... 1969 .... $20
J. W. D. Goodban:
"History of The English Golf Union
    1924-1984" .... 1984 .... $50
"Royal North Devon Golf Club, A
    Centenary Anthology 1864-1964" .... 1964 .... $75
"The History of Saunton Golf Club
    1897-1987" .... 1987 .... $55
Edward D. Goodman:
"Meadowbrook Country Club, A Descriptive
    History From Its Beginnings In 1957
    Through 1984" .... 1984 .... $25
Ross Goodner:
"The 75 Year History of Shinnecock Hills
    Golf Club" (500 Copies) .... 1966 .... $650
    With Spider Web Dust Jacket.............. 1966 ......$1250
    Signed limited edition (20 copies) .... 1966 ......$2500
"Golf's Greatest ..." .... 1978 .... $25
Ken Goodwin:
"Clacton-on-Sea Golf Club 1892-1992" .... 1992 .... $25
Stephen Goodwin:
"The Greatest Masters" .... 1988 .... $25
Goodwood G. C:
"Goodwood Golf Club Official Handbook" ...... 1972 .... $40
Patricia Goodyear:
"Baltimore Country Club. One Hundred

Years"... 1998 .... $75
Richard D. Gordin and Roderick W. Meyers:
"Golf Fundamentals".................................. 1973 .... $10
Bob Gordon:
"Basic Golf"... 1972 .... $45
Charles A. Gordon:
"The Gordon Caddie Guide" .... 1921 .... $95
Hugh H. Gordon:
"Repair Your Own Golf Clubs" .... 1959 .... $20
James Gordon:
"A Description of Both Touns of Aberdeen" ... 1842 .... $350
Jack Gordon:
"Ten Commandments of The Golf Stroke"..... 1929 .... $150
        Reprint... 1969 .... $20
"Understandable Golf" .... 1926 .... $95
John Gordon:
"The Grand Old Game" .... 1995 .... $45
"The Greatest Golf Gourses of America" .... 1997 .... $10
"The Greatest Golf Courses In Canada" .... 1991 .... $40
John Gordon & Michael French:
"The Great Golf Courses Of Canada"............ 1991 .... $55
Gorham Golf Book:
"The Gorham Golf Book" .... 1903 ......$1,500
Goring & Streatley Golf Club:
"Goring and Streatley Golf Club" .... 1938 .... $60
"Goring and Streatley Golf Club. The First
        Hundred Years 1895-1995" .... 1995 .... $35
Harry Gottlieb:
"Golf For Southpaws" .... 1953 .... $35
"I Have The Secret of Putting" .... 1965 .... $20
Gourock Golf Club:
"Gourock Golf Club" .... 1958 .... $25
Bobby Grace:
"Guide To Collecting Rare Ping Golf Clubs".... 1993 .... $55
Stan Graff:
"So You Want To Play Golf: The Golf Swing
        Explained Simply And Logically"......... 1974 .... $10
Herb Graffis:
"Easy Cures For Your Ailing Golf" .... 1959 .... $15
"Esquire's World of Golf"............................ 1965 .... $25
"Fun And Larceny" .... 1936 .... $45
"The Golf Club Organizers Handbook" .... 1931 .... $75
"Golf Facilities" .... 1949 .... $95
"Golfing's Dictionary of Golf Information" ..... 1960 .... $45

Thousands of color book illustrations visible at
www.rogeregilchrist.com

"Golfing's Digest of Golf Lessons" .... 1955 .... $20
"Golfing's Picture Story of Good Golf".......... 1954 .... $60
"Golfing's Treasury of Golf Tips" .... 1963 .... $15
"More Business For You" .... 1954 .... $15
"The PGA: The Official History of The
        Professional Golfer's Association
        Of America" .... 1975 .... $75
"Planning The Professionals Shop".............. 1951 .... $35
"The Primer of Good Golf" .... 1957 .... $15
"Simply Golf"... 1959 .... $40
"Six Champions Tell You How" .... 1953 .... $25
"A Treasury of Golf Tips"............................ 1940 .... $50
"TWA And Your Golf Professional Want You
        To Have This In Flight Golf Lesson" ..... 1971 .... $15
Graham:
    "Mayfair Golf and Country Club:
        75 Years, 1922-1997" .... 1997 .... $25
Alex S. Graham:
    "Graham's Golf Club"................................ 1965 .... $20
David Graham:
    "Your Way To Winning Golf" .... 1985 .... $20
    "David Graham's Guide To Golf Equipment" .. 1993 .... $25
Harry Graham:
    "Rhymes For Riper Years" .... 1917 .... $45
Ian R. Graham:
    "The Merchants of Edinburgh Golf Club
        1907-1982" .... 1982 .... $35
Julian P. Graham:
    " A Photographic Study of Pebble Beach
        Golf Links"...................................... 1952 .... $350
Lou Graham:
    "Mastering Golf" .... 1978 .... $10
Robert A. Grampsey:
    "St Mungo's Gowfers: A History of Glasgow
        Golf Club 1787-1987"....................... 1987 .... $150
Grange-Over-Sands:
    "Grange-Over-Sands New Golf Club" .... 1951 .... $25
Arthur Grant:
    "Golf: The Pocket Professional" .... 1930 .... $60
Donald Grant:
    "Personal Memories of Royal Dornoch
Golf Club 1900-1925".................................... 1978 .... $60
    "Donald Ross of Pinehurst and
        Royal Dornoch" .... 1973 .... $95

Thousands of color book illustrations visible at
www.rogeregilchrist.com

Roger E. Gilchrist's Guide to Collectible Golf Book Prices

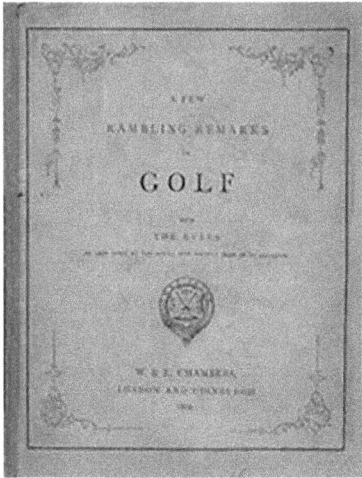

Chambers – A Few Rambling
Remarks on Golf

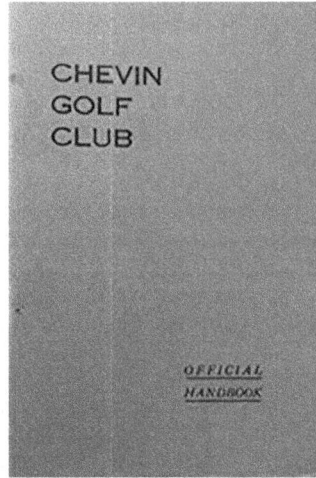

Chevin G. C. - Handbook

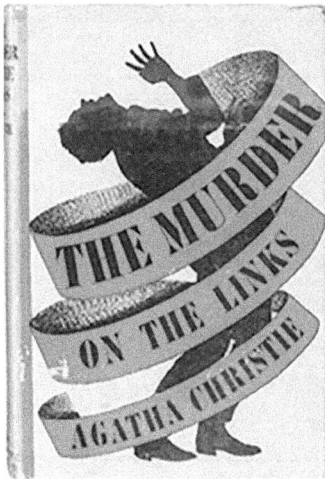

Christie – Murder on the Links

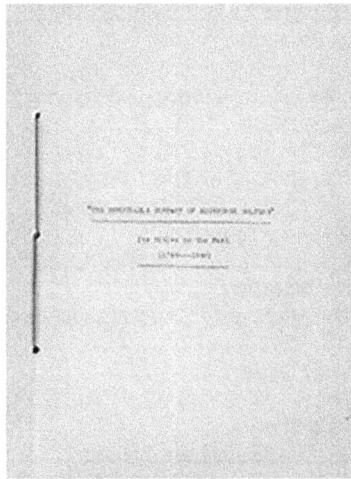

Clapcott – The Honorable Company
Of Edinburgh Golfers

Thousands of color book illustrations visible at
www.rogeregilchrist.com

Ellsworth S. Grant:
"The Club on Prospect Street. A History
of the Hartford Club" .... 1984 .... $75
H. R. J. Grant & John F. Moreton:
"Aspects of Collecting Golf Books" .... 1996 .... $100
Limited Edition of 425 .... 1996 .... $250
Julian I. Graubart:
"Golf's Greatest Championship".................... 1997 .... $20
Charles Graves & Henry Longhurst:
"Candid Caddies" .... 1935 .... $145
Revised Edition .... 1947 .... $75
Robert Muir Graves:
"A Practice Golf Facility For Athletic Fields" ... 1961 .... $15
Berkeley Gray:
"Dare Devil Conquest" .... 1950 .... $50
Bob Gray & Lou Messinger:
"A Line on Golf" .... 1952 .... $75
David Gray:
"Mr Carteret and Others............................. 1910 .... $50
Harry J. Gray:
"Last Blast At Wethersfield"........................ 1983 .... $10
Jonathon Gray:
"The Owl" .... 1937 .... $285
Maxwell Gray:
"The Great Refusal".................................. 1906 .... $55
Rick Grayson & John Andrisani:
"Super Golf..."... 1996 .... $20
Great Chebeague G. C:
"The History of The Great Chebeague
Golf Club" (250 Copies) .... 1962 .... $115
Green Meadow C. C:
"Green Meadow Country Club".................... 1928 .... $50
James Green:
"The History of Shooters Hill Golf Club
1903-1973 .... 1973 .... $45
Michael Green:
"The Art of Coarse Golf"............................. 1967 .... $10
Robert Green:
"Golf: An Illustrated History" .... 1987 .... $20
"The Illustrated Encyclopeadia of Golf"......... 1992 .... $20
Sandy Green:
"Don'ts For Golfers"................................. 1925 .... $150
Kell Greene:
"The Golf Swing of Bobby Jones".................. 1931 .... $300

Thousands of color book illustrations visible at
www.rogeregilchrist.com

Robert Greene & Brian Morgan:
"Classic Holes of Golf" .... 1989 .... $25
Ian Greenfield:
"Turf Culture" .... 1962 .... $50
Wayne Greenhaw:
"The Golfer" .... 1967 .... $25
Greenways:
"Fifty Golf Hints For Beginners" .... 1928 .... $65
George W. Greenwood:
"Golf Really Explained" .... 1926 .... $65
Edward Gregory:
"Country Club of Greenfield The Centennial
      History" (150 Copies) .... 1996 .... $35
Paul Gregory:
"Greatest Moments In Golf" .... 1987 .... $15
Gregory's Guide:
"Gregory's Guide For Golfers" .... 1939 .... $65
Gene Gregson:
"Hogan The Man Who Played For Glory" .... 1978 .... $35
J. M. Gregson:
"Dead On Course' .... 1991 .... $35
"Murder On The Nineteenth" .... 1989 .... $40
J. S. Gregson:
"Gimcrackiana .... 1833 ....$1500
Jim Gregson:
"Golf Rules" .... 1984 .... $10
Malcolm Gregson:
"Golf With Gregson" .... 1968 .... $15
Ian Greig:
"The King's Club Murder" .... 1930 .... $35
"The Silver King Mystery" .... 1930 .... $35
Gren:
"The Duffer's Guide To Golf" .... 1984 .... $10
Peter Gresswell:
"Weekend Golfer" .... 1977 .... $10
Thomas Gribbin:
"Correct Caddy Conduct" .... 1920 .... $95
Francis Grierson:
"Boomerang Murder" .... 1951 .... $25
James Grierson:
"Delineations of Saint Andrews" .... 1807 ......$7,500
      Revised Edition .... 1833 .... $995
      2nd Edition .... 1923 .... $625
"Saint Andrews As It Was And It Is,

Thousands of color book illustrations visible at
www.rogeregilchrist.com

Being The Third Edition of
Dr. Grierson's Delineations" .... 1838 ...... $2,000
Marcus Griffin:
"A History of The Concord Golf Club
1899-1939" .... 1939 .... $60
E .M. Griffiths:
"With Club And Caddie" .... 1909 .... $650
Bruce E. Griggs:
"Golfgraphs" .... 1933 .... $50
John Grime:
"The Royal Lytham and St. Annes Golf Club".. ???? $75
R. Grimsdell:
"Golf In South Africa" .... 1928 .... $525
Will Grimsley:
"Golf: Its History, People and Events" .... 1966 .... $125
Lewis Grizzard:
"Does A Wild Bear Chip In The Woods?" .... 1990 .... $10
James P. Grode:
"The Full Gospel Golfer As Revealed By
The Holy Spirit" .... 1983 .... $10
Milton Gross:
"Eighteen Holes In My Head" .... 1959 .... $20
S. Gross:
"Golf, Golf, Golf" .... 1989 .... $10
Jack Grout:
"Jack Grout's Golf Clinic" .... 1985 .... $15
"Let Me Teach You Golf As I Taught
Jack Nicklaus" .... 1975 .... $25
Guaranteed Golf Lesson:
"The Guaranteed Golf Lesson" .... 1968 .... $10
Larry Guest:
"Arnie, Inside The Legend" .... 1993 .... $20
Guide To Golf Clubs:
"A Guide To Golf Clubs In And Around
London" .... 1955 .... $30
David Guiney:
"The Dunlop Book of Golf" .... 1973 .... $65
"100 Years of Golf At Sutton" .... 1990 .... $35
Ralph Guldahl:
"Grove Your Golf Swing" .... 1939 .... $125
Guldahl, Revolta, Sarazen, & Shute:
"Four Masters" .... 1937 .... $95
Bill Gulick:
"The Country Club Caper" .... 1971 .... $30

Thousands of color book illustrations visible at
www.rogeregilchrist.com

Geoffrey M. Gullik:
"History of Lindrick Golf Club 1891-1951"..... 1951 .... $150
Philip Gundelfinger Jr.:
"Golf's Who's Who: Records of The Pros"...... 1958 .... $45
Harry E. Gunn:
"How To Play Golf With Your Wife
    And Survive".................................... 1976 .... $10
John Gurda:
"A Sense of Tradition: The Centennial History
    of the Milwaukee Country Club" .... 1993 .... $65
Lealand Gustavson:
"Enjoy Your Golf"...................................... 1954 .... $35
T. H.:
"A Barton Ballad" .... 1918 .... $50
Steve Haake:
"The Engineering of Sport" .... 1996 .... $65
Harry J. Haas:
"A Handbook For Caddies And Members"...... 1922 .... $225
"Golf Service Book For Caddies And
    Members"...................................... 1938 .... $95
James Haber:
"Golf Made Easy: How To Achieve A
    Consistently Effective Golf Swing" .... 1974 .... $20
"Mastering The Art of Winning Golf"............. 1976 .... $15
John C. Hackbarth:
"The Key To Better Golf" .... 1929 .... $225
Dave Hackenberg:
"Inverness Club: Its Vibrant Voice Chimes
    Through a Century 1903-2003" .... 2003 .... $175
Hackensack G. C:
"Hackensack Golf Club 1900"..................... 1900 .... $50
Alan J. Hackett:
"Manitoba Links"...................................... 1998 .... $20
Buddy Hackett:
"The Truth About Golf And Other Lies" .... 1968 .... $15
Bob Hackey:
"Golf Annual '74: World Golf Hall of Fame
    Edition".. 1974 .... $20
Tim Hackler & Amanda Robb:
"A History of the Washington Golf and Country
    Club: A Century of Tradition
    1894-1994" .... 1994 .... $55
Stewart Hackney:
"Bygone Days On The Old Course" .... 1990 .... $45

Signed Limited Edition of 200 .... 1990 .... $125
Signed 2nd edition (300 Copies) .... 1990 .... $30
"Carnoustie Links: Courses and Players" ...... 1989 .... $35

Haddington Municipal:
"Haddington Municipal Golf Course"............. 1953 .... $25

Philip S. Haffenden:
"Willingdon Golf Club....1898-1998" .... 1998 .... $35

Walter Hagen:
"Elements of the Golf Swing" .... 1930 .... $450
"Golf Clubs And How To Use Them" .... 1929 .... $145
"The Walter Hagen Story" (US edition)......... 1956 .... $125
Special Bound Edition....................... 1956 .... $150
"The Walter Hagen Story" (UK Edition) .... 1956 .... $75
Memorial Tournament Reprint
(250 Copies).................................. 1977 .... $165
Reprint... 2000 .... $15
"The How And Why of Golf" .... 1932 .... $135

James & Lynn Hahn:
"Nancy Lopez, Golfing Pioneer" .... 1979 .... $15
"Patty! The Sports Career of Patricia Berg" ... 1981 .... $15

Paul Hahn:
"From The Pen And Camera of Paul Hahn".... 1965 .... $10
"Paul Hahn Shows You How To Play
Trouble Shots" .... 1965 .... $25
"Links Logic" .... 1951 .... $35

Paul Hahn Jr.:
"No Trick To It" .... 1975 .... $10

William Halberg:
"The Rub of The Green" .... 1988 .... $20
"Perfect Lies: A Century of Good Golf
Stories"... 1990 .... $20
"Perfect Lies: A Century of Great Golfers"..... 1989 .... $20
"Perfect Lies" .... 1998 .... $20
"The Soul of Golf" .... 1997 .... $15

Lee M. Hale:
"Ninety Years in the Forefront of New Jersey
Golf. Echo Lake Country Club" .... 1988 .... $35

Richard Walden Hale:
"The Story of Bar Harbor" .... 1949 .... $75

Thomas Haliburton:
"Rabbit Into Tiger" .... 1964 .... $15

Halifax Golf And Country Club:
"Programme Commemorating The Official
Opening of The New Course, Halifax

Thousands of color book illustrations visible at
www.rogeregilchrist.com

Golf And Country Club"...................... 1970 .... $25
Gerald Hall:
"A History of The Santa Anna Country Club" . 1989 .... $35
Henry Hall:
"The Tribune Book of Open Air Sports.."....... 1887 .... $125
Holworthy Hall:
"Dormie One, And Other Golf Stories".......... 1917 .... $335
    Reprint (250 Copies) .... 1944 .... $50
    Gogarty reprint (500 Copies).............. 1995 .... $35
Jay Hall:
"The Executive Trap"................................. 1992 .... $20
John H. Hall:
"The Victoria Club 1903-1978".................... 1978 .... $30
Peter Hall:
"A History of Lindrick Artisans Golf
    Club 1899-1999" .... 1999 .... $20
Ray Hall:
"A Golf Plan For Schools" .... 1952 .... $45
A.E. Hallem:
"Straight Road To Golf"............................. 1928 .... $95
Michael Halliday & Gavin Caldwell:
"From College Courses to Lasting Links
    1909-2009" .... 2009 .... $25
Hallowes Golf Club:
"Hallowes Golf Club .... 1911 .... $250
Malcolm Hamer:
"The Ryder Cup"...................................... 1992 .... $25
"A Deadly Lie" .... 1992 .... $15
"Dead On Line"... 1996 .... $25
"Shadows On The Green"............................ 1994 .... $30
"Sudden Death"....................................... 1991 .... $65
B. C. Hamilton:
"Golf: A Treatise On The Royal And Ancient
    Game" .... 1947 .... $85
David Hamilton:
"Early Golf At Edinburgh & Leith: The Account
    Books of Sir John Foulis of Ravelston". 1988 .... $150
    Signed Limited Edition of 300 .... 1988 .... $250
"Early Aberdeen Golf, Golfing Small Talk In
    "1638" .... 1985 .... $95
    Signed Limited Edition (450 Copies) .... 1985 .... $195
"Early Golf At St. Andrews" .... 1986 .... $95
    Signed by Hamilton (350 Copies) .... 1986 .... $350
"Early Golf In Glasgow 1589-1787" .... 1985 .... $65

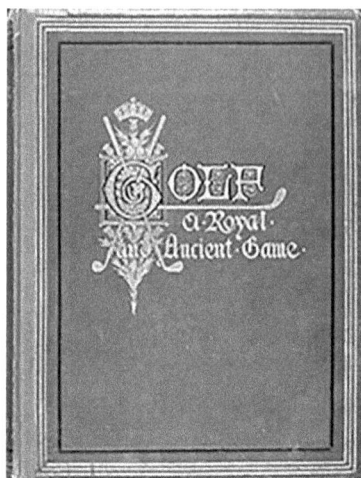

Clark – Golf A Royal and Ancient
Game (50 Copies)

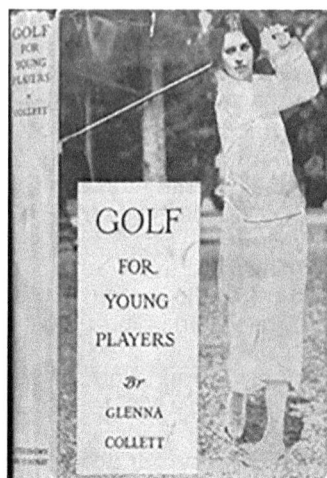

Collett – Golf For Young
Players (Dust Jacket)

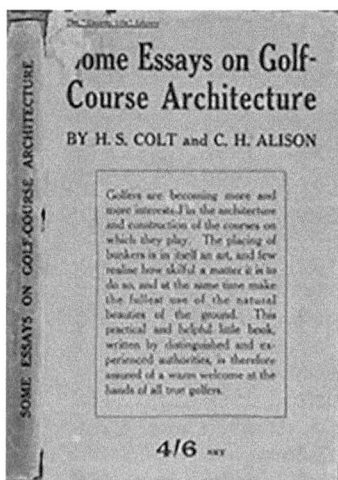

Colt & Alison – Some Essays on
Golf Course Architecture

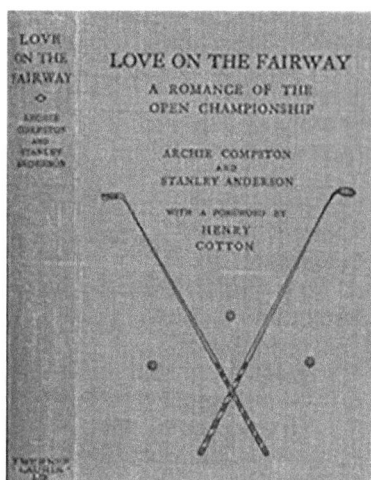

Compston & Anderson - Love
on the Fairway

Thousands of color book illustrations visible at
www.rogeregilchrist.com

Signed By Hamilton (250 Copies)........ 1985 .... $325
"Game At Golf" (70 signed copies) .... 1987 .... $750
"Golf: Scotlands Game" .... 1998 .... $100
Limited Edition of (350 Copies)........... 1998 .... $400
"Preicous Gum The Story of the Gutta Ball" .. 2004 .... $300
"The Beacon Golfing Handbook".................. 1984 .... $15
"The Good Golf Guide To Scotland"............. 1982 .... $20
"The South Sea Brithers" (150 Copies)........ 1992 .... $300
"John Kerr, The Sporting Padre" (90 Copies). 1989 .... $350
"The Britherhood" (300 Copies) .... 1992 .... $150
"The Thorn Tree Clique.." (50 Copies)........ 2001 .... $475
280 Copies .... 2001 ;....... $150
Eddie Hamilton:
"Golfing Gimmicks" .... 1958 .... $10
Edward A. Hamilton & Charles Preston:
"Golfing America"..................................... 1958 .... $60
Rory Hamilton:
"A Golfer's Guide To Wee Places: Luffness,
Gullane, Muirfield" .... 1980 .... $120
J. A. Hammerton:
"Mr. Punch's Golf Stories Told By His
Merry Men"...................................... 1909 .... $125
"Mr. Punch On The Links"........................... 1935 .... $75
"The Rubaiyat of A Golfer"......................... 1946 .... $75
Daryn Hammond:
"The Golf Swing, The Ernest Jones Method" .. 1920 .... $150
Ike S. Handy:
"How To Hit A Golf Ball Straight"................. 1967 .... $90
"It's The Dammed Ball".............................. 1951 .... $75
Hank Haney:
"The Only Golf Lesson You'll Ever Need"....... 1999 .... $10
Charles Steadman Hanks:
"Hints To Golfers" .... 1913 .... $95
Hanna:
"50 Years from the Olde English Restaurant
Ltd (1928) to Peace Portal G.C (1978)" 1979 .... $25
John Hanna:
" Malone Golf Club 1895-1995 A History" ..... 1995 .... $75
Chris Hannan:
"Outlands Golf Club Golden Anniversary
1931-1981" .... 1981 .... $25
Hannay & Blair:
"Stranraer Golf Club 1905-1995"................. 1996 .... $45

Thousands of color book illustrations visible at
www.rogeregilchrist.com

N. Ferguson Blair:
"Scraps on Golf – Manuscript of Golf Poetry". 1842 .... $1950
Sebastian Hannay:
"All Square....." .... 1980 .... $50
Frank Hannigan:
"Joseph C Dey Jnr. Golf's Most Influential
        Figure" (220 Copies) .... 1992 .... $175
Hansen:
"History of Chenequa Country Club
        1911-1986" .... 1986 .... $25
Rick Hanson:
"Splitting Heirs" .... 1997 .... $35
George Harbottle:
"The Northumberland Golf Club Story" .... 1978 .... $50
George & Stanley Harbottle:
"100 Years at "The Park". The
        Northumberland Golf Club Story
        1898-1998 .... 1999 .... $40
Harburn G. C:
"Harburn Golf Club" .... 1939 .... $35
Byron Harcke:
"Fore: Golf Fundamentals" .... 1960 .... $10
Michael Hardcastle:
"Aim For The Flag" .... 1969 .... $20
James C. Hardie:
"Western Gailes 1897-1997" .... 1997 .... $325
William H. Harding:
"Rainbow" .... 1979 .... $20
Merrill D. Hardy & Eleanor Walsh:
"Golf" .... 1980 .... $10
Burnham Hare:
"The Golfing Swing Simplified And Its
        Mechanism Correctly Explained" .... 1913 .... $150
Harry Harewood:
"A Dictionary of Sports" .... 1835 .... $195
Ernest Hargreaves:
"Caddie In The Golden Age" .... 1993 .... $30
J. R. Harker:
"The Finchley Golf Club" .... 1929 .... $95
Bob Harlow:
"Golf State, North Carolina" .... 1953 .... $15
"True Golf Facts" .... 1940 .... $70
Claude "Butch" Harmon Jr:
"The Four Cornerstones of Winning Golf" ...... 1996 .... $20

"Butch Harmon's Playing Lessons"............... 1998 .... $15
Paul Harney:
"Golf Is A Simple Game" .... 1972 .... $10
"How To Putt A Flip Vision Golf Manual"........ 1965 .... $65
Harpenden G. C:
"Harpenden Golf Club, 1894-1954"............. 1954 .... $40
Chandler Harper:
"My First Seventy Years in Golf".................. 1994 .... $35
Stephan K. Harper:
"Hawaii Golf Guide"................................... 1994 .... $10
Edward Harriman:
"The Story of Eastward Ho" .... 1978 .... $25
Mark G. Harris:
"New Angles On Putting And Chip Shots"...... 1940 .... $150
Richard Harris:
"Drive For Show Putt For Dough" .... 1972 .... $10
"How To Take The Fun Out of Golf"............. 1970 .... $10
Robert Harris:
"Proposed New Rules of Golf A Threat
    To The Game As A Sport" .... 1949 .... $75
"Sixty Years of Golf"................................. 1953 .... $125
Austin Harrison:
"Essays of Today And Yesterday" .... 1927 .... $25
Al Hart:
"Golfun: A Humorous Approach To
    A Serious Subject"............................ 1966 .... $10
Ken Hart-Thomas:
"Minehead And West Somerset Golf Club
    1882-1982" .... 1982 .... $60
George Hartley:
"A History of St. George's Hill Golf Club
    1913-1983" .... 1983......... $75
"The Perranporth Golf Club" .... 1961 .... $25
Syd Harriet & ol Grazi:
"The Senior Golfer's Answer Book" .... 1999 .... $10
J. R. Hartley:
"Golfing"... 1995 .... $15
Ray Hartley:
"The Perranporth Golf Club" .... 1970 .... $35
Hartford G.C:
"50th Anniversary"................................... 1946 .... $75
John C. Harvey:
"The Golfer's Repair And Maintenance
    Handbook".................................... 1984 .... $15

Thousands of color book illustrations visible at
www.rogeregilchrist.com

W. Hugh Harvey & E. J. Symons"
"A Century On The Towans" .... 1989 .... $45
Sam Hasegawa:
"Johnny Miller" .... 1975 .... $10
Peter Haslam:
"The World of Scottish Golf" .... 1985 .... $15
David Hassall:
"Golf: The Official Book of the Australian
  Open" .... 1984 .... $55
John Hassall:
"The Seven Ages of Golf" .... 1899 ..... $2,500
Hastings C C:
"The Hastings Country Club"....................... 1926 .... $45
H. A. Hattstrom:
"Golf After Forty" .... 1946 .... $30
"The In-Line Method of Putting and
  Approaching" .... 1959 .... $45
"On And Off The Green"............................. 1955 .... $45
Arnold Haultain:
"The Mystery Of Golf" (440 Copies) .... 1908 ..... $3,000
   Second Edition .... 1910 .... $225
   Reprint.. 1965 .... $250
   Reprint.. 1986 .... $50
   Reprint.. 1997 .... $15
Thomas Hauser:
"Arnold Palmer: A Personal Story" .... 1994 .... $20
Clem Hawke:
"A Century of Golf at Hokowhitu" .... 1995 .... $25
Hawera G. C:
"Rules of the Ladies Hawera Golf Club" .... 1932 .... $50
Ken Hawkes:
"BBC Book of Golf"................................... 1975 .... $10
Reginald Hawkins:
"Golf at Letchworth"................................. 1985 .... $20
F. W. Hawtree:
"The Golf Course: Planning, Design,
  Construction, & Maintenance"............. 1983 .... $35
Fred Hawtree:
"Colt & Co; A Biographical Study of Henry
   Shapland Colt 1869-1951 With His
   Partners C.H. Alison; J.S.F. Morrison
   and Dr.Mackenzie" (100 Copies) .... 1991 .... $225
    Reprint (900 Copies) .... 1991 .... $125
"Aspects of Golf Course Architecture"

(675 Copies) .... 1998 .... $120
Grant Books Ltd Edition of 75 .... 2008 .... $325
Contributors Copy Ltd Edition of 6 ...... 2008 .... $300
"Triple Bauge" .... 1996 .... $150
Alex Hay:
"The Golf Manual" .... 1980 .... $15
"The Handbook of Golf" .... 1984 .... $15
"The Mechanics of Golf" .... 1979 .... $15
"Skills & Tactics of Golf" .... 1980 .... $10
Alex Hay & Bill Robertson:
"Young Golfer" .... 1980 .... $10
Alex Hay & Julian Worthington:
'Golf School" .... 1986 .... $15
Hayes, Evans, & Isaac:
"The Care of The Golf Course" .... 1992 .... $40
Hayling G. C:
"Hayling Golf Club Centenary 1883-1983" .... 1983 .... $25
Sandra Haynie:
"Golf: A Natural Course For Women" .... 1975 .... $20
Abel Haywood:
"The Manchester Golf Club" .... 1909 ...... $1,250
Charles S. Haywood:
"The Summer Playground" .... 1902 .... $175
John C. Haywood:
"The Silver Creek" .... 1908 .... $295
Ann Hazell:
"A Slice of History, Blackwood Golf Club
        1930-1980" .... 1979 .... $25
Ronald Heager:
"Kings of Club" .... 1968 .... $25
James F. Healey:
"Golfing Before The Arch" .... 1997 .... $125
"Glen Echo Country Club 100 Years" .... 2001 .... $75
"Sunset Country Club" .... 2010 .... $50
Kay Healy:
"Heritage of Oakland Hills As Of 1982" .... 1982 .... $75
T. M. Healy:
"Glynn:" .... 1993 .... $95
"Portmarnock Golf Club 1894-1994" .... 1993 .... $40
William T. Healy:
"The History of the Tucson Country Club" ..... 1990 .... $75
Jerry Heard:
"The Golf Secrets of The Big Money Pros" ..... 1992 .... $10

Ian Heath:
"A Round With...." .... 1986 .... $10
"The Golden Rules of Golf" .... 1984 .... $10
Peter Heath:
"Humors of Golf" .... 1975 .... $15
"Towards 100 Years: Edgbaston Golf Club
     1896-1986" (750 Copies) .... 1986 .... $65
Michael Hebron:
"See And Feel The Inside Move The Outside" 1984 .... $10
Phyllis F. Heck:
"History of the Dayton Country Club
     1896-1976" .... 1996 .... $25
Genevieve Hecker:
"Golf For Women" .... 1904 ..... $2,100
Ethel F. Heddle:
"A Secret of St Andrews" .... 1923 .... $45
H. Richard Heilman:
"Golf At Merion 1896-1976" .... 1977 .... $95
Jack G. Heise:
"How You Can Play Better Golf Using
     Self-Hypnosis" .... 1961 .... $45
"Super Golf With Self-Hypnosis" .... 1962 .... $35
A. E. Heiss:
"The 19th Hole" .... 1933 .... $70
Jane Heller:
"The Club" .... 1995 .... $35
Eleanor E. Helme:
"After The Ball" .... 1931 .... $325
"The Best of Golf" .... 1925 .... $225
"Family Golf" .... 1938 .... $175
"The Lady Golfer's Tip Book" .... 1923 .... $325
Myra B. Helmer & Inez L. Klumph:
"Father Gander Golf Book" .... 1909 .... $450
Charles T. Helmes & Kenneth W. Price:
"Waccabuc Country Club: Seventy Years
     of History 1912-1982" .... 1982 .... $65
Henderson's Photographic:
"Henderson's Photographic Golf Instructor" .. 1923 .... $100
Edward Henderson:
"The Negro in Sports" .... 1939 .... $75
Ian Henderson:
"Edzell Golf Club – The First Hundred Years
     1895-1995" .... 1995 .... $35

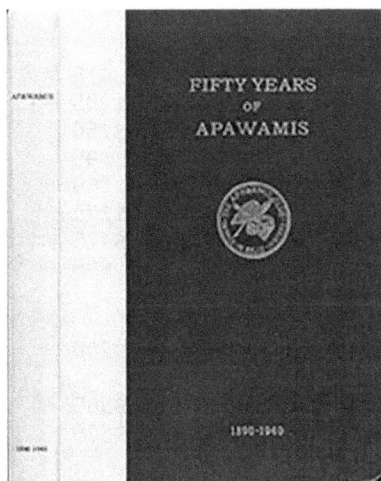

Conroy – Fifty Years of
Apawamis

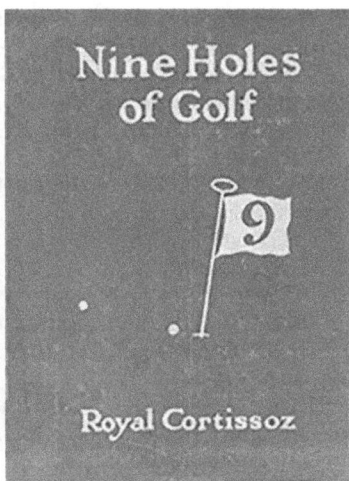

Cortissoz – Nine Holes of Golf

Cotton – My Swing

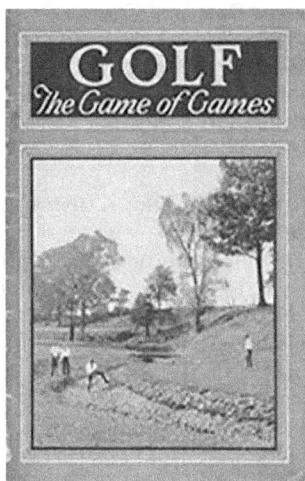

Crawford, MacGregor & Canby -
Golf The Game of Games

Thousands of color book illustrations visible at
www.rogeregilchrist.com

Ian T. Henderson & David I. Stirk:
"The Compleat Golfer: An Illustrated History
    of The Royal And Ancient Game"......... 1979 .... $75
"Golf In The Making" .... 1979 .... $295
    Revised Edition................................. 1982 .... $150
    Revised edition................................ 1994 .... $95
"The Heritage of Golf: An Illustrated History" 1985 .... $60
"Royal Blackheath".................................... 1981 .... $175
    Signed (100 Copies) .... 1981 .... $475
    Second Edition .... 1995 .... $95
"Shortspoon-Major F. P. Hopkins 1830-1913
    Golfing Artist and Journalist"
    (750 Copies)................................... 1984 .... $200
James Henderson:
"A History of the Royal Co. Down Golf Club" . 1958 .... $595
"Royal County Down Golf".......................... 1982 .... $525
J. Lindsay Henderson:
"The Records of The Panmure Golf Club" ...... 1926 ....$1450
L.J. Henderson:
"Golf By The Masters"............................... 1950 .... $30
"The P.G.A. Golfer's Guide" .... 1949 .... $30
Peter Henderson:
"Pitch And Putt Golf Courses"..................... 1930 .... $150
    1995 Reprint................................. .... $15
Robert W. Henderson:
"Line of Flight, A Manual of Golf"................. 1939 .... $225
W.C. Henderson & Son:
"Views of St Andrews: .... 1892 .... $850
J. Hendren:
"The Knock Golf Club, A History 1895-1982". 1982 .... $30
W. Garden Hendry:
"The Dynamic Anatomy of The Golf Swing, A
    Scientific Approach To Improvement
    At Golf"... 1985 .... $15
Henly G. C:
"Henly Golf Club"..................................... 1916 .... $175

Elizabeth Hennessy:
"A History of Roehampton Club 1901 to
    1986" .... 1986 .... $50
Harold Henning:
"Drive Around Southern Africa With Harold
    Henning".. 1974 .... $135
"Harold Henning's Golfer's Guide of Southern

Africa".. 1984 .... $15
James Henry:
"The Irvine Golf Club Bogside 1887-1987".... 1987 .... $45
Bill F. Hensley:
"North Carolina-Golf State U.S.A.".............. 1953 .... $15
Tom Hepburb & Selwyn Jacobson:
"America's Most Difficult Golf Holes" .... 1983 .... $20
"Australia's Most Difficult Golf Holes" .... 1982 .... $25
"Canada's Most Difficult Golf Holes"............ 1983 .... $20
"Even More Of Australia's Most Difficult
   Golf Holes" .... 1983 .... $25
"Great Britain And Ireland's Most Difficult
   Golf Holes" .... 1983 .... $20
"Great Golf Holes of New Zealand" .... 1981 .... $20
"Great Golf Holes of South Africa" .... 1984 .... $25
"New Zealand's Toughest Golf Courses
   Book II" .... 1983 .... $25
"South East Asia's Toughest Golf Holes" .... 1984 .... $20
"The World's 72 Toughest Golf Holes" .... 1984 .... $20
George H. Hepworth:
"Hiram Golf's Religion.."............................ 1898 .... $125
Sandy Herd:
"My Golfing Life" (London Edition) .... 1923 .... $425
         New York Edition .... 1923 .... $225
Hergenroeder, Wright, & Hillum:
"The Conduct Compendium of Golf"............ 1979 .... $10
Roger F. Hermanson:
"The Rules of Golf In Programmed Form" ..... 1968 .... $10
Hermes:
"Texas Golf"... 1987 .... $20
Charles Herndon:
"Golf Made Easier" .... 1930 .... $80
Donald Herold:
"Adventures In Golf" .... 1965 .... $15
"Love That Golf" .... 1952 .... $20
Steve Hershey:
"The Senior Tour" .... 1992 .... $20
Peggy Herz:
"La Quinta Country Club. Silver Anniversary
       1959-1984" .... 1984 .... $75
Kenneth G. Hess:
"The Golfer's Alphabet"............................. 1991 .... $20
Frederick W. Hetzel:
"You Can Improve Your Golf With A

Sling-Master" .... 1956 .... $10
Karla L. Heuer:
"Golf Course, A Guide To Analysis and
    Valuation" .... 1980 .... $10
Oliver Heuler:
"Golf Short Game Basics" .... 1996 .... $10
William Heuman:
"Famous American Athletes" .... 1963 .... $20
Cyril Hewertson:
"Walton Heath Golf Club, The Story of the
    First 75 Years, 1904-1979" .... 1979 .... $55
    Limited Edition of 200 signed copies .... 1979 .... $95
Karen Hewson:
"The Open Championship of Canada" .... 2004 .... $20
Lionel Hewson:
"The Irish Golf Directory" .... 1929 .... $275
Hexdown and Bigbury-On-Sea:
The Hexdown and Bigbury-On-Sea
    Golf Club" .... 1927 .... $95
Paul L. Hexter:
"You Can Play Golf Forever" .... 1979 .... $10
John Heywood:
"John Heywood's Guide To Lancashire,
    Cheshire, Derbyshire, Yorkshire And
    North Wales Golf" .... 1914 .... $950
May Hezlet:
"Ladies Golf" .... 1904 ......$1075
Hiawatha G. C:
"For Those Who Golf" .... 1932 .... $275
Angus Hibbard:
"Golf And The Glen View Club" .... 1970 .... $25
George Hibbard:
"Perfect Impact: .... 2000 .... $25
Keith C. Hick:
"The Hesketh Golf Club 1885-1985"
    (750 Copies) .... 1985 .... $45
Donal Hickey:
"Queen of Them All: A History of Killarney
    Golf and Fishing Club 1893-1993" .... 1993 .... $75
Darrell Hickok:
"Play Better Golf" .... 1966 .... $10
Elizabeth Mary Hicks:
"Fundamentals of Golf" .... 1948 .... $45

Elizabeth M (Betty) Hicks & Ellen J. Griffin:
"Golf Manual For Teachers" .... 1949 .... $225
Helen Hicks:
"Golf Hints For Women" .... 1935 .... $65
Highcliffe Castle G. C:
"Highcliffe Castle Golf Club"........................ 1961 .... $25
Highland C. C:
"Highland Country Club 50th Anniversary
    1901-1951" .... 1951 .... $35
Walter J. Highman:
"A Heavenly Meeting, A Sequel".................. 1925 .... $20
Patricia Highsmith:
"Mermaids On The Golf Course" .... 1985 .... $25
B. J. W. Hill & Peter Hill:
"A History of Royal St George's Golf Course". 1987 .... $45
Dave Hill & Nick Seitz:
"Teed Off"... 1977 .... $25
J. C. H. Hill:
"The Lyre On The Links And Other Verses" ... 1935 .... $250
Arthur Hills:
"Arthur Hills and Associates" .... 1980 .... $150
Hillbarn Golf Club
"Hillbarn Golf Club" .... 1959 .... $25
Hillcrest C. C:
"Hillcrest Country Club: 60 Years of
    Memories, 1920-1980"...................... 1980 .... $35
Hillerich & Bradsby:
"The First Step To Par Golf"........................ 1925 .... $475
"Grand Slam Golf Classics"......................... 1931 .... $300
"Points About Golf Clubs You Should Know" .. 1925 .... $225
Gerald Hillinthorn:
"Your First Game of Golf" .... 1891 ....$2295
A. J. Hills:
"Golf At Jasper Park" .... 1948 .... $200
Hilton Park G. C:
"Hilton Park Golf Club Jubilee Year
    1927-1977" .... 1977 .... $25
Harold H. Hilton:
"Modern Golf".. 1913 .... $225
    1916 edition .... 1916 .... $150
    1922 edition .... 1922 .... $95
    1926 edition .... 1926 .... $75
    1932 edition .... 1932 .... $150
"My Golfing Reminiscences"........................ 1907 .... $575

Reprint... 1998 .... $35
"The Rules of Golf"...................................... 1915 .... $400
Harold Hilton & Garden G. Smith:
"The Royal And Ancient Game of Golf"
    (100 Deluxe Copies) .... 1912 .... $15,000
    (900 leather Copies) .... 1912 ......$2750
    Reprint (500 Copies) .... 2001 .... $195
Maurice Hime:
"The Unlucky Golfer: His Handbook" .... 1904 .... $125
Darce Hindle:
"Links of Love, A Story of The Riviera" .... 1904 .... $275
Geneive Hingst & Mary E. McKee:
"The Game of Golf; Programmed Instructions
    of Playing Procedures"....................... 1968 .... $15
Hinsdale G. C:
"Hinsdale Golf Club, Clarendon Hills,Illinois" . 1916 .... $175
"Hinsdale Golf Club Centennial 1898-1998" .. 1998 .... $45
Ruth Hirst & Jean Lockwood:
"Meltham Golf Club" .... 1982 .... $15
Historian:
"Ashford Manor Golf Club".......................... 1966 .... $45
Thomas K. Hitch & Mary I. Kuranote:
"Ailae Country Club, The First Half Century".. 1981 .... $15
Jimmy Hitchcock:
"Master Golfer".. 1967 .... $20
Michael Hobbs:
"50 Masters of Golf" .... 1983 .... $30
"British Open Champions" .... 1991 .... $15
"Golf For The Connoisseur: A Golfing
    Anthology"...................................... 1979 .... $45
"Golf In Art"... 1996 .... $20
"Golf To Remember"................................. 1978 .... $45
"Golfer's Companion" .... 1997 .... $20
"The Golfer's Companion" .... 1988 .... $35
"Golf: A Visual History"............................. 1992 .... $30
"Great Opens: Historic British And
    American Championships 1913-1975".. 1976 .... $35
"In Celebration of Golf"............................. 1982 .... $35
"On The Green" .... 1991 .... $10
"The Ryder Cup: The Illustrated History"...... 1989 .... $35
    Presentation Copy (95 copies) .... 1989 .... $395
"The World's Great Golf Courses" .... 1988 .... $25
"Trouble Shooting"................................... 1991 .... $15

Michael Hobbs & Peter Alliss:
"Golf To Remember".................................. 1978 .... $20
Hobsen:
"Cohasset Golf Club 1894-1994" .... 1994 .... $45
William G. Hobson:
"It Ain't Necessarily So" .... 1959 .... $60
Howard H. Hoddinott:
"Out of the Rough: Kingsknowe Golf Club
    Limited 1908-1983" .... 1983 .... $95
R. D. Hodgson:
"An Eye Off The Ball At Littlestone.."
    (350 Copies) .... 1939 .... $250
Bert Hodson:
"Your Best Way To Play The Chigwell Golf
    Course"... 1952 .... $25
Arthur Hoffman:
"The Golfer's Catalog" .... 1984 .... $10
Bob Hoffman:
"The Functional Isometrics Contraction For
    Golf"... 1963 .... $10
Davy Hoffman:
"America's Greatest Golf Courses" .... 1987 .... $40
Ben Hogan:
"Five Lessons: The Modern Fundamentals
    of Golf" .... 1957 .... $135
"Here's Your Free Golf Lesson".................... 1949 .... $225
Smashing Drive".. 1943 .... $225
"Power Golf"... 1948 .... $95
"Power Golf" 1st English edition .... 1949 .... $75
Ben Hogan & Others:
"The Complete Guide To Golf".................... 1955 .... $50
Bill Hogan:
"Golf Gadgets".. 1989 .... $10
"Learning Golf".. 1993 .... $15
Chuck Hogan:
Five Days To Golfing Excellence" .... 1986 .... $10
Michael Hogan:
"Betchworth Park Golf Club, A History
    of the Club 1911-1991" .... 1991 .... $45
Hokitika G. C:
"Hokitiki Golf Club Inc, 1906-1981" .... 1981 .... $45
Hollingworth, Birmingham, & Pender:
"Golf: Par Fore" .... 1982 .... $10

Cundell – Rules of Thistle
Golf Club (1st Edition)

Cunningham – Upper Largo,
Lower Largo

Dalrymple – Golfer's Guide

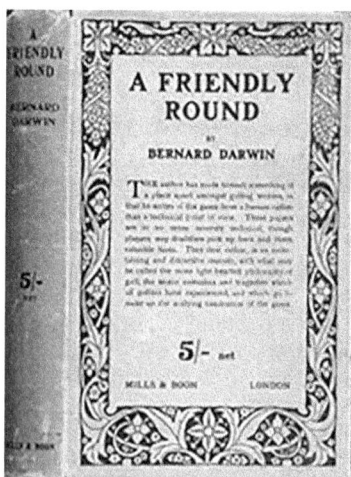

Darwin – A Friendly Round
(Dust Jacket)

Thousands of color book illustrations visible at
www.rogeregilchrist.com

Betsy Holloway:
"The Country Club of Orlando 1911-2000".... 2000 .... $45
William R. Holmes:
"Bushfoot Golf Club Centenary 1890-1990" .. 1990 .... $25
Homewood C. C:
"Your Book for Nineteen Hundred
    and Eleven .... 1911 .... $65
Richard Holt, Peter Lewis & Wray Vamplew:
"The Professional Golfers Association
    1901-2001 Limited Edition of 2000 ..... 2002 .... $250
Billy Hon:
"Prominent Golfers In Caricature"................. 1930 .... $395
Honourable Company of Edinburgh Golfers:
"Rules and Regulations of the Honourable
    Company of Edinburgh Golfers" .... 1888 ....$3995
"Rules and Regulations of the Honourable
    Company of Edinburgh Golfers" .... 1889 ....$3750
"Rules and Regulations of the Honourable
    Company of Edinburgh Golfers" .... 1935 .... $250
Richard W. Hooper:
"The Game of Golf In East Africa"................. 1953 ....$1250
Brad Hoot:
"Golf Is An Easy Game" .... 1983 .... $10
Bob Hope:
"Confessions of A Hooker"......................... 1985 .... $15
Hopkins:
"Woodway: Country Club 1916-1991".......... 1991 .... $25
Anthony Hopkins:
"Songs For Swinging Golfers" .... 1981 .... $10
Frank Hopkins:
"Golf Holes They Talk About" (880 Copies) ... 1927 .... $750
John Hopkins:
"Beacon Golfing Handbook"........................ 1983 .... $20
"Golf: - The Four Majors" .... 1988 .... $20
"Nick Faldo In Perspective"........................ 1985 .... $25
Cecil Hopkinson:
"A Catelogue of 101 Interesting Books
    Arranged by Subjects ..." .... 1935 ....$1250
"Collecting Golf Books 1743-1938" .... 1938 .... $500
    Reprint (250 Copies) .... 1980 .... $350
John Hornabrook:
"Golden Years of New Zealand Golf" .... 1967 .... $45
D. Hornby:
"The History of the Seaton Carew Golf

Club 1874-1974" .... 1974 .... $95
W. B. J. Horne:
"The History of The Royal Wimbleton
Golf Club 1865-1949"........................ 1949 .... $225
Paul Hornung:
"The Story of Muirfield Village Golf Club and
The Memorial Tournament"
(525 Copies).................................... 1985 .... $120
"Scioto Country Club - 75 Years of History
1916 - 1991". .... 1993 .... $125
G. T. Horrocks:
"From Seat Naze to Ewood Lane Head" .... 2003 .... $35
Chester Horton:
"Better Golf" .... 1930 .... $55
"Golf: The Long Game".............................. 1969 .... $10
"Golf: The Short Game" .... 1970 .... $10
"Chester Hortons Golf Lesson" .... 1925 .... $65
Mabel S. Hoskins:
"Golf for Women, By A Woman Golfer"......... 1916 .... $395
Dendra Hoskison:
Sutton Coldfield Ladies Golf Club,
1892-1992 Limited Edition of 270 .... 1992 .... $75
Howard C. Hosmer:
"From Little Acorns, The Story of Oak Hill
1901-1976" .... 1977 .... $80
"From Little Acorns, The Story of Oak Hill
1901-1986 .... 1986 .... $65
"Through Half A Century" (500 copies)......... 1945 .... $125
"The Year of The Diamond, Being An Account
of the First Seventy-Five Years of the
Country Club of Rochester"
(1000 Copies) .... 1971 .... $125
Colonel S. Hotchkin:
"The Principles of Golf Architecture"............. 1935 ......$5000
Horace L. Hotchkiss:
"Origin and Organization of The Senior's
Tournament".................................... 1922 .... $150
John F. Hotchkiss:
"500 Years of Golf Balls" .... 1997 .... $20
Neal Hotelling:
"Pebble Beach Golf Links" .... 1999 .... $75
George Houghton:
"Addict In Bunkerland" .... 1962 .... $30
"An Addicts Guide To British Golf" .... 1959 .... $75

"Believe It Or Not-That's Golf" .... 1974 .... $25
"Bridgport And West Dorset Golf Club"
    (1000 copies).................................... 1991 .... $45
"Confessions of A Golf Addict: An Anthology
    of Carefree Notes And Drawing".......... 1959 .... $45
"Confessions of A Golf Addict"...................... 1952 .... $45
"Full Confessions of A Golf Addict"............... 1966 .... $35
"Golf Addict Among The Irish" .... 1965 .... $30
"Golf Addict Among The Scots" .... 1967 .... $30
"Golf Addict Goes East"............................ 1967 .... $35
"Golf Addict In Gaucho Land"...................... 1970 .... $25
"Golf Addict Invades Wales" .... 1969 .... $30
"Golf Addict Strikes Again" .... 1963 .... $25
"Golf Addict Visits The USA" .... 1956 .... $30
"Golf Addicts Galore" .... 1968 .... $25
"Golf Addicts Omnibus: The Best of
    George Houghton" .... 1966 .... $45
"Golf Addicts On Parade"............................ 1959 .... $30
"Golf Addicts Through The Ages"................. 1956 .... $30
"Golf Addicts To The Fore"........................... 1985 .... $20
"Golf And The Stranglehold" .... 1986 .... $25
"Golf On My Pillow" .... 1958 .... $45
"Golf Visits".. 1955 .... $25
"Golf With A Whippy Shaft" .... 1971 .... $55
"Golfer's ABC" .... 1953 .... $45
"Golfers In Orbit"....................................... 1968 .... $20
"Golfers Treasury: A Personal Anthology" ..... 1964 .... $55
"How To Be A Golf Addict".......................... 1971 .... $25
"I Am A Golf Widow" .... 1961 .... $20
"Just A Friendly A Book of Golf Addict
    Cartoons" .... 1973 .... $20
"More Confessions of A Golf Addict"............. 1954 .... $30
"Portrait of A Golf Addict"........................... 1959 .... $30
"Secret Diary of A Golf Addict's Caddie" .... 1964 .... $35
"The Truth About Golf Addicts" .... 1957 .... $25
Houghton & Dutton:
    "The Rules of Golf".................................. 1900 .... $600
Rod Houston:
    "Golspie Golf Club 1889-1989".................... 1989 .... $20
Archie Hovanesian:
    "Golf Is Mental" .... 1960 .... $10
Morris T. Hoversten:
    "Onwentsia Club 1895-1995 A Centennial" ... 1995 .... $35

Thousands of color book illustrations visible at
www.rogeregilchrist.com

How to Be a Good Caddie:
 "How To Be A Good Caddie" .... 1952 .... $20
How to Cut Strokes:
 "How To Cut Strokes From Your Score" .... 1968 .... $10
How to Play the Old Course:
 "How To Play The Old Course, St. Andrews". 1932 .... $350
Eric Leigh Howard:
 "How I Beat Palmer, Player and Nicklaus"..... 1972 .... $25
Robert E. Howard:
 "Lessons From Great Golfers" .... 1924 .... $175
Audrey Howel:
 "Harry Vardon: The Revealing Story of
   A Champion Golfer" .... 1991 .... $35
Jeff Howson:
 "Golf: How To Look Good When You're Not".. 1988 .... $10
Edmund Hoyle:
 "Hoyle's Games Improved".......................... 1790 .... $450
   1796 edition (5th Edition) .... 1796 .... $400
   1800 Edition (6th Edition)................... 1800 .... $250
   1807 edition .... 1807 .... $200
   1814 American Edition .... 1814 .... $300
   1847 Edition .... 1847 .... $200
   1859 Edition .... 1859 .... $175
   1873 Edition .... 1873 .... $125
Huapai G. C:
 "Huapai Golf Club Golden Jubilee
   1939-1988" .... 1988 .... $45
Hubbard Trail C. C:
 "Hubbard Trail Country Club 50 Years
   1925-1975" .... 1975 .... $35
Charles E Hubbard:
 "Grasses" .... 1954 .... $50
D. C. N. Hudson:
 "Your Book of Golf" .... 1967 .... $35
John Huggan:
 "Cure Your Slice Forever"........................... 1994 .... $10
Brian Huggett:
 "Better Golf" .... 1964 .... $15
Percy Huggins:
 "The Golfer's Book of Days, Facts, Feats,
   and Folklore" .... 1993 .... $15
 "The Golfer's Miscellany"............................ 1971 .... $45
 "This Is Scottish Golf"................................ 1990 .... $10
 "Troon Golf Club"..................................... 1972 .... $35

C. E. Hughes & Fred Buchanan:
"Sport In A Nutshell" .... 1921 .... $45
E. H. Hughes:
"The History of the Spokane Country Club,
75th Anniversary" .... 1973 .... $45
Henry Hughes:
"Golf For The Late Beginner" .... 1911 .... $195
"Golf Practice For Players of Limited Leisure" 1913 .... $125
Margaret Hughes:
"A Round With Darwin" .... 1984 .... $40
W. E. Hughes:
"Chronicles of The Blackheath Golfers
(1st Ed)" .... 1897 ......$4,500
"Chronicles of The Blackheath Golfers" .... 1897 ......$1,500
Robert H. H. Hugman:
"Putting Know-How" .... 1963 .... $10
Gerald Hulme:
"Cheadle Golf Club 1885-1985" .... 1985 .... $60
Ronald W. Hulse:
"Dinsdale Spa Golf Club" .... 1960 .... $25
"Hexham Golf Club" .... 1960 .... $25
John Hulteng:
"Meeting Place by the Lake" .... 1992 .... $35
Pierre Humble:
"Caddy-Caddy" .... 1929 .... $95
Humorist On Golf:
"The Humorist On Golf" .... 1930 .... $225
Eric Humphreys:
"The Dunlop Golfer's Companion" .... 1977 .... $20
Hunstanton Links:
"Hunstanton Links: Portrayed by
F.H.Partridge From 1907-1921
(232 Copies) .... 2009 .... $75
Celebration edition (68 Copies) .... 2009 .... $150
Orrin T. Hunt:
"The Joy of Golf" .... 1977 .... $10
David S. Hunter:
"Golf Simplified" .... 1921 .... $150
Mac Hunter:
"Golf For Beginners" .... 1973 .... $15
N. C. Hunter:
"The Losing Hazard" .... 1951 .... $65
Robert Hunter:
"The Links" .... 1926 .....$1,450

Second Edition .... 1935 .... $350
USGA Reprint (1500 Copies) .... 1994 .... $125
Reprint.. 1998 .... $35
Robert E. Hunter:
"Royal & Ancient Game of Golf, A Golf
Diary of 72 Years"............................ 1966 $65
Wiles R. Hunter:
"The Links" .... 1999 .... $40
Willie Hunter:
"The Easy Way To Winning Golf" .... 1935 .... $175
Huntingdon Valley C. C:
"The Huntingdon Valley Country Club:
Charter By-Laws Officers..." .... 1910 .... $125
Huntly:
"Huntly, The Official Guide" .... 1938 .... $45
Dr Michael J. Hurdzan:
"Evolution of The Modern Green"................. 1985 .... $55
"Golf Course Architecture, Design
Construction & Restoration" .... 1996 .... $65
Presentation Copy............................ 1996 .... $900
Harry Hurt III:
"Chasing The Dream" .... 1997 .... $15
Mervyn J. Huston:
"Golf And Murphy's Law"............................ 1981 .... $30
"Great Golf Humor, A Collection of Stories
& Articles" .... 1977 .... $25
Horace G. Hutchinson:
"After Dinner Golf" .... 1896 ......$3,500
Reprint (400 Copies) .... 1986 .... $195
"Aspects of Golf"...................................... 1900 ......$7,500
"The Book of Golf and Golfers".................... 1899 .... $600
First American Edition .... 1900 .... $275
"British Golf Links, A Short Account of The
Leading Golf Links of The United
Kingdom" (250 Copies. Large Paper
Edition) .... 1897 ......$2,995
1st Trade Edition .... 1897 .... $500
Reprint .... 2005 .... $75
"Bert Edward, The Golf Caddie".................. 1903 ......$1000
"Famous Golf Links" .... 1891 ......$1,350
"Fifty Years of Golf".. 1919 .... $625
USGA Reprint (1500 Copies) .... 1985 .... $145
"Golf".. 1890 ......$2000

Thousands of color book illustrations visible at
www.rogeregilchrist.com

Roger E. Gilchrist's Guide to Collectible Golf Book Prices

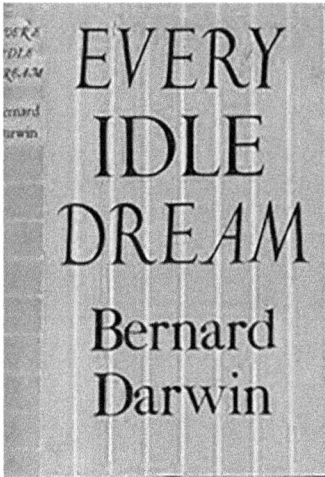

Darwin – Every Idle Dream

Darwin – Golf (1st Edition)

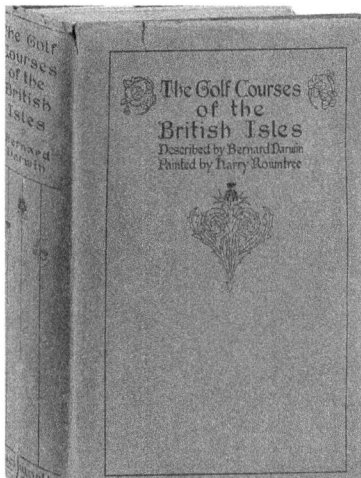

Darwin – Golf Courses of the British
Isles (1st Edition Dust Jacket)

Thousands of color book illustrations visible at
www.rogeregilchrist.com

Limited Large Paper Edition
(250 Copies).................................... 1890 ......$3,250
Badminton Library print..................... 1890 .... $450
June 1890 Edition .... 1890 .... $400
February 1892 Edition .... 1892 .... $250
December 1893 Edition .... 1893 .... $195
Reprint... 1987 .... $75
Reprint... 1998 .... $50
"Golf, A Complete History of The Game"....... 1900 .... $500
"Golf Greens and Greenskeeping"................ 1906 ......$1,500
"Golfing".. 1901 .... $550
"Golfing - The Oval Series of Games"........... 1893 .... $450
"A Golfing Pilgrim On Many Links" .... 1897 .... $850
"Hints On The Game of Golf" .... 1886 ......$3,500
Reprint... 1987 .... $45
"The Lost Golfer" .... 1930 ......$4,750
"The New Book of Golf"............................. 1912 .... $500
Jock Hutchinson:
"Better Golf" .... 1928 .... $175
"Underfoot Golf Diagrams: Jock Hutchinson
Series"... 1923 .... $450
R. E. Hutchison:
"Responsibilities of A Golfer"....................... 1952 .... $75
Laurence Hutton:
"Golf, And Some Of Its Ancient Traditions" ... 1895 .... $150
E. J. Hyde:
"The Story of The Pennant Hills Golf Club
1922-1959" .... 1959 .... $40
Theo B. Hyslop:
"Mental Handicaps In Golf"......................... 1927 .... $135
Grace Iarrobino & Elayne Slaughter:
"The Golfer's Cookbook" .... 1968 .... $15
Clete Idoux:
"Play Better Golf"..................................... 1966 .... $15
Ignotus:
"Golf in a Nutshell"................................... 1919 .... $150
James Igoe Jr.:
"Hooks And Slices".................................... 1950 .... $30
Ilfracombe G. C:
"Ilfracombe Golf Club" .... 1963 .... $30
"Ilfracombe Golf Club 1892-1992 .... 1992 .... $25
Betty P. Imhoff:
"The Country Club of York 1899-1975
History" (Ltd Edition of 1200) .... 1975 .... $55

India House:
"India House" .... 1930 .... $75
Indian Valley C. C:
"Indian Valley Country Club 1952-1977" ...... 1977 .... $25
Indian Wells C. C:
"Indian Wells Country Club, 1956-1990" ...... 1990 .... $25
John Ingham:
"Best Golfing Jokes" .... 1969 .... $10
Martin Inigo:
"Stone Dead" .... 1991 .... $20
David Innes:
"The Story of Golf In New South Wales
    1851-1987" .... 1987 .... $35
J. K. G. Innes:
"Guide to Elie and Earlsferry Golf Course"..... 1899 ....$2250
J, & G. Innes:
"How to Play the Old Course St. Andrews
    And all about it" .... 1933 .... $150
Michael Innes:
"An Awkward Lie" .... 1971 .... $35
Innis Arden G. C:
"The History of Innis Arden, 1899-1973" ...... 1974 .... $75
"The History of Innis Arden, 1905-1974" ...... 1975 .... $60
"The History of Innis Arden 1899-1992" .... 1992 .... $25
Instant Golf:
"Instant Golf" .... 1966 .... $25
"How To Do It In Slow Motion".................... 1973 .... $20
Interesting Facts:
"Interesting Facts For Every Golfer"............. 1932 .... $75
The International:
"The International".................................... 1968 .... $55
Inverness G. C:
"Inverness Club"....................................... 1979 .... $25
"Inverness Golf Club 1883-1983" .... 1983 .... $35
"Inverness Club.... 1903-2003" (2000 Copies)2003 .... $125
IPC Business Press:
"Guide To Golf Courses In The UK" .... 1973 .... $20
Ireland:
"Ireland: A Golfer's Paradise" .... 1968 .... $30
Irish Golf Courses:
"Irish Golf Courses 1983/84" .... 1984 .... $20
Irish Golfing Union:
"Yearbook 1957"...................................... 1957 .... $20

Philip Irlam:
"A Lively Octogenarian Hillside Golf Club
1911-1991" .... 1993 .... $35
Robert Ironside & Harry Douglas:
"A History of Royal Musselburgh Golf Club
1774-1999" .... 1999 .... $95
Ironwood C. C:
"Ironwood Country Club; 25th Anniversary" .. 1999 .... $25
Andrew Irving:
"Accumulated Golfing Hints" .... 1988 .... $10
Hale Irwin:
"Play Better Golf"................................... 1974 .... $20
"Smart Golf" .... 1999 .... $15
J. F. Irwin:
"Golf Sketches" .... 1892 ....$9500
N. L. Irwin:
"St. Georges Golf And Country Club 50 Years
1929-1979" .... 1979 .... $20
Ralph Irwin-Brown:
"Hindhead's Turn Will Come" .... 1991 .... $30
Kenneth Isenogle:
"Anatomy of Right Handed Golf" .... 1980 .... $10
Isle of Purbeck:
"Isle of Purbeck Golf Club" .... 1984 .... $20
Isles Of Scilly G. C:
"Isles Of Scilly Golf Club" .... 1950 .... $35
Islesmere G & C. C:
"Islesmere Golf & Country Club Inc" .... 1969 .... $45
Cho Ito:
"Golfers Treasures" .... 1925 .....$1,275
Ives Hill C. C:
"Ives Hill Centennial 1897-1997 .... 1997 .... $45
J.A.C.K.:
"Golf In The Year 2000" .... 1892 .....$2,500
Reprint.. 1984 .... $65
Tony Jacklin:
"100 Jacklin Golf Strips From The Daily
Express"... 1970 .... $20
"Golf Step By Step" .... 1969 .... $15
"Golf With Tony Jacklin"............................. 1969 .... $20
"Jacklin: The Champion's Own Story" .... 1970 .... $35
"Tony Jacklin, The First Forty Years" .... 1985 .... $45
"Tony Jacklin's Guide To Professional Golf" ... 1970 .... $10
"The Ryder Cup '85"................................. 1985 .... $30

"Your Game And Mine" .... 1990 .... $10
Tony Jacklin & Peter Dobereiner:
"Jacklin's Golf Secrets" .... 1983 .... $15
"The First 40 Years" .... 1985 .... $15
Alan F. Jackson:
"The British Professional Golfers 1887-1930
  A Register" (500 Copies) .... 1994 .... $75
  Limited signed edition of 100.............. 1994 .... $150
Dr. Arthur Jackson:
"Eye On The Ball, Mind On The Game" .... 1999 .... $15
Barney Jackson:
"History of The Canadian Open At Glenn
  Abbey".. 1984 .... $35
David Jackson:
"Golf Songs And Recitations" .... 1886 ......$9,000
  Second Edition .... 1895 ....$3500
  Reprint... 1988 .... $75
Rev. John Jackson & J. Gordon Dow:
"Official Guide To Crail And The Neigborhood
  Including The Isle of May"................... 1922 .... $95
Ken Jackson:
"Burton-On-Trent Golf Club"....................... 1993 .... $45
Robert B. Jackson:
"Supermex: The Lee Trevino Story"............. 1973 .... $20
John Jacobs:
"Another Consultation With Doctor Golf"....... 1965 .... $20
"Golf".. 1963 .... $25
"Golf Doctor"... 1979 .... $15
"John Jacobs Analyses Golf's Superstars" ..... 1974 .... $35
"Play Better Golf"...................................... 1972 .... $15
"Play Better Golf With John Jacobs" .... 1969 .... $15
"Practical Golf" .... 1972 .... $25
"Quick Cures For Weekend Golfers" .... 1979 .... $20
John Jacobs & Peter Dobereiner:
"Golf In A Nutshell" .... 1995 .... $25
Linda Jacobs:
"Laura Baugh: Golf's Golden Girl"................ 1975 .... $10
"Lee Elder, The Daring Dream" .... 1976 .... $15
"Ellen The Expert"..................................... 1974 .... $10
"50 Greatest Golf Lessons of The Century" ... 1999 .... $20
Timothy Jacobs:
"Great Golf Courses of The World".............. 1990 .... $30
"The Golf Courses of Jack Nicklaus" .... 1989 .... $30

Timothy Jacobs & John Kirk:
"The Golf Courses of Robert Trent Jones Jr".. 1988 .... $20
Peter Jacobsen:
"Buried Lies" .... 1993 .... $20
Henri Jakubowicz:
"Rusty Staples or Aspects of Collecting
    Golf Instructional Booklets (72 Copies) 2004 .... $500
James River C. C:
"James River Country Club Twenty-Fifth
    Anniversary" .... 1957 .... $45
"James River Country Club Commemorating
    The Fiftieth Anniversary" .... 1982 .... $25
Francis James:
"Bedfordshire Golf Club" .... 1957 .... $25
"Brancepeth Castle Golf Club".................... 1949 .... $50
"The Hesketh Golf Club"............................. 1951 .... $30
"Llandudo Golf Club" .... 1960 .... $25
"The Okehampton Golf Club" .... 1951 .... $35
"Sidmouth Golf Club"................................. 1952 .... $25
"Warren Golf Club".................................... 1960 .... $20
Joseph James:
"How To Give Up Golf"............................... 1970 .... $15
"Kill It Before It Moves" .... 1961 .... $10
"Quiet On The Tee" .... 1963 .... $15
"So You're Taking Up Golf?" .... 1969 .... $10
"What It Is, Is Golf" .... 1965 .... $15
Mark James:
"Into The Bear Pit".................................... 2000 .... $20
Michael T. James:
"The Centenary History of the
    Monmouthshire Golf Club".................. 1992 .... $45
Sid James:
"From Tee To Cup".................................... 1955 .... $15
Ken Janke:
"Golf Is A Funny Game" .... 1992 .... $20
"Ken Janke's Golf Library" .... 1998 .... $20
    Limited signed edition (100 Copies).... 1998 .... $195
Allen E. Jansson:
"How To Master The Art of One Putting" .... 1983 .... $15
Don January & Al Carrell:
"Golf Is A Funny Game" .... 1967 .... $20
Japanese Government Railways:
"Golf in Japan" .... 1932 .... $250
"Golf In Japan".. 1934 .... $200

Thousands of color book illustrations visible at
www.rogeregilchrist.com

"Golf In Japan" .... 1956 .... $175
Quentin Jardine:
"Skinner's Round" .... 1995 .... $20
T. G. Jarrett:
"A History of The New Club, St. Andrews" ..... 1982 .... $30
"St Andrews Golf Links. The First 600 Years" 1995 .... $35
Gordon Jarvie:
"Great Golf Stories" .... 1993 .... $20
Jasper Park:
"Golf at Jasper Park in the Canadian Rockies" 1916 .... $595
Susan Jeffreys:
"The Punch Book of Golf" .... 1986 .... $20
Robert P. Jelett:
"History of the Hermitage Country Club" ...... 1961 .... $75
Dan Jenkins:
"Dead Solid Perfect" .... 1974 .... $45
"The Dogged Victims of Inexorable Fate" ...... 1970 .... $55
"Life Its Ownself" .... 1983 .... $20
"Sports Illustrated's: The Best 18 Golf
    Holes In America" .... 1966 .... $40
"Fast Copy" .... 1988 .... $20
"You Call It Sports...." .... 1989 .... $20
"You Gotta Play Hurt" .... 1991 .... $20
"Fairways And Greens" .... 1994 .... $30
L. C. Jenkins:
"Golf In Hardy Country" .... 1993 .... $35
"Parkstone: A History of Its Golf Club" .... 1987 .... $40
Albert Jenny:
"The Royal Game: Stories Around A Little
    White Ball" .... 1962 .... $10
Owen Fox Jerome:
"The Golf Club Murder" .... 1929 .... $175
J. C. Jessop:
"Teach Yourself Golf" .... 1950 .... $40
    Revised .... 1964 .... $20
Gilbert Jessup & J. B. Salmond:
"The Book of School Sports" .... 1939 .... $35
C. Kevin Jett:
"History of the Muskogee Country Club"
    (100 Copies) .... 1991 .... $125
A. J. D. Johnson:
"The History of Royal Birkdale Golf Club
    1889-1989" .... 1988 .... $85

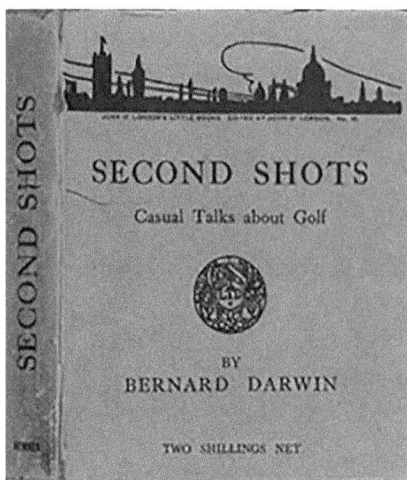

Darwin – Second Shots
(1st Edition Dust Jacket)

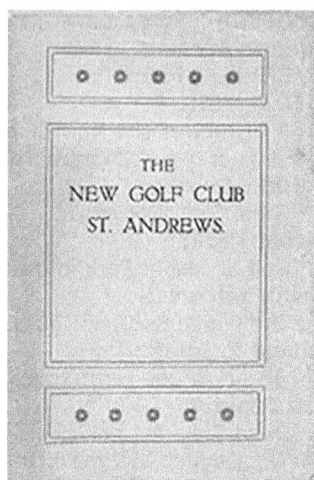

Darwin – The New Golf
Club St Andrews

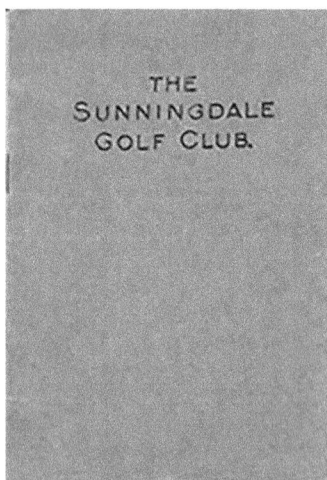

Darwin – The Sunningdale
Golf Club

Del Monte – Golf at Del Monte
California

Thousands of color book illustrations visible at
www.rogeregilchrist.com

Carol C. Johnson & Ann C. Johnstone:
"Golf: A Positive Approach" .... 1975 .... $10
Johnson, Oliver & Shields:
"Golf"... 1979 .... $10
Hank Johnson:
"End Your Fear of Sand Forever" .... 1981 .... $10
"How To Win The Three Games of Golf"........ 1993 .... $35
J. W. Johnson:
"A Wonderful Golf Score" .... 1920 .... $125
Joseph Johnson:
"From Eyrie to Eagles: The History of
    Yarra Yarra Golf Club 1898-1998" .... 1998 .... $40
"The Royal Melbourne Golf Club: A
    Centenary History" .... 1991 .... $75
Sal Johnson:
"The Otsego Golf Club" .... 1995 .... $20
Salvatore Johnson:
"The Official U.S Open Almanac" .... 1995 .... $15
Owen Johnson:
"Even Threes" .... 1930 .... $150
William O. Johnson & Nancy P. Williams:
"Whatta Gal: The Babe Didrikson Story"....... 1977 .... $35
Willis Johnson Jr.:
"Peachtree Golf Club" .... 1978 .... $95
    Leather Bound Edition .... 1978 .... $245
Alastair J. Johnston:
"The Clapcott Papers"............................... 1985 .... $150
    Subscribers edition of 400................. 1985 .... $400
    20 Presentation copies .... 1985 .... $850
"Vardon To Woods" (900 Copies) .... 1999 .... $150
Alastair J. Johnston & James F. Johnston
"The Chronicles of Golf" (900 Signed copies) 1993 ....$1250
Patrica C. Johnston:
"Reflections: The White Bear Yacht Club.
    1889-1989" .... 1989 .... $75
Alastair J. Johnston & Joseph Murdock:
"C. B. Clapcott and His Golf Library"
    (300 Copies)................................... 1989 .... $450
    Special Edition .... 1989 .... $400
Don Johnston:
"Golf Etiquette or Lack Thereof" .... 1985 .... $10
A. C. Jones:
"The Royal Country Down Golf Club"............ 1962 .... $75
"The Royal Country Down Golf Club"............ 1969 .... $50

Thousands of color book illustrations visible at
www.rogeregilchrist.com

Elwood H. Jones:
"Peterborough Golf & Country Club
1897-1997" .... 1997 .... $75
Ernest Jones:
"Swing The Clubhead" .... 1952 .... $75
      Reprint... 1977 .... $20
"Swing's The Thing In Golf" .... 1940 .... $75
Ernest Jones & Innes Brown:
"Swinging Into Golf"................................ 1937 .... $95
Lyndon Jones:
The Cataraqui Golf and Country Club: The
First Seventy Years, 1917-1987" .... 1987 .... $75
Molly S. Jones:
"Golden Jubilee: The Story of the
Southerdown Ladies Golf Club
1905-1955" .... 1957 .... $95
W. Pete Jones:
"A Directory of Golf Courses By Designer
Donald J Ross" .... 1992 .... $20
Rees L. Jones & Guy L. Rando:
"Golf Course Development" .... 1974 .... $20
Rees L. Jones & John Paul Newport:
"Bethpage Black Course Field Notes" .... 2002 .... $350
Robert Jones:
"British Golf Odyssey"................................ 1977 .... $25
"Gulls On The Golf Course"......................... 1975 .... $20
"Sherlock Holmes Saved Golf" .... 1986 .... $45
"Sherlock Holmes The Golfer" .... 1981 .... $45
Robert E. Jones:
"A History of The Missoula Country Club"...... 1979 .... $25
Robert Trent Jones:
"Description of The Golden Horseshoe
Golf Course At Williamsburg Inn" .... 1965 .... $150
"Golf Course Architecture" (In Enveople) ...... 1938 ....$2595
      Reprint of 50 copies .... 2015 .... $100
"Great Golf Stories".................................. 1982 .... $20
"Golf's Magnificent Challenge"..................... 1988 .... $50
Robert Trent Jones Jr:
"The Golf Courses of Robert Trent Jones Jr".. 1988 .... $45
"Golf By Design" .... 1993 .... $40
"Great Golf Stories"................................... 1982 .... $35
Robert Tyre Jones Jr.:
Flicker No 11b Brassie and Iron.................. 1930 .... $200
      Harrods Edition .... 1926 .... $300

"Flicker No 11a Drive and Mashie .... 1930 .... $225
    Harrods Edition .... 1926 .... $300
"Flicker No 11c Out the Rough and Putt" ...... 1930 .... $150
    Harrods Edition .... 1926 .... $225
"Golf Is My Game" .... 1960 .... $125
    1st British Edition .... 1961 .... $55
"Golf Shots By Bobby Jones-Brassie
    And Iron Shots"................................. 1930 .... $475
"Golf Shots By Bobby Jones-Driver
    And Mashie Shots"............................. 1930 .... $475
"Golf Shots By Bobby Jones- Out of The
    Rough And Putt"............................... 1930 .... $475
"How A College or School Should Publicize
    the Showing of a Motion Picture
    on Golf"... 1936 ....$1250
"How To Organize Golfers In A Municipality" . 1936 .... $450
"How To Play Golf".................................... 1929 .... $550
    Revised edition................................. 1930 .... $250
"How I Play Golf" .... 1935 .... $275
    Japanese Edition............................... 1938 .... $295
"How to Run A Golf Tournament" .... 1936 .... $575
"Bobby Jones on The Basic Golf Swing" .... 1969 .... $95
    Classics of Golf reprint....................... 1994 .... $25
"Bobby Jones On Golf"............................... 1930 .... $475
    Japanese Edition............................... 1931 ....$1250
    Reprinted edition .... 1966 .... $95
    UK Edition .... 1968 .... $75
    Reprint... 1984 .... $20
"My Twelve Most Difficult Shots" .... 1929 .... $995
"Publicity Manual and Handbook for
    University And College Teams............. 1930 ....$1250
"Short Cuts to Par Golf" .... 1931 .... $495
"Rights and Wrongs of Golf" .... 1935 .... $150
    Revised Edition (8 more Pages) .... 1935 .... $175
    A G Splading & Brothers Edition......... 1939 .... $175
"A Short Love Story: The People of St.
    Andrews And Robert T. (Bobby)
    Jones Jr." .... 1973 .... $95
"Some Tips From Bobby Jones"................... 1935 ....$1400
"The Masters Tournament" .... 1960 .... $450
Robert T. "Bobby" Jones & Ben Crenshaw:
"Classic Instruction" .... 1998 .... $30
Robert Tyre Jones Jr. & O.B. Keeler:
"Down The Fairway" .... 1927 ....$3000

Thousands of color book illustrations visible at
www.rogeregilchrist.com

1st UK Edition (Dust Jacket)............... 1927 .... $725
Reprint.. 1958 .... $35
Classics Of Golf reprint .... 1985 .... $30

Robert Tyre Jones Jr. & Harold Lowe:
"Group Instruction In Golf"......................... 1939 .... $400

Robert Tyre Jones Jr. & Clifford Roberts:
"The Masters Tournament"......................... 1952 ....$2150

Tony Jones:
"A Brief History of Abergele And Pensarn
    Golf Club 75th Anniversary Year
    1910-1985" .... 1985 .... $30

G. Gumby Jordan & Don Wade:
"Caddies"... 1987 .... $30

Harry H. Jordan:
"Ye Golf Booke" .... 1928 .... $275

Alex Josey:
"Golf In Singapore" .... 1969 .... $20

David Joy:
"The Scrapbook of Old Tom Morris" .... 2001 .... $50

Michael Joyce:
"Edinburgh: The Golden Age 1769-1832" ..... 1951 .... $65

Jubilaums-Chronik G. & C. C:
"Jubilaums-Chronik Golf and Country Club" .. 1992 .... $35

H. Stanley Judd:
"How To Play Golf The Easy Way"............... 1980 .... $10

Judge, Ramsell & Gilmour:
"Shrewsbury Golf Club, 100 Years
    1891-1991" .... 1991 .... $25

Marcia E. Julius:
"For The Good of Golf And St Andrews"........ 1998 .... $45
    Limited Edition of 500

John Junkermeier:
"The Glorious Past of Stockdale Country
    Club" .... 1978 .... $25

Nancy Jupp:
"Nairn Golf Club" .... 1957 .... $30

Liz Kahn:
"The LPGA: The Unauthorized Version" .... 1996 .... $25
"Tony Jacklin: The Price of Success" .... 1979 .... $15

Marilyn M. Kahn:
"Inwood Country Club Seventy-Fifth
    Anniversary 1901-1976".................... 1976 .... $25

Kane, Kane Jr., & MacDonald:
"Tedesco Country Club 1903-1978" .... 1978 .... $25

Thousands of color book illustrations visible at
www.rogeregilchrist.com

Kansas City Sports Co:
"You And Your Golf Course" .... 1955 .... $15
Jim Kaplan:
"Hillerich & Bradsby: History - Catalogs" ...... 1982 .... $35
"MacGregor Golf: History - Catalogs" .... 1980 .... $35
   Revised .... 2000 .... $25
"Wilson Golf: History - Catalogs" .... 1981 .... $35
   Revised .... 2000 .... $25
Karen C. C:
"Karen Country Club, Past and Future" .... 1978 .... $10
Peter V. Karpovich:
"A Study of Some Physiological Effects
  of Golf" .... 1928 .... $150
Shirli Kaskie:
"A Woman's Golf Game" .... 1982 .... $15
Leonard J Katosky:
"The Story of Golf In Waterloo IA" .... 1994 .... $10
James E. Kavanagh:
"Golf Made Easy" .... 1953 .... $15
L. V. Kavanagh:
"The History of Golf In Canada" .... 1973 .... $45
Herbert I. Kavet:
"Golf" .... 1992 .... $15
John Kay:
"A Series of Original Portraits and Caricature
  Etchings" (4 Vols) .... 1837 .... $1150
Thomas Kay:
"The Prestwick St. Nicholas Golf Club" .... 1947 .... $85
Christopher Keane:
"The Tour" .... 1974 .... $25
Tom Kearney:
"A Funny Thing Happened" .... 1985 .... $10
Kebo Valley Club:
"The Kebo Valley Sixtieth Anniversary Year
  1888-1948" .... 1948 .... $95
O. B. Keeler:
"The Autobiography of The Average Golfer" .. 1925 .... $625
"The Boy's Life of Bobby Jones" .... 1931 .... $595
"Golf In North Carolina" .... 1938 .... $750
Francis B. Keene:
"Lyrics of The Links" .... 1921 .... $375
Nicholas Keith:
"Golf: Sportsviewers Guide" .... 1984 .... $15

Konrad Kellen:
"Talk On The Golf Course"............................ND.......... $65
Homer Kelley:
"The Golfing Machine: Geometric Golf"......... 1969.......... $40
James E. Kelley:
"Minnesota Golf: 75 Years of Tournament
    History".. 1976.......... $30
Robert F. Kelley:
"The Sportsman's Anthology" .... 1944.......... $20
G. M. Kelly:
"Golf In New Zealand; A Centennial History". 1971.......... $50
Jeff Kelly & Antonio Sanchez:
"Ryder Cup 97"... 1997.......... $25
Liam Kelly:
"Balbriggan Golf Club Golden Jubilee
    1945-1995" .... 1995.......... $25
William E. Kelly:
"Birth of the Birdie: Atlantic City Country
    Club Centennial 1897-1997"............... 1997.......... $95
Kelso G. C:
"Kelso Golf Club Bazaar Cookery Book"........ 1914........ $475
Charles F. Kemp:
"Smart Golf: A Study of The Mental And
    Emotional Side of Golf"...................... 1974.......... $10
"The World of Golf & The Game of Life"........ 1978.......... $10
Barbara K. Keogh & Carol E. Smith:
"Personal Par" .... 1985.......... $15
Kendal G. C:
"Kendal Golf Club" .... 1965.......... $25
Kenilworth G. C:
"Kenilworth Golf Club" .... 1951.......... $35
Mrs. Edward Kennard:
"The Golf Lunatic And His Cycling Wife"........ 1902........ $500
"The Sorrows of a Golfers Wife" .... 1896........ $625
Henry Kennedy:
A History of the Rolling Hills Golf Club
    1926-1994" .... 1994.......... $25
Daniel E. Kennedy:
"Golf In Sapphira's Days"........................... 1910.......... $80
Des Kennedy & Harry Georgiades:
"A Slice of Fun" .... 1965.......... $10
James Kennedy:
"Folklore And Reminiscences Of Strathtay
    And Grandtully".................................. 1927.......... $25

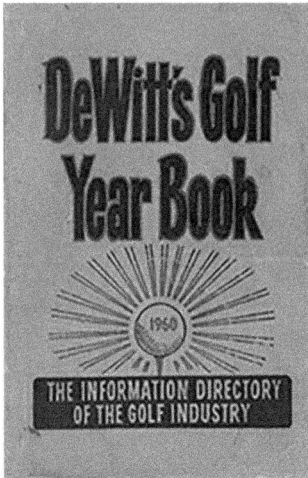

Dewitt – Dewitt's Golf Year Book

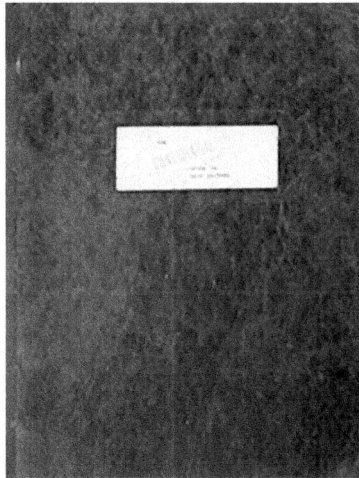

Doak – The Confidential Guide to Golf Courses (40 Copies)

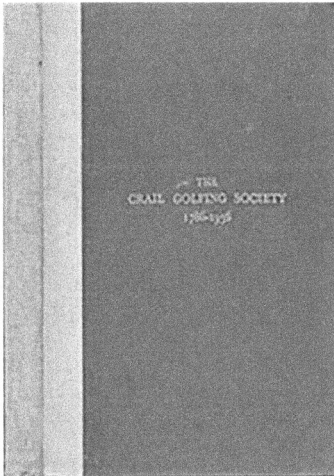

Dow – The Crail Golfing Society 1786-1936 (250 Copies)

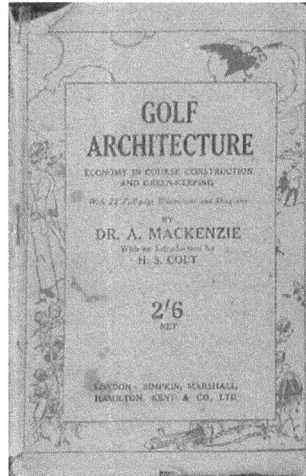

MacKenzie–Golf Architecture (Dust Jacket)

Thousands of color book illustrations visible at
www.rogeregilchrist.com

John H. Kennedy:
"A Course Of Their Own" .... 2000 .... $20
Patrick Kennedy:
"Golf Clubs Trademarks: American
    1898-1930" .... 1984 .... $30
Don Kennington:
"The Source Book of Golf" .... 1981 .... $45
Kent C. C:
Kent County Club, Grand Rapids Michigan" ... 1901 .... $75
John H. Kent:
"Rhythm Golf" .... 1958 .... $10
Kenwood G. & C. C:
"Kenwood 50 Years 1928-1978" .... 1978 .... $25
Michael Kenyon:
"The Shooting of Dan McGrew" .... 1972 .... $10
Barbara K. Keogh & Carol E. Smith:
"Personal Par: A Psychological System of
    Golf For Women" .... 1985 .... $15
Jerry Kearney:
"Co. Meath Golf Club 1898-1998 The Road
    from Effernock" .... 1998 .... $150
Shirley K. Kerns:
"Fifty Years of Brae Burn 1897-1947" .... 1947 .... $95
John Kerr:
"The Golf Book of East Lothian" .... 1896 ...... $1,500
    Small Paper Edition (500 Copies) .... 1896 ...... $2500
    Large Paper Edition Signed
    (250 Copies) .... 1896 ...... $4500
    Reprint (500 Copies) .... 1987 .... $600
"The Golf Song Book" .... 1903 .... $700
John Kerr:
"One Hundred Years at the Boat" .... 1998 .... $65
George F. Kerr:
"The Year of the Old Goats" .... 1987 .... $10
William M. Kerr:
"The History of the Royal Durban Golf
    Club 1892-1992 .... 1992 .... $45
Michal Kerry & Dick Glynne-Jones:
"Piltdown 1904-2004" .... 2004 .... $40
Kaye W. Kessler:
"The Golf Club" .... 1982 .... $20
"The International At Castle Pines Golf Club". 1986 .... $35
Kettering G. C:
"Kettering Golf Club 1891-1991" .... 1991 .... $45

Mohamed Khnichich:
"Golf In Morocco"..................................... 1996 .... $30
Ted Kiegiel:
"Balanced Golf" .... 1999 .... $15
Bob Kiehl:
"Duffer Golf Or How To Break 100".............. 1979 .... $10
John Kiernan:
"The American Sporting Scene".................... 1941 .... $55
Thomas Kiernan:
"Woodirons".. 1981 .... $15
Killarney Golf And Fishing Club:
"Killarney Golf And Fishing Club"................. 1951 .... $80
Albert E. Killeen:
"The Ten Million Dollar Golf Ball" .... 1983 .... $20
Julia Kilmer:
"The Club. Celebrating Seventy Years.
    Hendersonville Country Club
    1933-2003" .... 2003 .... $50
Alfred King:
"Banstead Downs Golf Club The First
    Hundred Years 1890-1990"................ 1989 .... $15
J. B. King:
"St. Austell Golf Club"............................... 1924 .... $60
Leslie King:
"Master Key To Good Golf" .... 1976 .... $60
"The Master Key To Success At Golf" .... 1962 .... $65
Leslie J. King:
"The Hamilton Golf and Country Club One
    Hundred Years of Golf 1894-1994"...... 1993 .... $75
W. R. King:
"Mohawk Golf Club, Three Quarters of
    A Century"...................................... 1973 .... $30
Kings Norton G. C:
"Kings Norton Golf Club Ltd:
    The Official Handbook" .... 1918 .... $225
"Kings Norton Golf Club Ltd:
    The Official Handbook" .... 1962 .... $45
Kingussie G. C:
"Kingussie Golf Club 1891-1991 .... 1991 .... $45
H.A. Kinney:
"Brighton And Hove Golf Club, 1887-1973"... 1973 .... $35
Charles Kip:
"The Amateur Championship Golf
    Competition At Morris County Golf

Thousands of color book illustrations visible at
www.rogeregilchrist.com

Club" (100 Copies)........................... 1898 ....$3250
Rudyard Kipling & Walter De la Mere:
"St Andrews: Two Poems".......................... 1926 .... $55
John Kirk & Timothy Jacobs:
"The Golf Courses of Robert Trent Jones Jr".. 1988 .... $75
Andra Haultain Kirkaldy:
"Fifty Years of Golf, My Memories".............. 1921 .... $525
USGA Reprint (1500 Copies) .... 1993 .... $125
Kirkcudbright G. C:
"Kirkcudbright Golf Club 1892-1993" .... 1993 .... $45
Joe Kirkwood:
"The Links of Life".................................... 1973 .... $85
Kiswauketoe C. C:
"Loramoor the Home of the Kishwauketoe
Country Club.................................. 1928 .... $145
John Kissling:
"Seventy Years: A History of The Metropolitan
Golf Club, Oakleigh Victoria".............. 1973 .... $75
Tom Kite:
"How To Play Consistent Golf".................... 1992 .... $15
Donald M. Kladstrup:
"The Crown Jewels of Oak Hill" .... 1989 .... $50
Ernie Klappenbach:
"A Forty-Two Year History 1935-1971
Southern Hills Country Club"
(1500 Copies) .... 1977 .... $175
"A Fifty-Seven Year History 1935-1992
Southern Hills Country Club"
(1500 Copies) .... 1992 ....$120
Gene Kleese:
"Gene's Golf Guide - Chicago".................... 1992 .... $10
Bradley S. Klein:
"Rough Meditations"................................. 1997 .... $15
Bradley S. Klein & Carol Haralson:
"Building Sabonack" .... 2006 .... $75
Dave Klein:
"Golf's Big Three".................................... 1973 .... $10
"Great Moments In Golf".......................... 1971 .... $20
Linda Klinger:
"Celebrating 75 Years".............................. 1999 .... $95
Jerry Kloppenburg:
"Cure The Yips" .... 1985 .... $5
Elizabeth & James Klugness:
"The Nongolfers Cookbook" .... 1982 .... $10

Thousands of color book illustrations visible at
www.rogeregilchrist.com

Mary C. Klute:
"Golfers Always Say" .... 1984 .... $10
Knaresborough G. C:
"Knaresborough Golf Club" .... 1929 .... $80
Bob Kneedler:
"Golfitis: Golf It Is" .... 1965 .... $5
Professor K. Knight:
"Andreapolis, Being Writings In Praise
    of St Andrews" .... 1903 .... $75
Reg Knight:
"Golf For Beginners" .... 1970 .... $10
"Learn Golf Backwards" .... 1965 .... $10
William A. Knight & T. T. Oliphant:
"Stories of Golf" .... 1894 .... $800
    Revised Edition .... 1894 .... $250
Knock G. C:
"Knock Golf Club 1895-1995 .... 1995 .... $45
Knollwood C. C:
"Knollwood Country Club 1894-1969,
    75 Years of Golf" .... 1969 .... $20
Cargill G. Knott:
"Life and Scientific Work of Peter Guthrie
    Tait" .... 1911 .... $650
Philip Knowles:
"A History of Bruntsfield Allied Golf Club
    1856-1996" (600 Copies) .... 1997 .... $45
Bill Knox:
"The Killing Game" .... 1963 .... $45
Edmund G. V. Knox:
"Mr. Punch On The Links" (Dust Jacket) .... 1929 .... $600
Ronald A. Knox:
"The Viaduct Murder" .... 1926 .... $120
George Knudson:
"The Natural Golf Swing" .... 1988 .... $35
Eric Knutson:
"Innis Arden: 100 Years In The
    Neighborhood, 1899-1999: .... 2000 .... $50
Margaret Koch:
"The Pasatiempo Story" .... 1990 .... $50
C. P Kochanski:
"Pro-Motion – Driver" .... 1959 .... $125
William Kociemba & Eric A Kaufman:
"The Three Stooges Country Club " .... 1998 .... $10

Lee Kocsis:
"Kinks On The Links: With Spiked Footnotes" 1982 .... $25
Koebler:
"Wawashkamo Golf Club, Mackinac Island" ... 1982 .... $75
Albert E. Koehl:
"Ardsley Country Club" .... 1955 .... $125
Elaine B. Koehl:
"Ponte Vedra Club 1927-1982 The First
    Fifty-Five Years" .... 1982 .... $30
Aileen P. Koehler:
"Wawashkame Golf Club" .... 1982 .... $20
Kathryn Korchok:
"The St Catherine's Golf and Country Club
    1889-1989" .... 1990 .... $25
Peter Kostis:
"The Inside Path To Better Golf" .... 1982 .... $15
Ruben Kraetz:
"Golf In Ten Lessons" .... 1938 .... $25
Kenneth Krakauer:
"When Golf Came To Kansas" .... 1986 .... $20
Mark H. Kramer:
"Kramers Guide To Golf Courses of The
    Hawaiian Islands" .... 1990 .... $20
John B. Kritzer:
"Butterfield Country Club 1920-1970" .... 1970 .... $15
Robert Kroeger:
"The Golf Courses of Old Tom Morris" .... 1995 .... $175
    limited edition of 1975
        Signed Limited Edition (50 Copies) ...... 1995 .... $495
"Complete Guide To The Golf Courses
    of Scotland" .... 1992 .... $15
"To The 14th Tee"
    Collectors edition of 195 .... 2001 .... $185
    Signed limited edition of 750 .... 2001 .... $65
William C. Kroen:
"A Hacker No More" .... 1987 .... $15
"The Why Book of Golf" .... 1988 .... $10
Dr. Tom Kubistant:
"The Bibliography On The Psychology
    of Golf" .... 2000 .... $20
"Links Golf" .... 1999 .... $20
Susan Kuchinskas:
"The Drive To Win" (7500 Copies) .... 1992 .... $20

Thousands of color book illustrations visible at
www.rogeregilchrist.com

Thomas Kuhl:
"Collecting Memories"................................. 1995 .... $45
Jared Jay Kullman:
"101 Winning Golf Tips" .... 1980 .... $5
"How To Play Winning Golf"........................ 1980 .... $5
Bob Kuntz with Mark Wilson:
"Antique Golf Clubs"................................. 1990 .... $75
      Subscribers Edition of 500 .... 1990 .... $150
Vartan Kupelian:
"Stalking The Tiger" .... 1997 .... $10
Shela & Joel Kushell:
"Golf Resorts"... 1983 .... $15
Bob Labbance:
"The Centennial History of the the
      Bethlehem Country Club".................... 1998 .... $30
"The Centennial History of the Keene
      Country Club" .... 1997 .... $35
"The Centennial History of the
      Woodstock Country Club" .... 1994 .... $35
      Authors Edition of 100 signed............. 1994 .... $85
"The Old Man" .... 2000 .... $25
"The Vardon Invasion"............................... 2008 .... $75
Bob Labbace & David Cornwell:
"The Golf Courses of New Hampshire".......... 1989 .... $20
"The Maine Golf Guide"............................. 1991 .... $20
Bob Labbance & Gordon Witteveen:
"Keepers of The Green" .... 2002 .... $25
Bob Labbance & Patrick White:
"The Country Club of Pittsfield: More than a
      Century of History" .... 2004 .... $35
"The History of the Springhaven Club
      1896-2004" .... 2004 .... $35
Rudy Lachenmeir:
"Are You A Gope Or A Golfer" .... 1952 .... $15
Ladies Championship:
"Ladies Championship Golf 1893-1932 In
      Aid of The Golfers Cot" .... 1932 .... $195
Ladies Golf Union
"The Ladies Golf Union Annual".................. 1894 ......$1475
"The Ladies Golf Union Official Year Book" .... 1902 ....$1000
Andre-Jean Lafaurie:
"Trophy Lancome" .... 1999 .... $125
La Grange C. C:
"Historical Review of La Grange Country

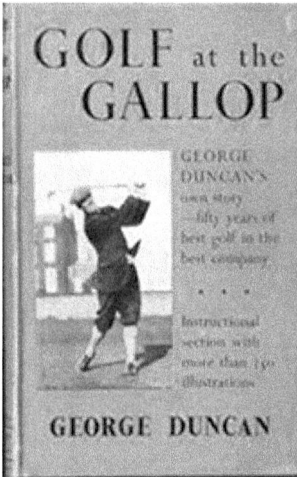

Duncan – Golf at the Gallop

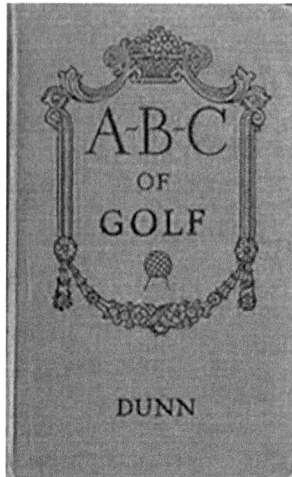

Dunn – A-B-C of Golf

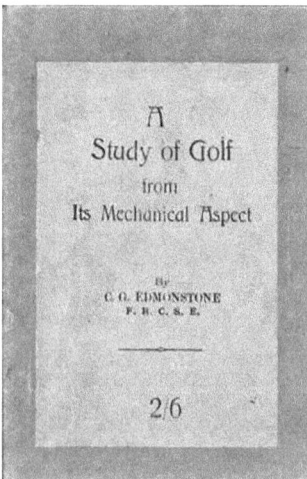

Edmonstone – A Study of Golf

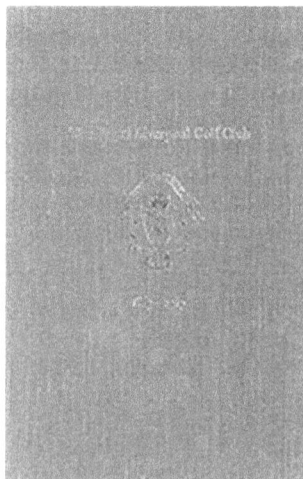

Edwards – The Royal Liverpool
Golf Club 1869-1969

Thousands of color book illustrations visible at
www.rogeregilchrist.com

Club, 1899-1949" .... 1949 .... $60
Renton Laidlaw:
"Golfing Heroes" .... 1989 .... $10
"Play Better Golf" .... 1986 .... $10
"The European Open" .... 1988 .... $30
"Wentworth: A Host of Happy Memories" ...... 1993 .... $50
"The Sunningdale Centenary 1900-2000" ..... 2000 .... $35
Laidlaw & Mason:
"A Very Pleasant Golfing Place" .... 1991 .... $55
Lake Placid:
"Lake Placid Club Golf Courses" .... 1910 .... $295
"Lake Placid Club Handbook " .... 1914 .... $225
"Lake Placid Golf Club" .... 1915 .... $150
Ivan Lake:
"Falmouth Golf Club" .... 1974 .... $20
Lakes Entrance G. C:
"Lakes Entrance Golf Club New Links, 25th
    Anniversary 1962-1986"
    (1500 Copies) .... 1986 .... $30
Lakes G. C:
"Prospectus of The Lakes Golf Club Limited" . 1937 .... $45
Lake Swannanoa G. & C. C:
"Lake Swannanoa: The Beautiful Trail .... 1925 .... $125
Lake Zurich G. C:
Lake Zurich Golf Club Him Book" .... 1915 .... $250
Roy Lalande:
"Inverness Golf Club 1926-1974" .... 1974 .... $35
Lamberhurst G. C:
"Lamberhurst Golf Club" .... 1951 .... $30
Harry J. Lambeth:
"A Directory of The Leading Builders
    of The Nation's Golf Courses" .... 1974 .... $25
Lamborn & Harberl:
"Golf at the Stanley Hotels" .... 1923 .... $350
Lancaster G. & C. C:
"Lancaster Golf Club" .... 1933 .... $90
"Lancaster Golf Club 50th Anniversary" .... 1983 .... $20
"Ashton Hall A Golfers Paradise" .... 1933 .... $60
H. Boswell Lancaster:
"Ridiculous Golf, In Story And In Verse" .... 1938 .... $195
Al Laney:
"Following The Leaders" .... 1991 .... $30
Andrew Lang:
"A Batch of Golfing Papers" .... 1892 .... $575

"A Batch of Golfing Stories" .... 1892 .... $350
"A Monk of Fife" .... 1896 .... $125
"Ballades And Verses Vain" .... 1884 .... $750
"Ballades And Rhymes" .... 1911 .... $95
"Echoes Re-Echoed: An Anthology of
     St. Andrews Verse" .... 1934 .... $90
"New Rules for the Game of Mail" .... 1910 .... $495
"Old Friends: Essays in Epistolary Parody" .... 1890 .... $125
"The Poetic Works of Andrew Lang"
     (4 Vols) 1075 copies .... 1923 .... $135
"St Andrews" (107 Large paper copies) .... 1893 ..... $1,250
     First Trade Edition .... 1893 .... $495
"The Red True Story Book" .... 1895 .... $150
David Langdon:
    "How To Play Golf And Stay Happy" .... 1964 .... $15
    "How To Talk Golf: A Glossary of Golf Terms" 1975 .... $15
Harry Langton:
    "Thomas Hodge: Golf Artist of St Andrews" .. 2000 .... $150
Bernhard Langer:
    "While The Iron Is Hot" .... 1988 .... $15
William B. Langford:
    "Golf Course Architecture In The Chicago
      District" .... 1915 .... $125
Lansdown G. C:
    "Lansdown Golf Club" .... 1939 .... $65
Bruce Lansky:
    "Golf: It's Just A Game" .... 1996 .... $5
Robert Lapham:
    "Twenty Years of Life Begins At Forty" .... 1972 .... $30
Roger D. Lapham:
    "The History of Cypress Point Club" .... 1996 .... $75
Gary Larrabee:
    "Salem Country Club – One Hundred
      Years 1895-1995" .... 1995 .... $125
    "Wenham Country Club 100 Years" .... 1999 .... $75
George E. Lardner:
    "Cut Your Score" .... 1933 .... $175
    "Golf Technique Simplified" .... 1933 .... $95
    "How To Play Golf" .... 1927 .... $125
Rex Lardner:
    "Downhill Lies And Other Falsehoods Or
      How To Play Dirty Golf" .... 1973 .... $15
    "The Great Golfers" .... 1970 .... $35
    "Out of The Bunker And Into The Trees Or

The Secret of High Tension Golf"......... 1960 .... $20

Lawrence Larier:
"Golf And Be Damned"............................... 1954 .... $15
"You've Got Me In A Hole".......................... 1955 .... $15

Mary Liz Larmore:
"The Resort Book For Swingers, A Golfer's
Vacation Guide"................................ 1981 .... $10

Gary Larrabee:
"Wenham Country Club, 100 Years"............. 2000 .... $25
"The Green & Gold Coast: The History of
Golf On the Boston's North Shore
1893-2001" .... 2001 .... $75

Herbert Larsen:
"Women's Metropolitan Golf Association
1899-1974" .... 1975 .... $40

Lucy Larson:
"Garden State Women's Golf Association
1953-1978" .... 1978 .... $35

Lauder G. C:
"Royal Burg of Lauder Golf Club 1896-1996". 1996 .... $45

Michael Laughlin:
"Radical Golf" .... 1996 .... $15

Mario Laureti:
"All Putts Should Count 1/2 Stroke"............. 1981 .... $10

Janice Law:
"Death Under Par" .... 1981 .... $30

Peter Lawless:
"The Golfer's Campanion" .... 1937 .... $250
Signed Deluxe edition .... 1937 .... $375

Don Lawrence:
"Victoria Golf Club 1903-1988" .... 1988 .... $50

Stewart Lawson:
"The Original Rules of Golf" (100 Copies) ..... 1981 .... $350

A. P. Layer:
"The Simplicity of The Golf Swing"............... 1911 .... $175

Joe Lazaro:
"The Right Touch" .... 1978 .... $35

Roland Lazenby:
"Golden West Golf" .... 1988 .... $10

Henry Leach:
"Great Golfers In The Making" .... 1907 .... $425
USGA reprint (1500 Copies) .... 1988 .... $135
"The Happy Golfer" .... 1914 .... $700
"Letters of A Modern Golfer To His

Thousands of color book illustrations visible at
www.rogeregilchrist.com

Grandfather"..................................... 1910 .... $550
"The Spirit of The Links" .... 1907 .... $750
Rod Leach:
"The Buxton & High Peak Golf Club" .... 1987 .... $25
David Leadbetter:
"Faults And Fixes"..................................... 1993 .... $10
"Lessons From The Golf Greats".................. 1995 .... $25
"The Golf Swing"....................................... 1990 .... $20
"Positive Practice" .... 1997 .... $15
Brendan D. Leahey:
"One Hundred Years At Vesper Country
        Club" .... 1979 .... $95
Leamington G. C:
"Leamington Golf Club"............................. 1937 .... $60
David Lee:
"Gravity Golf"... 1994 .... $20
Jack Lee:
"Royal Perth: The History of Royal Perth" ..... 1978 .... $65
James P. Lee:
"Golf And Golfing: A Practical Manual".......... 1895 ......$1,450
"Golf In America"...................................... 1895 ......$1,550
        USGA reprint (1500 Copies) .... 1986 .... $250
        Reprint... 2001 .... $20
Phil Lee MD & Jeff Warne:
"Shrink Your Handicap"............................. 2000 .... $20
Stan Lee:
"Golfers Anonymous"................................. 1961 .... $10
Lee-On-The-Solent G. C:
"Lee-On-The-Solent Golf Club The First
        75 Years A Brief History" .... 1980 .... $25
Peter W. Lees:
"Care of the Green".................................. 1918 ......$2,500
Leicestershire G. C:
"Leicestershire Golf Club".......................... 1938 .... $65
Dell Leigh:
"Golf at its Best on the L.M.S."................... 1925 .... $250
"Twelve of The Best On The L.M.S.".............. 1930 .... $375
Ernest P. Leigh-Bennett:
"An Errant Golfer" .... 1929 .... $125
"Some Friendly Fairways"........................... 1930 .... $155
"Southern Golf" .... 1935 .... $125
Cecil Leitch:
"Golf".. 1922 .... $275
"Golf For Girls" .... 1914 .... $235

"Golf Simplified" .... 1924 .... $295
Tony Lema:
  "Champagne Tony's Golf Tips" .... 1966 .... $40
  "Golfers' Gold: An Inside View of The
      Pro Tour"... 1964 .... $55
      Classics of Golf Reprint...................... 1987 .... $30
  "How To Break 100/90/80"........................ 1965 .... $45
G. E. Leman:
  "A Short History of The Origins of Golf At
      Northam And The Foundation of The
      Present Royal North Devon Golf Club".. 1926 .... $450
George J. Lemmon:
  "About Golf".. 1941 .... $200
Kim Lenaghan:
  "A Little History of Golf" .... 1996 .... $10
John Leng:
  "Leng's Golfer's Manual" .... 1907 .... $150
Lord William P. Lennox:
  "Sport at Home and Abroad" (2 Vols).......... 1872 .... $150
Mark Lerner:
  "Golf Is For Me" .... 1982 .... $10
Bill Leslie & Gene O'Brien:
  "Aim and Hang Loose" .... 1976 .... $10
Letchworth G. C:
  "Letchworth Golf Club"............................. 1938 .... $75
  "Letchworth Golf Club Official Handbook" ..... 1972 .... $45
Jack Level:
  "St. George's Golf And Country Club
      Thirtieth Anniversary" .... 1945 .... $90
Stephen M. Levine:
  "Woodcrest Country Club - A History" .... 1985 .... $150
John G. Levison:
  "A Short History of The Presidio Golf Club" ... 1964 .... $25
Levy, Kiely, & Horton:
  "Construction, Renovation and Care of
      The Golf Course" .... 1923 ....$1250
Lawrence Levy & Brian Morgan:
  "Golf: Tours And Detours"......................... 1988 .... $25
Beverly Lewis:
  "Golf For Women" .... 1989 .... $15
Catherine Lewis:
  "The Story of The Atlanta Athletic Club
      A Host To History" .... 2005 .... $50

Thousands of color book illustrations visible at
www.rogeregilchrist.com

Don Lewis:
"After Dinner Golf" .... 1976 .... $10
I. G. Lewis:
"Turf: A Book About Golf Greens, Tennis
    Courts, Bowling Greens, And Playing
    Pitches Etc." .... 1948 .... $75
Peter Lewis:
"The Dawn of Professional Golf" .... 1995 .... $45
    Limited Edition of 850 signed .... 1995 .... $95
    Limited Edition of 150 Copies .... 1995 .... $195
Lewis, Clark, & Grieve:
"A Round of History" .... 1998 .... $15
Lewis, Grieve, & Mackie:
"Art And Architecture of The Royal And
    Ancient Golf Club" (195 Copies) .... 1997 ......$1150
Robert Lewis:
"Win Those Saturday Games" .... 1979 .... $10
Liberton G. C:
"Liberton Golf Club: Through the Millennium
    1980-2000" .... 1999 .... $45
Glenn Liebman:
"Golf Shorts" .... 1995 .... $10
Life Magazine:
"Fore! Life's Book For Golfers" .... 1900 .... $450
Life's Comedy:
"Life's Comedy Out of Doors" .... 1897 .... $125
John A. Lillie:
"Ninety Years A Golfer" .... 1981 .... $10
Lucy C. Lillie:
"The Family Dilemma" .... 1894 .... $150
Lindy Lindberg:
"Lindy Lindberg's Spot System of Chipping" .. 1977 .... $10
R. C. Lindholm:
"Lindy's Golf Course Guide For The
    Washington-Baltimore Area" .... 1983 .... $10
Walter C. Lindley:
"Oahu Country Club Seventy-Five Years" ...... 1981 .... $25
Harvey Lindsay:
"Penalties on the Link" .... 1915 .... $250
Robert Lindsay:
"Chronicles of Scotland" .... 1814 .... $295
Stuart Lindsay:
"The Nairn Golf Club 1887-1987" .... 1987 .... $75

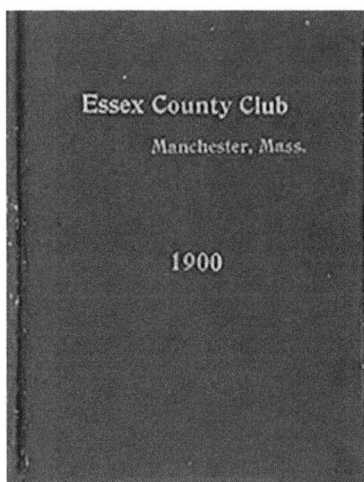

Essex C.C. – Essex Country
Club 1900

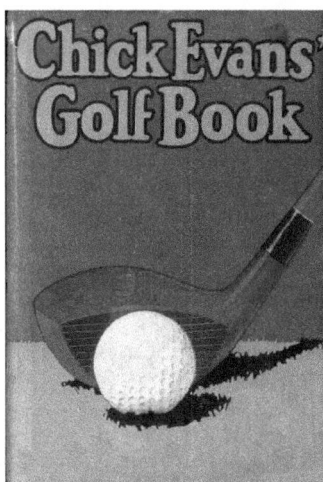

Evans – Chick Evans Golf Book
(1st Trade edition Dust Jacket)

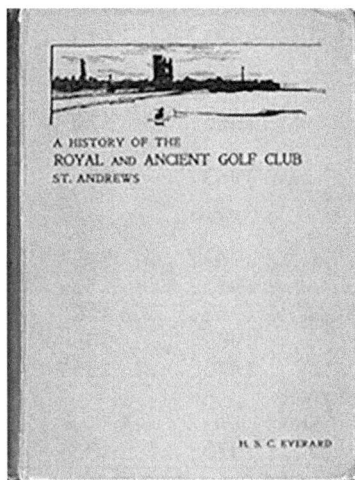

Everard – A History of the
Royal and Anciemt Golf Club

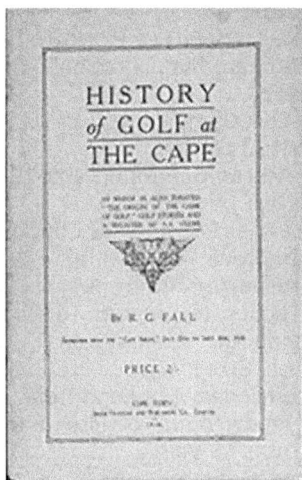

Fall – History of Golf at
The Cape

James E. Lindslay:
"Breaking a Hundred: A Centenary History
of the Castine Golf Club".................... 1997 .... $35
Lo Linkert:
"Around The Course In 19 Holes" .... 1983 .... $15
"Duffers, Hackers, and Other Golfers".......... 1981 .... $10
"Golftoons" .... 1977 .... $15
Bo Links:
"Follow The Wind"..................................... 1995 .... $20
"Riverbank Tweed and Roadmap Jenkins"..... 2001 .... $20
W. T. Linskill:
"Golf".. 1889 .... $750
"St Andrews Golf Stories"........................... 1921 .... $195
Liphook G. C:
"The Liphook Golf Club" .... 1925 .... $80
Horace M. Lippincott:
"A History of The Philadelphia Cricket
Club 1854 To 1954" .... 1954 .... $75
Howard Liss:
"The Masters Tournament" .... 1974 .... $35
Listen To This One:
"Listen To This One".................................. 1933 .... $20
David Lister:
"I'd Like To Help The World To Swing" .... 1977 .... $10
"The Ultimate Simplification" .... 1981 .... $10
John Lister:
"The Short Game".................................... 1996 .... $10
Little Ashton G. C:
"Little Ashton Golf Club 1908-1983" .... 1983 .... $25
Gene Littler:
"Gene Littler Presents 38 Checkpoints To
Improve Your Swing" .... 1962 .... $45
"How to Master The Irons" .... 1962 .... $35
"Iron Tactics, My Secrets To Winning Golf" ... 1962 .... $10
"The Long And Medium Irons".................... 1965 .... $65
"The Real Score"...................................... 1976 .... $35
"Stroke Minder: The Long Irons: The Driver:
Sandwedge: The Pitch Shot: The Short
Irons" 5 Vols................................... 1978 .... $85
Littlestone G. C:
"Littlestone Golf Club" .... 1951 .... $55
R. H. Littleton:
"Outdoor Games - Cricket and Golf" .... 1901 .... $125

Thousands of color book illustrations visible at
www.rogeregilchrist.com

John Littlewood:
"Oxford & Cambridge Golfing Society The
President's Putter, 50 Putters;
1920-1976" .... 1976 .... $60
"North Hants Golf Club Centenary History
1904-2004" .... 2004 .... $125
Royal Liverpool G. C:
"The Royal Liverpool Golf Club Official
Handbook" .... 1967 .... $50
Llandrindod G. C:
"The Llandrindod Golf Club".......................... 1948 .... $50
B. Lloyd:
"Wirral Ladies Golf Club: Centenary Portrait"
(500 Copies) .... 1993 .... $45
F. B. Lloyd:
"The Seniors: Being The Story of
Senior Golf" .... 1975 .... $10
Lloyd's G. C:
"A History of Lloyd's Golf Club" (52 Copies) .. 1997 .... $300
Bobby Locke:
"The Basis of My Game"............................ 1950 .... $65
"Golf Hints".. 1955 .... $75
"How To Improve Your Putting".................... 1949 .... $75
"Bobby Locke On Golf"................................ 1953 .... $75
"Bobby Locke's South African Golf Annual" ... 1948 .... $250
Tony Locke:
"Golf Is My Mistress: Memoirs of A Club
Profesional" .... 1981 .... $15
Richard Lockridge:
"Murder Can't Wait" .... 1964 .... $30
Joseph N. Lockyer & W. Rutherford:
"The Rules of Golf".................................... 1896 .... $850
Robert L. Loeffelbein:
"How To Goof-Proof Your Golf Game"........... 1971 .... $10
Dr. John Logan:
"Masserene Golf Club 1895-1995" .... 1995 .... $25
John Logue:
"A Rain of Death"...................................... 1998 .... $15
"Follow The Leader" .... 1979 .... $35
"The Feathery Touch of Death" .... 1997 .... $35
"Murder On The Links"............................... 1996 .... $15
Carl Lohren:
"One Move To Better Golf" .... 1975 .... $35
"Getting Set For Golf"................................ 1995 .... $20

Thousands of color book illustrations visible at
www.rogeregilchrist.com

E. L. Lomax:
"Union Pacific Overland..." .... 1900 ....$425
A. Q. London:
"The Swing In Golf And How To Learn It" ..... 1919 .... $625
London, Midland Scottish Railway Services:
"Gleneagles Hotel" .... 1924 .... $950
London & North Eastern Railway:
"Golf Courses Served by Stations on the
London and North Eastern Railway".....???? $295
London Scottish G. C:
"London Scottish Golf Club " .... 1899 .... $175
R. Brent Long:
"The First One Hundred Years: The
Mississaugua Golf and Country Club"... 2006 .... $125
Long Ashton G. C:
"Long Ashton Golf Club"............................. 1939 ....$6
Long Ball:
"The Long Ball, Add 50 Yards Or More To
Your Drive".................................... 1978 .... $10
Gordon Long:
"A History of The Geelong Golf Club
1892-1967" (700 Copies) .... 1967 .... $95
Longcliffe G. C:
"Longcliffe Golf Club"................................ 1938 .... $65
Henry Longhurst:
"Addington Golf Club" .... 1953 .... $40
"The Best of Henry Longhurst: On Golf
And Life" .... 1978 .... $40
U.S Edition .... 1979 .... $35
"Golf In Ireland" .... 1953 .... $175
"Golf Mixture".. 1952 .... $75
"Golf"... 1937 .... $125
Reprint... 1949 .... $30
"How To Get Started In Golf"....................... 1967 .... $25
"I Wouldn't Have Missed It"......................... 1941 .... $75
"It Was Good While It Lasted"...................... 1941 .... $150
"John O'Gaunt Golf Club" .... 1950 .... $45
"Mere Golf And Country Club" .... 1947 .... $50
"My Life and Soft Times"............................. 1971 .... $75
"Never On Weekdays" .... 1968 .... $50
"Only On Sundays"..................................... 1964 .... $55
"Round In Sixty-Eight"................................ 1953 .... $85
"Southport: Golf Centre of Europe".............. 1969 .... $35
"Spice of Life"... 1963 .... $55

"Talking About Golf" .... 1966 .... $75
"The Best of Henry Longhurst" .... 1978 .... $45
"The Essential Henry Longhurst" .... 1988 .... $30
"Turnberry Hotel And Its Golf Courses" .... 1958 .... $100
"Turnberry Hotel And The Ailsa Golf Course". 1953 .... $150
"Unwritten Golf Contract" .... 1952 .... $75
"West Sussex Golf Club" .... 1960 .... $40
"The Wilderness Country Club" .... 1937 .... $60
"You Never Know Until You Get There" .... 1949 .... $55
Henry Longhurst & Geoffrey Cousins:
"The Old Course At St. Andrews" .... 1961 .... $250
"Ryder Cup 1965" .... 1965 .... $45
Peter Longo:
"Simplified Golf: There's No Trick To It" .... 1980 .... $10
Doreen Longrigg:
"Ladies On The Fairway" .... 1981 .... $10
Longue Vue Club:
"Longue Vue Club Fiftieth Anniversary
        1920-1970" .... 1970 .... $30
Looe Bin G. C:
"Looe Bin Golf Club" .... 1964 .... $25
Samuel L. Looker:
"On The Green: An Anthology For Golfers" .... 1922 .... $375
Nancy Lopez:
"Lopez On Golf" .... 1988 .... $15
"The Complete Golfer" .... 1987 .... $15
"The Education of A Woman Golfer" .... 1979 .... $20
LeRoy B. Lorenz:
"The Science of Golf" .... 1955 .... $125
Henry Lord & Oliver Gregory:
"St Andrews: The Home of Golf" .... 2010 .... $50
Phillip Q. Loring:
"Rhymes of A Duffer" .... 1915 .... $750
Los Altos G. C:
"Los Altos Golf and Country Club" .... 1949 .... $65
Los Altos Golf and Country Club" .... 1950 .... $45
"Los Altos Golf and Country Club
        Yearbook 1967-68" .... 1968 .... $20
Los Altos Golf and Country Club. Our First
        Seventy-Five Years. 1923-1998 .... 1998 .... $45
Los Angeles C. C:
"Constitution, By Laws, Rules, Officers, and
        Members" .... 1911 .... $125
"Golden Anniversary of The Clubhouse

1911-1961" .... 1961 .... $125
"The History of the Los Angeles Country Club
    1898-1973" .... 1973 .... $125
Dic Loscalzo:
"On The Links" .... 1926 .... $250
Davis Love III:
"Every Shot I Take"................................. 1997 .... $10
George Low:
"The Master of Putting"............................ 1983 .... $50
John L. Low:
"Concerning Golf" .... 1903 .... $245
    USGA Reprint.................................. 1987 .... $125
"F. G. Tait, A Record Being His Life, Letters,
    And Golfing Diary" .... 1900 .... $475
    Classics of Golf reprint...................... 1988 .... $25
Douglas Lowe:
"The Glasgow Herald Book of Golf" .... 1990 .... $15
W. W. Lowe:
"Bedrock Principles of Golf" .... 1937 .... $55
Laddie Lucas:
"Five Up: A Chronicle of Five Lives" .... 1978 .... $30
"John Jacobs And His Impact On Golf" .... 1987 .... $20
"The Sport of Prince's, Reflections of
    A Golfer" .... 1980 .... $35
Patricia L. Lucas:
"Overlake; the Land, The Club the People" ... 1979 .... $20
Ted Lucock:
"Golf Mad" .... 1981 .... $10
"Golfing With Lu" .... 1980 .... $10
Eleanor Luedtke:
"In Good Company: A Centennial History of
    the Country Club of Detroit
    1897-1997" .... 1997 .... $20
Luffness G. C:
"A Brief Histroy of Luffness Golf Club
    And Kilspinde Golf Club" .... 1967 .... $30
Nick Lumb:
"A Beginners Guide To Golf" .... 1987 .... $10
Lumb, Hobbs, & Pinner:
"The Complete Book of Golf" .... 1988 .... $20
Robert N. Lundberg:
Bass Rocks Golf Club".............................. 1995 .... $45
Steve Lunderstedt & Dave Wilson:
"The Kimberley Golf Club 1890-1990".......... 1991 .... $125

Thousands of color book illustrations visible at
www.rogeregilchrist.com

Evelyn Lunemann:
"Fairway Danger"...................................... 1969 .... $35
Maxine V. E. Lupo:
"How To Master A Great Golf Swing"............ 1991 .... $15
Norman Lupovich:
"Elm Ridge Country Club 1924-1974" .... 1974 .... $30
Douglas Lutz:
"Metropolitan Golf Guide: New York Edition" . 1973 .... $25
Theodore Luxton:
"The Dynamics Golf Correspondence Course" 1973 .... $10
"The Real Truth About The Golf Swing" .... 1985 .... $15
David W. Lyle:
"Images of St Andrews Past" .... 1998 .... $15
Sandy Lyle:
"The Championship Courses Of Scotland"..... 1982 .... $75
"Dunlop Golf Guide - Carnoustie" .... 1982 .... $20
"Dunlop Golf Guide - Muirfield" .... 1982 .... $20
"Dunlop Golf Guide - Royal Troon"............... 1982 .... $20
"Dunlop Golf Guide - Turnberry" .... 1982 .... $20
"Learning Golf The Lyle Way"...................... 1986 .... $15
Lyme Regis G. C:
"Lyme Regis Golf Club" .... 1951 .... $50
Michael Lynch & Ben Cligain:
"The Ryder Cup Handbook" .... 1993 .... $15
John M. Lynham:
"The Chevy Chase Club: A History
       1885-1957" .... 1958 .... $125
R. Milton Lynnes:
"Exmoor Country Club 1896-1996".............. 1996 .... $95
Rev C. J. Lyon:
"History of St Andrews" (Two Vols).............. 1843 ....$2750
Harry Lyons & Dick Johnson:
"The Hazards of Golf: A Complete
       How-Not-To Book" .... 1979 .... $10
R. H. Lyttleton:
"Out-Door Games: Cricket And Golf"............ 1901 .... $350
       Signed Limited Edition (150 Copies) .... 1901 .... $925
P. J. M.:
"Golfing Trifles" .... 1985 .... $25
J. C. Macabe:
"The First Eighty Years, Douglas Park
       Golf Club"...................................... 1982 .... $50
Bob MacAlindin:
"James Braid – Champion Golfer"

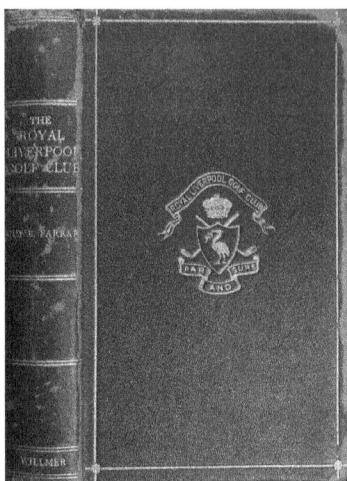

Farrar – The Royal Liverpool
Golf Club (Deluxe 1St Edition)

Fleming – Goldfinger
(1St Edition Dust Jacket)

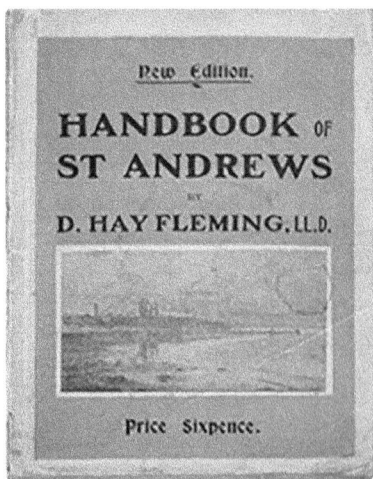

Fleming – Handbook of St
Andrews

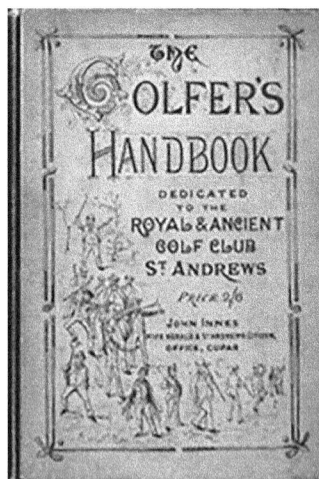

Forgan – The Golfer's
Handbook (1St Edition)

Thousands of color book illustrations visible at
www.rogeregilchrist.com

(550 Copies) .... 2003 .... $125
Charles MacArthur:
"The Golfer's Annual for 1869-1870" .... 1870 .... $18,500
James C. MacBeth:
"Golf From A To Z" .... 1935 .... $95
"Golf: Professional Methods British And
    American" .... 1930 .... $95
"Golf: Professional Methods British And
    American" .... 1933 .... $75
"Modern Golfing Methods By British And
    American Experts" .... 1933 .... $45
"Methods of The Golf Masters" .... 1934 .... $75
"One Way Golf" .... 1935 .... $85
"One Way Golf, The Secret And Simplicity
    of The Perfect Swing" .... 1935 .... $60
Eddie MacCabe:
"The Ottawa Hunt Club, 75 Years of History
    1908-1983" .... 1983 .... $90
Maccauvlei G. C:
"Maccauvlei Golf Club" .... 1948 .... $50
Terrence MacClure:
"Golf Ching" .... 1997 .... $15
Alistair Macdonald:
"The History of Langley Park Golf Club
    1910-1985" .... 1985 .... $50
"Deeside Golf Club Centenary 1903-2003" .... 2004 .... $95
Bob MacDonald:
"Golf" .... 1927 .... $45
Charles B. MacDonald:
"National Golf Links of America" .... 1912 ....$1750
"Scotland's Gift: Golf" .... 1928 ....$1275
    Signed Limited Edtion (260 Copies) ... 1928 ....$6500
    Classics of Golf reprint .... 1985 .... $50
George MacDonald:
"Gutta Percha Willie" .... 1908 .... $75
John MacDonald:
"Crail Golfing Society, 1836-1986" .... 1986 .... $95
John S. MacDonald:
"Deck And Home Golf" .... 1905 .... $125
Robert G. MacDonald:
"Golf" .... 1927 .... $250
"Golf At A Glance" .... 1931 .... $95
Robert G. MacDonald & Leo Bolstad:
"Golf" .... 1961 .... $15

Thousands of color book illustrations visible at
www.rogeregilchrist.com

R. S. MacDonald:
"The Happy Golfer A Collection of Articles
    From The American Golfer Magazine
    1922-1936" .... 1997 .... $40
C. A. Macey:
"Golf Through Rhythm" .... 1957 .... $35
Udo Machat:
"Golf Courses of the Monterey Peninsula" ..... 1998 .... $20
"Poppy Hills Golf Course" .... 1998 .... $75
Machrihanish G. C.:
"Machrihanish Golf Club" .... 1919 .... $375
Jean MacKay:
Royal Dornoch Golf Club 1877-1977" .... 1977 .... $60
    Reprint .... 1997 .... $45
Thomas Mackay:
"A History of The Liverpool Golf Club" .... 1972 .... $30
Alister Mackenzie:
"The Spirit of St Andrews" .... 1995 .... $60
    Leather Bound Limited Edition .... 1995 .... $375
"Dr. Mackenzie's Golf Architecture"
    (700 Copies) .... 1982 .... $300
    Leather Bound Presentation Copy .... 1982 .... $695
Alister J. Mackenzie:
"Golf Architecture: Economy In Course
    Contruction And Green Keeping" .... 1920 ...... $3995
    Reprint .... 1987 .... $50
    Japanese Reprint .... 1997 .... $50
Alister J. Mackenzie, L. A. & P. J. A. Berkmans:
"Description of The Bobby Jones Golf Course
    With An Historical Sketch of Fruitlands" 1924 ...... $1,250
David A. MacKenzie:
"A History of The Melrose Golf Club" .... 1979 .... $30
Marlin MacKenzie:
"Golf The Mind Game" .... 1990 .... $10
Richard MacKenzie:
"A Wee Nip At The 19th Hole" .... 1997 .... $15
Mrs. Louie Mackern & M. Boys:
"Our Lady of The Green" .... 1899 .... $950
Richard T. Mackey:
"Golf" .... 1962 .... $10
"Golf: Learn Through Auditory And Visual
    Cues" .... 1978 .... $10
A. C. Makie:
"Stonehaven Golf Club 1888-1988" .... 1988 .... $65

Keith Mackie:
"Piccadilly World of Golf" .... 1972 .... $30
"Golf At St Andrews" .... 1995 .... $60
Keith Mackie & Iain Crawford:
"Capital Golf: A Colour Guide To More Than
    35 Courses In And Around Edinburgh" . 1984 .... $15
Ian M. Mackintosh:
"Troon Golf Club Its History From 1878" .... 1974 .... $20
Mackintosh & Sweet:
"Troon Golf Club 1878-1978" .... 1978 .... $65
Muir Maclaren:
"The Australian and New Zealand Golfer's
    Handbook" .... 1957 .... $35
"The Golfer's Bedside Book" .... 1976 .... $15
G. A. MacLean:
"Golf Through The Ages" .... 1923 .... $125
John MacLean:
"Coventry Golf Club 1887-1987" .... 1987 .... $25
R. J. Maclennan:
"Golf At Gleneagles" .... 1921 .... $950
John MacLeod:
"The Golfer's Dictionary" .... 1935 .... $350
John Macleod:
"A History of The Royal Dornoch Golf Club
    1877-1999" .... 2000 .... $95
Ray MacMillan:
"Masterminding Golf" .... 1960 .... $10
T. J. Macnamara:
"The Gentile Golfer" .... 1905 .... $450
Jeff MacNelly:
"A Golf Handbook" .... 1996 .... $20
Maco Publishing:
"Pro's Handbook of Golf" .... 1968 .... $10
Peter MacPhee:
"Ballater Golf Club 1892-1992" .... 1992 .... $75
Duncan MacPherson:
"Golf Simplified" .... 1936 .... $125
A. J. Macself:
"Lawns And Sports Greens" .... 1932 .... $55
Angus MacVicar:
"Dunaverty Golf Club - The First 100 Years" .. 1989 .... $45
"Golf In My Gallowses" .... 1983 .... $20
"Murder At The Open" .... 1965 .... $145
"The Painted Doll Affair" .... 1973 .... $425

Thousands of color book illustrations visible at
www.rogeregilchrist.com

Paul MacWeeney:
 "Woodbrook Golf Club 1926-1976" .... 1976 .... $30
Rev. Thomas McWilliam:
 "Around The Fireside" .... 1927 .... $30
Rob Maetzig:
 "Ngamotu 1893-1993 A Centennial History".. 1993 .... $45
David Magowan:
 "The Scarsdale Golf Club 1898-1948"
 (800 Copies) .... 1948 .... $185
James J. Mahon:
 "Baltusrol, 90 Years In The Mainstream of
 American Golf" .... 1985 .... $45
Jack Mahoney:
 "The Golf History of New England" .... 1973 .... $85
 "Centennial Edition" .... 1995 .... $50
Mahood:
 "Fore!" .... 1959 .... $15
Mahopac G. C:
 "Mahopac Golf Club 1898-1980"
 (500 Copies) .... 1980 .... $60
Stewart Maiden:
 "Ten Lessons In Golf" .... 1930 .... $550
James Maidment:
 "A Book of Scotish Pasquils 1568-1715" .... 1868 .... $300
Alex Main:
 "Fortrose And Rosemarkie Golf Club
 1888-1988" .... 1988 .... $40
Sal Maiorana:
 "Through The Green" .... 1993 .... $15
 "Oak Hill Centennial 1901-2001" .... 2001 .... $55
Lewine Mair:
 "The Dunlop Lady Golfer's Companion" .... 1980 .... $10
Norman Mair:
 "Muirfield, Home of The Honorable Company
 1744-1994" .... 1994 .... $95
 Signed Limited Edition (100 Copies) .... 1994 .... $575
 "Pillars of The Temple" .... 1995 .... $20
Robert Majoribanks:
 "A History of the Royal Ottawa Golf Course
 1891-1991" .... 1991 .... $45
Malden G. C.:
 "The Story of The Malden Golf Club
 1893-1990" .... 1990 .... $30

Thousands of color book illustrations visible at
www.rogeregilchrist.com

Bill Mallon MD:
"The Golf Doctor".................................... 1996 .... $10
Ralph Maltby:
"Golf Club Assembly Manual"...................... 1981 .... $30
"Golf Club Design, Fitting, Alteration
        And Repair" .... 1974 .... $35
"Golf Club Repair In Pictures" .... 1978 .... $20
Manchester C. C:
"Manchester Country Club 1923-1973" .... 1973 .... $65
Manchester Courier:
"Manchester Courier Guide To Lancashire,
        Cheshire, Derbyshire And North
        Wales Golf"..................................... 1914 .... $95
Manchester G. C:
"The Manchester Golf Club" .... 1936 .... $350
Manchester Guardian:
"Golf In 1938"....................................... 1938 .... $75
"Golf In 1939"....................................... 1939 .... $50
Lloyd Mangrum:
"Fine Points of Golf" .... 1958 .... $55
"Golf: A New Approach"............................ 1949 .... $25
"How To Break 90 At Golf" .... 1952 .... $15
"How To Drive A Golf Ball"......................... 1955 .... $20
"How To Play Better Golf"........................... 1954 .... $20
James S. Manion:
"Culbertson's Contract Golf" .... 1932 .... $120
Manito Golf & C. C:
"Manito Golf And Country Club 50
        Years 1922-1972"............................ 1972 .... $30
Carol Mann:
"The 19th Hole"..................................... 1992 .... $15
Frederick G. Mann:
"Lord Rutherford On The Golf Course".......... 1976 .... $35
Reg Manning:
"From Tee To Cup".................................. 1954 .... $35
Mannings Heath G. C:
"Mannings Heath Golf Club"....................... 1955 .... $10
Clifford Mansfield:
"A Hundred Years of Golf In Glossop".......... 1994 .... $35
Gary Mansfield:
"A History of Golf In Victoria Australia" .... 1987 .... $35
Will Manson:
"A Deadly Game" .... 1967 .... $35

Thousands of color book illustrations visible at
www.rogeregilchrist.com

Manual for Caddies:
"Manual For Caddies" .... 1937 .... $150
Manufactuers' G. C:
"Proposed Country and Golf Club..." .... 1923 .... $600
G. E. Mappin:
"The Golfing You"...................................... 1948 .... $45
Major G. F. Mappin:
"The Haunted Major" .... 1937 .... $25
Ray March:
"A Paradise Called Pebble Beach" .... 1992 .... $45
David Marchuk:
"The Golf Log Book" .... 1989 .... $10
John Margolies:
"Miniature Golf" .... 1987 .... $40
Marietta:
"Golf Stories" .... 1905 .... $750
Robert Marjoribanks:
"Royal Ottawa Golf Club 1891-1991" .... 1991 .... $85
Sara W. Marks:
"Fore! Women Only; An Anatomy of A
         Woman's Golf Club" .... 1966 .... $15
John P. Marquand:
"Life At Happy Knoll" .... 1957 .... $45
Dave Marr:
"Woods From The Tee And Fairway,
         A Flip Vision Golf Manual" .... 1965 .... $35
Julie Mars:
"Golf. Life On The Course"........................... 1994 .... $10
Irving T. Marsh and Edward Ehre:
"Best Sports Stories"................................. 1944 .... $35
Thomas Marsh:
"Blackheath Golfing Lays" .... 1873 ....$6250
Harry Marshall:
"Sixty Years And More A History of Low
         Laithes Golf Club" .... 1985 .... $25
Keith B. Marshall:
"Golf Galore"... 1960 .... $40
"In Golf We Trust"..................................... 1988 .... $30
Robert Marshall:
"The Haunted Major" .... 1902 .... $250
         Reprint.. 1937 .... $50
         Reprint.. 1951 .... $35
         Reprint.. 1960 .... $30
         Reprint.. 1973 .... $20

Thousands of color book illustrations visible at
www.rogeregilchrist.com

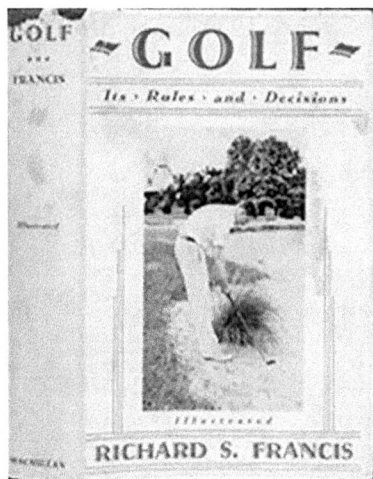

Francis – Golf It's Rules and
Decisions

Gimcrack - Gimcrackiana

Golf at a Glance
(1st Edition)

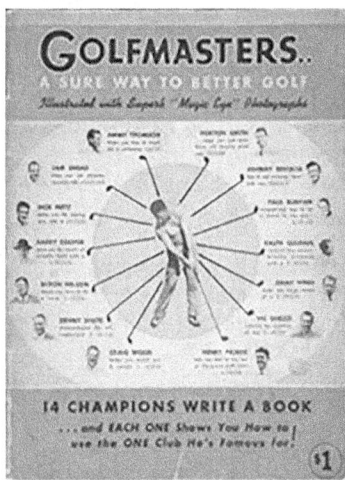

Golf Masters – A Sure Way to
Better Golf

Reprint.. 1999 .... $15
"The Enchanted Golf Clubs"........................ 1920 .... $145
Stuart Marshall:
"One Up And One To Go" .... 1997 .... $10
David Martin:
"Minchinhampton Golf Club Centenary
    History 1889-1989" .... 1989 .... $45
Harry B. Martin:
"Fifty Years of American Golf"..................... 1936 .... $650
    Signed Limited Edition (355 copies)..... 1936 ......$1250
    Argosy Reprint .... 1966 .... $95
"The Garden City Golf Club 1899-1949"
    (600 Copies).................................... 1949 .... $250
"Golf For Beginners".................................. 1930 .... $75
"Golf Made Easy" .... 1932 .... $75
"Golf Yarns" .... 1913 .... $450
"Great Golfers In The Making" .... 1932 .... $65
"How To Play Golf".................................... 1936 .... $85
"The Making of A Champion" .... 1928 .... $425
"Pictorial Golf"... 1928 .... $75
"Sketches Made At The Winter League of
    Advertising Interests, At Pinehurst,
    North Carolina, January 1915"............ 1915 .... $175
"St. Andrews Golf Club 1888-1963"............. 1963 .... $350
    Limited Edition (500 Copies) .... 1963 .... $695
"What's Wrong With Your Game"................. 1930 .... $65
Harry B. Martin & A.B. Halliday:
"Saint Andrews (New York) Golf
    Club 1888-1938" (500 Copies) .... 1938 .... $750
"Saint Andrews Golf Club 1888-1963".......... 1963 .... $400
J. Peter Martin:
"Adirondack Golf Courses..."...................... 1987 .... $35
    Second Edition .... 1993 .... $25
"The Centennial History of the Whiteface
    Golf Club 1898-1998 .... 1998 .... $45
James J. Martin:
"Torresdale-Frankford Country Club
    1896-1996" .... 1996 .... $45
John S. Martin:
"The Curious History of The Golf Ball" .... 1968 .... $250
    Signed by Martin (500 Copies)........... 1968 .... $425
Thomas J. Martin:
"Riverside Golf Club An American Landmark
    1893-1993" .... 1993 .... $35

Dr. Wayne E. Martin:
"An Insight Into Sports"............................ 1984 .... $50
George Martine:
"Reliquiae divi Andreae"............................ 1797 .... $750
Martini:
"Martini Course Charts of Famous British
    Golf Courses".................................... 1958 .... $495
Maryland Interclub Seniors:
"A History of MISGA 1976-1985"................. 1985 .... $40
Marco Mascardi:
"World Cup Golf"...................................... 1991 .... $20
Gard Mason:
"Durand Eastman Golf Club Member
    Information Package"......................... 1978 .... $10
J. T. Mason:
"Build Yourself A Golf Swing By The Seven
    Steps of The Mason Methods"............. 1974 .... $10
Jerry Mason:
"The Golf Club At Aspetuck" .... 1974 .... $65
Massachusetts Golf Association:
"1914 Yearbook"...................................... 1915 .... $95
"1939 Yearbook....................................... 1939 .... $55
"Caddie Instruction Manual" .... 1946 .... $65
    1955 Edition .... 1955 .... $35
    1958 Edition .... 1958 .... $35
"Massachusetts Golf Association"..................... 1927 .... $75
"Massachucetts Golf Association Rule Book .... 1931 .... $50
"Massachusetts Golf Association
    50th Anniversary"............................. 1953 .... $25
"Massachusetts Golf Association Official
    Handicap List" .... 1920 .... $25
S. M. Masse:
"Caddy Savvy" .... 1947 .... $60
Massereene G. C:
"Massereene Golf Club 1895-1974" .... 1975 .... $55
I. H. Masson & M. H. Hill:
"Littlestone Golf Course 1888-1988"
    (600 Copies) .... 1988 .... $75
Arnaud Massy:
"Golf" French Edition .... 1911 .... $450
    English Edition .... 1914 .... $150
    U.S Edition .... 1922 .... $95

Master Golf:
"Learn Golf With The Stars, The Neil
Coles Way" .... 1977 .... $15
Nick Mastroni;
"The Insiders Guide To Golf Equipment" .... 1997 .... $15
Donald Mackay Mathieson:
"The Golfer's Handbook" .... 1899 ....$1750
Thomas Mathison:
"The Goff"... 1743 .... $75,000
Second Edition .... 1763 .... $75,000
Third Edition .... 1793 .... $50,000
USGA Reprint (1400 Copies) .... 1981 .... $650
Bruce H. Matson:
" Golf in the Commonwealth"...................... 2004 .... $50
"Hermitage Country Club. A History of the
First Hundred Years. 1900-2000" .... 2000 .... $50
Geoffrey J. Matson:
"Off The Tee: Favourite Golfing Stories
and Anecdotes of The Famous" .... 1963 .... $15
D. B. Matthew:
"Broughty Golf Club History 1878-1978" ...... 1978 .... $25
William Mauchan:
"Picturesque Musselburgh And its Golf Links . 1906 .... $600
William Charles Maughan:
"Picturesque Musselburgh And Its Golf Links" 1906 ......$1,695
Reprint.. 1986 .... $75
Maxfli:
"Golf Penalties".. 1959 .... $50
Jessica Maxwell:
"Driving Myself Crazy" .... 2000 .... $20
Sir John Maxwell:
"A Diurnal of Remarkable Occurences That
Have Passed Within The Country
of Scotland...." .... 1833 .... $600
R. Stanley Maxwell:
"Clandeboye 2000" .... 2000 .... $10
George S. May:
"Highlights Of George S. May's Tam
O'Shanter Golf Tournaments
1941-1956" .... 1956 .... $45
John Allan May:
"Bedside Duffer" .... 1969 .... $20
"Duffer's A.B.C." .... 1970 .... $20
"Duffer's Discoveries" .... 1972 .... $20

"Duffer's Guide"... 1967 .... $25
"Duffer's Progress".................................... 1968 .... $20
Julian May:
   "The Masters".. 1975 .... $15
   "The PGA Championship Tournament".......... 1976 .... $15
   "Lee Trevino, The Golf Explosion"............... 1974 .... $15
   "The U.S. Open Championship".................... 1975 .... $15
Dick Mayer:
   "How To Think And Swing Like A Golf
      Champion"....................................... 1958 .... $20
Mayfield C. C:
   "The Mayfield Country Club 1912" .... 1912 .... $75
   "75th Anniversary: Mayfield 1911-1986"...... 1986 .... $45
John F. Mayhew:
   "Par Excellence, Highlights of Sixty-Five
      Years At Barton Hills Country Club
      1917-1982" .... 1983 .... $10
Cliff McAdam:
   "Golf Illustrated Presents Arnie".................. 1976 .... $15
   "How To Break 90/80/Par" .... 1973 .... $10
Alexander J. McAlister:
   "The Eternal Verities of Golf" .... 1911 .... $350
Evelyn Ditton McAllister:
   "Golf For Beginners. A Golfing Handbook"..... 1969 .... $15
Troon McAllister:
   "The Foursome"..................................... 2000 .... $20
Bert McAndrew & T. McClurg:
   "Basic Principles And Practice of Golf" .... 1975 .... $10
J. McAndrew:
   "Golfing Step By Step".............................. 1910 .... $350
J. McBain & W. Fernie:
   "Golf: Dean's Champion Handbooks" .... 1899 ......$2,995
John.O McCabe:
   "The First Eight Years: Douglas Park
      Golf Club"....................................... 1982 .... $95
Brian McCallen:
   "Golf Resorts of The World" .... 1993 .... $25
George McCallister:
   "Golfercises" .... 1960 .... $10
Colman McCarthy:
   "The Pleasures of The Game: The Theory
      Free Guide To Golf".......................... 1977 .... $30
John F. McCarthy:
   "The Beauty of Golf In New York State"........ 1989 .... $45

Keith McCartney:
"Tom Morris of St Andrews"......................... 1998 .... $15
Harry McCaw & Brum Henderson:
"Royal County Down Golf Club: The First
    Century" .... 1988 .... $100
"The Royal County Down Ladies Golf Club
    A Memoire"..................................... 1989 .... $75
R. M. McClaren:
"The Honorable Company of Edinburgh
    Golfers 1744-1944".................................. 1944 .... $650
Peter McCleery:
"More Instant Golf Lessons" .... 1985 .... $10
Whitney McClelland:
"The 1992 Viewer's Guide To Professional
    Golf"... 1991 .... $15
J. W. McClung:
"Edmonton Country Club. The Early Years.
    1896-1986" .... 1986 .... $35
Tom McCollister:
"Golf In Georgia" .... 1993 .... $20
Bob McCollum:
"Guide To Golf Course Marking" .... 1988 .... $60
John McConachie:
"The Moray Golf Club of Lossiemouth
    1889-1989" .... 1989 .... $35
James McConnaughey:
"Just Swing The Clubhead"......................... 1946 .... $40
Gary McCord:
"Golf For Dummies"................................... 1996 .... $5
"Just A Range Ball In A Box of Tiltleists"....... 1997 .... $5
Robert McCord:
"The Golf Book of Days"............................. 1995 .... $20
"Golf. An Album of Its Hiistory"................... 1998 .... $30
Mark H. McCormack:
"Arnie: The Evolution of A Legend".............. 1967 .... $25
"Success Secrets" .... 1989 .... $10
"Dunhill Golf Yearbook 1979"...................... 1979 .... $25
"Dunhill Golf Yearbook 1980"...................... 1980 .... $15
"Dunhill World of Professional Golf 1981" ..... 1981 .... $15
"Dunhill World of Professional Golf 1982" ..... 1982 .... $15
"Dunhill World of Professional Golf 1983" ..... 1983 .... $15
"Ebel World of Professional Golf 1984" .... 1984 .... $15
"Ebel World of Professional Golf 1985" .... 1985 .... $15
"Golf '67: World Professional Golf:

The Facts And Figures" .... 1968 .... $35
"The Wonderful World of Professional Golf"... 1973 .... $65
"The World of Professional Golf 1968" .... 1968 .... $35
"The World Of Professional Golf:
    Golf Annual 1969" .... 1969 .... $25
"The World of Professional Golf: Mark H.
    McCormack's Golf Annual 1970" .... 1970 .... $25
"The World of Professional Golf: Mark H.
    McCormack's Golf Annual 1971" .... 1971 .... $20
"The World of Professional Golf: Mark H.
    McCormack's Golf Annual 1972" .... 1972 .... $20
"The World of Professional Golf: Mark H.
    McCormack's Golf Annual 1973" .... 1973 .... $35
"The World of Professional Golf: Mark H.
    McCormack's Golf Annual 1974" .... 1974 .... $25
"The World of Professional Golf: Mark H.
    McCormack's Golf Annual 1975" .... 1975 .... $25
"The World of Professional Golf: Mark H.
    McCormack's Golf Annual 1976" .... 1976 .... $20
"The World of Professional Golf: Mark H.
    McCormack's Golf Annual 1977" .... 1977 .... $20
"The World of Professional Golf: Mark H.
    McCormack's Golf Annual 1978" .... 1978 .... $20
"The World of Professional Golf: Mark H.
    McCormack's Golf Annual 1979" .... 1979 .... $20
"The World of Professional Golf: Mark H.
    McCormack's Golf Annual 1980" .... 1980 .... $20
"The World of Professional Golf: Mark H.
    McCormack's Golf Annual 1981" .... 1981 .... $20
"The World Of Professional Golf: Mark H.
    McCormack's Golf Annual 1982" .... 1982 .... $20
"The World of Professional Golf: Mark H.
    McCormack's Golf Annual 1983" .... 1983 .... $20
"The World of Professional Golf: Mark H.
    McCormack's Golf Annual 1984" .... 1984 .... $20
"The World of Professional Golf: Mark H.
    McCormack's Golf Annual 1985" .... 1985 .... $20
"The World of Professional Golf:Mark H.
    McCormack's Golf Annual 1986" .... 1986 .... $20
"The World of Professional Golf: Mark H.
    McCormack's Golf Annual 1987" .... 1987 .... $20
"The World of Professional Golf: Mark H.
    McCormack's Golf Annual 1988" .... 1988 .... $20
"The World of Professional Golf: Mark H.

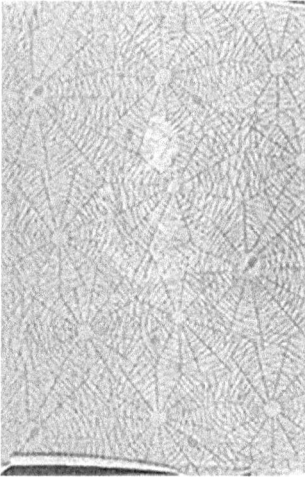

Goodner – The 75 History of
Shinnecock Hills (Spider Web
Dust Jacket)

Grierson – Delineations of
St Andrews

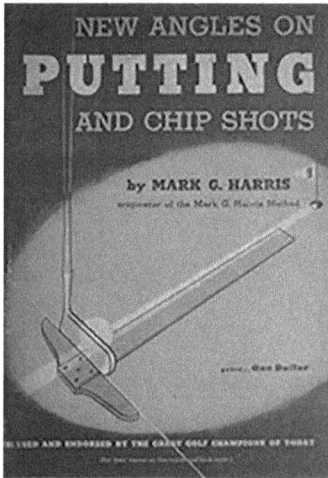

Harris – New Angles on Putting
And Chip shots

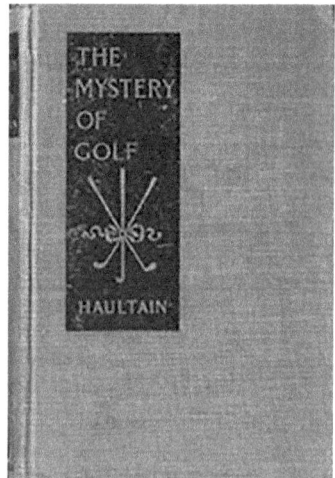

Haultain – The Mystery of Golf

Thousands of color book illustrations visible at
www.rogeregilchrist.com

McCormack's Golf Annual 1989"......... 1989 .... $20
"The World of Professional Golf: Mark H.
    McCormack's Golf Annual 1990"......... 1990 .... $20
"The World of Professional Golf: Mark H.
    McCormack's Golf Annual 1991"......... 1991 .... $20
"The World of Professional Golf: Mark H.
    McCormack's Golf Annual 1992"......... 1992 .... $20
"The World of Professional Golf: Mark H.
    McCormack's Golf Annual 1993"......... 1993 .... $20
"The World of Professional Golf: Mark H.
    McCormack's Golf Annual 1994"......... 1994 .... $20
"The World of Professional Golf: Mark H.
    McCormack's Golf Annual 1995"......... 1995 .... $20
"The World of Professional Golf: Mark H.
    McCormack's Golf Annual 1996"........ 1996 .... $20
"The World of Professional Golf: Mark H.
    McCormack's Golf Annual 1997"......... 1997 .... $30
"The World of Professional Golf: Mark H.
    McCormack's Golf Annual 1998"......... 1998 .... $20
"The World of Professional Golf: Mark H.
    McCormack's Golf Annual 1999"......... 1999 .... $20
"The World of Professional Golf: Mark H.
    McCormack's Golf Annual 2001"......... 2001 .... $25
Bill McCormick:
"The Complete Beginner's Guide To Golf" ..... 1974 .... $15
J. McCormick:
"Fore: How To Play Good Golf".................... 1932 .... $150
Clint McCowan:
"The Member Guest" .... 1995 .... $25
Bill McCreath:
"One Hundred Years of Golf at Goswick"....... 1990 .... $45
Andrew McCredie:
"Capilano Golf and Country Club. The
    Making of a Legend" (100 Copies)....... 2004 .... $95
Carol McCue:
"How To Conduct Golf Club Championships" . 1964 .... $10
Vade McCum:
"The Golfers"... 1909 .... $150
J. McCullough:
"Golf: Containing Practical Hints With
    Rules of The Game" .... 1899 ......$2,750
D. J. McDiardmid:
"100 Years of Golf At Machrihanish
    1876-1976" .... 1976 .... $65

Thousands of color book illustrations visible at
www.rogeregilchrist.com

Bob McDonald & Les Bolstad:
"Golfers Handbooks" (Set Of 4).................. 1951 .... $95
"How To Improve Your Golf"....................... 1958 .... $15
Doug McDonald:
"Home On The Range".............................. 1996 .... $10
H. Spencer McDonald:
"Pacific Coast Golf And Outdoor Sports" .... 1913 .... $200
Norman McDonald:
"Strathfield Golf Club Golden Jubilee
    1931-1981".................................... 1981 .... $35
Michael McDonnell:
"The Complete Book of Golf" .... 1985 .... $20
"Golf: The Great Ones" .... 1971 .... $25
"Great Moments In Sport: Golf" .... 1974 .... $30
"The World of Golf 1971-1972" .... 1972 .... $30
Bill McDonough:
"Common Sense Golf" .... 1975 .... $10
Stan McDougal:
"101 Great Golf Jokes and Stories".............. 1968 .... $10
"The World's Greatest Golf Jokes" .... 1980 .... $10
Donald McDougall:
"Boswell & Son"...................................... 1978 .... $35
"Davie"... 1977 .... $20
Roy L. McFrederick:
"The Golfer's Handbook, A Manual On Golf
    As It Is Played And Taught By The
    Old Masters".................................... 1926 .... $850
Charles McGehee:
"History of The Southern Seniors Golf
    Association Fifty Years On 1930-1980" 1980 .... $35
Mike McGetrick:
"The Scramblers Dozen" .... 2000 .... $15
Kevin McGimpey:
"The Story of the Golf Ball" .... 2003 .... $275
    Limited Edition of 20 .... 2003 .... $750
Donald McGraw:
"The Full Bag, Or The Golf Duffer's Golf Book:
    How To Keep From Breaking 100"....... 1962 .... $15
George F. McGregor:
"Open Reflections" .... 1948 .... $30
"Open Reflections" .... 1949 .... $20
"Open Reflections" .... 1950 .... $20
"Open Reflections" .... 1952 .... $20

Ian McGregor:
"Tain Golf Club 1890-1990"......................... 1990 .... $20
Peter McGuire:
"Riverside and the People Who Made it
    Special"... 1997 .... $150
Robert McGurn & S.A. Williams:
"Golf Power In Motion"............................... 1967 .... $25
John C. McHose:
"The Wilshire Country Club 1919-1979" .... 1979 .... $40
"The Wilshire Country Club 1919-1989" .... 1989 .... $30
Hugh McHugh:
"Down the Line With John Henry"................ 1901 .... $75
Ralph McInerny:
"Law And Arbor" .... 1995 .... $25
"Lying Three: A Father Dowling Mystery"...... 1979 .... $35
Jan McIntosh:
"Hooked On Golf"....................................... 1982 .... $10
Dugald McIntyre:
"Beyond Mount Pisgah: The History of
    Millport Golf Club"............................. 1988 .... $45
David McKay:
"Leith And The Origins of Golf".................... 1984 .... $15
Archibald McKinlay:
"Our First 100 Years: Rockford Country Club"1999 .... $35
S. L. McKinlay:
"Gleneagles Hotel Golf Courses, Scotland".... 1961 .... $75
"The Millport Golf Club"............................... 1948 .... $35
"The Belleisle Golf Courses"......................... 1952 .... $35
"Western Gailes 1897-1947"......................... 1947 .... $35
"Scottish Golf And Golfers"......................... 1992 .... $35
Richmond McKinney:
"The Honourable Company of Edinburgh
    Golfers 1744-1944" .... 1944 .... $800
Iaen McLachlan:
"Attack The Flag" .... 1977 .... $10
"One Hundred Golf Tips By Leading
    Australian And New Zealand Golfers"... 1973 .... $20
"Putting Tips From The Top" .... 1980 .... $10
"Swing To Win, The Story And Techniques of
    Leading Proette, Judy Perkins"............ 1975 .... $10
Louis R. McLain:
"St Augustine Golf Club 1909-1910" .... 1010 .... $250
"St Augustine Golf Club 1910-1911" .... 1911 .... $175

Thousands of color book illustrations visible at
www.rogeregilchrist.com

Owen P. McLain:
"Hooks & Slices: The First Eighty Years at
      the Everett Golf and Country Club"...... 1992 .... $60
R. M. McLaren:
"The Honorable Company of Edinburgh
      Golfers 1744-1944"......................... 1944 ....$1050
Jack McLean:
"One Knuckle Grip" .... 1939 .... $70
"Why Not Beat Bogey"............................. 1938 .... $75
Jim McLean:
"Clontarf Golf Club 1912-1987".................... 1987 .... $35
Terry McLean:
"A Simpler Place In Time, Golfing In
      New Zealand" .... 1980 .... $20
Callum McLeod:
"What St Andrews Means To Me"................. 1992 .... $35
Rod McLeod:
"St. Andrews Old" .... 1970 .... $25
Vickie McLeod:
"Comox Golf Club. The First Fifty:
      1934-1984" .... 1984 .... $35
Leo McMahon:
"Royal Porthcawl Golf Club 1891-1991"........ 1991 .... $95
Terrence A McMahon:
"Country Club of Scranton. A History
      1896-1987" .... 1987 .... $55
Thomas G. McMahon:
"Golf's Professional Man".......................... 1935 .... $45
"What Price Uniformity? The Golf
      Handicap Situation" .... 1966 .... $30
Valarie McMahan:
"Bumpsies: The Golf Ball Kids".................... 1929 .... $275
P. McMaugh:
"Golf Green Construction" .... 1955 .... $65
John McMillan:
"Darley Golf Course Centenary 1911-2011" .. 2011 .... $225
Robin McMillan:
"The Golfers Home Companion" .... 1993 .... $15
"365 One Minute Golf Lessons" .... 1994 .... $10
John McMurtie:
"The Golfers' Guide And Official Handbook
      For Scotland 1901-1902" .... 1902 .... $975
H. B. McNally:
"Mt Bruno Country Club Some Historical

Notes 1918-1978" .... 1978 .... $125
"Bruno 1918-1993" .... 1993 .... $75
Rand McNally:
"All About Golf" .... 1975 .... $20
J. Gordon McPherson:
"Golf And Golfers, Past And Present" .... 1891 ...... $1,000
USGA Reprint (1550 Copies) .... 1991 .... $150
Eoin McQuillan:
"The Fred Daly Story" .... 1978 .... $55
D. G. McRae:
"The Principle of Human Automation As
Applied To Golf" .... 1945 .... $20
Joseph W. McSpadden:
"How To Play Golf" .... 1907 .... $100
Michael McSweeney:
"Galway Golf Club 1895-1995" .... 1995 .... $25
Michael McTeigue:
"The Keys To The Effortless Golf Swing" .... 1985 .... $15
Paul McWeeney:
"Milltown Golf Club Golden Jubilee" .... 1981 .... $20
Mrs L. T. Meade:
"The Heart of Gold" .... 1902 .... $45
Paul Meadows:
"Cape Cod Golf Guide" .... 1986 .... $15
James A. G. Mearns:
"200 Years of Golf 1780-1980 Royal
Aberdeen Golf Club" .... 1980 .... $75
Standish F. Medina:
"A History of The Westhampton Country
Club 1890-1955" .... 1955 .... $125
Tom Meateer:
"Warrenport Golf Club 1893-1993" .... 1993 .... $40
Ross Mehalski & John Skinner:
"The Christchurch Golf Club 1873-1973,
A Century of Golf In Christchurch" ...... 1973 .... $50
Bill Mehlhorn:
"Golf Secrets Exposed" .... 1984 .... $40
Joseph G. Mele & Charles R. Wayne Jr.:
"A Golfer's Guide To Public Golf Courses
In New Jersey Vol. 1 North Jersey" ...... 1985 .... $25
Michael Melford & Bob Fenning:
"Denham Described. A History of Denham
Golf Club 1910-1992" .... 1992 .... $65

Thousands of color book illustrations visible at
www.rogeregilchrist.com

Mendip G. C:
"Mendip Golf Club" .... 1965 .... $25
Al Mengert:
"Master The Pro's Swing With Al Mengert's
 Rythym Master"............................... 1981 .... $25
Frank G. Menke:
"Encyclopedia of Sports" .... 1944 .... $25
"The All Sports Record Book"...................... 1950 .... $25
William A. Menton:
"The Golfing Union of Ireland 1891-1991" .... 1991 .... $50
Gordon Menzies:
"The World of Golf" .... 1982 .... $25
Scott Meredith:
"The Best of Wodehouse".......................... 1949 .... $35
Merion Cricket Club:
"The Merion Cricket Club: Charter, By Laws,
 Officers and Members" .... 1917 .... $195
"The Merion Cricket Club 1865-1965" .... 1965 .... $650
Merion G. C:
"Golf At Merion 1896-1976"....................... 1977 .... $35
Anthony F. Merrill:
"The Golf Course Guide" .... 1950 .... $35
Eddie Merrins:
"Golf For The Young" .... 1983 .... $10
"Swing The Handle-Not The Clubhead"........ 1973 .... $65
Ben Merwin:
"Idylwylde, First Fifty Years 1922-1972"...... 1972 .... $75
Leigh Metcalfe & Ted Mertz:
"Today's Humor, The Golf Number" .... 1927 .... $60
Don A. Metivier:
"A Club in the Country"............................. 1995 .... $30
Evelyn R. Metke:
"Ninety Years of Golf, a Chronology of Golf
 in Kelowna" .... 1992 .... $25
Metropolitan Golf Association:
"Caddie Management Manual" .... 1946 .... $30
"Electric Golf Survey In The Metropolitan
 New York Area" .... 1956 .... $25
"Golf Car Usage And Control In The
 Metropolitan New York Area".............. 1960 .... $25
"Manual of Caddie Instruction"................... 1957 .... $45
"Manual Caddie Management" .... 1932 .... $95
"Metropolitan Association Yearbook .... 1936 .... $35
"Metropolitan Golf Association" .... 1929 .... $125

Thousands of color book illustrations visible at
www.rogeregilchrist.com

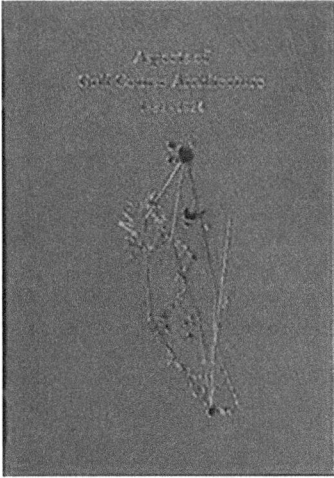

Hawtree – Aspects of Golf
Course Architecture (75 Copies)

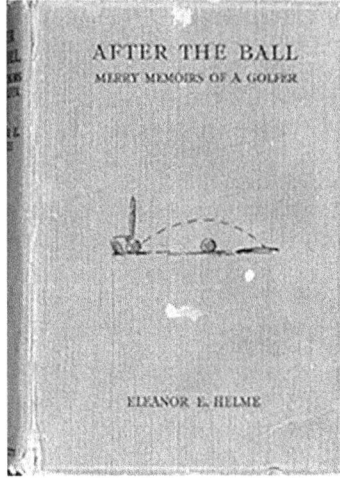

Helme – After the Ball
(1st Edition Dust Jacket)

Herd – My Golfing Life

Heywood – Guide To Golf

Thousands of color book illustrations visible at
www.rogeregilchrist.com

Metropolitan G. C:
 "Seventy Years: A History of the
    Metropolitan Golf Club"...................... 1973 .... $65
Dick Metz:
 "The Secret To Par Golf" .... 1940 .... $65
 "Short Cuts To Improve Your Golf" .... 1940 .... $45
Richard Metz:
 "The Graduated Swing Method".................... 1981 .... $20
Sol Metzger:
 "Putting Analyzed" .... 1929 .... $155
D. Swing Meyer:
 "The Method: A Golf Success Strategy" .... 1981 .... $25
Fred Meyer:
 "The Golf Special, A Musical Foozle,
    A Musical Comedy In Three Acts"........ 1909 .... $275
Meyrick & Queens Park G. C:
 "The Meyrick & Queens Park Golf Club"........ 1938 .... $175
 "The Meyrick & Queens Park Golf Club"........ 1948 .... $125
Rita R. Mhley:
 "Woodmont Country Club. A History" .... 1988 .... $25
Ron Michael:
 "More Birds Than Birdies: The Story of the
    Shepparton Golf Club"....................... 1985 .... $50
Thomas Michael:
 "The Encyclopedia For All Golfers" .... 1968 .... $20
 "Golf's Winning Stroke: Putting".................. 1967 .... $20
Cliff Michaelmore:
 "The Businessman's Book of Golf" .... 1981 .... $25
Herb Michaelson:
 " Sportin' Ladies"...................................... 1975 .... $30
Edward C. Michener:
 "The Everglades Club, A Retrospective
    1919-1985" .... 1985 .... $75
G. H. Micklem:
 "Help In The Interpretation of the Rules
    of Golf" .... 1979 .... $15
Mickleover G. C:
 "Mickleover Golf Club" .... 1938 .... $40
Cary Middlecoff:
 "Advanced Golf".. 1957 .... $35
 "Golf Doctor".. 1950 .... $45
 "The Golf Swing"....................................... 1974 .... $35
 "The Positive Approach To Better Golf"......... 1959 .... $35
 "Cary Middlecoff's Master Guide To Golf" ...... 1960 .... $35

Cary Middlecoff & Tom Michael:
"14 Classic Tips For The Year From The
 CBS Classic At Firestone C.C." .... 1967 .... $15
Ralph Middleton:
"Alwoodley Golf Club 1907-1983" .... 1985 .... $25
Midlothian C. C:
1898-1998 Midlothian Country Club" .... 1998 .... $15
Midvale G. & C. C:
"You Should Join the Midvale Golf
 And Country Club .... 1929 .... $125
Midwick C. C:
"Midwick Country Club Bylaws, House Rules,
 Roster of Members" .... 1930 .... $75
Vic Milburn & John Amy:
"History Of Bonnie Doon Golf Club
 1897-1997" .... 1997 .... $45
Alfred H. Miles:
"Golfer's Calendar" .... 1913 .... $75
Keith Miles:
"Bullet Hole" .... 1986 .... $30
"Double Eagle" .... 1987 .... $20
"Flagstick" .... 1991 .... $45
"Green Murder" .... 1991 .... $20
Rex Miles:
"From Morning Hill To Kirklands. A History
 of Peebles Golf Club. 1892-1992" .... 1992 .... $35
Mill Creek Park G. C:
"Mill Creek Park Golf Course 50th
 Anniversary 1927-1977" .... 1977 .... $35
Mill Hill G. C:
"Mill Hill Golf Club" .... 1963 .... $25
Beryl Buck Miller:
"Play A Round With Beryl Buck Miller" .... 1979 .... $10
Dick Miller:
"America's Greatest Golfing Resorts" .... 1977 .... $25
"Triumphant Journey" .... 1980 .... $65
Douglass B. Miller:
"So You Want To Play Golf" .... 1947 .... $15
Hack Miller:
"The New Billy Casper: More Important
 Things In Life Than Golf" .... 1968 .... $15
Helen M. Miller:
"So You Want To Be A Champion: Babe
 Didrickson Zaharias" .... 1961 .... $45

Johnny Miller:
"Pure Golf".. 1976 .... $35
Richard Miller:
"The Town & Country World of Golf" .... 1992 .... $50
Robert V. Miller:
"Golf, The Ageless Game" .... 1985 .... $10
Rev. T. D. Miller:
"Famous Scottish Links And Other Golfing
    Papers" .... 1911 ......$1,450
"The History of The Royal Perth Golfing
    Society" (150 Copies)........................ 1935 ......$1,900
    First Edition .... 1935 .... $600
Theodore T. Miller:
"Essex Country Club, Its History, Its
    Traditions"...................................... 1954 .... $30
Donald Millus:
"On The Southern Greens" .... 1983 .... $15
John Milton:
"A History of Royal Eastbourne Golf
    Club 1887-1987" .... 1987 .... $35
Milwaukee C. P. G. C:
"Golf on Milwaukee County Public Golf
    Courses" .... 1931 .... $300
"Golf on Milwaukee County Public Golf
    Courses" .... 1932 .... $195
H. Craig Miner:
"A History of The Wichita Country Club
    1900-1975" .... 1975 .... $25
Jeff Mingay:
"100 Years: A History of Essex Golf and
    Country Club: 1902-2002" .... 2002 .... $75
Richard V. Mirams:
"Moseley Milestones 1892-1992"................. 1993 .... $25
Charles Miron:
"Murder On The 18th Hole" .... 1978 .... $20
Abe Mitchell:
"Down To Scratch"   .... 1933 .... $90
"Essentials of Golf"................................... 1927 .... $155
    Swedish Edition .... 1928 .... $125
"Length On The Links" .... 1935 .... $75
Peter Mitchell:
"The Complete Golfer: Peter Thomson" .... 1991 .... $45
William F. Mitchell:
"Cochrane Castle Golf Club, Its History

From 1895" .... 1980 .... $45
"Centenary History of Cochrane Castle
    Golf Club".. 1995 .... $35
William M. Mitchell:
"Chislehurst Golf Club" (750 Copies)............ 1994 .... $45
George Mobbs:
"Northamptonshire Country Club,
    History of the Course" .... 1969 .... $25
Alex Moffat:
"Aloa Golf Club 1891-1991 a Centenary
    History"... 1991 .... $25
F. C. Moffatt:
"Seventy-Five Years of Golf, Morpeth
    Golf Club 1906-1981"........................ 1981 .... $25
Mohawk G. G:
"Mohawk Golf Club 1906"........................... 1906 .... $95
"Mohawk Golf Club 1912"........................... 1912 .... $75
Charles Monagan:
"The Country Club of Waterbury 1899-1999" 1999 .... $35
Hilario C. Moncado:
"360 Power Swing".................................... 1951 .... $10
Lord Moncrieff:
"Rufus Hickman of St Botolph's And Other
    Short Stories and Sketches"............... 1898 .... $135
Margorie M. Moncrieff:
"History of the Ladies Putting Club
    1867-1992" .... 1992 .... $75
Sil Monday:
"Golf In The Ohio Sun" .... 1970 .... $15
Monifieth G. C:
Monifieth Golf Club 1858-1958" .... 1958 .... $225
Monifieth G. L:
"Monifieth Golf Links Bazaar Book"
    (Hard Cover).................................... 1899 .... $10,000
"Monifieth Golf Links Bazaar Book" .... 1899 ....$1500
Monks of St Giles:
"Reminiscences of the Monks of St
    Giles" (3 Vols)......................... 1883-1911 .....$1350
William K. Montague:
"The Golf of Our Fathers" .... 1952 .... $350
"Rule Changes".. 1961 .... $25
Montclair G. C:
"Montclair Golf Club" .... 1935 .... $200
"Montclair Golf Club Club Book" .... 1936 .... $150

"Montclair Golf Club Club Book" .... 1959 .... $30
Monte Carlo C. C:
"Monte Carlo Country Club Presents
    The Lighter Side of Golf".................... 1982 .... $15
Monticeto:
"The Valley Club of Montecito 1928-1998"
    (1500 Copies) .... 1998 .... $75
Monterey Peninsula C. C:
"Monterey Peninsular Country Club" .... 1924 .... $400
"Membership List"..................................... 1926 .... $300
"Monterey Peninsula Country Club, Pebble
    Beach, The First fifty Years.
    1925-1975" .... 1975 .... $350
"Monterey Peninsula The Golf Capital
    of the World" .... 1960 .... $45
Ivan Montgomery:
"Dufftown Golf Club" .... 1996 .... $25
Orville Moody:
"Golf By Orville Who?" .... 1972 .... $15
Theodore Moone:
"Golf From A New Angle" .... 1934 .... $175
Moor Allerton G. C:
"A History of Moor Allerton Golf Club
    1923-1993" .... 1993 .... $25
Moore Park G. C:
"Moore Park Golf Club" .... 1968 .... $30
Bertha Moore:
"Bunkered: A Duologue For Two Women"..... 1922 .... $250
Charles Moore:
"The Mental Side of Golf" .... 1929 .... $95
Charles Moore:
"Reflections of Turtle Point. A 44 Year
    History"... 2004 .... $35
Kath Stewart Moore:
"Royal Portrush Ladies – a backward glance" 1992 .... $45
Moorestown Field:
"Four Score And Twenty Years of the
    Moorestown Field Club 1892-1992" ..... 1992 .... $30
Moortown G. C:
The Ryder Cup Memories Festival".............. 2000 .... $15
R. M. Morphett:
"Race Course to Fairways: A History of
    Long Island Country Club. Frankston".. 1988 .... $35

Frank W. Moran:
"Book of Scottish Courses" .... 1939 .... $95
"Golfers' Gallery" .... 1946 .... $50
"Gullane Golf Club" .... 1955 .... $65
"Scotland For Golf".................................... 1962 .... $35
"Westlinks Golf Course New Club, North
　　Berwick".. 1954 .... $45
Sharron Moran:
"Golf Is A Woman's Game Or How To Be
　　A Swinger On The Fairway" .... 1971 .... $15
Moray G. C:
"The Moray Golf Club At Lossiemouth
　　1889-1989" .... 1988 .... $40
John F. Moreton:
"The Golf Courses of James Braid".............. 1996 .... $250
　　Limited Edition of 525
"A Century of Golf at Huntercombe" .... 2001 .... $45
"A Century of Warwickshire County Golf"...... 2006 .... $45
"Crompton's Bounty: Erewash Valley Golf
　　Club 1905-2000" .... 2005 .... $45
"Ladbrook Park Golf Club: The Frst
　　Hundred Years 1908-2008 .... 2008 .... $45
"Porters Park Golf Club"............................ 1998 .... $45
"The Centenary History of the Worcester
　　Union of Golf Clubs"........................ 2005 .... $40
"The Story of Saddleworth Golf Club".......... 1998 .... $15
John F. Moreton & Iain Cunningham:
"James Braid and his Four Hundred Golf
　　Courses" .... 2013 .... $150
Albert A. Morey:
"Tee Time, Enjoy It And Live" .... 1952 .... $10
Brian Morgan:
"A World Portrait of Golf" .... 1988 .... $45
Jerome E. Morgan:
"Golf Analysis Log"................................... 1979 .... $10
John Morgan:
"Golf".. 1976 .... $15
W. A. Morgan:
"The House On Sport".............................. 1898 .... $95
Jim Moriarty:
"Tee Off!" .... 1991 .... $15
William Morison:
"Memorabilia of The City of Perth".............. 1806 .... $550

Thousands of color book illustrations visible at
www.rogeregilchrist.com

Hilton & Smith – The Royal &
Ancient Game of Golf
(100 Copies)

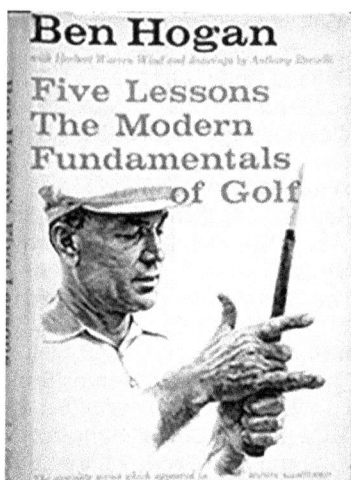

Hogan – Five Lessons
(Dust Jacket)

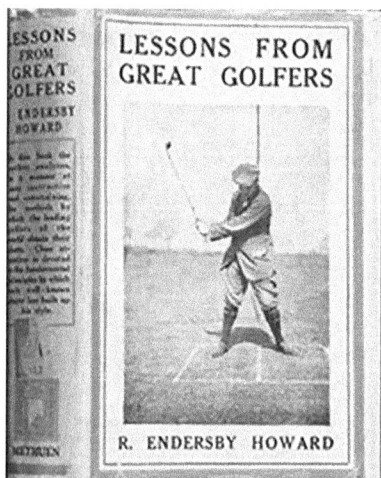

Howard – Lessons from Great
Golfers

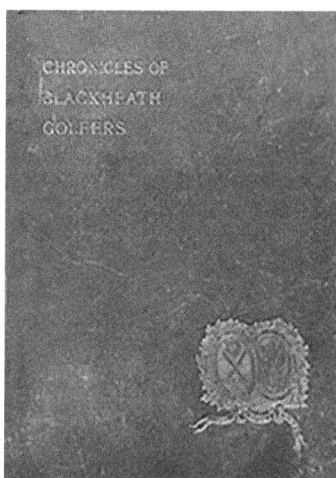

Hughes – Chronicles of Blackheath
Golfers   (1st Edition)

David C. Morley:
"The Missing Links: Golf And The Mind" .... 1976 .... $25
Michael E. Morley:
"The Art and Science of Putting" .... 1982 .... $15
Sam Morley:
"If It Wasn't For Golf" .... 1988 .... $20
"By Yon Bonnie Links!" .... 1990 .... $15
Don Morrell:
"The Dunes Club, A Chronicle of one of
    America's Finest Golfing Institutions" .. 1990 .... $35
H. Messon Morris:
"Church Stetton Golf Club" .... 1967 .... $25
John Morris & Leonard Cobb:
"Great Golf Holes of Hawaii" .... 1977 .... $50
"Great Golf Holes of New Zealand" .... 1971 .... $35
Robert Morris:
Hillwood Country Club: Excellence for
    Fifty Years 1953-2003 .... 2004 .... $35
Warren E. Morris:
"The Toltec Twist, Or My Dad's Notebook
    on Golf" .... 1955 .... $150
Elaine Morrison:
"Peace Portal Golf Club 75 Year 1928-2003" . 2003 .... $25
Alex J. Morrison:
"A New Way To Better Golf" .... 1932 .... $75
"Better Golf Without Practice" .... 1940 .... $55
"Pocket Guide To Better Golf" .... 1934 .... $75
Erwin G. Morrison:
"Here's How In Golf" .... 1949 .... $20
"Here's How To Play Money Golf" .... 1953 .... $15
"Life With Par" .... 1958 .... $10
Ian Morrison:
"Great Moments In Golf" .... 1987 .... $15
"The Hamlin Encyclopedia of Golf" .... 1986 .... $25
"100 Great Golfers" .... 1988 .... $15
"Golf Facts" .... 1993 .... $15
"Who's Who In Golf" .... 1988 .... $10
J. S. F. Morrison:
"Around Golf" .... 1939 .... $250
Gertrude W. Morrison:
"The Girls of Central High On Track
    And Field" .... 1914 .... $75
Morie Morrison:
"Heres How In Golf" .... 1949 .... $95

Thousands of color book illustrations visible at
www.rogeregilchrist.com

"Life With Par"... 1958 .... $20
Stuart Morrison:
"Golf Faults: How To Improve Your
    Game Fifty Percent" .... 1912 .... $95
Charles & Ann Morse:
"Lee Trevino" .... 1974 .... $15
Malcolm Mortimer:
"The Spirit of Cavendish Golf With Burbage
    Ladies Golf Club 1899-1999"
    (650 Copies)................................... 2000 .... $35
Charles Mortimer & Fred Pignon:
"The Story of The Open Championship
    1860-1950" .... 1952 .... $95
Cecil W. Morton:
"Golf: The Confessions of A Golf Club
    Secretary" .... 1963 .... $45
John F. Morton:
"Porters Park Golf Club"............................ 1998 .... $45
Jerry Mosca:
"Experiencing Golf In Scotland: A Guide To
    Scottish Courses" .... 1984 .... $15
Moseley G. C:
"Moseley Golf Club"................................. 1939 .... $45
H. Vincent Moses:
"Victoria Club. Centennial Edition
    1903-2003 .... 2003 .... $65
R. J. H. Moses:
"Fore" .... 1937 .... $275
Ian Mosey & Don Mosey:
"On The Golf Tour".................................. 1989 .... $15
Most Convenient Setting Forth:
"A Most Convenient Setting Forth of Much
    Interesting Information Regarding
    Golf"... 1900 .... $120
Mount Maunganui G. C:
"Mount Maunganui Golf Club Goden Jubilee
    1935-1985" .... 1985 .... $45
Mountain Ash G. C:
"Mountain Ash Golf Club 1908-1983" .... 1983 .... $15
Mountain Lake:
"Mountain Lake 1927-1928" .... 1928 .... $300
Mountain View C. C:
"Early Days of The Mountain View
    Country Club 1898-1927" .... 1927 .... $125

"The Mountain View Country Club,
    Greensboro, Vermont, 1898-1976"...... 1977 .... $35
Paul Mousset:
    "Physiologie du Golf" 1949 150
Mowbray G. C:
    "Mowbray Golf Club" .... 1932 .... $125
Mt. Anthony:
    "The Mount Anthony Club of Bennington
    Centre Vermont" .... 1898 .... $150
    "The Mt Anthony Country Club".................... 1944 .... $75
Steve Mucha:
    "How To Break 100: Golfing Shortcuts
    The Pros Don't Teach You" .... 1982 .... $10
Graham Muir:
    "Dumfries and Galloway Golf Club
    1880-1980" .... 1980 .... $15
Muirfield:
    "Rules And Regulations of The Honorable
    Company of Edinburgh Golfers" .... 1899 ......$3,000
Muirfield Village G. C:
    "Muirfield Village Golf Club" .... 1977 .... $25
T. B. Mullholland:
    "Killymoon The First Century 1889-1989" ..... 1989 .... $75
Richard Mullins:
    "The Phoenix Open - A 50 Year History" .... 1984 .... $15
Richard J. Mullins:
    "Portarlington Golf Club: A History
    1908-1987" .... 1987 .... $25
Charlie Mulqueen:
    "The Baltray Century 1882-1992"................ 1992 .... $65
    "Kilkenny Golf Club Centenary Year
    1896-1996" .... 1996 .... $35
Mark Mulvoy:
    "Sports Illustrated Golf"............................ 1983 .... $10
Mark Mulvoy & Art Spander:
    "Golf: The Passion And The Challenge"......... 1977 .... $30
Thomas F. Mulvoy Jr.:
    "Wollaston Golf Club   " .... 1970 .... $75
Carey G Mumford:
    "Golf's Best Kept Secret"........................... 1988 .... $15
Rainer Mund & Gunther Munch:
    "Straight Golf"....................................... 1998 .... $10
Joseph S. F. Murdoch:
    "The Library of Golf 1743-1966"

(3300 copies) .... 1968 .... $125
"The Library of Golf 1743-1977".................. 1978 .... $200
"The Murdoch Golf Library" (950 Copies)...... 1991........ $125
    Subscribers Edition of 215 .... 1991........ $150
Joseph Murdoch & Janet Seagle:
    "Golf: A Guide To Information Sources" .... 1979 ...... $225
Judith Murdock & Heather Parker:
    "History of Naracoorte"............................. 1963.......... $50
John Murphy:
    "The Bathroom Golf Book"......................... 1990.......... $15
Michael Murphy & Rhea White:
    "In The Zone".. 1978.......... $10
Thomas J. Murphy:
    "Woodland Golf Club, A 75 Year History
        1902-1977" .... 1977.......... $30
    "50 Golden Years with the New England
        Senior Golfers' Association
        1922-1972" .... 1972.......... $75
Tom Murphy:
    "Official Used Glub Guide 1965" .... 1964.......... $45
Alan Murray & Marlene Roeder:
    "Courses Without Par" .... (nd).......... $55
Dr. C. M. Murray:
    "Greenkeeping In South Africa".................. 1932 .... $750
Francis Murray:
    "The British Open" .... 2000.......... $35
Henry A. Murray:
    "The Golf Secret" .... 1953.......... $30
    "More Golf Secrets"................................. 1954.......... $15
J. P. Murray:
    "Golfing In Ireland" . ... 1952........ $350
Robinson Murray:
    "Are Golfers Human?".............................. 1951.......... $25
David Musgrove:
    "Life With Lyle"...................................... 1989.......... $30
Musselburgh News:
    "Guide to Musselburgh and District.............. 1901........ $150
H. Burton Musser:
    "Turf Management" .... 1950........ $195
        Revised Edition.................................. 1962.......... $75
Bill Mutter:
    "Golf on Ayrshire Coast" .... 1981.......... $15
Charles Mutter:
    "The Story of The Piltdown Golf Course

1904-1974" .... 1974 .... $30
Edward L. Myers:
"Experiences of a Caddy" (with Dust Jacket) . 1927 ......$1125
Kent Myers:
"Golf In Oregon" .... 1977 .... $30
D. T. Mylrea:
"Sale Golf Club, Twenty-First Anniversary
1913-1934" .... 1934 .... $65
Rawson Myrick:
"Golfing in Vermont" .... 1934 .... $150
Naas Co. Kildare G. C:
"100 Years in the Short Grass 1898-1998" ... 1998 .... $65
C. J. Naden:
"Golf" .... 1970 .... $10
Charles S. Naftal:
"Games That Golfer's Play" .... 1984 .... $10
Kel Nagle & Others:
"The Secrets of Australia's Golfing Success".. 1961 .... $30
Nagoya G. C:
Nagoya Golf Club Wago Course 50 Years" ..... 1982 .... $275
Nairn G. C:
"The Nairn Golf Club 1887-1987" .... 1987 .... $45
Ted Naismith:
"Golf" .... 1948 .... $125
Virginia L. Nance & Elwood C Davis:
"Golf" .... 1966 .... $15
Napa Valley C. C:
"Napa Valley Country Club 1915-2004" .... 2004 .... $60
Mark Napier:
"Memoirs of The Marquis of Montrose"
(2 Vols) .... 1856 .... $375
Bruce Nash & Allan Zullo:
"Amazing But True Golf Facts" .... 1992 .... $10
"The Golf Hall of Shame" .... 1989 .... $10
"The Hole Truth" .... 1995 .... $10
George C. Nash:
"Letters To The Secretary of A Golf Club" ..... 1935 .... $225
"General Forecursue And Co.: More Letters
to The Secretary of A Golf Club" .... 1936 .... $125
With Dust Jacket .... 1936 .... $400
"Golfing In Northern Ireland" .... 1955 .... $275
"Golfing In Ulster" .... 1949 .... $350
"Whelks Postbag" .... 1937 .... $500

Joseph Nason:
"Beginning Golf, The Game" .... 1948 .... $20
"Golf Coach's Guide" .... 1975 .... $10
"Golf Fundamentals"................................. 1949 .... $15
"Golf In Physical Education"........................ 1941 .... $45
"Golf Instructor's Guide" .... 1972 .... $30
"Golf Lessons" .... 1950 .... $15
"Golf Operations Handbook And Golf
      Facility Development Guide"............... 1985 .... $35
"Golf Market Report" .... 1969 .... $15
"Golf Operator's Handbook"........................ 1956 .... $65
"Golf Range Operator's Handbook" .... 1947 .... $40
"How To Improve Your Golf"....................... 1952 .... $25
"Minature Golf Courses"............................. 1949 .... $35
"Miniature Putting Course And Golf Driving
      Range Manual"................................. 1971 .... $15
"Municipal Golf Course"............................. 1955 .... $65
"Organizing And Operating Public Golf
      Courses" .... 1971 .... $15
"Par 3 And Executive Golf Course, Planning
      And Operation Manual"...................... 1974 .... $15
"Planning And Building The Golf Course" ...... 1958 .... $25
"Planning And Building The Par-3 Or
      Executive Golf Course Manual" .... 1960 .... $15
"Planning And Conducting Competitive
      Golf Events"................................... 1973 .... $45
"Planning Information For Private And
      Daily Fee Golf Clubs".......................... 1978 .... $10
"Planning Information For Private Golf
      Clubs"... 1965 .... $20
"Public Opinion Survey" .... 1955 .... $10
"Planning The Professionals Shop"............... 1951 .... $45
"Skills & Tactics of Golf"............................. 1980 .... $10
"Speedy Golf"... 1969 .... $10
"Suggestions For Conducting Intramural
      Golf Tournaments"........................... 1950 .... $15
"The Easy To Learn Golf Rules" .... 1941 .... $40
National G. L:
"National Golf Links of America".................. 1916 ....$1000
"National Golf Links of America:
      Shinnecock Hills Long Island" .... 1927 .... $425
Michael Neary:
"Golf Quizz Book"..................................... 1994 .... $20

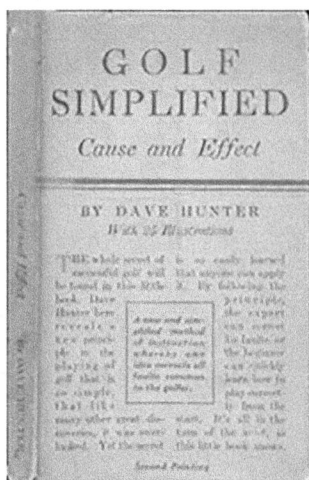

Hunter – Golf Simplified
(Dust Jacket)

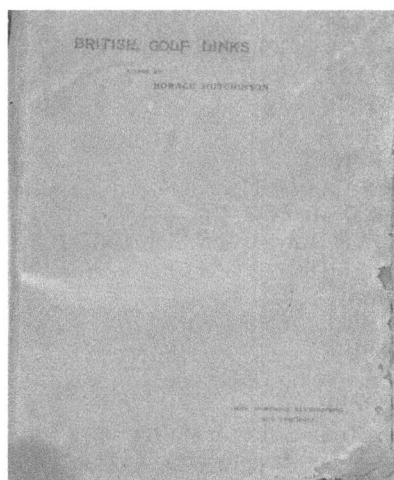

Hutchinson – British Golf Links
(1St Large Paper Edition in DJ)

Hutchinson – Hints on the
Game of Golf (1st Edition)

Jones Jr. – Bobby Jones on Golf

Thousands of color book illustrations visible at
www.rogeregilchrist.com

Cliff Neate:
"A History of Kingwood Golf Club
    1937-1987" .... 1987 .... $35
Neath G. C:
"Neath Golf Club"..................................... 1951 .... $25
Sylvia K. Neff:
"Know Your Golf" .... 1940 .... $45
Nefyn & District G. C:
"Nefyn & District Golf Club 1907-1982" .... 1982 .... $45
"Nefyn & District Golf Club" .... 1993 .... $25
Mark Neil:
"The Awful Golfer's Book"........................... 1957 .... $10
A.S. Neill:
"The Booming Of Bunkie" .... 1925 .... $150
Nancy Neill:
"More Than Bricks & Mortar: A History
    of the Atlanta Athletic Club" .... 1987 .... $35
Jim Nelford:
"Seasons In A Golfer's Life" .... 1984 .... $10
Adele Nelson:
"Somerset Hills Country Club 1899-1999" .... 1998 .... $200
Byron Nelson:
"How I Played The Game" .... 1993 .... $25
    Limited Edition of 500 signed .... 1993 .... $195
"How To Score Better Than You Swing"........ 1955 .... $35
"Pecora's Golf With Byron Nelson"
    (12 Pamphlets) .... 1951 .... $175
"The Little Black Book" .... 1995 .... $15
"Shape Your Swing The Modern Way" .... 1976 .... $25
"Winning Golf" .... 1946 .... $35
"The Byron Nelson Story"
    (600 Signed copies) .... 1980 .... $295
    Memorial Edition (300 Copies) .... 1980 .... $125
Kevin Nelson:
"The Golfer's Book of Daily Inspiration"........ 1996 .... $10
"The Greatest Golf Shot Ever Made" .... 1992 .... $10
Walter J. Nester Jr:
"New Haven Country Club 1898-1998 .... 1998 .... $20
Dwayne Netland:
"The Crosby: Greatest Show In Golf" .... 1975 .... $25
New Canaan C. C:
The Country Club of New Canaan
    1893-1998 .... 1998 .... $45

Roger E. Gilchrist's Guide to Collectible Golf Book Prices

T. Palmer Newbould:
"The Dieppe Golf Club" .... 1912 .... $175
Newbury And Crookham G. C:
"Newbury And Crookham Golf Club
    1873-1973" .... 1973 .... $25
Ernie Newell:
"Marlborough Golf Club 1888-1988" .... 1988 .... $45
Steve Newell:
"Golf Rules" .... 1995 .... $10
Steve Newell & Paul Foston:
"Achieving Better Golf" .... 1999 .... $10
"How To Play Golf" .... 1996 .... $20
New England Senior Golf Association:
"Bi Laws" .... 1960 .... $50
New Hampshire:
"The White Mountains of New Hampshire" ... 1917 .... $55
"Golf Courses Of New Hampshire" .... 1927 ....$1250
    Second Edition .... 1929 .... $950
    Fourth Edition .... 1931 .... $150
Joseph Newman:
"The Official Golf Guide of America For 1900" 1900 .... $900
Josiah Newman:
"The Official Golf Guide of The United States
    And Canada" .... 1899 ....$7500
    Second Edition .... 1900 ....$4500
"Newman's Guide To London Golf" .... 1913 ....$1075
M. H. Newmark:
"Something About Golf" .... 1922 .... $35
Newport G. C:
"New Port Golf Club Constitution and
    By-Laws" .... 1912 .... $150
Newton Abbot G. C:
"Newton Abbot Golf Club" .... 1954 .... $25
New York Newspaper:
"Fore" .... 1916 .... $375
New Yorker Magazine:
"Fore!" .... 1967 .... $10
New Zealand G. C:
"Around and About New Zealand Golf" .... 1989 .... $150
New Zealand Ladies Golf Union:
"Official Year Book" .... 1965 .... $75
"Official Year Book .... 1980 .... $25
"Official Year Book" .... 1981 .... $25
"Official Year Book" .... 1982 .... $25

"Official Year Book" .... 1985 .... $25
Niblick (Charles S. Hanks):
"Hints To Golfers" .... 1902 .... $450
        Limited Edition of 250) .... 1902 .... $750
        Limited edition of 1000 .... 1903 .... $150
"The Rules of Golf Authorised by the
        Royal and Ancient...." .... 1907 .... $450
Niblick (R. L. Kitching):
"Introduction To Golf" .... 1932 .... $155
Niblick (Reginald Sigel):
"Par Golf" .... 1926 .... $210
Niblick Club:
"The Niblick Club 1922-1947" .... 1947 .... $60
Bobby Nichols:
"Never Say Never: The Psychology of
        Winning Golf" .... 1965 .... $20
Lois Nichols:
"Green Hills Country Club 1930-1980" .... 1980 .... $20
Mary Nicholson:
"The Kittansett Club 1969-1999" .... 1999 .... $125
William Nicholson:
"An Almanac of 12 Sports" .... 1898 .... $395
Elinor Nickerson:
"Golf: A Woman's History" .... 1987 .... $30
Jack Nicklaus:
"18 Holes: The Master Professional Describes
        His Tee To Green Technique To You" ... 1970 .... $15
"All About The Grip" .... 1965 .... $15
"The Best Way To Better Golf" .... 1966 .... $15
"The Best Way To Better Golf Number 2" ...... 1968 .... $10
"The Best Way To Better Golf Number 3" ...... 1969 .... $10
"The Full Swing" .... 1984 .... $20
"Golf My Way" .... 1974 .... $20
"The Greatest Game of All: My Life In Golf" .. 1969 .... $50
"My 55 Ways To Lower Your Golf Score" .... 1964 .... $15
"Jack Nicklaus Golf Handbook: 25 Self
        Contained Lessons By The World's
        Greatest Golfer" .... 1973 .... $15
"Jack Nicklaus Plays The NCR South" .... 1969 .... $20
"Jack Nicklaus, Profile of A Champion" .... 1968 .... $20
"Jack Nicklaus' Lesson Tee: Back To Basics" . 1977 .... $15
"Jack Nicklaus' Lesson Tee" .... 1977 .... $15
"Jack Nicklaus' Playing Lessons" .... 1981 .... $20
"On And Off The Fairway: A Pictorial

Autobiography" .... 1978 .... $30
"My Story" .... 1997 .... $20
"Play Better Golf, The Swing From A-Z" .... 1980 .... $15
"Play Better Golf, Volume II The Short
    Game and Scoring" .... 1981 .... $15
"Play Better Golf Volume III Short Cuts
    To Lower Scores" .... 1983 .... $15
"Power Plus" .... 1966 .... $15
"Practice Tips" .... 1965 .... $15
"Reading And Controlling Putts" .... 1965 .... $15
"Take A Tip From Me" .... 1968 .... $15
"Total Golf Techniques" .... 1977 .... $15
"Winning Golf" .... 1969 .... $15
"The Worlds Great Golf Courses" .... 1989 .... $20

E. A. Nickson:
"The Lytham Century, A History of the Royal
    Lytham and St. Anne's Golf Club
    1886-1986" .... 1986 .... $165
"The Lytham Century and Beyond, A History
    of The Royal Lytham and St. Anne's
    Golf Club 1886-2000" .... 2000 .... $100

Eric Nicol & Dave More:
"Golf -The Agony & The Ecstacy" .... 1982 .... $15

Tom Nieporte & Don Sauers:
"Mind Over Golf: What 50 Top Pros Can
    Teach You About The Mysterious
    Mental Side of Golf" .... 1968 .... $25

Nippersink Lodge:
"Ye Golf Resort" .... 1924 .... $175

Nisbet's Yearbook:
"Nisbet's Golf Yearbook 1905" .... 1905 .... $475
"Nisbet's Golf Yearbook 1906" .... 1906 .... $400
"Nisbet's Golf Yearbook 1907" .... 1907 .... $400
"Nisbet's Golf Yearbook 1908" .... 1908 .... $400
"Nisbet's Golf Yearbook 1909" .... 1909 .... $375
"Nisbet's Golf Yearbook 1910" .... 1910 .... $400
"Nisbet's Golf Yearbook 1911" .... 1911 .... $350
"Nisbet's Golf Yearbook 1912" .... 1912 .... $375
"Nisbet's Golf Yearbook 1913" .... 1913 .... $350
"Nisbet's Golf Yearbook 1914" .... 1914 .... $350

Kwan-Yichi Nishimura:
"A Bibliography of Golf" .... 1960 .... $75
"History of Golf In Japan" .... 1976 .... $125

Thousands of color book illustrations visible at
www.rogeregilchrist.com

John Noble:
"The Official Duffer's Rules of Golf".............. 1981 .... $10
O. J. Noer:
"The O. J. Noer Memorial Turfgrass
      Collection"....................................... 1973 .... $300
James Nolan:
"Golf Antiques"... 1962 .... $65
"Of Golf And Dukes And Princes: Early Golf
      In France" (500 Copies).................... 1982 .... $50
William H. Nolan:
"Caddie Routine"....................................... 1951 .... $25
David Noonan:
"Memoirs of A Caddy".............................. 1991 .... $20
Jim Norland:
"Fifty Years of Mostly Fun: The History of
      Cherry Hills Country Club 1922-1972"
      (1000 Copies) .... 1972 .... $150
Greg Norman:
"Greg Norman: My Story" .... 1983 .... $20
"Shark Attack".. 1988 .... $15
"Advanced Golf".. 1995 .... $15
"Greg Norman's Instant Lessons" .... 1993 .... $15
Northbourne G. C:
"Northbourne Golf Club" .... 1951 .... $35
North Carolina, Golf State USA:
"North Carolina, Golf State USA" .... 1974 .... $15
North Foreland G. C:
"The North Foreland Golf Club" .... 1951 .... $125
North Jersey C. C:
"The North Jersey Country Club 1928" .... 1928 .... $125
"North Jersey Country Club 75th Anniversary"1970 .... $45
North Manchester G. C:
"North Manchester Golf Club" .... 1938 .... $150
"North Manchester Golf Club. 1894-1994" .... 1994 .... $50
Northumberland G. C:
Northumberland Golf Club"......................... 1955 .... $25
North Wales G. C:
"North Wales Golf Club Llandudno Centenary
      1894-1994" .... 1994 .... $45
Northwood G. C:
"Northwood Golf Club".............................. 1958 .... $25
Northwood Press:
"Back Then" .... 1990 .... $20

Ronald Norval:
"Gone To The Golf" .... 1965 .... $10
"King of The Links".................................... 1951 .... $175
Bev Norwood:
"The Open Championship 1984".................. 1984 .... $20
"The Open Championship 1985".................. 1985 .... $20
"The Open Championship 1986".................. 1986 .... $20
"The Open Championship 1987".................. 1987 .... $20
Joe Norwood:
"Help Yourself To Joe Norwood's Swing"....... 1941 .... $40
"Joe Norwood's Golf-O-Metrics".................. 1978 .... $20
Joe Novak:
"Fore!: Is Golf a Game or is it an Expedition" 1925 .... $150
"Golf Can Be An Easy Game" .... 1962 .... $20
"How To Put Power And Direction In
        Your Golf"...................................... 1954 .... $15
"The Novak System of Mastering Golf" .... 1969 .... $10
"Par Golf In 8 Steps" .... 1950 .... $15
"The Bel-Air Story".................................... 1975 ....$1250
Novak & Stump:
"Bel-Air Country Club" .... 1993 .... $75
Nuneville:
"Illustrated Lessons In Golf" .... 1924 .... $145
Jan Nyquist:
"Oslo Golfklubb 1924-1974" .... 1974 .... $75
Eddy Nunn:
"Mechanics of Golf" .... 1962 .... $15
Peter H. Nunn:
"100 Years of Golf At Flempton".................. 1995 .... $40
Oahu C. C:
"Oahu Country Club" .... 1956 .... $25
Oak Bluff C. C:
"Oak Bluff Country Club"............................ 1914 .... $60
Oakland Hills:
"75 Years at Oakland Hills"........................ 1991 .... $65
Oakley C. C:
"The Oakley Country Club 1909" .... 1909 .... $175
"The Oakley Country Club 1916" .... 1916 .... $125
"Oakley Country Club 1926 .... 1926 .... $95
"Oakley Country Club 1934" .... 1934 .... $50
"Oakley Country Club 1898-1948, Notes
        on a Happy Half Century ".............. 1948 .... $125
"Oakley Country Club 1898-1973: .... 1973 .... $75

Thousands of color book illustrations visible at
www.rogeregilchrist.com

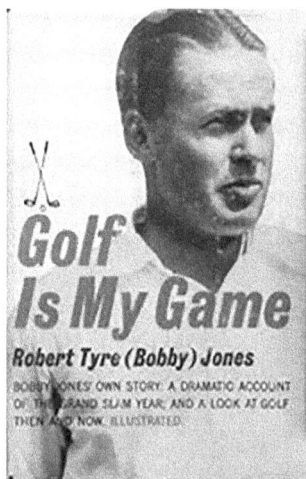

Jones – Golf is my Game
(Dust Jacket)

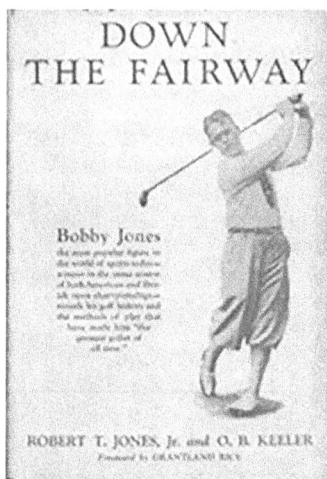

Jones & Keeler – Down the
Fairway (1st Trade Ed DJ)

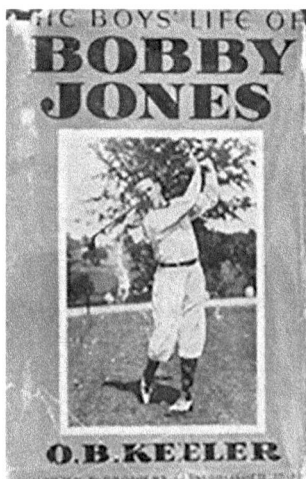

Keeler – The Boys Life of
Bobby Jones (Dust Jacket)

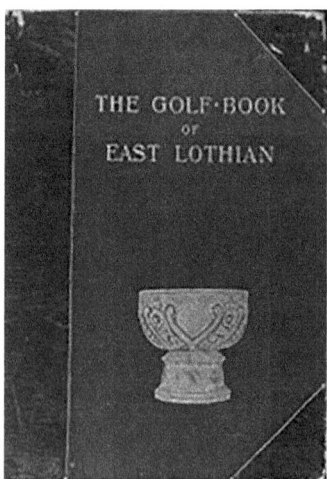

Kerr – The Golf Book of East
Lothian (250 Signed Copies)

Thousands of color book illustrations visible at
www.rogeregilchrist.com

Oakmont C. C:
Oakmont Country Club 1920 .... 1920 .... $250
Oak Park C. C:
"Oak Park Country Club Fifth Anniversary
  1914-1919" .... 1919 .... $75
Oakwood Club:
"Oakwood Club 1905-1955, Fiftieth
  Anniversary" .... 1955 .... $40
"Oakwood Club 75th Anniversary
  1905-1980" .... 1980 .... $35
Oban G. C:
"Oban Golf Club" .... 1915 .... $60
Harry Obitz & Dick Farley:
"Six Days To Better Golf: The Secrets of
  Learning The Golf Swing" .... 1977 .... $25
  Reissue .... 1988 .... $15
Gene O'Brien:
"Aim And Hang Loose" .... 1985 .... $10
Robert O'Byrne:
"Senior Golf" .... 1977 .... $15
Anthony O'Connor:
"Golfing In The Green" .... 1977 .... $15
Christy O'Connor:
"Christy O'Connor, His Autobiography" .... 1985 .... $30
Tim O'Connor:
"The Feeling Of Greatness" .... 1995 .... $25
"From The Wood To The Tees" .... 1992 .... $10
C. F. Odell:
"History of The Pretoria Country Club
  1909-1975" .... 1977 .... $95
Richard W Odermatt:
"New Haven Country Club 1898-1998" .... 1998 .... $30
Paddy O'Donnell:
"South Africa's Wonderful World of Golf" ...... 1973 .... $65
Official Golf Guide:
"Official Golf Guide 1947" .... 1947 .... $20
"Official Golf Guide 1948" .... 1948 .... $20
"Official Golf Guide 1949" .... 1949 .... $20
Willie Ogg:
"Golf As I Know It" .... 1961 .... $15
Jack O'Hare:
"County Armagh Golf Club: The Centenary
  Story" .... 1993 .... $35

Thousands of color book illustrations visible at
www.rogeregilchrist.com

Jack Ohman:
    "Why Johnny Can't Putt" .... 1993 .... $10
William Olcutt:
    "The Greenbrier Heritage" .... 1967 .... $45
Oldest Member:
    "The Etiquette And Tradition of Golf" .... 1920 .... $150
        Second Edition .... 1928 .... $100
        Finnigans Edition .... 1928 .... $75
Old Link G. C:
    "The Old Link Golf Club"............................. 1938 .... $60
Old Player:
    "Golf And How To Play It" .... 1905 .... $195
        Second Edition .... 1912 .... $75
Old Warson C. C:
    "Old Warson Country Club, 10th
        Anniversary".................................... 1964 .... $25
Olgiata G. C:
    "Circolo Golf Olgiata, Roma" .... 1961 .... $95
Jake Olgiati:
    "Pocket Golf Book Illustrated" .... 1924 .... $85
Oliver & Boyd:
"Oliver & Boyd's New Edinburgh Almanac" .... 1812 .... $295
"Oliver & Boyd's New Edinburgh Almanac" .... 1817 .... $275
"Oliver & Boyd's New Edinburgh Almanac" .... 1823 .... $255
"Oliver & Boyd's New Edinburgh Almanac" .... 1826 .... $225
    "Oliver & Boyd's New Edinburgh Almanac" .... 1865 .... $195
John M. Olman:
    "The Squire: The Legendary Golfing Life
        of Gene Sarazen"............................. 1987 .... $50
        (300 signed copies) .... 1987 .... $250
John M. & Morton W. Olman:
    "The Encyclopedia of Golf Collectibles" .... 1985 .... $35
        Limited Edition .... 1985 .... $195
    "Golf Antiques & Other Treasures of The
        Game" .... 1992 .... $20
    "Olman's Guide To Golf Antiques"................ 1992 .... $35
        Signed Subscribers Edition 250 Copies. 1992 .... $150
    "St Andrews And Golf" .... 1995 .... $55
        Signed Subscribers Edition 300 Copies. 1995 .... $275
Morton W. Olman:
    "The Byron Nelson Story" Signed By
        Nelson (600 Copies)......................... 1980 .... $175
    "Golfing Memories" (1000 Copies) .... 2004 .... $150
        Limited Edition of 20 Copies .... 2004 .... $400

James T. Olsen:
"Arnold Palmer: The King On The Course" .... 1974 .... $20
Arv Olson:
"Backspin: 100 Years of Golf In British
    Columbia".. 1992 .... $45
Bill Olson & Lo Linkert:
"Beat The Links" .... 1979 .... $10
George W. Olson:
"Bamboozled And Hornswogled".................. 1962 .... $10
Olympia Fields C. C:
"Olympia Fields Country Club" .... 1923 .... $750
"Olympia Fields Country Club: 75th
    Anniversary".................................... 1990 .... $65
Olympic Club:
"One Hundred Years: The Olympic Club
    Centennial"...................................... 1960 .... $750
John O'Mahony:
"The Sunny Side of Ireland" .... 1898 .... $175
Bill O'Malley:
"Fore And Aft" .... 1969 .... $10
"Golf Fore Fun".. 1953 .... $25
Mark Oman:
"Portrait of A Golfaholic" .... 1984 .... $10
"The Sensuous Golfer"................................ 1976 .... $10
Currey O'Neil:
"The Age Pro Golf Tips"............................... 1984 .... $75
William P. O'Neill:
"History of Overbrook Golf Club 1900-1975" ..... 1977 .... $65
Onwentsia Club:
"Book of the Onwentsia Club 1896-1923"..... 1922 .... $225
E. Philips Oppenheim:
"A Lost Leader".. 1907 .... $75
Oliver Optic:
"The Bunkers of Rippleton"........................ 1900 .... $75
Roy Orason:
"Five Iron" .... 1994 .... $20
Orchard Ridge C. C:
"Orchard Ridge Country Club 1924-1984
    60th Anniversary"............................... 1984 .... $30
Nan O'Reilly:
"Bobby Jones Had To Defeat Himself" .... 1927 .... $45
Original Golf Facts:
"The Original Golf Facts 1971" .... 1971 .... $20

Ormeau G. C:
   "From Demesne to Domain Ormeau Golf
         Club Centenary Brochure"................... 1993 .... $45
Ormskirk G. C:
   "Ormskirk Golf Club Golden Jubilee
         1899-1949" .... 1949 .... $50
Randall M. O'Rourke:
   "To Golf Here's How To Teach It" .... 1960 .... $10
   "The Truth About Golf" .... 1955 .... $10
Robert Osborn:
   "How To Play Golf".................................... 1949 .... $45
Shaughnessy G. & C. C:
   "Clubhouse Opening October 1st 1983"......... 1983 .... $20
   "Shaugnessy Golf and Country Club
         Founed in 1911"............................... 2006 .... $25
Gil O'Shaughnessy:
   "New Zealand Golf Guide" .... 1968 .... $20
Mary Jo O'Shea:
   "Laura Baugh"... 1976 .... $10
H. T. Ostermann:
   "Golf In Europe 1961" .... 1961 .... $35
   "Golf In Europe 1962" .... 1962 .... $30
   "Golf In Europe 1963" .... 1963 .... $20
   "Golf In Europe 1964" .... 1964 .... $20
   "Golf In Europe 1965" .... 1965 .... $20
   "Golf In Europe 1966" .... 1966 .... $20
   "Golf In Europe 1967" .... 1967 .... $20
   "Golf In Europe 1968" .... 1968 .... $20
   "Golf In Europe 1969" .... 1969 .... $15
   "Golf In Europe 1970" .... 1970 .... $15
   "Golf In Europe 1971" .... 1971 .... $15
   "Golf In Europe 1972" .... 1972 .... $15
Neville C. Oswald:
   "Thurlestone Golf Club, A Short History
         1897-1983" .... 1983 .... $30
Francis Ouimet:
   "A Game of Golf, A Book Of Reminiscence"... 1932 .... $325
         Signed First Edition (550 Copies)   .... 1932 ......$1,500
         Reprint... 1963 .... $95
         250 Memorial Tournament Reprint ...... 1978 .... $175
   "Golf Facts For Young People".................... 1921 .... $325
   "The Rules of Golf"................................... 1948 .... $55
Francis Ouimet & Others:
   "The Story of An Old Club, Commemorating

Wollaston's Fiftieth Anniversary
1895-1945" .... 1945 .... $70
David Outerbridge:
"Champion In A Man's World" .... 1998 .... $20
David Owen:
"My Unusual Game" .... 1995 .... $25
"The Making of The Masters" .... 1999 .... $20
De De Owens:
"Teaching Golf To Special Popualtions" .... 1984 .... $10
Oxford And Cambridge Golfing Society:
"Oxford And Cambridge Golfing Society
American Tour 1978" .... 1978 .... $20
T. H. Oyler:
"The Golfers Glossary" .... 1920 .... $995
Ozone Club:
"Down The Fairway And In The Rough With
The Ozone Club 1901-1927" .... 1927 .... $395
Lee Pace:
"Pinehurst Stories: A Celebration of Great Golf
And Good Times" .... 1991 .... $20
Al Pach:
"Artists And Writers Golf Association" .... 1948 .... $15
Pacific Book Auction Galleries:
"The Premier Golf Library Formed By J.S.F.
Murdoch" Special Edition of 100 signed by
four .... 1998 .... $200
John Pacini:
"It's Your Honour: An Account of The First Fifty
Years of The Peninsula Golf Club"
(1000 Copies) .... 1975 .... $55
Alfred H. Padgham:
"The Par Golf Swing" .... 1936 .... $225
Martin A. Padley:
"Nehoiden Golf Club and the History of
Wellesley College 1893-2005" .... 2005 .... $45
Par Golf:
"Fore" .... 1934 .... $95
Barry Pain:
"The One Before" .... 1902 .... $125
R. A. Page:
"Tales of Pinehurst" (2 Vols) .... 1988 .... $45
Steve Page:
"Putting Secrets For The Weekend Golfer" .... 1997 .... $15

Kevin Pakenham:
"The Gathering Bunker" .... 1996 .... $10
Luis Palangue:
"Portugal 1984, The Golfer's Paradise" .... 1984 .... $15
L. S. Paletou:
"The 19th Hole" .... 1933 .... $45
Arnold Palmer:
"Arnold Palmer's Scrapbook .... 1964 .... $1500
"495 Golf Lessons" .... 1973 .... $25
"Go For Broke: My Philosophy of Winning
　　Golf" .... 1973 .... $35
　　　220 Memorial Tournament Edition ...... 1993 .... $150
　　　Limited edition of 1000 signed .... 1999 .... $400
"Golf Journal" .... 1997 .... $10
"Golf Tactics" .... 1970 .... $15
"Graph-Check System For Golf" .... 1963 .... $15
"How To Improve Your Putting" .... 1964 .... $35
"My Eight Majors" (240 Copies) .... 1987 .... $175
"My Game And Yours" .... 1965 .... $20
"Arnold Palmer The Man And The Golfer" ...... 1966 .... $45
"The Arnold Palmer Method" .... 1968 .... $15
"Arnold Palmer Plays Merion" .... 1971 .... $25
"Arnold Palmer's Best 54 Golf Holes" .... 1977 .... $35
"Arnold Palmer's Golf Book: Hit It Hard" .... 1961 .... $45
"Arnold Palmer's Handbook of Golf" .... 1971 .... $20
"Play Great Golf" .... 1987 .... $25
"Portrait of A Professional Golfer" .... 1964 .... $50
"The Rolex Book of Golf" .... 1975 .... $20
"Situation Golf" .... 1970 .... $25
"Turning Point" (Signed Limited Edition) .... 1983 .... $250
"A Golfers Life" .... 1999 .... $20
　　　Leather Bound Ltd Ed of 2500 signed . 1999 .... $350
　　　Limited Edition of 1000 signed .... 1999 .... $250
Arnold Palmer & Peter Dobereiner:
"Arnold Palmer's Complete Book of Putting" .. 1986 .... $25
Colin Palmer:
"The Essential Guide to Collecting Golf Balls .. 2010 .... $65
Norman Palmer & William V. Levy:
"Five Star Golf" .... 1964 .... $30
Palmerston North G. C:
Rules of the Palmerston North Golf Club" ...... 1937 .... $75
John Panton:
"My Way of Golf" .... 1951 .... $25

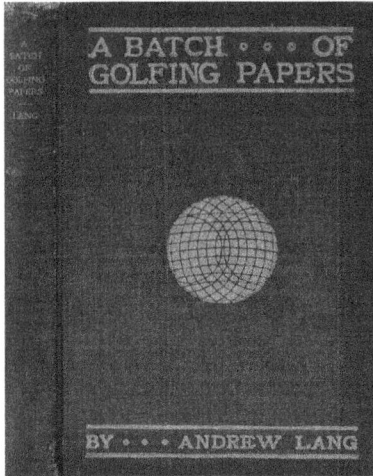

Lang – A Batch of Golfing
Papers (1st American Edition)

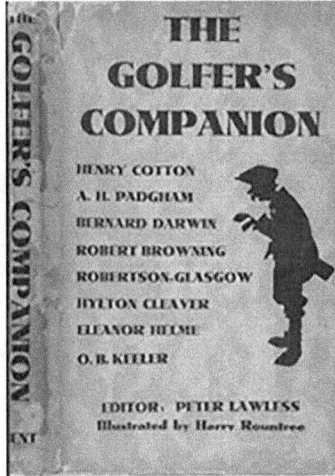

Lawless – The Golfer's Companion

Lee – Golf in America
(1st Edition)

MacDonald – Scotlands Gift Golf
(250 Copies)

Thousands of color book illustrations visible at
www.rogeregilchrist.com

Charles Papp:
"Swing It Like A Pendulum" .... 1965 .... $20
Marino Parascenzo:
"Oakmont 100 Years" .... 2003 .... $30
Parmily Paret:
"The Women's Book of Sports" .... 1901 .... $245
Par Excellance Magazine:
"Par Excellance Guide To Wisconsin" .... 1984 .... $10
William Park Jr.:
"The Art of Putting" .... 1920 .... $900
    American Edition .... 1921 .... $650
    Art of Putting reprint (50 Copies) .... 2011 .... $50
"The Game of Golf" .... 1896 ......$1250
    Second Edition .... 1896 .... $300
    Reprinted .... 1991 .... $45
Marty Parkes:
"Up on the Hill: A History of Essex Fells
    Country Club 1896-1996" .... 1996 .... $45
Parkstone G. C:
"Parkstone Golf Club" .... 1959 .... $25
Samuel L. Parrish:
"Some Facts, Reflections And Personal
    Reminiscences, Connected With The
    Introduction of The Game of Golf Into
    The United States, More Especially As
    Associated With The Foundation of
    The Shinnecock Hill Golf Club" .... 1923 ......$1,450
Mark Parsinen:
"Golf As It Should Be" .... 1996 .... $20
R. Parsons:
"Golfing Thinking" .... 1983 .... $10
W. Julian Parton:
"History of the Northampton Country Club
    1889-1999" .... 1999 .... $45
H. M. Paskow:
"Instant Golf" .... 1965 .... $15
Russ Pate:
"Colonial Country Club 1936-1986" .... 1986 .... $45
Es. L. Patenaude:
"Laval-sur-le-lac" (1000 Copies) .... 1967 .... $75
J. S. Paterson:
"The Eastwood Golf Club. 1893-1993" .... 1993 .... $45
Bob Patey:
"Welcome To The Club" .... 1981 .... $10

Robert E. Patmont:
"The History of the Claremont Country Club" 1988 .... $30
James Paton:
Scottish History And Life" .... 1902 .... $125
G. Z. Patten:
"Birth of Greatness: The Story of The
Honors Course" .... 1984 .... $25
William Patten:
"The Book of Sport"
(450 Deluxe Copies) .... 1901 .... $365
(1500 Deluxe Copies .... 1901 .... $225
A. Willing Patterson:
"The Story of Gulph Mills Golf Club
1916-1976" .... 1976 .... $35
George Patterson:
"A Short History of the Royal Sydney
Golf Club .... 1949 .... $95
James Patterson & Peter DeJonge:
"Miracle On The Seventeenth Green" .... 1996 .... $10
Wylde Patterson & Co:
"Golf Courses,Tennis Lawns Etc" .... 1922 .... $250
H. Pattison & Co:
"Golf Course And Sports Ground Equipment" 1962 .... $65
Carol S. Patton:
"Memories And Golf Stories" .... 1977 .... $20
E. Ted Patton:
"Wyoming Valley Country Club 1896-1984,
A History" .... 1984 .... $50
Pau G. C:
"Statutes" .... 1927 .... $125
Carl F. Paul:
"Club Making And Repair" .... 1984 .... $15
"Golf Club Design And Repair" .... 1978 .... $15
Donald G. Paulhus:
"Wannamoisett Country Club 1898-1998" .... 1998 .... $45
Carl Paulson & Louis Janda:
"Rookie On Tour" .... 1998 .... $10
Rachel C. Payes:
"O Charitable Death" .... 1968 .... $45
Corey Pavin:
"Corey Pavin's Shotmaking" .... 1996 .... $15
Edward F. Pazdur:
"Golf And Country Club Directory" .... 1976 .... $10
"Golf And Country Club Guest Policy

Thousands of color book illustrations visible at
www.rogeregilchrist.com

Directory".. 1977 .... $10
"Private Country Club Guest Policy
Directory".. 1980 .... $10
V. J. Pazzetti Jr.:
"Saucon Valley Country Club" .... 1951 .... $45
Peachtree G. C:
"Peachtree Golf Club" .... 1980 .... $45
Gene Pearce:
"The History of Tennessee Golf 1894-2001".. 2002 .... $60
Issette Pearson:
"The Ladies Golf Union Official Year Book" .... 1906 .... $450
"The Ladies Golf Union Official Yearbook" ..... 1909 .... $200
John Pearson & Peter Cusack:
"Golf at Silloth 1890-2000" .... 2002 .... $50
Leonard Pearl:
"The Big Secret of Golf" .... 1962 .... $10
Samuel M. Peck:
"The Golf Girl" .... 1899 .... $400
Michael W. Peers:
"A History of the Manchester Golf Club
1882-1982" .... 1982 .... $35
Pentland Peile:
"Clanbrae: A Golfing Idyll" .... 1908 .... $500
Thomas Pelly & C.G. Nickum:
"The Story of Restoration Point and the
Country Club.." .... 1984 .... $300
Alex Pendleton:
"Better Golf With Brains .... 1952 .... $75
Peninsula G & C. C:
"Peninsula Golf & Country Club" .... 1993 .... $35
Toney Penna:
"My Wonderful World of Golf" .... 1965 .... $45
Pennard G. C:
"Pennard Golf Club"................................ 1941 .... $50
Harvey Pennick & Bud Shrake:
"Harvey Pennick's Little Red Book" .... 1992 .... $15
"And If you Play Golf Your My Friend" .... 1993 .... $15
"For All Who Love The Game" .... 1995 .... $15
"The Game For A Lifetime" .... 1996 .... $15
Frank Pennink:
"Golfer's Companion" .... 1962 .... $45
"Homes of Sport: Golf" .... 1952 .... $45
"Frank Pennink's Choice of Golf Courses"...... 1976 .... $40
"Royal Ashdown Forest Golf Club The

Old And The New Courses"................. 1965 $55

Penrith G. C:
"A Century of Golf: Penrith Golf Club,
1890-1990".................................... 1990 $25

Penzance G. C:
"Penzance Golf Club"............................... 1914 .... $275

George Peper:
"Golf Courses of The PGA Tour" .... 1986 .... $25
"Golf In America-The First 100 Years".......... 1988 .... $25
    500 Copies signed by Nicklaus............ 1988 .... $450
"Golf's Supershots: How The Pros Played
Them" .... 1982 .... $20
"Grand Slam Golf"................................... 1991 .... $25
"The PGA Championship 1916-1984" .... 1984 .... $65
"Scrambling Golf:" .... 1977 .... $15
"Shinnecock Hills Golf Club 1881-1991"
(1000 Copies) .... 1991 .... $125
"The Story of Golf".................................... 1999 .... $35

Percorsi de Golf:
"Persorsi de Golf in Italia" .... 1985 .... $35

Helen B. & Roy F. Perkins:
"Wannamoisett Country Club 1898-1948" .... 1948 .... $175
Reprint... 1985 .... $25

W. F. Perkins:
"Golfer's Guide To Emotional Management" .. 1981 .... $10

Louis J. Perrottet:
"A History of Canoe Brook Country Club
1901-1965" .... 1965 .... $75

Byron Perry:
"75 Years at Oakland Hills Country Club"...... 1991 .... $50

Phyllis Perry:
"From Green To Gold: The First Fifty Years
of the Australian Ladies Golf Union"..... 1976 .... $30

J. D. Peden:
"Uplands Golf Club 1922-1982: Sixtieth
Anniversary" .... 1982 .... $45

Gordon Petch:
"Ashdown Over The Years"......................... 1973 .... $20

H. Thomas Peter:
"Reminiscences of Golf And Golfers" .... 1890 .... $10,000
Reprint (250 Copies) .... 1985 .... $225

Peterhead G. C:
"Peterhead And The Peterhead Golf Club"..... 1939 .... $65

Thousands of color book illustrations visible at
www.rogeregilchrist.com

Ettienne Petitjean:
"Golf: Quelques Civilites Pueriles er
    Honnetes" .... 1930 .... $650
Andrew Petnuch:
"T-U-R-N To Golf" .... 1969 .... $20
Roy A. Pettitt:
"The Straight-Line Golf Swing".................... 1946 .... $25
PGA:
"The Book On Golf: On The Occasion of The
    Ninth Biennial Ryder Cup Matches
    Pinehurst N.C. Nov 2nd and 4th 1951". 1951 .... $225
"Education And Teaching Clinics And
    Seminars" .... 1956 .... $20
"European Tournament Players' Division
    Tournament Guide 1977".................... 1977 .... $20
"European Tournament Players' Division
    Tournament Guide 1978".................... 1978 .... $20
"European Tournament Players' Division
    Tournament Guide 1979".................... 1979 .... $20
"European Tournament Players' Division
    Tournament Guide 1980".................... 1980 .... $20
"European Tournament Players' Division
    Tournament Guide 1981".................... 1981 .... $20
"European Tournament Players' Division
    Tournament Guide 1982".................... 1982 .... $15
"The Golf Professional At A Military Course" .. 1981 .... $10
"The Golf Professional At A Public Course" .... 1983 .... $15
"Golf's Professional Man"............................ 1943 .... $75
"Greener Pastures At Dunedin Isles"............ 1946 .... $35
"Ideas To Assist Golf Clubs And Courses
    Make Money To Reduce Costs" .... 1981 .... $15
"Official Record Book 1936-37" .... 1937 .... $75
"Official Record Book 1938-39" .... 1939 .... $70
"Official Tournament Guide 1972" .... 1972 .... $20
"Official Tournament Guide 1973" .... 1973 .... $20
"Official Tournament Guide 1974" .... 1974 .... $20
"Official Tournament Guide 1975" .... 1975 .... $20
"Official Tournament Guide 1976" .... 1976 .... $20
"Official Tournament Record Book 1940-41" . 1941 .... $75
"Official Tournament Record Book 1941-49" . 1949 .... $50
"Official Tournament Record Book 1950-58" . 1958 .... $50
"Official Tournament Record Book 1959-64" . 1965 .... $50
"PGA Book of Golf 1968"............................ 1968 .... $25
"PGA Book of Golf 1969"............................ 1969 .... $20

"PGA Book of Golf 1970" .... 1970 .... $25
"PGA Book of Golf 1973" .... 1973 .... $25
"PGA Book Of Golf 1974" .... 1974 .... $25
"PGA Book Of Golf 1975" .... 1975 .... $25
"PGA Book of Golf 1976" .... 1976 .... $20
"PGA Book of Golf 1977" .... 1977 .... $20
"PGA Book of Golf 1978" .... 1978 .... $20
"PGA Book of Golf 1979" .... 1979 .... $25
"PGA Book of Golf 1980" .... 1980 .... $25
"PGA Caddie Manual" .... 1964 .... $20
"PGA European Tour Official Guide 1983" ..... 1983 .... $15
"PGA European Tour Official Guide 1984" ..... 1984 .... $15
"PGA European Tour Official Guide 1985" ..... 1985 .... $15
"PGA Golf Professionals Guide" .... 1963 .... $20
"PGA Teachers Guide" .... 1951 .... $20
"Success Stories In The Golf Business" .... 1978 .... $20
"Teaching Manual" .... 1950 .... $20
"Tour 1980" .... 1980 .... $20
"Tour 1981" .... 1981 .... $20
"Tour 1982" .... 1982 .... $15
"Tour 1983" .... 1983 .... $15
"Tour 1984" .... 1984 .... $15
"Tour 1985" .... 1985 .... $15
"Tournament And Player Record Book For
    1934" .... 1935 .... $75
"Tournament And Player Record Book For
    1935" .... 1936 .... $75

Philadelphia C. C:
"Philadelphia Country Club Charter, By-Laws,
    Rules" .... 1910 .... $155
"The Philadelphia Country Club 1890-1965" .. 1965 .... $75

Geraldine Philbrick:
"A History of the Menio Country Club" .... 1978 .... $50

W. R. Philbrick:
"Slow Dancer" .... 1984 .... $45

Phil Philley:
"Golfing Art" .... 1988 .... $35
"Heather And Heaven Walton Heath G. C.
    1903-2003" (148 Subscriber Copies) ... 2003 .... $550

Betty Lou Phillips:
"Picture Story of Nancy Lopez" .... 1980 .... $15

Michael J. Phillips:
"How To Play Miniature Golf" .... 1930 .... $150

Thousands of color book illustrations visible at
www.rogeregilchrist.com

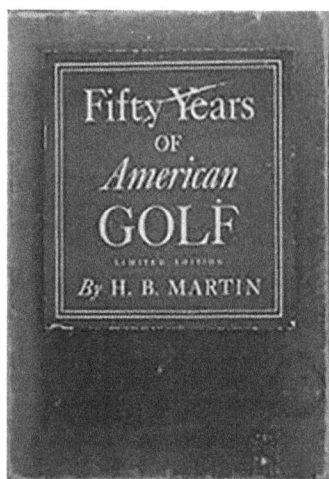

Martin – Fifty Years of American
Golf (355 Copies)

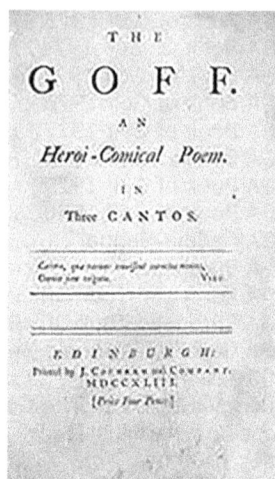

Mathison – The Goff
(1743 1st Edition)

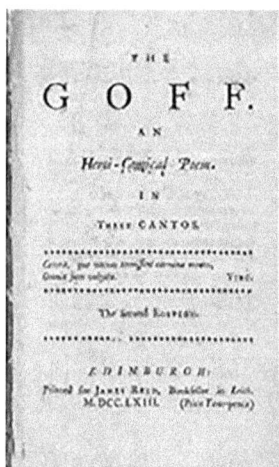

Mathison - The Goff
(1763 2nd Edition)

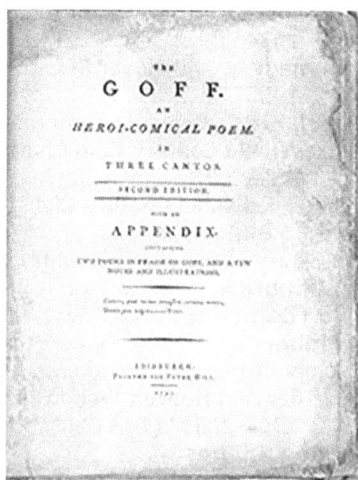

Mathison - The Goff
(1793 3rd Edition)

Thousands of color book illustrations visible at
www.rogeregilchrist.com

Philmont C. C:
   "Since The Spring of 1906" .... 1946 .... $50
   "Things A Caddy Should Know" .... (nd) $35
George A. Philpot:
   "The Birstall Golf Club" .... 1938 .... $55
   "The Bournemouth Golf Club" .... 1936 .... $70
   "The Bridport & West Dorset Golf Club" .... 1946 .... $50
   "The Chigwell Golf Club" .... 1939 .... $40
   "The Cleethorpes Golf Club" .... 1937 .... $65
   "The Grimsley Golf Club" .... 1938 .... $65
      "The North Wales Golf Club" .... 1947 .... $50
   "The Reading Golf Club" .... 1947 .... $65
Photographic Study of Pebble Beach:
   "Photographic Study of Pebble Beach
      Golf Links Stroke By Stroke" .... 1952 .... $325
Arthur E. Pickens Jr.:
   "The Golf Bum" .... 1970 .... $30
H. O. Pickworth:
   "Golf The Pickworth Way" .... 1949 .... $40
Pietzcker Photo:
   "A.C Wheeler Flip Book" .... 1920 .... $750
   "Eddie Williams" .... 1920 .... $400
   "Herbert E Skinner" .... 1920 .... $300
   "Frank Allen" .... 1920 .... $600
Charles P. Piers:
   "Sport And Life In British Columbia" .... 1923 .... $65
Fred J. C. Pignon:
   "Spalding Golfer's Year Book" .... 1960 .... $25
Phil Pilley:
   "Golfing Art" .... 1988 .... $40
   "Heather and Heaven: Walton Heath Golf
      Club 1903-2003" (Ltd Edition of 148) .. 2003 .... $495
      Regular Edition .... 2003 .... $150
Pinehurst Golf Resort:
   "Pinehurst A Winter Resort in North Carolina" 1901 .... $375
   "The Game at Pinehurst...." .... 1924 .... $465
   "Pinehurst and the Village Chapel" .... 1957 .... $125
Pine Valley G. C:
   "Pine Valley Golf Club" .... 1947 .... $225
   "Pine Valley Golf Club" .... 1974 .... $75
John Pinner:
   "The History of Golf" .... 1988 .... $20
Charles V. Piper & Russell A. Oakley:
   "Turf for Golf Courses" .... 1917 .... $850

Thousands of color book illustrations visible at
www.rogeregilchrist.com

Second Edition .... 1929 .... $395

Piping Rock Club:
"Piping Rock Club: Locust Valley..." .... 1914 .... $225

Turk Pipkin:
"Fast Greens" .... 1996 .... $15

Edward Pira:
"A Guide To Golf Course Irrigation System
Design And Drainage" .... 1997 .... $75

Plainfield C. C:
"Plainfield Country Club Club Book" .... 1913 .... $95
"The First Hundred Years" .... 1990 .... $45

Kin Platt:
"The Kissing Gourami" .... 1970 .... $35
"Murder In Rosslare .... 1986 .... $35

Jules Platte:
"Better Golf Through Better Practice" .... 1958 .... $15

Michael Platts:
"The Ryder Cup '85" .... 1985 .... $35
"Illustrated History of Golf" .... 1988 .... $35
"RAC Golf Guide" .... 1991 .... $10

Play It Pro:
"Golf From Beginner To Winner" .... 1960 .... $20

Gary Player:
"124 Golf Lessons" .... 1968 .... $25
"395 Golf Lessons" .... 1972 .... $25
"Bunker Play" .... 1996 .... $20
"Golf Begins at 50" .... 1988 .... $15
"Golfing S.A." .... 1980 .... $25
"Good Test For The U.S. Open, Haziltine
National Golf Club" .... 1970 .... $20
"Grand Slam Golf" .... 1966 .... $15
"Improve Your Golf" .... 1962 .... $15
"The Medium Iron To The Green" .... 1971 .... $15
"More Tips From Gary Player" .... 1968 .... $15
"Play Better Golf With Gary Player" .... 1970 .... $15
"Play Golf With Player" .... 1962 .... $20
"Gary Player On Fitness And Success" .... 1979 .... $10
"Gary Player Tells You All About The
Shakespeare Fiberglass Wondershaft
And What It Can Do For You" .... 1964 .... $25
"Gary Player World Golf Pro" .... 1974 .... $25
"Gary Player's Golf Book For Young People" .. 1980 .... $15
"Gary Player's Golf Class Book 1 100
Lessons" .... 1967 .... $25

"Gary Player's Golf Class Book II 100
Lessons"... 1969 .... $20
"Gary Player's Golf Class Book III 162
Lessons"... 1975 .... $15
"Gary Player's Golf Class Book IV 170
Lessons"... 1980 .... $15
"Gary Player's Golf Clinic" .... 1981 .... $20
"Gary Player's Golf Guide"......................... 1974 .... $20
"Gary Player's Golf Secrets"......................... 1962 .... $25
"Positive Golf: Understanding And Applying
The Fundamentals of The Game" .... 1967 .... $25
"The Tee Shot" .... 1971 .... $15
"To Be The Best"....................................... 1991 .... $20
   200 Memorial Tournament reprint....... 1997 .... $125
"Weathering The Sand And Storm"............... 1971 .... $20

Pleasington G. C:
"Pleasington Golf Club" .... (nd) $25

George Plim:
"Golf in Redditch 1891-1991" .... 1992 .... $25

George Plimpton:
"The Bogey Man" .... 1967 .... $15

Chris Plumridge:
"Almost Straight Down The Middle" .... 1993 .... $20
"The Book of Golf Disasters & Bizarre
Records" .... 1985 .... $20
"Golf's Lighter Side" .... 1989 .... $20
"How To Play Golf"..................................... 1979 .... $15
"The Essential Henry Longhurst" .... 1988 .... $35
"The Illustrated Encyclopedia of World Golf" . 1988 .... $20
"The Volvo Tour Yearbook 1990".................. 1991 .... $25

C. Plumridge & J. Hopkins:
"A Golfer's Companion".............................. 1990 .... $20

Pocket Pro:
"Pocket Pro".. 1948 .... $35

Podmore:
"From Lightcliffe to Ogden: The Halifax
Golf Club 1895-1995"........................ 1995 .... $20

P. Byron Polakoff:
"Arnold Palmer And The Golfin' Dolphin"....... 1984 .... $75

Frank B. Pollard:
"Golf On The Peninsula: An Illustrated Guide
To The World Famous Courses On
The Monterey Peninsula" .... 1973 .... $60

Jack Pollard:
"Golf: The Australian Way" .... 1970 .... $20
"Gregory's Australian Guide To Golf" .... 1964 .... $25
"Australian Golf" .... 1990 .... $45
A. J. E. Pollock:
"Golf At Seacroft, The First One Hundred
        Years" .... 1994 .... $25
William H. Pollock:
"You The Golfer" .... 1937 .... $125
Harold M. Pond:
"Guide To 1,870 North American Golf
        Courses" .... 1954 .... $40
Pontypridd G. C:
"Pontypridd Golf Club" .... 1924 .... $85
Kelly Pool:
"Selected Drawing of Clare Briggs" .... 1930 .... $175
William Poole:
"The History of Onwentsia 1895-1945" .... 1985 .... $65
Nicholas Popa:
"Caddy Tip$" .... 1953 .... $65
Mary Kay Poppenberg & Marlene Parrish:
"I'd Rather Play Golf Than Cook" .... 1976 .... $10
Portland G. C:
"Portland Golf Club. A Seventy-Five Year
        History 1914-1989" .... 1989 .... $45
Portmarnock G. C:
"Portmarnock Golf Club" .... 1939 .... $200
Portsea G. C:
"Portsea Golf Club History 1925-1975
        50th Anniversary Souvenir" .... 1975 .... $15
Sandra Post & Loral Dean:
"Sandra Post And Me" .... 1998 .... $15
Mitchell P. Postel:
"History of The Burlingame Country Club"
        (1500 Copies) .... 1982 .... $30
"The University Club of San Francisco
        Centennial History 1890-1990" .... 1990 .... $65
"The History of the Peninsula Golf
        And Country Club .... 1993 .... $65
E. C. Potter:
"Midlothian Melodies, Mnemonic
        Maunderings of The Merry Muse" .... 1900 .... $500
Stephen Potter:
"The Complete Golf Gamesmanship" .... 1968 .... $20

"Golfmanship" .... 1968 .... $20
Potters Bar G. C:
"The Potters Bar Golf Club" .... 1926 .... $80
George Pottinger:
"Muirfield And The Honorable Company" ...... 1972 .... $50
W. A. Poucher:
"The Surrey Hills" .... 1949 .... $45
M. Powersland:
"Great Yarmouth & Caister Golf 1882-1982" . 1982 .... $65
Eric M. Prain:
"Live Hands: A Key To Better Golf" .... 1946 .... $45
    Reprint..................................... 1994 .... $10
"The Oxford And Cambridge Golfing
    Society 1898-1948" .... 1949 .... $200
Prairie Dunes:
"Prairie Dunes: The First 50 Years
    1937-1987" .... 1987 .... $30
John Lowell Pratt:
"Golf, Swimming, Tennis"......................... 1966 .... $15
William Pratt and Keith Jennison:
"Year-Round Conditioning For Part Time
    Golfers"... 1979 .... $20
Arthur Preedy:
"Home Park Golf Club"............................. 1950 .... $75
A. E. Prentice:
"Royal Dublin Golf Course" .... 1945 .... $950
Prestatyn G. C:
"Prestatyn Golf Club"............................... 1951 .... $45
Prestbury & Upton G. C:
"The Prestbury & Upton Golf Club" .... 1950 .... $45
Charles Preston:
"Fore: Golf Cartoons From The Wall Street
    Journal" .... 1962 .... $20
Prestwick G. C:
"A Players Guide"................................... 1982 .... $35
"The Official Guide to Prestwick (Ayershire) .. 1915 .... $225
Charles Price:
"A Golf Story"....................................... 1986 .... $95
"The American Golfer" .... 1964 .... $75
"Black's Picture Sports: Golf"..................... 1976 .... $20
"Esquire's Golfer's Guide"......................... 1972 .... $35
"Golf Magazine's Pro Pointers And Stroke
    Savers" .... 1960 .... $20
"Golfer-At-Large: New Slants On

The Ancient Game" .... 1982 .... $35
"Scotland's Golf Courses" .... 1989 .... $75
"Shell's Wonderful World of Golf 1963" .... 1963 .... $60
"Sports Illustrated Book of Golf" .... 1970 .... $40
"Sports Illustrated Golf" .... 1972 .... $20
"The World of Golf: A Panorama Of Six
    Centuries of The Games' History" .... 1962 .... $95

Charles Price & George C. Rogers Jr.:
"The Carolina Low Country, Birthplace of
    American Golf 1786" .... 1980 .... $75

Robert Price:
"The Golf Industry In Scotland" .... 1998 .... $55

Prince's G. C:
"Prince's Golf Club Sandwich" .... 1932 .... $200

Syd Pritchard:
"A Golfers Guide To Shakespeare" .... 1988 .... $10

Pro Am Guide To Golf:
"Pro Am Guide To Golf" .... 1982 .... $15

Pro's Handbook of Golf:
"Pro's Handbook of Golf" .... 1967 .... $15

Robert D. Pryde:
"The Early History of Golf in New Haven
    Connecticut" .... 1952 .... $225

Barbara Puett & Jim Affelbaum:
"Golf Etiquette" .... 1992 .... $10

Peter Pugh:
"The Belfry The Making of a Dream" .... 1989 .... $25

P. C. Pulver:
"The American Annual Golf Guide" .... 1916 .... $625
"The American Annual Golf Guide" .... 1921 .... $425

Punch Magazine:
"The Funny Side of Golf" .... 1909 .... $500
"Mr. Punch On The Links" .... 1935 .... $200
"Mr. Punch's Golf Stories Told By His Merry
    Men" .... 1909 .... $150
"That Game Of Golf And Some Other
    Sketches" .... 1902 .... $300

Purley Downs G. C:
"Purley Downs Golf Club 1894-1994"
    (1000 Copies) .... 1994 .... $45

Puttenham G. C:
"Puttenham Golf Club" .... 1951 .... $45

Nancy Quantz:
"Tee Party" .... 1969 .... $10

Thousands of color book illustrations visible at
www.rogeregilchrist.com

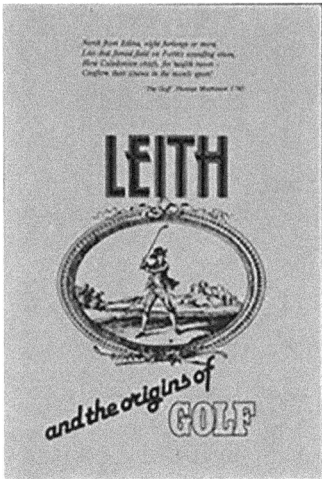

McKay – Leith and the Origins
Of Golf

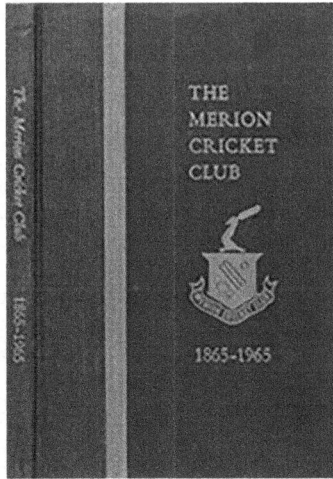

Merion C.C. – Merion Cricket Club
1865-1965

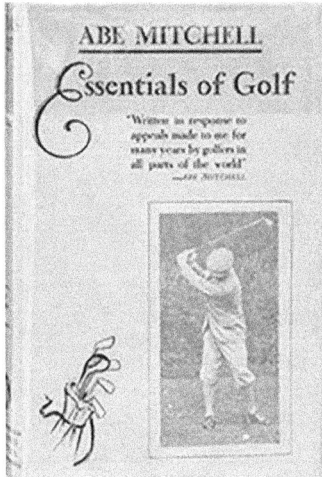

Mitchell – Essentials of Golf
(Dust Jacket)

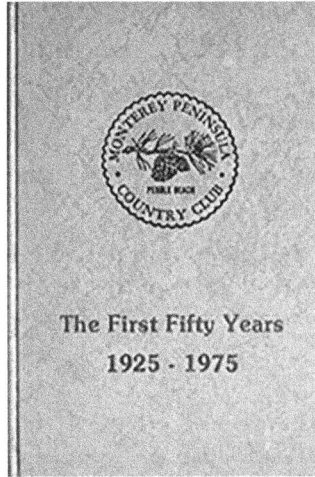

Monterey Peninsular - The
First Fifty Years

Thousands of color book illustrations visible at
www.rogeregilchrist.com

Joe Queenan:
"Imperial Caddy" .... 1992 .... $15
Harve Quelin:
"Saint-Nom-La-Breteche Golf Club" .... 2003 .... $75
Joseph Quinzi:
"Back To The Basics In Golf"....................... 1980 .... $10
Joseph Quinzi & Catherine McKenzie Shane:
"The Women's World of Golf"...................... 1980 .... $15
William L. Quirin:
"Golf Clubs of The MGA" .... 1997 .... $45
"Scarsdale Golf Club. The First Hundred
        Years".. 1998 .... $75
"Wee Burn: The First Century, 1896-1996"... 1996 .... $25
Quirin, Stowell & Coveney:
"The Greenwich Country Club 1892-1992".... 1993 .... $125
Qvist:
"Golfermania".. 1985 .... $10
Claude Radcliffe:
"Holed Out In One" .... 1919 .... $175
Radyr G. C:
"Radyr Golf Club 1902-1977"...................... 1977 .... $15
Tony Rafty:
"Tony Rafty's Golfing Greats"...................... 1983 .... $25
Martin A. Ragaway:
"Golfer's Dictionary"................................. 1984 .... $20
"Sex Before Golf"..................................... 1982 .... $10
"The Worlds Worst Golf Jokes".................... 1974 .... $10
William Ralston & C. W. Cole:
"North Again, Golfing This Time" .... 1894 .... $250
Neil Ramsay:
"Scotland's Golfing Heritage" .... 1984 .... $20
Paul E. Ramsdell:
"Our Story: The First 75 Years of Fircrest
        Golf Club" (300 Copies) .... 1999 .... $75
Allan Ramsey:
"West Sussex Golf Club Golden Jubilee
        1931-1981" .... 1981 .... $20
Lon W. Ramsey:
"Secrets of Winning Golf Matches"............... 1960 .... $10
Tom Ramsey:
"25 Great Australian Golf Courses" .... 1981 .... $20
"Discover Australia's Golf Courses".............. 1987 .... $15
"Golfer's Gift Book" .... 1983 .... $10
"How To Cheat And Hustle At Golf".............. 1983 .... $10

"Tom Ramsey's World of Golf" .... 1977 .... $15
Ray W. Rancourt:
"Shennecossett: The History of a Golf
Course"... 1989 .... $25
Richard C. Randolph:
"You Will Win Betting On The Golf
Course-I'll Betcha"............................. 1983 .... $10
E. Cyril Rands:
"Ipswich Golf Club" .... 1930 .... $50
Rangitikei G. C:
"Rangitikei Golf Club Golden Jubilee,
1925-1975" .... 1975 .... $40
D. Helen Rankin:
"Greenisland Golf Club 1894-1994" .... 1994 .... $45
Judy Rankin:
"A Natural Way To Golf Power" .... 1976 .... $15
Milton Rappoport:
"Oh No! A Golf Duffer's Handbook".............. 1956 .... $25
Bertil Rarald:
"Get Fit For Golf" .... 1985 .... $10
Roy & Betty Rasmussen:
"1981 Michigan Golfers Map And Guide"....... 1981 .... $10
Wally Rasmussem:
"The Preaching Pro" .... 1979 .... $10
Ratho Park G. C:
"Ratho Park Golf Club"............................... 1948 .... $50
Jeanette E. Rattray & Julian Myrick:
"Fifty Years of The Maidstone Club
1891-1941"(500 Copies) .... 1941 .... $225
Facsimilie Edition .... 1991 .... $100
Anthony Ravielli:
"What Is Golf" .... 1976 .... $15
Ravisloe C. C:
"House, Ground and Caddy Rules".............. 1917 .... $150
Chris Rawson:
"Where Stone Walls Meet the Sea. Sakonnet
Golf Club 1899-1999"......................... 1999 .... $65
Edward Ray:
"Driving, Approaching, Putting"................... 1923 .... $175
"Golf Clubs And How To Use Them" .... 1922 .... $195
"Golf: My Slice of Life".............................. 1972 .... $25
"Inland Golf" .... 1914 .... $185
Raymond G. C:
"Golf at The Raymond" .... 1919 .... $150

Milton Reach:
"Night Golf".. 1955 .... $10
Dai Read:
"Maldon Golf Club 1891-1991".................... 1991 .... $25
Professor John Read:
"Historic St Andrews And Its University"....... 1939 .... $35
Opie P. Read:
"Opie Read On Golf".................................. 1925 .... $145
"The Gold Gauze Veil"............................... 1927 .... $175
Rebar, Jaske, & Doran:
"Cross Word Golf: A Game For Two Players" . 1933 .... $25
Redditch G. C:
"Redditch Golf Club".................................. 1936 .... $65
"Golf in Redditch 1891-1991" .... 1991 .... $30
Ken Redford & Nick Tremayne:
"Success In Golf" .... 1977 .... $10
Red Hill C. C:
"History of Red Hill Country Club. Golden
        Anniversary 1971" .... 1971 .... $50
Redlands C. C:
"Redlands Country Club. A Centennial
        History, 1896-1996" (1000 Copies)..... 1996 .... $50
John Redman:
"Essentials of The Golf Swing" .... 1993 .... $15
Jack Redmond:
"Golf Training"... 1930 .... $95
John Redmond:
"Great Golf Courses of Ireland".................. 1992 .... $45
"Ballybunion - An Illustrated Centenary
        History 1893-1993" .... 1994 .... $85
John Reece:
"Golf of Course"....................................... 1983 .... $15
A. Reed:
"The History of Brook Hollow Golf Club" .... 2006 .... $15
Betty Jane Reed:
"Golfin With A Dolphin"............................. 1968 .... $20
Dai Rees:
"Golf My Way" .... 1951 .... $65
"Golf Today".. 1962 .... $55
"The Key To Golf" .... 1961 .... $45
"Dai Rees On Golf" .... 1959 .... $45
"Thirty Years Of Championship Golf"............ 1968 .... $65
Enoch Rees:
"Death Ball" .... 1943 .... $95

Dean Refram & Arthur Burgone:
"Golf-O-Genics" .... 1978 .... $15
Conrad H. Rehling:
"Golf For The Physical Education Teacher
    and Coach" .... 1954 .... $15
Austin Reid:
"A History of Limerick Golf Club 1891-1991". 1991 .... $25
Hastings C. Reid:
"The Key To The Rules of Golf And
    Definitions" .... 1946 .... $75
Nat B. Reid:
"The Jonathan Club Story" .... 2005 .... $50
Steven Reid:
"Get To The Point At The County Sligo
    Golf Club" (500 Copies) .... 1991 .... $65
William Reid:
"Golfing Reminiscences: The Growth
    of The Game 1887-1925".................... 1925 .... $950
William Reid:
"Seventy-Five Years of Golf At Cathkin
    Braes 1888-1963" .... 1963 .... $40
Leonard Remis:
"Glendale Golf and Country Club: 50th
    Anniversary Yearbook, 1946-1996" ..... 1996 .... $25
Marion Renick:
"Champion Caddy" .... 1943 .... $75
John Ressich:
"Thir Braw Days" .... 1933 .... $175
John Retallick & Michael Campbell:
Wagga Wagga Country Club 75 Years" .... 2005 .... $25
Alexander H. Revell:
"The Pro And Con of Golf" .... 1915 .... $450
Ralph H. Reville:
"Golf In Canada"...................................... 1926 .... $150
Johnny Revolta:
"6 Lessons From Johnny Revolta" .... 1954 .... $15
Johnny Revolta & Charles Cleveland:
"Johnny Revolta's Short Cuts To Better Golf" 1949 .... $35
Frank Reynolds:
"Hamish McDuff"....................................... 1937 .... $50
"Punch Pictures" .... 1922 .... $175
"The Frank Reynolds Golf Book: Drawings
    From Punch" .... 1932 .... $125
"The Frank Reynolds Golf Collection" .... 1970 .... $125

Thousands of color book illustrations visible at
www.rogeregilchrist.com

Morgan B. Reynolds:
"Seventy Years Of Belle Meade Country
Club 1901-1971" .... 1971 .... $150
Rhode Island C. C:
"Rhode Island Country Club 1911-1951" ...... 1952 .... $45
Hal Rhodes:
"Fundamental Principles Of Golf" .... 1952 .... $25
Louis Rhodes:
"Stop Action Golf: The Driver" .... 1971 .... $10
W. H. Ricardo:
"Golfing Parodies" .... 1930 ....$1250
"Out of Bounds No. 1" .... 1927 .... $150
"Out of Bounds No. 2" .... 1927 .... $150
Rice, Ross, Ryder, Rawls & MacFarlane:
"The Centennial History of the Worcester
Country Club. 1900-2000
(1000 Copies) .... 2000 .... $75
Grantland Rice:
"Fore-With A Glance Aft"............................ 1929 .... $445
"Golf Wonderland: Asheville – Biltmore
Forest .... 1925 .... $450
"Sam Snead, Mystery Man of Golf" .... 1949 .... $25
"The Bobby Jones Story"............................ 1953 .... $150
1st British Edition .... 1953 .... $125
100 Memorial Tournament Reprint ..... 1980 .... $450
"Sport Lights of 1923" .... 1924 .... $95
"The Golf Course That Surprised Me" .... 1927 .... $200
"The Tumolt and The Shouting" .... 1954 .... $40
Grantland Rice & Clare Briggs:
"The Duffers Handbook of Golf".................... 1926 .... $175
Signed Limited Edition (500 Copies ..... 1926 ....$1250
Grantland Rice & Harford Powell:
"The Omnibus of Sport" .... 1962 .... $15
Rice, Richardson, & Morrison:
"Golfer's Year Book 1938" .... 1938 ....$110
Jonathan Rice:
"Curiousities of Golf" 1994   .... $25
Robert Rice:
"Scotlands Golf Courses"............................ 1989 .... $35
Wallace & Frances Rice:
"The Little Book of Sports .... 1910 .... $125
Endicott Rich & Foley Johnson:
"You Can Think Ten Strokes Off
Your Game, We Did" .... 1931 .... $45

Thousands of color book illustrations visible at
www.rogeregilchrist.com

F. T. Richards:
"The Royal Game of Golf"............................ 1901 ....$5995
Philip Richards:
"Between The Church And The Lighthouse
    The History of Bernham and Berrow
    Golf Club" (750 Copies) .... 2001 .... $125
    Limited Edition of 50 .... 2001 .... $225
Bruce Richardson:
"Richardson's Common Sense Golf" .... 1984 .... $10
Donald H. Richardson:
"World Wide Golf Directory"......................... 1973 .... $20
Forest B. Richardson:
"Broadmoor Golf Club: An Historical
    Perspective".................................... 1983 .... $75
G. A. Richardson:
"The Shipley Century 1896-1996" .... 1996 .... $20
William D. Richardson:
"Richardson's Annual Golf Review of The
    48 States" .... 1933 .... $55
"The National Golf Review 1936".................. 1936 .... $55
"The Eastern Golfer".................................. 1939 .... $55
"The Official Golf Guide"............................. 1947 .... $30
William D. Richardson & Lincoln A. Werden:
"Annual Golf Review 1931".......................... 1932 .... $150
"Annual Golf Review 1933".......................... 1934 .... $45
"Annual Golf Review 1934".......................... 1935 .... $45
"Golfer's Yearbook 1930" .... 1930 .... $150
"Golfer's Yearbook 1931" .... 1931 .... $35
"Golfer's Yearbook 1932" .... 1932 .... $30
"Golfer's Yearbook 1933" .... 1933 .... $50
Nason Richmond:
"Patented Golf Games, Gimmicks, and
    Gadgets".. 1991 .... $15
Richmond C. C:
"Richmond Country Club Constitution and
    By Laws" .... 1914 .... $125
"Historical Souvenir Book of The Fiftieth
    Anniversary of The Richmond
    Country Club 1888-1938" .... 1938 .... $90
Bill Rickard:
"Army Golf Club 1883-1983" .... 1983 .... $15
C. A. P. Ricornus:
"The Goat Club Golf Book" .... 1911 .... $450

Thousands of color book illustrations visible at
www.rogeregilchrist.com

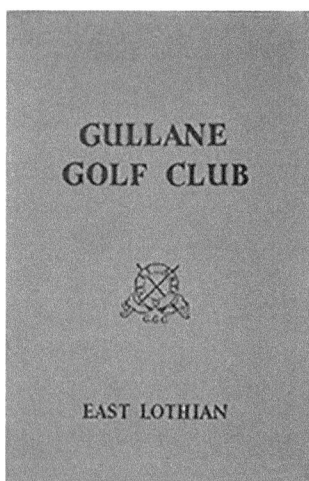

Moran – Gullane Golf Club

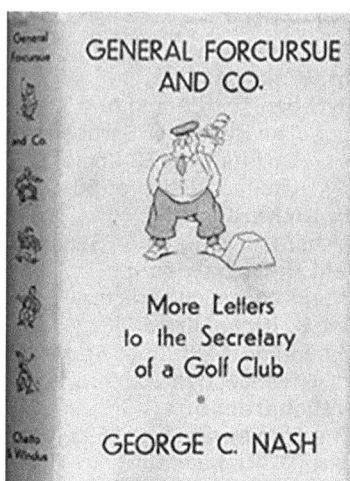

Nash – General Forcursue and Co

Nelson – Winning Golf

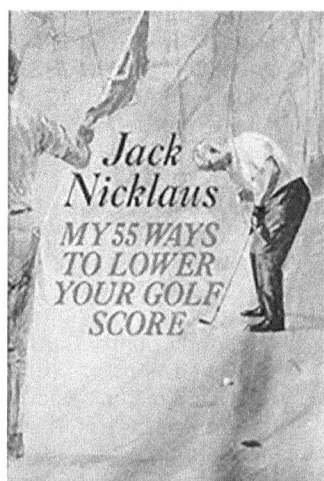

Nicklaus – My 55 Ways to
Lower Your Golf Score

Thousands of color book illustrations visible at
www.rogeregilchrist.com

Bruce Richter:
"The Fairway is Mine – One Hundred Years
of the Brisbane Golf Club" .... 1996 .... $45
Gervase C. Riddell:
"Practical Golf Course Design And
Construction" .... 1973 .... $60
Ridgewood C. C:
"The Ridgewood Country Club History
1890-1940" .... 1940 .... $75
Harold Riley:
"Following the Open" .... 2010 .... $350
"Golf Sketches 1967 Open Championship
at Hoylake" (100 Copies) .... 1967 .... $225
"Golf Sketches Jack Nicklaus Turnberry
1977" .... 1977 .... $225
"Golf Sketches 1990 LA Open .... 1990 .... $95
"Golf Sketches 1991 Ryder Cup"
(150 Copies) .... 1991 .... $1100
"Golf Sketches 2005 Open Championship ..... 2005 .... $250
"Golf Studies Harold Riley at Dunhill" .... 2001 .... $225
"The Belfry" .... 2001 .... $225
"Henry Cotton at Eighty" .... 1987 .... $150
"Jack Nicklaus Muirfield 1993"
(10 Signed Copies) .... 1993 .... $750
"Sketches From the Belfry" (500 Copies) ...... 1993 .... $125
Signed Copies (200 Copies) .... 1993 .... $250
"Some Golfing Dogs" (100 Copies) .... 1998 .... $95
"Turnberry 1994" .... 1994 .... $350
"World Cup Golf" (100 Copies) .... 1993 .... $195
John Riley:
"Royal Salisbury Golf Club Commemorative
Brochure" .... 1968 .... $25
Norman H. Rimmer:
"Mere Golf And Country Club Golden
Jubilee 1934-1984" .... 1985 .... $15
Ringway G. C:
"Ringway Golf Club 75th Anniversary
1909-1984" .... 1984 .... $20
Robert K. Risk:
"Songs of The Links" .... 1904 .... $225
Carol Rissel:
"The 1982 US Open Book" .... 1982 .... $45
Phil Ritson:
"Golf Your Way" .... 1992 .... $10

Roanoke C. C:
"Golf in Roanoke Va. "The Magic City" .... 1916 .... $650
Beverley Robb:
"Collectible Golfing Novelties" .... 1992 .... $25
George Robb:
"Historical Gossip About Golf and Golfers" .... 1863 .... $10,000
    USGA Reprint (1500 Copies) .... 1991 .... $95
James Robb:
"Murrayfield Golf Club, The Story of Fifty
    Years" .... 1947 .... $75
J. Cameron Robbie:
"The Chronicle of the Burgess Golfing
    Society of Edinburgh 1735-1935" .... 1936 .... $575
    Reprint .... 1983 .... $85
"The Chronicle of the Burgess Golfing
    Society of Edinburgh 1936-1985" .... 1987 .... $95
J. & P. Robins:
"One hundred Years of Golf –Some Rhyl
    Golf Club History - 1890 –1990 .... 1990 .... $45
Roberts:
"Thurlestone Golf Club, The Centenary" .... 1997 .... $25
Graham Roberts:
"Townsville Golf Club Centenial History
    1893-1993" .... 1993 .... $35
Arthur E. Roberts:
"Handbook For Caddies" .... 1914 .... $125
Clifford Roberts:
"The Story of the Augusta National
    Golf Club" .... 1976 .... $300
    Limited Edition presented to Staff .... 1976 .... $600
G. P. Roberts:
"Southport & Ainsdale Golf Club.
    The Ryder Cup 1933" .... 1991 .... $150
Henry Roberts:
"The Green Book of Golf: Pacific Coast" .... 1914 .... $750
"The Green Book of Golf 1923-1924" .... 1924 .... $325
"The Green Book of Golf 1925-26" .... 1926 .... $225
Palmer W. Roberts:
"Fore: The Golfer's International Cookbook" . 1978 .... $15
A .J. Robertson:
"The A.B.C. of Golf" .... 1904 .... $275
Frank N. Robertson:
"Golf Gleanings Old And New And The
    History of The Maritime Seniors'

Golf Association" .... 1953 .... $250
G. S. Robertson:
"A History of The Stromness Golf Courses,
  With Notes On The Kirkwall And Isles
  Courses" .... 1974 .... $20
J. S. Robertson:
"A Century of Golf On Dartford Heath
  1891-1991" (1000 Copies)................. 1992 .... $55
James K. Robertson:
"About St Andrews - And About" .... 1973 .... $35
"St. Andrews: Home of Golf" .... 1967 .... $55
  60 Copies signed by Nicklaus............. 1967 .... $250
  Revised Edition............................... 1974 .... $25
Kolin Robertson:
"Some Yorkshire Golf Courses" .... 1935 .... $525
Maud Gordon Robertson:
"Hints To Lady Golfers"............................ 1909 .... $700
W. Heath Robinson:
"Humors of Golf"...................................... 1923 .... $650
  Reprint... 1975 .... $35
Larry Robinson:
"Golf Secrets of The Pros" .... 1956 .... $25
Lawrence Robinson:
"History of The Blind Brook Club" .... 1947 .... $75
  Facsimile Reprint .... 1992 .... $25
Lawrence Robinson & James Graham:
"Golfer's Digest" .... 1966 .... $20
Robby Robinson:
"Golf Guide To The Caribbean, Including
  The Bahamas & Bermuda" .... 1983 .... $20
Spencer Robinson:
"Festina Lente A History of the the Royal
  Hong Kong Golf Club 1889-1989 .... 1989 .... $85
Nancy Robison:
"Nancy Lopez: Wonder Woman of Golf"........ 1979 .... $15
William J. Roche:
"Wollaston Golf Club 50th, 75th and
  100 Anniversary (3 Volumes) .... 1995 .... $195
Rock Island Arsenal G. C:
"Rock Island Arsenal Golf Club".................. 1982 .... $15
"Rocky Mountain G. C.:
"Rocky Mountains Country Club" .... 1905 .... $150
Phil Rodgers:
"Play Lower Handicap Golf" .... 1986 .... $15

Phillip H. Rodgers:
"How To Play St. Andrews Old Links Course". 1951 .... $55
Robert Rodrigo:
"The Birdie Book"...................................... 1967 .... $35
Chi Chi Rodriguez:
"101 Super Shots" .... 1990 .... $10
"Chi Chi's Secrets of Power Golf"................ 1967 .... $15
"Everybody's Golf Book" .... 1975 .... $15
Chi Chi Rodriguez & Harry Stroiman:
"Chi Chi's Golf Secret" .... 1964 .... $20
Rev. Charles Roger:
"History of St Andrews" .... 1849 ...... $1495
      2nd Edition .... 1849 .... $400
Rolling Rock:
"Rolling Rock Club" .... 1939 .... $75
O. B. Rominger:
"The Desert Valley Country Club" .... 1975 .... $15
Romsey G. C:
"Romsey Golf Club".................................. 1951 .... $70
"Romsey Golf Club Official Handbook".......... 1971 .... $40
John Ronald:
"Royal Colwood Golf Club: The First 90
      Years".. 2003 .... $35
Eric Room:
"Wrexham Golf Club Its History Since 1906". 1996 .... $45
J. P. Rooney:
"Play Good Golf" .... 1939 .... $65
Tim Rosaforte:
"Heartbreak Hill .... 1996 .... $15
"PGA Tour '90" .... 1991 .... $25
Bob Rosburg:
"The Putter Book" .... 1963 .... $20
William G. Rose & Charles M. Newcomb:
"Cut Down That Score: The Psychology
      of Golf" .... 1925 .... $350
Joel Rosen:
"The Philosophy of Dub McDub" .... 1933 .... $55
Art Rosenbaum:
"Golf at the Presidio 1895-1995"................ 1994 .... $60
A. C. Gordon Ross:
"A Mixed Bag of Golfing Verse" .... 1977 .... $10
Campbell Ross:
"The Fun of the Fairway"........................... 1943 .... $195
"More Fun of the Fairway" .... 1945 .... $175

Charles Ross:
"The Haunted Seventh" .... 1922 .... $300
Donald J. Ross:
"The Partial List of Prominent Golf Courses
    Designed By Donald J. Ross" .... 1930 .... $775
"Golf Has Never Failed Me" (400 Copies) ..... 1996 .... $250
John M. Ross:
"Golf Businessman's Almanac 1968" .... 1968 .... $10
"Golf Businessman's Almanac 1969" .... 1969 .... $10
"The Golfer's Coloring Book" .... 1962 .... $15
"Liberty Mutual's 18 Tips From18 Legends
    of Golf" .... 1986 .... $15
Rossbach:
"A History of the Century Country Club
    1898-1973" .... 1973 .... $65
Reverand T. Norman Rowsell:
"Eltham Lodge, The Eltham Golf Clubhouse" . 2010 .... $25
    Ltd Edition of 50 Hardbound .... 2010 .... $50
Robert J. Rotella:
"Golf Is A Game of Confidence" .... 1996 .... $10
"The Golf of Your Dreams" .... 1997 .... $10
Robert J. Rotella & Linda Bunker:
"Mind Mastery For Winning Golf" .... 1981 .... $10
Bob Rotella & Bob Cullen:
"Golf Is Not A Game of Perfect" .... 1995 .... $15
"Golf Is A Game of Confidence" .... 1995 .... $15
"Putting Out of Your Mind" .... 2005 .... $10
Rother G. C:
"The Rother Golf Club" .... 1924 .... $75
John Rotherfield:
"The Official Handbook of Golf In
    Somerset 1938-1939" .... 1939 .... $125
J. H. Rothwell and F. Purchas:
"Brighton And Hove Golf Club Jubilee
    1887-1973" .... 1973 .... $50
Rough & The Fairway:
" The Rough and the Fairway" .... 1922 .... $550
Round Hill Club:
"Round Hill Club 1922-1979" (600 Copies) ... 1979 .... $75
Anthony Rowan-Robertson:
"Aldeburgh Golf Club" .... 1973 .... $55
Ralph Rowland:
"The Humors of Golf" .... 1903 .... $2995

Thousands of color book illustrations visible at
www.rogeregilchrist.com

Rowlands Castle G. C:
Rowlands Castle Golf Book Centenary
Handbook"....................................... 2001 .... $40
Reginald H. Roy:
"The Vancouver Club. First Century
1889-1989" .... 1989 .... $75
Royal & Ancient Game of Golf:
"The Royal and Ancient Game of Golf" .... 1950 .... $45
Royal & Ancient Golf Club of St. Andrews:
"Decisions By The Rules of Golf Committee
Of The Royal And Ancient Golf Club
1909-1910" .... 1911 .... $225
"Decisions By The Rules of Golf Committee
of The Royal And Ancient Golf Club
1909-1913" .... 1914 .... $175
"Decisions By The Rules of Golf Committee
of The Royal And Ancient Golf Club
1909-1919" .... 1920 .... $155
"Decisions By The Rules of Golf Committee
of The Royal And Ancient Golf Club
1909-1924" .... 1925 .... $125
"Decisions By The Rules of Golf Committee
of The Royal And Ancient Golf Club
1909-1928" .... 1929 .... $125
"Decisions By The Rules of Golf Committee
of The Royal And Ancient Golf Club
1934" .... 1935 .... $125
"Golf Rules Illustrated" .... 1969 .... $20
"Golf Rules Illustrated" .... 1980 .... $10
"Royal and Ancient Golf Club of
St. Andrews Reports For 1948"........... 1949 .... $350
"Rules & List of Members" .... 1927 .... $400
"Rules of Golf"... 1888 ......$1750
"Rules of Golf"... 1891 .... $500
"Rules of Golf"... 1939 .... $25
"rules of Golf"... 1949 .... $20
"Rules of Golf"... 1984 .... $5
"Rules of the Royal and Ancient Golf
Club of St. Andrews With
Alphabetical List of Members 1910"..... 1914 .... $265
"The Rules of Golf as Adopted by the R&A"... 1899 ....$1750
Royal Antwerp G. C:
"Royal Antwerp Golf Club 1888-1988".......... 1988 .... $95

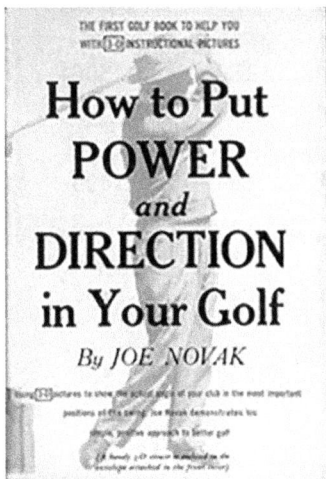

Novak – How to Put Power
And Direction in Your Golf

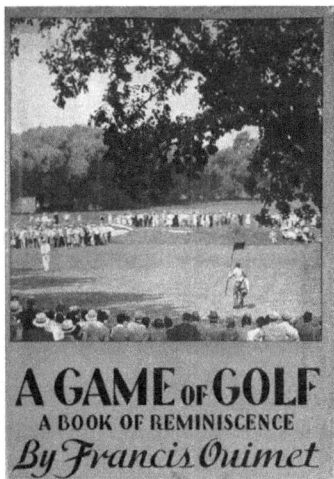

Quimet – A Game of Golf A Book
of Reminiscence

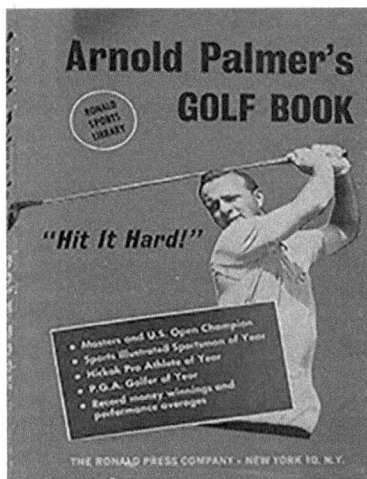

Palmer – Arnold Palmer's
Golf Book Hit it Hard

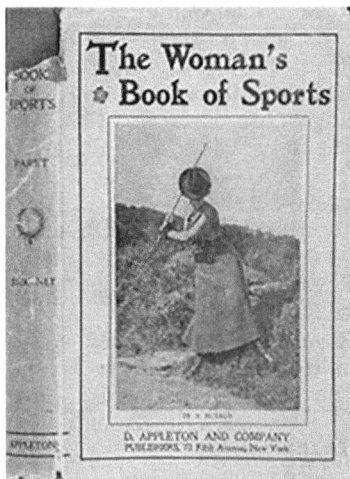

Paret – The Womens Book of
Sports (1st Edition Dust Jacket)

Thousands of color book illustrations visible at
www.rogeregilchrist.com

Royal Blackheath G. C:
"Rules for the Government of the Royal
Blackheath Golf Club" .... 1868 .... $2500
"Royal Blackheath Golf Club" .... 1970 .... $100
Royal Bombay G. C:
"Centenary Souvenir Handbook of The Royal
Bombay Golf Club 1842-1942" .... 1942 .... $495
Royal Burgess Golfing Society:
"Royal Burgess Golfing Society of Edinburgh
1735-1985 250th Anniversary
Celebration" .... 1985 .... $35
Royal Canberra G. C:
"Royal Canberra Golf Club: The First
75 Years 1926-2001" .... 2001 .... $50
Royal Cape G. C:
"Royal Cape Golf Club Centenary Year
1885-1985" .... 1985 .... $65
Royal Cinque Ports G. C:
"Royal Cinque Ports Golf Club" .... 1921 .... $150
Royal Cromer G. C:
"Royal Cromer Golf Club 1888-1988" .... 1988 .... $25
Royal Dublin G. C:
"Royal Dublin Golf Club. Diamond
Jubilee Year 1885-1945 .... 1945 .... $950
"Royal Dublin Golf Club 1885-1963" .... 1963 .... $95
Royal Eastbourne G. C:
"Royal Eastbourne Golf Club" .... 1938 .... $90
"The Royal Eastbourne Golf Club
1887-1987" .... 1987 .... $20
Royal Golf Balls:
"The Most Violated Golf Rules" .... 1957 .... $50
Royal Guernsey G. C:
"Royal Guernsey Golf Club" .... 1961 .... $35
Royal Harare G. C:
"Royal Harare 1898-1998" .... 1998 .... $35
Royal Hong Kong G. C:
"The Royal Hong Kong Golf Club
Members Handbook" .... 1980 .... $20
Royal Insurance:
"Revised Rules of Golf" .... 1908 .... $65
"Revised Rules of Golf .... 1912 .... $50
Royal Jersey G. C:
"The Royal Jersey Golf Club" .... 1950 .... $45

Royal Lytham & St. Annes:
"Royal Lytham And St. Annes Golf Club" ...... 1938 .... $150
"Royal Lytham And St. Annes Golf Club
    Diamond Jubilee 1898-1958"............. 1958 .... $60
Royal Montreal G. C:
"The Royal Montreal Golf Club 1873-1923" ... 1923 .... $475
"The Royal Montreal Golf Club 1873-1973" ... 1973 .... $95
Royal Musselburgh G. C:
"Royal Musselburgh Golf Club 1774-1974".... 1974 .... $150
Royal North Devon G. C:
"The Royal North Devon Golf Club Rules
    for the Game 1889" .... 1889 .... $650
"Rules of The Royal North Devon Golf Club".. 1903 .... $350
Royal Oaks C. C:
"Royal Oaks Country Club: Celebrating
    50 Years 1945-1995" .... 1984 .... $50
Royal Poinciana G. C:
"Royal Poinciana Golf Club, Naples Florida:
    Twentieth Anniversary Celebration
    1969-1989" .... 1989 .... $45
"Royal Poinciana Golf Club, The First
    Twenty-Five Years 1969-1994".......... 1994 .... $45
Royal Portrush G. C:
"Royal Portrush Golf Club Official Handbook " 1975 .... $50
Royal Salisbury G. C:
"Royal Salisbury Golf Club, 75th
    Anniversary 1898-1973".................... 1973 .... $85
Royal Singapore G. C:
"Royal Singapore Golf Club" .... 1957 .... $75
Royal Sydney G. C:
"Short History of The Royal Sydney Golf
    Club" .... 1949 .... $225
Royal Tarlair G. C:
"On our Own Braesides. Royal Tarlair Golf
    Club The Founding Years 1920-1926".. 1993 .... $45
Royal Worlington & Newmarket G. C:
"The Royal Worlington And Newmarket
    Golf Club".. 1950 .... $85
Lorne Rubinstein:
"Links" .... 1990 .... $10
"Summit: The Story of the First
    Seventy-five Years" .... 1987 .... $45
Lorne Rubenstein & J. Briggs:
"Brantford Golf And Country Club

Thousands of color book illustrations visible at
www.rogeregilchrist.com

1879-1979" .... 1979 .... $35
Earl Ruby:
  "The Caddy-Cism: A Manual For Caddies"..... 1937 .... $65
Mason Rudolph:
  "The Short Irons".................................. 1965 .... $20
Rugby G. C:
  "Rugby Golf Club" .... 1951 .... $45
Bob Rule:
  "Champions Golf Club 1957-1976" .... 1976 .... $70
Paul Runyan:
  "Golf Is A Game" .... 1939 .... $35
  "Paul Runyan's Book For Senior Golfers" ...... 1962 .... $10
  "Short Way To Lower Scoring" .... 1979 .... $15
Jack Ruppert:
  "The ABC of Golf".................................. 1946 .... $35
Benjamin Rush:
  "Sermons To Gentlemen Upon
      Temperance And Exercise"................. 1772 ......$2,000
Lorraine Rush:
  "Golf Lessons" .... 1981 .... $10
Dermot J. Russell:
  "Cork Golf Club 1888-1988" .... 1988 .... $65
Edwin F. Russell:
  "Siwanoy Country Club 1901-1976
      75th Anniversary"............................. 1976 .... $50
  "Siwanoy Country Club 1901-2001"............. 2001 .... $50
George C. Russell:
  "The Williamwood Golf Club 1906-1981
      Three Over Fours" .... 1981 .... $25
Jean M. Russell:
  "Old Manchester Golf Club" .... 1988 .... $20
Joe Rutlin:
  "Clinton Country Club: A History and
      Celebration of 100 Years of Golf.
      1895-1995" .... 1995 .... $60
Joseph E. G. Ryan:
  "Golfers' Green Book 1902"...................... 1902 .... $575
  "Golfers' Green Book 1906"...................... 1906 .... $500
William Ryan:
  "The History of Innes Arden 1899-1973" ...... 1973 .... $75
  "The History of Innes Arden 1899-1980" ...... 1980 .... $35
Peter Ryde:
  "Halford Hewitt: A Festival of Foursomes"..... 1984 .... $100
  "Mostly Golf: A Bernard Darwin Anthology"... 1976 .... $85

"Royal And Ancient Championship
    Records 1860-1980" .... 1981 .... $60
"Strokesaver The Official Course Guide,
    The Royal St. George's Golf Club" .... 1981 .... $25
Ogier Rysden:
"The Book of Blues".................................. 1900 .... $75
G. S.:
"Northern Golf Club, Abridged History
    1896-1946" .... 1946 .... $45
R. A. S:
"The Links: An Auld Kirk Allegory" .... 1895 ....$1495
Ernie Sabayrac:
"Professionalizing The Golf Pro Shop"........... 1975 .... $35
Edwin L. Sabin:
"The Magic Mashie And Other Golfish
    Stories"... 1902 .... $495
Allan Sadler & Allen C Sears:
"The Magic Move of Golf" .... 1974 .... $15
Harold Sagar:
"A History of Purley Downs Golf Club" .... 1983 .... $45
Salisbury and South Wilts G. C:
"Salisbury And South Wilts Golf Club" .... 1939 .... $75
J. B. Salmond:
"Andrew Lang and St Andrews, A
    Centenary Anthology" .... 1944 .... $325
"The Story of The R&A"............................. 1956 .... $285
Ross Salmon:
"Devon Golf Clubs".................................. 1984 .... $20
"Golf Clubs Of Cornwall, Isles of Scilly,
    and Jersey"...................................... 1985 .... $20
Daphne Salt & Leo Freestone:
"From Causeway To Clubhouse"................... 1991 .... $20
Saltburn-By-The-Sea G. C:
"Saltburn-By-The-Sea Golf Club".................. 1949 .... $40
Victor Salvatore Jr.:
"The Otsego Golf Club" .... 1994 .... $15
Curt Sampson:
"Hogan"... 1996 .... $30
"The Eternal Summer"............................... 1992 .... $20
"Texas Golf Legends"................................ 1993 .... $45
"The Masters".. 1998 .... $15
"Royal And Ancient" .... 2000 .... $20
Harold A. Sampson:
"Golf Instruction Simplified" .... 1950 .... $40

"Primer of Golf Instruction" .... 1932 .... $350
San Jose Golf & C. C:
"San Jose Golf and Country Club 75th
     Anniversary. 1912-1987. .... 1987 .... $50
Don A. Sanders:
"Go For The Green".................................. 2001 .... $15
Doug Sanders:
"Come Swing With Me" .... 1974 .... $30
"Compact Golf".. 1964 .... $20
T. W. Sanders:
"Lawns And Greens"................................. 1911 .... $75
San Diego C. C:
San Diego Country Club Book. First
     Hundred Years" .... 1998 .... $50
Amelia Sands:
"Indian Hill Club 1914-1964" .... 1964 .... $15
Sandwich:
"Sandwich Borough & Cinque Port Official
     Guide" .... 1952 .... $45
Sandy Says:
"Sandy Says" .... 1934 .... $250
Sandy Lodge G. C:
"Sandy Lodge Golf Club" .... 1965 .... $35
"Sandy Lodge Golf Club 1910-1960" .... 1960 .... $35
San Francisco G. & C. C:
"San Francisco Golf And Country Club, San
     Francisco, California: Constitution and
     By-Laws with Rules and List of
     Members".. 1921 .... $155
"The History of The San Fransisco Golf Club" 1978 .... $145
Santa Anita G. C:
"Ten Commandments of Golf Etiquette" .... 1948 .... $50
Sante Fe Railroad:
"Come and Golf In California" .... 1931 .... $150
"Golf in California" (3rd Edition) .... 1902 .... $600
Ross Santee:
"The Bar X Golf Course"............................. 1933 .... $155
     With Scorecard................................. 1933 .... $195
     Reprint.. 1971 .... $30
Sapphire Valley C. C:
"The Country Club of Sapphire Valley" .... 1990 .... $50
Sapper:
"51 Stories" .... 1934 .... $35
"Out of The Blue"..................................... 1925 .... $175

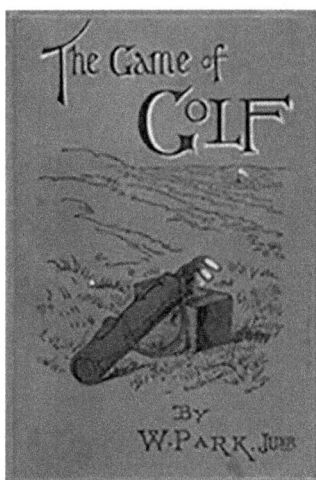

Park – The Game of Golf

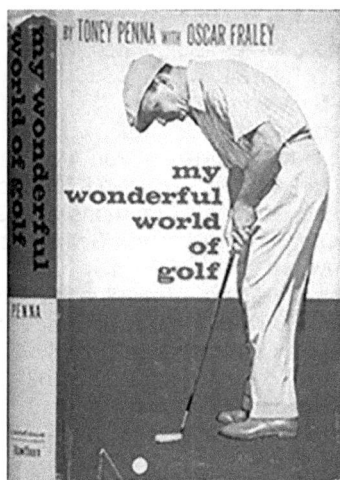

Penna – My Wonderful World Of Golf

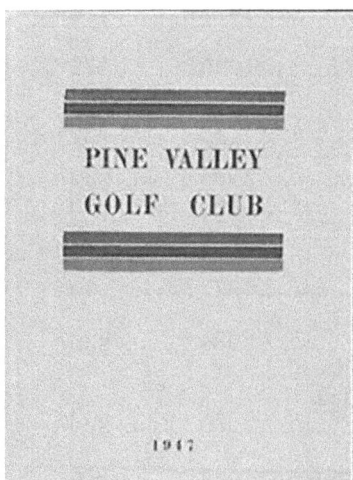

Pine Valley G. C. – 1947

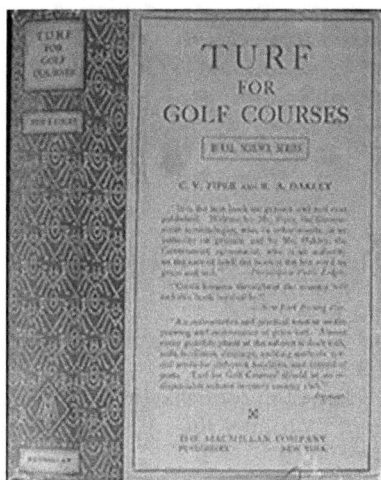

Piper & Oakley – Turf for Golf Courses (Dust Jacket)

Thousands of color book illustrations visible at
www.rogeregilchrist.com

Reprint.. 1935 .... $45
"Uncle James' Golf Match"........................... 1932 .... $150
Reprint.. 1942 .... $50

Gene Sarazen:
"Better Golf After Fifty"............................... 1967 .... $30
"Golf: New Horizons, Pan Am's Guide To
    Golf Courses Round The World" .... 1966 .... $50
"Gene Sarazen's Commonsense Golf Tips".... 1924 .... $125
"Gene Sarazen's World Golf Directory" .... 1977 .... $25
"How to Drive" .... 1933 .... $875
"Thirty Years of Championship Golf" .... 1950 .... $85
    260 Memorial Tournament Reprint ...... 1979 .... $125
    Reprint.. 1987 .... $20
"Want To Be A Golf Champion?".................... 1945 .... $60

Gene Sarazen & Others
"From Tee To Cup".................................... 1937 .... $50
"The Golf Clinic"....................................... 1949 .... $35

D. A. Sargent:
"The Out of Door Library"........................... 1897 .... $95

George Sargent:
"Golf, The Proper Way" .... 1912 .... $75

Howard A. Sasse:
"Putting Facts And Fallacies"...................... 1972 .... $15

Archie Satterfield:
"Sahalee Country Club" (250 Copies)........... 1990 .... $75

Vivien Saunders:
"Advanced Golf"...................................... 1995 .... $25
"The Complete Woman Golfer".................... 1975 .... $55
"The Golfing Mind" .... 1984 .... $30
"Successful Golf" .... 1980 .... $30
"The Golf Handbook For Women" .... 2000 .... $15

Vivien Saunders & Clive Clark:
"The Young Golfer".................................... 1977 .... $10

Saunton G. C:
"Saunton Golf Club" .... 1984 .... $35

E. J. Savage:
"The Story of Felixstowe Ferry Golf Club
    1880-1980" .... 1980 .... $20

Savannah G. C:
"Brief History of The Savannah Golf Club" .... 1975 .... $40

John G. Saxe:
"The Jones' Golf Swing And Other
    Suggestions"...................................... 1948 .... $225
"The Jones' Golf Swing, With Practical

Suggestions By Many Experts"............ 1951 .... $185
Doreen Sayers:
"Ben Sayers 100 Years of Golf In North
  Berwick 1857-1962".......................... 1994 .... $30
John Saywell:
"The Ilkley Centenary: A History of the
  Ilkley Golf Club 1890-1990" .... 1990 .... $95
Neil Scaife:
"Four Hundred Years of The Blackheath
  Goffer" Deluxe Leather Edition of 100 .. 2008 .... $200
Dennis R. Scanlan:
"Scanlan Golf-Kards" .... 1928 .... $195
Vernon Scannell:
"Sporting Literature An Anthology" .... 1987 .... $15
Scarborough South Cliff G. C:
'Scarborough South Cliff Golf Club" .... 1956 .... $25
Arthur C. Scarlett:
"Index And Representitive Price Guide To
  Golf Books 1743-1970"...................... 1970 .... $150
Charles Scatchard:
"Guide to Yorkshire Golf............................ 1955 .... $250
"The Pannal Golf Club"............................... 1960 .... $15
Michael T. Schaefer:
"Across The Pond".................................... 1993 .... $15
Dick Schapp:
"Massacre At Winged Foot"......................... 1974 .... $20
"The Masters" .... 1970 .... $45
"Pro: Frank Beard On The Golf Tour" .... 1970 .... $15
Robert Scharff:
"The Collier Quick And Easy Guide To Golf"... 1963 .... $15
"Golf: Collier Quick And Easy Series" .... 1966 .... $10
"Golf" .... 1968 .... $10
"Golf Magazine's Encyclopedia of Golf" .... 1970 .... $25
"Golf Magazine's Great Golf Courses
  You Can Play" .... 1973 .... $15
"Golf Magazine's Handbook of Golf Strategy" 1971 .... $10
Ann Scheid:
"The Valley Hunt Club: One Hundred Years
  1888-1988 .... 1988.......... $65
Helen B. Schleman:
"Group Golf Instruction"............................ 1934 .... $95
Chuck Schmitt:
"My Golf Clinic"....................................... 1967 .... $10

Jackson Scholz:
 "Fairway Challenge" .... 1964 .... $10
Leslie Schon:
 "The Psychology of Golf" .... 1922 .... $95
J. Ellsworth Schrite:
 "Divots For Dubs" .... 1934 .... $130
Cliff Schrock
 "Rules Of Golf Applied" .... 1995 .... $15
 "Women's Golf Handbook".......................... 1995 .... $10
 "Youth Golf" .... 1994 .... $10
Reg Schroeter:
 "Rivermead Golf Club 1910-1985:
     The First 75 Years" .... 1985 .... $45
Lowell Schulman:
 "Miracle on Breeze Hill: The Making of
     Atlantic Golf Club"............................ 2002 .... $25
Charles M. Schultz:
 "Snoopy's Grand Slam"............................ 1972 .... $65
 "An Educated Slice"................................. 1990 .... $15
Alan T. Schumacher:
 "The Newport Country Club: Its Curious
     History"... 1986 .... $65
Craig Schumacher:
 "Nancy Lopez" .... 1979 .... $15
Gary H. Schwartz:
 "The Art of Golf" .... 1990 .... $25
Clinton Scollard:
 "The Epic of Golf"................................... 1923 .... $195
A Scot:
 "Consistent Golf or, How To Become A
     Champion".. 1934 .... $125
Scotland For Golf:
 "Scotland For Golf"................................... 1961 .... $60
Scotland Home of Golf:
 "Scotland Home of Golf" .... 1960 .... $50
 "Scotland Home of Golf" .... 1978 .... $30
 "Scotland Home of Golf" .... 1981 .... $25
Garnet Scott:
 "A Centenary History of the
     Worcestershire Golf Club" .... 1979 .... $45
Lewis Scott:
 "Par Golf: With 1934 Rule Changes" .... 1934 .... $75
Mike Scott:
 "The Crazy World of Golf"........................... 1985 .... $10

Thousands of color book illustrations visible at
www.rogeregilchrist.com

O.M. Scott and Sons:
"The Seeding and Care of Golf Courses" .... 1922 .... $675
"The Putting Green: Its Planting and Care" ... 1931 .... $550
Patrick W. Scott:
"Huntly Golf Club 1892-1992" .... 1993 .... $45
Tom Scott:
"AA Guide To Golf In Great Britain" .... 1977 .... $45
"Aberdare Golf Club" .... 1953 .... $25
"A Centenary History of The
    Worcestershire Golf Club" .... 1979 .... $25
"A Century of Golf 1860-1960" .... 1960 .... $95
"Adleburgh Golf Club" .... 1957 .... $25
"Ashridge Golf Club" .... 1955 .... $30
"Axe Cliff Golf Club" .... 1962 .... $25
"Barton-On-Sea Golf Club" .... 1958 .... $45
"The Bedford And Country Golf Club" .... 1948 .... $45
"The Berkshire Golf Club" .... 1955 .... $30
"The Bigbury Golf Club" .... 1957 .... $30
"Boldon Golf Club" .... 1953 .... $25
"Bramshaw Golf Club" .... 1962 .... $20
"Brookmans Park Golf Club" .... 1955 .... $75
"Burnham & Berrow Golf Club" .... 1957 .... $25
"Bury St Edmunds Golf Club" .... 1952 .... $45
"Camberley Heath Golf Club" .... 1950 .... $45
"Chipstead Golf Club" .... 1960 .... $35
"Club Golfer's Handbook" .... 1972 .... $15
"The Concise Dictionary of Golf" .... 1978 .... $35
"Dartford Golf Club" .... 1955 .... $40
"The Dyke Golf Club" .... 1952 .... $125
"Ealing Golf Club" .... 1960 .... $25
"The Ferndown Golf Club" .... 1957 .... $65
"Ferndown Golf Club" .... 1968 .... $45
"Fifty Miles of Golf Round London" .... 1952 .... $40
"Filey Golf Club" .... 1957 .... $35
"Formby Golf Club" .... 1968 .... $45
"Golf At Brighton: Hollingsbury Park,
    Dyke And Waterhall Courses" .... 1951 .... $35
"Golf With The Experts" .... 1959 .... $35
"Golf-Begin The Right Way" .... 1974 .... $15
"Golfing Technique In Pictures" .... 1957 .... $30
"Haywards Heath Golf Club Ltd" .... 1973 .... $35
"Hayling Golf Club" .... 1955 .... $40
"Hillside Golf Club" .... 1958 .... $45
"Hornsea Golf Club" .... 1960 .... $35

"Hull Golf Club".. 1960 .... $25
"Hythe & Dibden Golf Club" .... 1951 .... $35
"King's Lynn Golf Club"............................... 1960 .... $25
"Knole Park Golf Club" .... 1955 .... $65
"Knole Park Golf Club" .... 1971 .... $40
"Lytham Green Golf Club" .... 1955 .... $35
"Moor Park Golf Club"................................ 1960 .... $25
"More Golf With The Experts"...................... 1965 .... $25
"Northamptonshire County Golf Club .... 1954 .... $25
"Notts Golf Club"....................................... 1955 .... $20
"The Observer's Book of Golf".................... 1975 .... $15
"Prince's Sandwich".................................. 1960 .... $25
"Portstewart Golf Club" .... 1972 .... $40
"The Royal Birkdale Golf Club Southport" ..... 1955 .... $60
"The Royal Cinque Ports Club" .... 1951 .... $45
"The Royal Cinque Ports Golf Club".............. 1968 .... $35
"Royal Cromer Golf Club" .... 1960 .... $25
"The Royal Eastbourne Golf Club"................ 1951 .... $40
"The Royal Norwich Golf Club" .... 1960 .... $25
"Royal Porthcawl Golf Club"........................ 1960 .... $35
"Saunton Golf Club" .... 1960 .... $20
"Scarborough South Cliff Golf Club"............. 1951 .... $35
"Seacroft Golf Club" .... 1960 .... $20
"The Seaford Golf Club And Dormy House
        Club" .... 1960 .... $25
"Secrets of The Golfing Greats".................... 1965 .... $25
"Sixty Miles Of Golf Around London" .... 1975 .... $15
"Sonning Golf Club".................................... 1965 .... $15
"The South Herts Golf Club" .... 1955 .... $35
"The Stoke Poges Golf Club"....................... 1963 .... $20
"The Story Of Golf" .... 1972 .... $45
"Sunningdale Ladies Golf Club" .... 1960 .... $15
"Swanage And Studland Golf Club".............. 1970 .... $45
"Teignmouth Golf Club" .... 1960 .... $15
"Thurlestone Golf Club Official Handbook" .... 1968 .... $40
"The Observer's Book of Golf".................... 1975 .... $10
"The Trentham Golf Club" .... 1954 .... $25
"Tyrrells Wood Golf Club" .... 1955 .... $25
"West Cornwall Golf Club Book" .... 1955 .... $25
"The Western-Super-Mare Golf Club" .... 1955 .... $25
"Westgate And Birchington Golf Club".......... 1951 .... $20
"The Wilderness Golf Club"......................... 1960 .... $15
"Wimbledon Park Golf Club" .... 1951 .... $30
"Windemere Golf Club" .... 1972 .... $15

Thousands of color book illustrations visible at
www.rogeregilchrist.com

"Woodhall Spa Golf Club" .... 1960 .... $15
"Worcestershire Golf Club" .... 1967 .... $15
"Workington Golf Club" .... 1956 .... $25
"Yelverton Golf Club" .... 1960 .... $15
Tom Scott & Geoffrey Cousins:
"Golf Begins At 45" .... 1960 .... $25
"The Golf Immortals" .... 1968 .... $45
    American Edition .... 1969 .... $25
"Golf For The Not So Young" .... 1960 .... $15
"Golf Secrets of The Masters" .... 1968 .... $25
"The Ind Coope Book of Golf" .... 1965 .... $35
"The Wit of Golf" .... 1972 .... $25
Tom Scott & Webster Evans:
"The Golfer's Year" .... 1950 .... $45
"The Golfer's Year Volume II" .... 1951 .... $35
Scottish Exhibition:
"Scottish Exhibition of Natural History, Art &
    Industry Glasgow 1911"
    (Two Volumes) .... 1911 .... $175
Scottish Golfer:
"Swing Minded" .... 1932 .... $95
Scottish Golf Union:
"Scottish Golf Union Official Yearbook" .... 1961 .... $25
Scottish Ladies Golf Union:
"Official Yearbook" .... 1984 .... $15
Scrabo G. C:
"Scrabo Golf Club 1907-1982 75th
    Anniversary Souvenir Brochure" .... 1983 .... $20
Scriba:
"Tour Round Scottish Golf Links" .... 1888 ......$1,500
Romeyn B. Scribner:
"Senior Golf, Golf Is More Fun After
    Fifty-Five" .... 1960 .... $95
    1000 Copies signed by Chick Evans .... 1960 .... $250
Edward Scudmore:
"Royal Wimbleton Golf Club Centenary 1965" 1965 .... $60
Dick Scuse & Richard G Smith:
"The Olympic Club of San Francisco
    1860-1960" .... 1960 .... $195
Janet Seagle:
"The Club Makers" .... 1980 .... $25
Seagle & Pyne III:
"A Special Place: A History of Somerset Hills
    Country Club" .... 1990 .... $150

Thousands of color book illustrations visible at
www.rogeregilchrist.com

Ray – Golf Clubs and How
To Use Them (1st Edition)

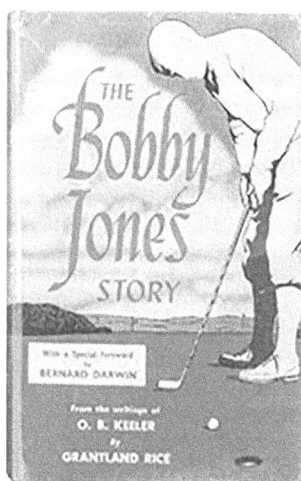

Rice – The Bobby Jones Story

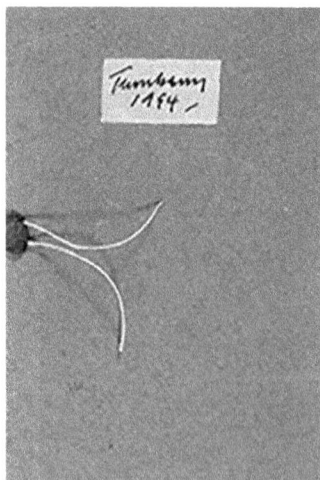

Riley – Turnberry

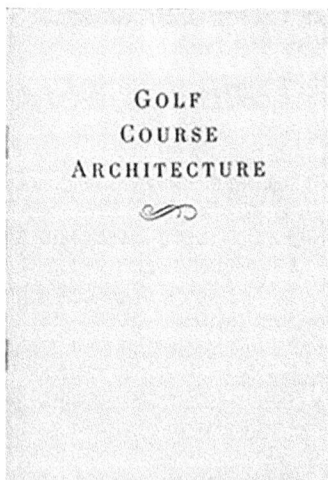

Robert Trent Jones - Golf
Course Architecture

Thousands of color book illustrations visible at
www.rogeregilchrist.com

Alice D. Seagrave:
"Golf Retold: The Story of Golf In Cleveland" 1940 .... $115
Henry Seaton-Karr:
"Golf: Greenings Useful Handbook Series" .... 1907 .... $475
Seattle G. C:
"Seattle Golf Club 1900-1950" .... 1950 .... $35
Secrets of Winning Golf Matches:
"Secrets of Winning Golf Matches With
   A Total Concept For Winning Golf
   And 12 Winning Golf Discoveries" .... 1959 .... $15
Secrets To The Short Game:
"Secrets To The Short Game: Pitching,
   Chipping, Putting"............................. 1976 .... $20
F. H. Seeley:
Eltham Warren Golf Club 1890-1990" .... 1990 .... $45
Segovia G. C:
"Segovia Golf Club in Chiyoda" .... 1993 .... $275
H. A. Seifert:
"The First 75 Years of The Manawatu Golf
   Club 1895-1970" .... 1970 .... $75
Nick Seitz:
"Quick Tips From the CBS Golf Spot" .... 1982 .... $10
"Super Stars of Golf" .... 1978 .... $25
Selangor G. C:
"Twelve Under Fours: An Informal History
   of the Selangor Golf Club; Diamond
   Jubilee 1953" .... 1953 .... $95
Don Selby:
"Examiner Golf Foto Lessons" .... 1955 .... $15
Jack Selleck & Art Bernard:
"Golf is a Trap".. 1968 .... $20
Seminole G. C:
"Seminole Golf Club 1955 Club Book" .... 1955 .... $700
Eric Sen:
"The Lodhi-Delhi Golf Club" .... 1977 .... $15
Prosper L. Senat:
"Through The Greens And Golfers Year
   Book"... 1898 ....$4500
Tom Serpell:
"Golf On Old Picture Postcards".................. 1988 .... $25
Lancelot C. Servos:
"Practical Instruction In Golf"..................... 1905 .... $195
Henry Seton-Karr & Others:
"Golf"... 1907 .... $595

Thousands of color book illustrations visible at
www.rogeregilchrist.com

Burt Seymour:
   "All About Golf: How To Improve Your
      Game" .... 1924 .... $125
Shaker Heights C. C:
   The Shaker Heights Country Club:
      Our Diamond Jubilee"........................ 1988 .... $45
Geoff Shackelford:
"Alister MacKenzie's Cypress Point Club" .... 2000 .... $300
"Masters of The Links" .... 1997 .... $35
   "The Captain. George C Thomas Jr
      And His Golf Architecture"................. 1998 .... $50
   "The Golden Age of Golf Design" .... 1999 .... $20
   "The Good Doctor Returns" .... 1998 .... $20
   "The Riviera Country Club. A Definitve
      History"... 1995 .... $175
Alexander I. Shand:
   "Memories of Gardens" .... 1908 .... $45
Craig Shankland:
   "The Golfer's Stroke-Saving Handbook"........ 1978 .... $15
   "Stroke-Saving For The Handicap Golfer" ..... 1979 .... $10
Shanklin & Sandown G. C:
   "The Shanklin & Sandown Golf Club" .... 1939 .... $30
   "The Shanklin & Sandown Golf Club" .... 1950 .... $60
Andrew Shanley:
   "Fathers, Sons, And Golf"......................... 1997 .... $10
Harold Shapiro:
   "Get Golf Straight" .... 1972 .... $15
Mel Shapiro:
   "Golf: A Turn Of The Century Treasury" .... 1986 .... $30
Sharon C. C:
   "The Sharon Country Club Sixtieth
      Anniversary 1895-1955".................... 1955 .... $35
James E. Shaw:
   "Prestwick Golf Club, A History and Some
      Records" .... 1938 ....$1475
Joseph T. Shaw:
   "Out of The Rough" .... 1934 .... $195
      Reprint... 1991 .... $25
Arthur Shay:
   "40 Common Errors In Golf And How To
      Correct Them"................................. 1978 .... $10
Jim Sheard & Wally Armstrong:
   "In His Grip"... 1997 .... $10
   "Playing The Game" .... 1998 .... $15

Thousands of color book illustrations visible at
www.rogeregilchrist.com

Joseph M. Sheehan:
"How Maureen Orcutt Won 10
    Metropolitan Golf Championships" .... 1969 .... $25
Larry Sheehan:
"Best Golf Humor From Golf Digest" .... 1972 .... $20
"Great Golf Humor From Golf Digest" .... 1979 .... $15
"The Whole Golf Catalog" .... 1979 .... $15
Laurence Sheehan:
"A Passion For Golf" .... 1994 .... $30
Patty Sheehan & Betty Hicks:
"Patty Sheehan On Golf" .... 1996 .... $15
Alan Sheldon:
"Rhode Island Country Club 1911-1961
    Fiftieth Anniversary" .... 1962 .... $20
Colin Sheldon:
"Reigate Heath And Its Golf Club" .... 1982 .... $15
Jeff Shelley:
"Golf Courses of The Pacific Northwest" .... 1990 .... $15
"The Northwest Golfers Almanac" .... 1991 .... $10
Jeff Shelley & Michael Riste:
"Championships And Friendships" .... 1999 .... $25
Warner Shelly:
"Pine Valley Golf Club, A Chronicle" .... 1982 .... $145
Shell Oil Co.:
"Shell's Wonderful World of Golf 1966" .... 1966 .... $65
"Shell's Wonderful World of Golf 1967" .... 1967 .... $45
"Shell's Wonderful World of Golf 1968" .... 1968 .... $40
"Shell's Wonderful World of Golf 1969" .... 1969 .... $40
"Shell's Wonderful World of Golf 1970" .... 1970 .... $30
J. H. Shennan:
"A History of Lancaster Golf Club" .... 2001 .... $10
F. S. Shenstone:
"Golf Rules of Golf Decisions, Tables of
    Penalties and General Index" .... 1924 .... $350
"Golf Rules and Decisions...." .... 1927 .... $150
"Golf Rules And Decisions..." .... 1935 .... $95
James Shepherd Jr.:
"Golf Shots" .... 1924 .... $225
Thomas H. Shepherd:
"Modern Athens" .... 1829 .... $395
James Sheridan:
"Sheridan of Sunnydale: My Fifty Six
    Years As A Caddie Master" .... 1967 .... $65

Thousands of color book illustrations visible at
www.rogeregilchrist.com

John D. Sheridan:
"It Stands To Reason" .... 1947 .... $35
James W. Sherman:
"Joey Gets The Golf Bug" .... 1961 .... $10
Sherwood Forest G. C:
"Sherwood Forest Golf Club"........................ 1924 .... $75
Alexander Shewan:
"Homeric Games at an Ancient St Andrews".. 1911 .... $165
Shinnecock Hills G. C.:
"Constitution By-Laws, List of Officers
    and Members"................................... 1906 .... $400
"National Golf Links Of America" .... 1913 .... $400
"Shinnecock Hills Golf Club Revised
    Constitution".................................... 1930 .... $150
Robert L. Shinnie:
"The Book of Kingussie"............................ 1911 .... $200
Robert L. Shirley:
"Brae Burn Country Club. One Hundred Years
    of Golf and Family Life 1897-1977" ..... 1997 .... $75
Shirley Park G. C:
"The Shirley Park Golf Club" .... 1955 .... $85
R. K. Shone:
"Bedford Golf Club 1892-1967".................... 1967 .... $45
    Reprint.. 2000 .... $20
Alan Shore:
"Wells Golf Club Centenary 1893-1993" .... 1993 .... $60
Josselyn M. Shore:
"The Story of The Fresh Meadow
    Country Club" .... 1985 .... $50
Julian Shore:
"Rattle His Bones"................................... 1941 .... $25
Cleeke Shotte:
"The Golf Craze: Sketches and Rhymes" ...... 1907 ....$1550
I. Robert M. Shultz:
"Directory of Municipal And Tax Supported
    Golf Courses".................................. 1959 .... $15
Gil Sibley:
"Northampton Golf Club. A Centenary
    History 1893-1993........................... 1992 .... $50
Sidcup G. C:
"Sidcup Golf Club".................................... 1911 .... $65
Sidmouth G. C:
"The Sidmouth Golf Club"........................... 1931 .... $60

Terence Sieg:
"Golf Travels Guide To The Worlds
      Greatest Golf Destinations" .... 1997 .... $20
Charlie Sifford:
"Just Let Me Play" .... 1992 .... $20
Silver King:
"The Silver King Handbook The Rules of
      Golf" .... 1934 .... $50
"This Golf" .... 1946 .... $35
Silver Niblick:
"The Silver Niblick: A Fond Remembrance
      And Good Times" .... 1972 .... $15
Jim Silvey:
"Golf As I See It" .... 1969 .... $15
"How To Learn The Total Game" .... 1982 .... $10
Richard Simek & Richard O'Brien:
"Total Golf: A Behavioral Approach" .... 1981 .... $15
Gordon G. Simmonds:
"The Walker Cup 1922-1999 Golf's Finest
      Contest" (1950 Copies) .... 2000 .... $125
      Limited Edition of 200 Copies .... 2000 .... $475
Marlin L. Simmons:
"Golf And The Subconscious Mind" .... 1984 .... $10
Richard Simmons:
"The Young Golfer" .... 1999 .... $10
George Simms:
"John Player Golf Yearbook 1973" .... 1973 .... $15
"John Player Golf Yearbook 1974" .... 1974 .... $15
"John Player Golf Yearbook 1975" .... 1975 .... $15
"John Player Golf Yearbook 1976" .... 1976 .... $15
"The World of Golf 1977" .... 1977 .... $15
"The World of Golf 1978" .... 1978 .... $15
"The World of Golf 1979" .... 1979 .... $15
"The World of Golf 1980" .... 1980 .... $15
Leonard Simons:
"The Royal & Ancient Beginning of
      Franklin Hills Country Club" .... 1985 .... $20
O. C. Simons:
"Landscape Gardening" .... 1939 .... $75
R. G. Simons:
"The History of West Herts Golf Club
      1890-1989" .... 1988 .... $35
Gordon Simpson:
"Golfing Greats" .... 1989 .... $10

Thousands of color book illustrations visible at
www.rogeregilchrist.com

Harold Simpson:
"The Seven Stages of Golf, and Other
Golf Stories In Picture And Verse" .... 1909 ...... $1250
Simpson, Mize, & Roberts:
"Focus - The Name of The Game"................ 1999 .... $15
S. Raleigh Simpson:
"A Green Crop"... 1937 .... $250
"The Lyre Of The Links" .... 1920 .... $475
Walter Grindley "Bart" Simpson:
"The Art of Golf" .... 1887 ...... $2150
USGA Reprint (1400 Copies) .... 1982 .... $275
John Sinclair:
"The Statistical Account of Scotland"
(21 Volumes) .... 1791 ...... $1750
Singapore Island C. C:
"Golf Rules In Pictures"............................. 1969 .... $75
Mrs. James Singleton & Eliot Thorpe:
"Sara Bay Country Club 1926-1976"............ 1976 .... $15
Calvin H. Sinnette:
"Forbidden Fairways"................................. 1998 .... $15
Sirrah:
"Slaves of The Links"................................ 1914 .... $275
Sitwell Park G. C:
"Sitwell Park Golf Club"............................. 1937 .... $40
Billy Sixty:
"Golfax".. 1946 .... $45
Billy Sixty Sr. & Billy Sixty Jr.:
"Have Fun Golfing In The 60's" .... 1960 .... $15
John Skene:
"The Lawes and Acts of Parliament…".......... 1597 ...... $2500
Three Volumes from 1597 to 1621)
Skerries G. C:
"Skerries Golf Club".................................. 1977 .... $15
Skosie C. C:
Skosie Country Club 1897-1997 .... 1997 .... $45
Dick Skuse:
"One Hundred Years, the Centennial
1860-1960" .... 1960 .... $125
Ann Slack:
"The Mountain View Country Club
1898-1976" .... 1976 .... $35
Charles Slack:
"Blue Fairways" .... 1999 .... $15

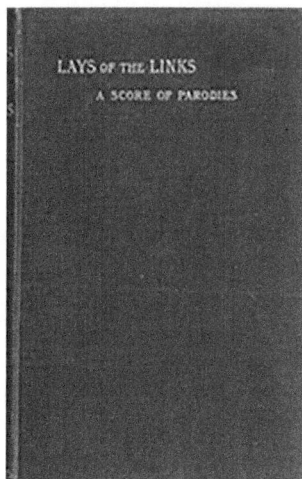

Ross – Lays of the Links

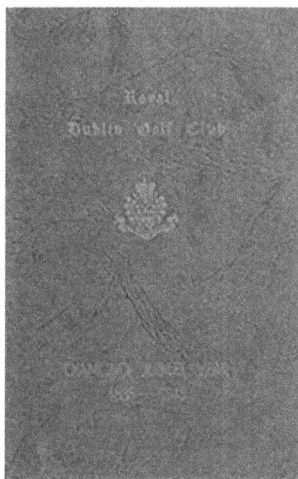

Royal Dublin G. C. - Diamond Jubilee Year 1885-1945

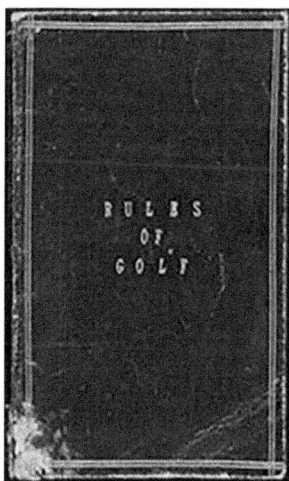

Royal Perth Golfing Society - Rules of the Game of Golf

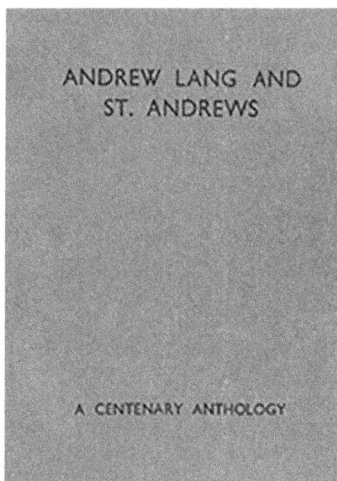

Salmond – Andrew Lang and St Andrews

L. Ert Slack:
"Golf Putting" .... 1936 .... $40
Slattery & Gray:
"The Days We Went A-Golfing: The First
    Hundred Years of West Linton
    Golf Club .... 1990 .... $45
Slazengers:
"Hitting Straight Into Golf With Slazengers"............. 1951.............. $25
Bill Sliger:
"Washtenaw Country Club 1899-1999".................. 1999.............. $45
Sleepy Hollow C. C:
"The Sleepy Hollow Country Club" .... 1919 .... $185
"The Sleepy Hollow of Today" .... 1931 .... $65
John Sleight:
"The City Centenary 1891-1991".................. 1991 .... $25
H. Slocum:
"The Easy Way To Learn Golf Rules" .... 1961 .... $25
David C. Smail:
"Prestwick Golf Club 1851-1989"
    (1250 Copies) .... 1989 .... $195
John Smart:
"A Round of The Links: Views of
    The Golf Greens of Scotland".............. 1893 .... $18,000
                Reprint .... 1986 .... $250
Patrick Smartt:
"Golf Grave And Gay" .... 1964 .... $25
"If You Must Play Golf".............................. 1963 .... $20
"Sussex Golf, The 19th Century Club" .... 1977 .... $15
Allan E. Smith:
"History of The Seattle Golf Club 1960-1972"
    (1000 Copies) .... 1972 .... $75
Alex Smith:
"Lessons In Golf" .... 1907 .... $200
Banjo Smith:
"Columbia Country Club 1948-1952" .... 1952 .... $35
Charles Smith:
"The Aberdeen Golfers: Record and
    Reminiscences" (150 Copies) .... 1909 ..... $2,950
    Reprint (200 copies) .... 1982 .... $350
David Smith:
"Royal Winchester Golf Club Centenary
    1888-1988" .... 1988 .... $25
David L. Smith & John P. Holmes:
"The Gods of Golf" .... 1996 .... $25

Don Smith:
"The Young Sportsman's Guide To Golf" .... 1961 .... $20
Douglas LaRue Smith:
"Winged Foot Story: The Golf, The People,
    The Friendly Trees" .... 1984 .... $95
Emil Smith:
"Golf Laffs: 150 Cartoons To Suit You
    To A Tee" .... 1964 .... $10
Everett M. Smith:
"Synonym Golf: A New Indoor Game" .... 1931 .... $115
Frank S. Smith:
"How You Can Become A Good Putter" .... 1925 .... $110
Frederick W. Smith:
"Skytop-An Adventure" .... 1963 .... $15
Garden C. Smith:
"Golf" .... 1897 .... $550
"Side Lights On Golf" .... 1907 .... $525
"The World of Golf: The Isthmian Library" .... 1898 .... $725
George F. Smith:
"Hints To Golfers" .... 1929 .... $175
Horton Smith & Marian Benton:
"The Velvet Touch" .... 1965 .... $95
Horton Smith & Dawson Taylor:
"The Master's Secrets of Holing Putts" .... 1982 .... $15
"The Secret of Holing Putts" .... 1961 .... $35
"The Secret of Perfect Putting" .... 1963 .... $35
James Smith:
"The Machrihanish Golf Club" .... 1910 ....$1350
James Greig Smith:
"Woodspring" .... 1898 ......$2,000
Jim Smith:
"Acton Golf Club, A History" .... 1981 .... $20
Joseph S. K. Smith & B. S. Weastell:
"The Foundations of Golf" .... 1925 .... $195
    1st US Edition .... 1926 .... $55
Julian C. Smith:
"Breaking Ninety: A History of The Country
    Club Of Ithaca 1900-1989" .... 1990 .... $30
Kenneth Smith:
"Golf Club Alterations And Repairs" .... 1965 .... $15
Larry Smith:
"Golf Pix: A Pictorial Guide To Golfing, Palm
    Beach County Including Tequesta" ..... 1984 .... $15

Thousands of color book illustrations visible at
www.rogeregilchrist.com

Mel Smith:
"Golf Mel's Way" .... 1975 .... $10
Parker Smith:
"Golf Techniques: How To Improve Game" ... 1973 .... $10
Patricia Jean Smith:
"The Golf Widows Revenge"........................ 1986 .... $10
Peter D. Smith:
"Master Class Golf" .... 1993 .... $15
Peter Smith:
"Single Figure Golfer" .... 1995 .... $10
R. B. Smith:
"Blackburn Golf Club: 100 Years 1894-1994" 1994 .... $95
R. Boyd Smith:
"The History of The Sylvania Country Club" .. 1959 .... $35
R. Craig Smith:
"Enjoy Golf And Win"................................ 1981 .... $10
Rick Smith:
"How To Find Your Perfect Golf Swing"......... 1998 .... $20
Robert Howie Smith:
"The Golfer's Yearbook For 1866"................ 1867 .... $18,500
Seamus Smith:
"Grange Golf Club"................................... 1977 .... $15
Shirlee H. Smith:
"The Tacoma Country and Golf Club"
     (1000 Copies) .... 1980 .... $100
"The Tacoma Country And Golf Club
     Centennial 1894-1994" (1000 Copies) . 1994 .... $55
T.A. Smith & K.R Parker:
"On Fulwood Green: The Story of Preston
     Golf Club 1892-1992"....................... 1992 .... $55
Terry Smith:
"Aussie Golf Trivia" .... 1985 .... $10
"Australian Golf, The First 100 Years" .... 1982 .... $45
"The Complete Book of Australian Golf"........ 1975 .... $35
"Tony Rafty's Golfers: A Treasury of
     Stars in Caricature"........................... 1975 .... $15
W. H. Smith:
"Symposium On Golf"............................... 1912 .... $75
Wiley Smith:
"Homer!"... 1954 .... $150
Bryan Smyth:
"Wetherby Golf Club, A Short History" .... 1985 .... $15
J. C. Snaith:
"Lord Cobbleigh Disappears"...................... 1936 .... $40

"Curiouser And Curiouser".......................... 1935 .... $45
Myrene Snarr & Patricia Corn:
"An Illustrated Guide To Northern
 California Golf Courses".................... 1978 .... $20
Sam Snead:
"Correcting Common Golf Faults" .... 1952 .... $20
"The Driver Book".................................... 1963 .... $25
"The Education of A Golfer" .... 1962 .... $25
 Memorial Tournament Reprint
 (410 Copies)................................... 1984 .... $125
 Ltd Edition (2000 Copies) .... 1997 .... $95
"Golf Begins At Forty"............................... 1978 .... $30
"How To Hit A Golf Ball From Any Sort
 of Lie"... 1950 .... $25
"How To Play Golf, And Professional Tips
 On Improving Your Score" .... 1946 .... $30
"Natural Golf"... 1953 .... $30
"Pigeons, Marks, Hustlers and Other Golf
 Bettors You Can Beat"...................... 1986 .... $25
"Short Cuts To Long Drives" .... 1965 .... $15
"Sam Snead On Golf" .... 1961 .... $25
"Sam Snead Teaches You His Simple Key
 Approach To Golf"............................ 1975 .... $40
"Sam Snead's Basic Guide To Good Golf"...... 1968 .... $15
"Sam Snead's Celebrity Golf Tips" .... 1960 .... $15
"Sam Snead's Quick Way To Better Golf"...... 1938 .... $35
"Sam Snead's Secrets of Golf" .... 1960 .... $15
"Slammin' Sam" .... 1986 .... $20
"Stop-Action Golf Book, 2-4 Iron"................ 1960 .... $25
"The Game I Love"................................... 1997 .... $15
"The Greenbriers Sam Snead Teaches Golf".. 1966 .... $25
"The Lessons I've Learned" .... 1989 .... $15
Sam Snead & Bob Considine:
"How To Cut Strokes Off Your Game".......... 1945 .... $40
Richard Sneddon:
"The Golf Stream".................................... 1941 .... $115
George P. Snell:
"Golf At Hotel Del Monte" .... 1904 .... $200
Hal Snow:
"Royal Johannesburg Golf Club 1890-1990".. 1990 .... $35
Franklin B. Snyder:
"Early Days of the Mountain View Country
 Club 1898-192".............................. 1927 .... $175

Thousands of color book illustrations visible at
www.rogeregilchrist.com

Jerry Snyder:
"The Golf Collectors Handbook"................... 1997 .... $20
Fred Solar:
"Manual For Learning The Natural Golf
    Swing For Men And Women" .... 1993 .... $10
Clyne Soley:
"How Well Should You Putt? A Search For
    A Putting Standard" .... 1977 .... $15
Mark Soltau:
"California Golf"...................................... 1989 .... $15
Somerset and Its Golf:
"Somerset And Its Golf"............................ 1932 .... $95
Somerset & Gloucestershire:
"Golf in Somerset and Gloucestershire"........ 1962 .... $35
Robert Sommers:
"Golf Anecdotes"..................................... 1995 .... $20
"The US Open" .... 1987 .... $20
"1988 U.S Open Championship Rules
    Committee" .... 1988 .... $45
Robert Sommers & Cal Brown:
"Great Shots"... 1989 .... $15
John Sommerville:
"A Foursome At Rye" .... 1898 .....$1,500
Songs of the Azooks:
"Being a Collection of Verse and Worse Sung
    by That Ancient and Honorable Society
    of Golfers, by One of 'Em"................. 1940 .... $395
Gary L. Sorensen:
"The Architecture of Golf".......................... 1976 .... $125
Souchak, Middlecoff, & Snead:
"Improve Your Golf" .... 1959 .... $15
Daniel C. Soutar:
"The Australian Golfer" .... 1906 .... $525
    Second Edition .... 1908 .... $395
Neil Soutar:
"Northamptonshire County Golf Club
    1910-1995" .... 1995 .... $30
South African Golf:
"Golfing In Southern Africa" .... 1958 .... $175
South Herts G. C:
"A Year to Remember South Herts Golf Club
    Centenary 1899-1999 .... 1999 .... $45
South Leeds G. C:
"South Leeds Golf Club 1914-1989"............. 1989 .... $25

South Shore C. C:
South Shore Country Club Year Book".......... 1910 .... $125
South Wales Golf Courses:
"A Guide to South Wales Golf Courses" .... 1956 .... $200
Southern California Golf Association:
"History of Golf in Southern California".......... 1925 .... $350
"Southern California Directory of Golf" .... 1990 .... $15
Southern Hills C. C:
"Brief History And Guide To The Golf Course
    of Southern Hills Country Club".......... 1977 .... $35
"Southern Hills Country Club: A Fifty-Seven
    Year History, 1935-1992"
    (1500 Copies) .... 1992 .... $45
Southern Pacific Rail Road:
"Del Monte Golf Links" .... 1903 .... $250
Southerness G. C:
"Southerness Golf Club 1947-1997.............. 1997 .... $40
Southhampton C. C:
"Southhampton Golf Club 1925-1975" .... 1975 .... $20
Southport Municipal G. L:
"The Southport Municipal Golf Links" .... 1933 .... $125
David Sowell:
"Ike, Golf, & Augusta" .... 2012 .... $20
A. G. Spalding:
"Golf Reporters Almanac"........................... 1958 .... $20
"Kro-Flite Kronicles Or Grey Matter
    For Golfers" .... 1935 .... $60
"Rules of Golf".. 1897 .... $550
"Some Tips from Bobby Jones" .... 1935 .... $300
"Spalding's Spring and Summer Sports"....... 1897 .... $250
"The Seasons Golf Score Report Including
    USGA Golf Rules"............................. 1937 .... $45
"The Uses of the Golf Club Explained" 1927 175
Anthony Spalding:
"Golf for Beginners" .... 1935 .... $20
Spalding's Atheltic Library:
"Spalding's Golf Guide for 1893" .... 1893 ......$1350
Spalding's Official Golf Guide:
"Spalding's Official Golf Guide" .... 1895 ......$2700
Sparrow & Bull:
"100 Years of Ladies Golf: The Christchurch
    Ladies Golf Club 1892-1992".............. 1992 .... $75
Spectator's Guide to Golf:
"A Spectator's Guide To Golf" .... 1969 .... $15

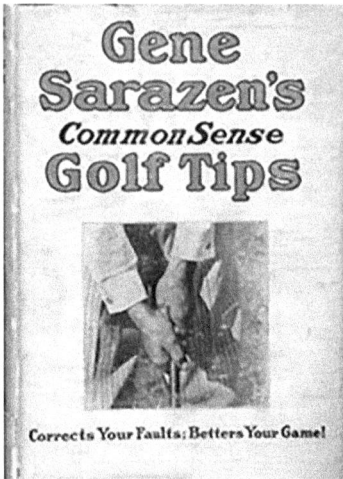

Sarazen – Common Sense
Golf Tips

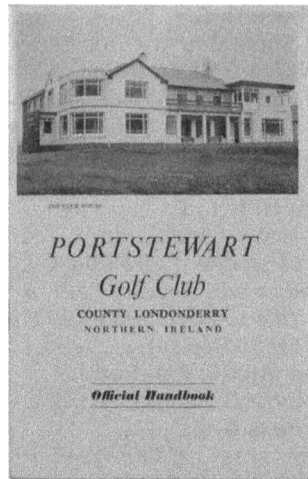

Scott – Portstewart
Golf Club

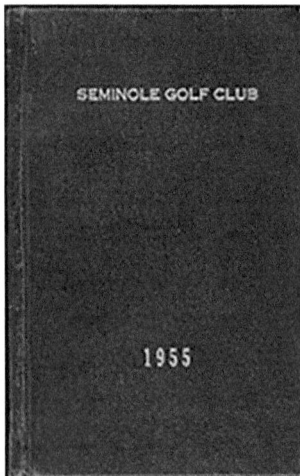

Seminole G. C. – 1955

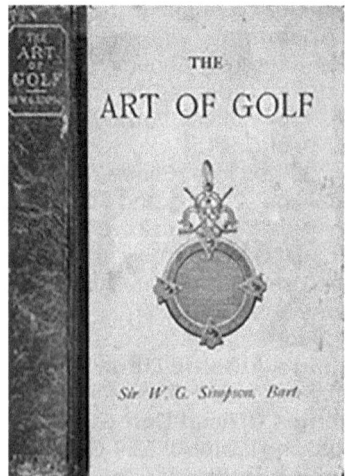

Simpson – The Art of Golf

Thousands of color book illustrations visible at
www.rogeregilchrist.com

Johnny Spence:
"Golf Pro For God"..................................... 1965 .... $10
"How To Lose At Golf" .... 1971 .... $10
Sydney Spicer:
"Boomerang Golf" .... 1968 .... $10
Milo Spillane:
"Adare Manor Golf Club 1900-2000" .... 2000 .... $35
Burton Spooner:
"A History Of Montague Golf Club"............... 1985 .... $45
John Spooner:
"Golf Facts: Product Knowledge–Basic
    Information on The Art of Selling
    Golf Equipment" .... 1973 .... $15
"The Foursome"... 1993 .... $15
The Sportfolio:
"The Sportfolio: Portraits And Biographies
    of Heros And Heroines of Sport
    And Pastime" .... 1896 .... $175
Sportoscope:
"Long Irons by Tommy Armour".................. 1932 .... $100
"The Approach by Leo Diegel"..................... 1932 .... $100
"The Drive by Johnny Farrell" .... 1932 .... $100
"The Grip by Johnny Farrell"....................... 1932 .... $100
"The Niblick by Leo Diegel"......................... 1932 .... $100
"The Putt by Johnny Farrell" .... 1932 .... $100
Sports Illustrated:
"Golf".. 1994 .... $10
"Golf Lessons From The Pros" .... 1961 .... $20
"Sports Illustrated Golf Tips From The
    Top Professionals" .... 1961 .... $15
"Ten Top Tips"... 1958 .... $10
"Tips On Top Performance:
    With Golf Tips From
    Sam Snead And Mickey Wright" .... 1955 .... $15
"The Wonderful World of Sport" .... 1967 .... $20
"Tiger Woods. The Making of A Champion" ... 1996 .... $15
Sports Trader:
"W. B. Tattersall Ltd Golf Rules".................. 1940 .... $50
Gerald Sprayregen:
"The Soul of Tiger Woods".......................... 1998 .... $10
Jack Springman:
"The Beauty of Pebble Beach"..................... 1964 .... $375
"The Many Faces of The American Golf
    Course"... 1963 .... $400

Shirley Sprung & Jerry Sprung:
"Decorated Golf Collectibles" .... 1991 .... $35
Craig Stadler:
"Craig Stadlers Secrets of The Short Game".. 1987 .... $15
"I Am The Walrus" .... 1995 .... $10
J. H. Stainton:
"The Golf Courses of Yorkshire" .... 1912 .... $375
Stambaugh G. C:
"Henry Stambaugh Golf Course
        50th Anniversary 1923-1973".............. 1973 .... $35
Stancliffe (Stanley Clifford):
"An Astounding Golf Match"........................ 1914 .... $350
"The Autobiography of A Caddy-Bag".......... 1924 .... $375
"Golf Do's And Don't's" .... 1902 .... $125
"Quick Cuts To Good Golf"......................... 1920 .... $125
Stanley G. C:
"Stanley Golf Club House" .... 1933 .... $60
Carl Stanley & H. R. Warner:
"Hotel Del Monte" .... 1915 .... $150
Dave Stanley:
"A Treasury of Golf Humor" .... 1949 .... $30
Dave Stanley & George C. Ross:
"The Golfer's Own Book" .... 1957 .... $35
Jeremy Stanley & Paula Campbell:
"Bangor Golf Club. One Hundred Years
        1903-2003" .... 2003 .... $25
Louis T. Stanley:
"A History of Golf"................................... 1991 .... $25
"The Book of Golf" .... 1960 .... $35
"Fontana Golf Book" .... 1957 .... $15
"Fresh Fairways"...................................... 1949 .... $65
"Golf With Your Hands".............................. 1966 .... $25
"The Golfer's Bedside Book" .... 1955 .... $40
"Green Fairways" .... 1947 .... $65
"How To Be A Better Woman Golfer"............ 1952 .... $30
"Legends of Golf"..................................... 1997 .... $20
"Master Golfers In Action" .... 1950 .... $20
"Pelham Golf Year".................................... 1981 .... $35
"St. Andrews"... 1986 .... $55
"Style Analysis" .... 1951 .... $35
"Swing To Better Golf"............................... 1957 .... $25
"This Is Golf".. 1954 .... $35
"This Is Putting" .... 1957 .... $35
"The Woman Golfer".................................. 1952 .... $30

Thousands of color book illustrations visible at
www.rogeregilchrist.com

Max & Louis T. Stanley:
"The Faulkner Method" .... 1952 .... $35
H. Stanners:
"Newbattle Golf Club Ltd 1896-1996"........... 1996 .... $30
Stanwich Club:
"The Stanwich Club".................................. 1972 .... $55
A. Stark:
"Physical Training For Golfers" .... 1937 .... $125
Jim Stark & Douglas Lowe:
"Helensburgh Golf Club First 100 Years"...... 1993 .... $25
Allan D. Starr:
"The Easy Way To Lower Your Golf Score" .... 1975 .... $10
Paul D. Staudohar:
"Golfs Best Short Stories" .... 1997 .... $15
St Andrews:
"St Andrews Rules of Golf" .... 1888 ....$1850
"St Andrews Links. Bye-Laws and Regulations
        for Starting .... 1898 ....$1250
"The Book of St Andrews Links. Plan of
        Golf Courses".................................. 1898 ....$1500
St. Andrews G. C:
"How to Play the Old Course, St Andrews".... 1947 .... $45
"Officers, Members, Constitution and Rules..."1896 .... $450
"St. Andrews Golf Club" .... 1934 .... $195
"St. Andrews Golf Club 1888-1963"............. 1963 .... $130
"St Andrews Golf Club Yearbook" .... 1932 .... $150
St. Andrews Preservation Trust:
"St. Andrews: Its Character and Traditions".. 1951 .... $65
St. Augustine G. C:
"St. Augustine Golf Club 1909-1910" .... 1909 .... $75
"The St. Augustine's Golf Club" .... 1951 .... $45
St. Austell G. C:
"St. Austell Golf Club 1911-1991"................ 1991 .... $15
St. Charles C. C:
"St. Charles Country Club 1905-1965" .... 1966 .... $40
St. Cloud C. C:
"The St. Cloud Country Club"...................... 1927 .... $75
St. Deiniol G C:
"St Deiniol Golf Club Bagor, North Wales"..... 1964 .... $45
Donald Steel:
"The Golfer's Bedside Book" .... 1965 .... $20
"The Golfer's Bedside Book" .... 1971 .... $15
"Guiness Book of Golf Facts And Feats" .... 1980 .... $25

Thousands of color book illustrations visible at
www.rogeregilchrist.com

"Classic Golf Links of Great Britain And
    Ireland"... 1992 .... $50
"Traditions and Change.. 1939-2004"
    (250 Copies).................................... 2004 .... $500
    Limited edition of 1754...................... 2004 .... $125
Donald Steel & Peter Ryde:
"The Encyclopedia of Golf" .... 1975 .... $45
"The Shell International Encyclopedia
    of Golf" .... 1975 .... $65
Chester K. Steele:
"The Golf Course Mystery" .... 1919 .... $200
Eldon P. Steeves:
"Nineteenth & Twentieth Century Golf
    Literature And Memorabilia" .... 1996 .... $150
St. George's C. C:
"St George's Country Club 1929-1979" .... 1979 .... $35
John de St. Jorre:
"Legendary Golf Clubs of Scotland, England,
    Wales & Ireland".. 1999 .... $150
"Legendary Golf Clubs of the American East" 2003 .... $100
    Deluxe Edition................................. 2003 .... $250
"Legendary Golf Links of Ireland" .... 2006 .... $95
"The Story of Golf at the Country Club"
    (1300 Copies) .... 2009 .... $450
St Louis C .C:
"St Louis Country Club, Clayton,St Louis" ..... 1904 .... $150
Jennette A. Stein & Emma F. Waterman:
"Golf For Beginning Players" .... 1934 .... $45
Harris B. Steinberg:
"The Hackers: Twelve Golf Drawings" .... 1956 .... $225
John Steinbreder:
"Golf Courses of the US Open".................... 1996 .... $35
St Stephen's Club:
"Rules And Regulations And List of Members
    of The St Stephen's Club" .... 1928 .... $125
H. G. Stephenson:
"A History of Todmorden Golf Club" .... 1983 .... $15
Leonard Stern & Ed Powers:
"The World's Greatest And Funniest Golf
    Awards" .... 1985 .... $10
Peter Stevens:
"Links Lore" .... 1998 .... $15
Elizabeth S. Stevenson:
"The Belvedere Club, Memoirs of

Members 1878-1968"........................ 1969 .... $15

Robert Louis Stevenson:
"The Pavillion on the Links" .... 1913 .... $75

W. Grant Stevenson:
"Wee Johnnie Paterson & Other Humorous
Sketches".. 1914 .... $75

Alan Stewart:
"Kilmarnock Golf Club 1887-1987" .... 1987 .... $25

Earl Stewart Jr. & Dr. Harry E. Gunn:
"Golf Begins At Forty"................................ 1977 .... $10
"Left Hander's Golf Book"........................... 1976 .... $10

Hal D. Stewart:
"The Nineteenth Hole A Play In One Act"...... 1933 .... $295

James L. Stewart:
"Golfiana Miscellanea, Being A Collection
Of Interesting Monographs on the
Royal And Ancient Game of Golf" .... 1887 .... $1450

Jerry Stewart:
Pebble Beach : Golf and the Forgotten Men" . 2005 .... $25

John W. Stewart:
"Roland: A Short Story About Roland
MacKenzie's Golfing Career"
(2000 Copies) .... 1987 .... $35

Ron Stewart:
"Saratoga Golf & Polo Club Centenial
Celebration 1896-1996"..................... 1996 .... $25

Thomas P. Stewart:
"A Tribute To Golf" .... 1990 .... $45

Thomas P Stewart & Russell Shoeman:
"The Nature of Golf" .... 1999 .... $35

T. Ross Stewart:
"Lays of The Links: A Score of Parodies" ...... 1895 .... $750

Tracy Stewart:
"Payne Stewart" .... 2000 .... $10

Fred Stibbons:
"Norfolk's Caddie Poet" .... 1923 .... $350

Ezra Stiles:
"Landscape Architecture Illustrated" .... 1955 .... $500

Leo Stillings:
"Golf Fundamentals and Helpful Hints"......... 1935 .... $40

Charley Stine:
"1983 Golf Directory" .... 1983 .... $15

Frank M. Stipe:
"The Australian"...................................... 1980 .... $15

Thousands of color book illustrations visible at
www.rogeregilchrist.com

David Stirk:
"Carry Your Bag Sir?" .... 1989 .... $25
"Golf: The Great Clubmakers" .... 1991 .... $65
"Golf: The History of An Obsession" .... 1987 .... $40
"Golf: History Tradition 1500-1945 .... 1998 .... $175
    Deluxe Edition of 100 .... 1998 ......$1250
John de St Jorre:
"Legendary Golf Clubs of Scotland, England,
    Wales and Ireland" .... 1998 .... $225
"The Story of Golf at the Country Club" .... 2009 .... $350
Stirling G. C:
"Stirling Golf Club Centenary 1869-1969" ..... 1969 .... $15
John Stirling:
"Fit For Golf" .... 1984 .... $10
"Golf: The Skills of the Game" .... 1985 .... $25
Lauren St John:
"Greg Norman" .... 1998 .... $20
"Out of Bounds" .... 1995 .... $20
"Seve, Ryder Cup Hero" .... 1993 .... $20
"Shark" .... 1998 .... $10
St. Joseph C. C:
"Fore: St. Joseph Country Club Yearbook" .... 1953 .... $25
Alicia St. Ledger:
"Monkstown Golf Club 1908-1983" .... 1983 .... $15
M. A. Stobart:
"Won At The Last Hole: A Golfing Romance" . 1893 ......$2,200
John Stobbs:
"An A.B.C. of Golf" .... 1964 .... $20
"The Anatomy of Golf: Technique And Tactic" 1962 .... $30
"At Random Through The Green" .... 1966 .... $20
"The Camberley Heath Golf Club" .... 1955 .... $65
"The Dulwich And Syndenham Hill Golf Club" 1953 .... $25
"The Fulwell Golf Club" .... 1953 .... $20
"Tackle Golf This Way" .... 1961 .... $15
Dave Stockton & Al Barkow:
"Dave Stockton's Putt To Win" .... 1996 .... $15
William L. Stoddard:
"The Near Golfer's Almanac" .... 1909 .... $350
"The Near Golfer's Almanac" .... 1910 .... $245
"The New Golfer's Almanac" .... 1909 .... $350
Sydney Stokes:
"A History of Ekwanok" .... 1974 .... $50
"Centennial History of The Ekwanok
    Country Club" .... 2000 .... $50

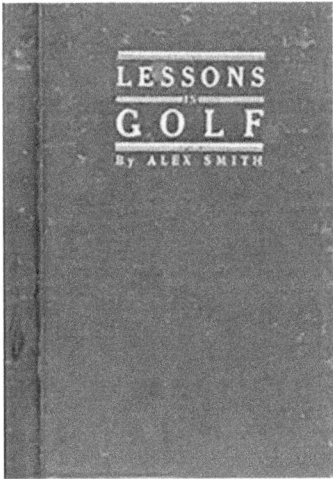

Smith – Lessons in Golf
(1st Edition)

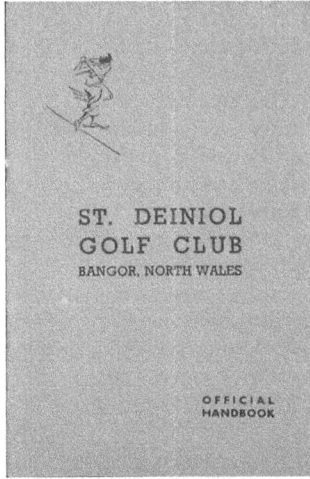

St. Deiniol – Golf Club

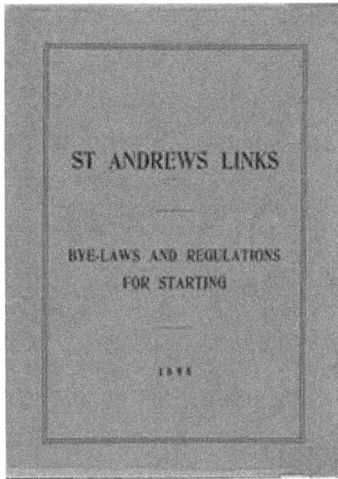

St Andrews Links – By Laws

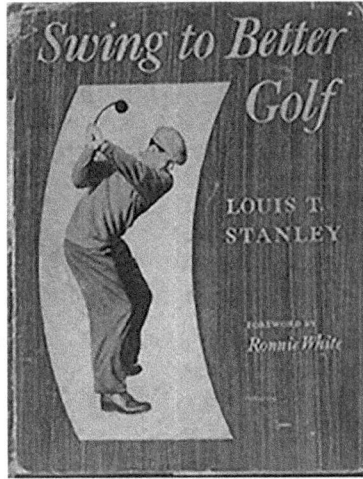

Stanley – Swing to Better Golf

Hal Stone:
"Salt Spring Golf and Country Cllub
1928-1988" .... 1988 .... $25
Story of The Open:
"The Story of The Open 1860-1960" .... 1960 .... $40
A. Stowell & Co:
The Seven Ages of Golf" .... 1906 .... $275
Carlton Stowers:
"The Unsinkable Titanic Thompson" .... 1982 .... $95
Lewis Strang:
"Golf and Business" .... 1925 .... $65
Curtis Strange:
" Win And Win Again" .... 1990 .... $15
Stratford-On-Avon G. C:
"The Stratford-On-Avon Golf Club" .... 1946 .... $55
Strathfield G. C:
"Strathfield Golf Club Silver Jubilee
1931-1956" .... 1956 .... $45
Stratton & Landon:
"The Mohawk Golf Club 1898-1998" .... 1998 .... $45
Straus & Dunnigan:
"Walk a Crooked Trail: A Centennial History
of the Wawashkamo Golf Club" .... 2000 .... $35
John Strawn:
"Driving The Green: The Making of A
Golf Course" .... 1991 .... $30
Frank Strazza:
"Golf's Inside Secrets" .... 1955 .... $15
John Strege:
"Tiger" .... 1997 .... $10
"Tournament Week" .... 2000 ....$5
Felix B. Streyckmans:
"The Story of Our Club" .... 1968 .... $75
Art Stricklin:
"A History of Northwood Club 1946-2002" .... 2002 .... $35
Mabel A. Stringer:
"Golfing Reminiscences" .... 1924 ......$1,950
Horace D. Strong:
"Thru The Years At The Brooklawn Country
Club 1895-1945 50th Anniversary" ...... 1945 .... $50
Joseph Strutt:
"The Sports and Pastimes of the People
of England" .... 1801 ......$1,875
1810 Edition .... 1810 .... $350

1833 Edition .... 1833 .... $200
1867 Edition .... 1867 .... $150
1876 Edition .... 1876 .... $125
1900 Edition .... 1900 .... $100

Ian Stuart:
"Golf In Hertfordshire" .... 1972 .... $25

Stump & Walter Co:
"Golf Turf of High Quality" .... 1922 .... $450

Don Sturgess:
"Basic Golf" .... 1954 .... $40

J. Hamilton Stutt:
"The Reclamation of The Derelict Lands For
   Golf" .... 1980 .... $35

Suburban Club of Baltimore:
"The Suburban Club of Baltimore County
   1900-1995" .... 1995 .... $60

Louise Suggs:
"Par Golf For Women" .... 1953 .... $25

Louise Suggs & Others:
"Golf For Women" .... 1960 .... $30

Des Sullivan:
"Essex Falls Country Club 1896-1950" .... 1950 .... $20

George Sullivan:
"The Champions Guide To Golf" .... 1966 .... $25

Sunset Magazine:
"Golf Course Directory For California" .... 1964 .... $45

Sunset Ridge C. C:
"Sunset Ridge Country Club: Our First 50
   Years 1923-1972" (1500 Copies) .... 1972 .... $50

Surbiton G. C:
"Surbiton Golf Club 1895-1995" .... 1995 .... $25

Pearson Surita:
"The Royal Calcutta Golf Club 150th
   Anniversary 1829-1979" .... 1979 .... $125

Eddie Sussalla:
"Tournament Players Magazine" .... 1979 .... $15

Susie Takes Up Golf:
"Susie Takes Up Golf" .... 1940 .... $60

Helen G. Sutin & Beatrice Quinn:
"Chips And Putts" .... 1969 .... $10

Martin A. F. Sutton:
"The Book of the Links: A Symposium on
   Golf" .... 1912 .... $500
"Golf Courses, Design, Construction And

Upkeep" .... 1933 .... $975
Second Edition .... 1950 .... $400
"Laying Out And Upkeeping of Golf
    Courses And Putting Greens".............. 1906 ......$2,650
Sutton Coldfield G. C.:
"Sutton Coldfield G.C. Jubilee 1889-1939".... 1939 .... $45
Henry E. Swanson:
"Fifty Years of Woodland G.C. 1902-1952".... 1952 .... $40
Swanston G. C:
"Swanston Golf Club" .... 1948 .... $55
Brian Swarbrick:
"The Duffer's Guide To Bogey Golf" .... 1973 .... $20
Rory Sweetman:
"The Hutt Golf Club A Centennial
    History 1982-1992" .... 1992 .... $45
Harry R. Sweny:
"Keep Your Eye On The Ball..." .... 1898 ......$2,450
O. F. T.:
"Aldeburgh G.C. The First 100 Years
    1884-1984" .... 1984 .... $25
S. Takahata:
"The Story of The Kobe Golf Club" .... 1966 .... $250
Jimmy Tarbuck:
"Tarbuck On Golf" .... 1983 .... $15
Jerry Tarde:
"How To Hit Crisp Iron Shots"..................... 1980 .... $10
Haruo Tashiro:
"Turfgrass Insects Of The United States
    And Canada".................................... 1987 .... $65
Tavistock C. C:
"Tavistock Country Club 1921-1971" .... 1971 .... $25
Arthur V. Taylor:
"Origines Golfianae: The Birth of Golf And
    Its Early Childhood As Revealed In A
    Chance Discovered Manusript From
    A Scottish Monastery" (500 Copies)..... 1912 .... $400
Bert L. Taylor:
"A Line O'Gowf Or Two" .... 1923 .... $175
Chip Taylor:
"What You Should Know To Putt For Bread" . 1976 .... $10
Dawson Taylor:
"How To Talk Golf".................................... 1985 .... $20
"Inside Golf" .... 1978 .... $25
"The Masters"... 1973 .... $75

Deluxe Edition $175
"The Masters: An Illustrated History" .... 1981 .... $55
"The Masters, Golf's Most Prestigious
    Tradition" .... 1986 .... $35
"St. Andrews Cradle of Golf" .... 1976 .... $55
Hugh Taylor:
    "Golf Dictionary" .... 1970 .... $15
J. Fred Taylor & W. D. Kerr:
    "The Beaconsfield Golf Club 1904-1979
      Seventy-Fifth Anniversary" .... 1979 .... $125
J. H. Taylor:
    "Golf: My Life's Work" .... 1943 .... $325
      2nd Edition .... 1943 .... $150
    "Southampton Public Golf Courses" .... 1935 .... $60
    "Taylor On Golf, Impressions, Comments,
      And Hints" .... 1902 .... $875
    "The Golfer's Record of Games" .... 1906 .... $195
J. H. L. Taylor:
    "Langland Bay Golf Club, Mumbles, Swansea"1953 .... $25
James Taylor:
    "Formby Golf Club 1884-1984" .... 1984 .... $30
John L. Taylor:
    "Golf Collectors Price Guide" .... 1983 .... $65
Joshua Taylor:
    "The Art of Golf" .... 1913 .... $400
    "The Lure of The Links" .... 1920 .... $375
Neville Taylor:
    "Via the 19th Hole Barwon Heads Golf Club" . 1987 .... $20
Paula Taylor:
    "Golf's Greatest Winner: Jack Nicklaus" .... 1977 .... $20
Thomas T. Taylor:
    "The Golf Murders Collection"
      (400 signed Copies) .... 1997 .... $250
William D. Taylor:
    "Wallasey Golf Club 1891-1953" .... 1953 .... $25
Tedesco C. C:
    "Tedesco Country Club 50th Anniversary
      1903-1953" .... 1953 .... $65
    "Tedesco Country Club 75th Anniversary
      1903-1978" .... 1978 .... $50
Lawrence Teeman:
    "Consumer Guide Complete Guide To Golf" ... 1975 .... $10
Tee Party On The Green:
    "Tee Party On The Green" .... 1925 .... $125

Thousands of color book illustrations visible at
www.rogeregilchrist.com

David Shea Teeple:
"How to Cheat at Golf"................................ 1958 .... $50
Tee Time At The Masters:
"A Collection of Recipies" .... 1977 .... $15
Tee Tree Gully G. C:
"Tee Tree Gully Golf Club Inc. A Summary
of the First 50 Years......................... 1982 .... $50
Tee Up:
"Tee Up"... 1962 .... $15
Tehidy Park G. C:
"Tehidy Park Golf Club"............................. 1947 .... $40
Jacques Temmerman:
"Golf And Kholf"...................................... 1993 .... $65
H. A. Templeton:
"Vector Putting: The Art And Science of
Reading Greens and Computing Break" 1984 .... $15
The Country Club:
"The Country Club" .... 1937 .... $450
"The Country Club" .... 1941 .... $400
"Its First 75 Years 1889-1964".................... 1964 .... $195
The Golfer:
"The Golfer: Devoted to the Game of Golf
and the Golfer's of the United States
of America".................................... 1895 ....$3000
1896 Edition .... 1896 ....$1000
1897 Edition .... 1897 .... $500
"The Golfer: 50 Golden Years 1926-1976" ... 1976 .... $35
The Graphic Score Book Company:
"Club Tournaments And Events".................. 1939 .... $50
The Greenbrier:
"Three Championship Courses" .... 1984 .... $35
Norman Thelwell:
"Play It As It Lies".................................... 1988 .... $10
Allan Thinwell:
"Formby Golf Club 1884-1984" .... 1984 .... $25
This Golf From Tee To Green:
"This Golf From Tee To Green".................... 1936 .... $150
Alan Thom:
"From Westlands to Eastlands: The History
of Rothesay Golf Club, 1892-1992." .... 1992 .... $45
M. D. Thom:
"Instructions To Young Golfers" .... 1959 .... $15
"It's A Golf Rule"...................................... 1951 .... $35
"Tricky Golf Rules" .... 1952 .... $125

Thousands of color book illustrations visible at
www.rogeregilchrist.com

Bob Thomas:
"Ben Hogan's Secret" .... 1998 .... $20
David Thomas:
"Instructions To Young Golfers" .... 1959 .... $25
"Modern Golf"... 1967 .... $25
George C. Thomas Jr.:
"Golf Architecture In America, Its Strategy
      And Construction"............................. 1927 ......$1,200
      Reprint... 1997 .... $85
Ivor S. Thomas:
"Formby Golf 1884-1972" .... 1972 .... $45
Jack Thomas:
"Axe Cliff Golf Club 1894-1994" .... 1994 .... $20
P. Richard Thomas:
"The Country Club of Meadville 1905-1976".. 1977 .... $15
Peter H. Thomas:
"Golf Reminiscences By An Old Hand" .... 1890 ....$3500
      (Reprint of 250 Copies) .... 1985 .... $225
Robert E. Thomas:
"Wyantenuck Country Club Centennial
      History 1896-1996" .... 1996 .... $35
James K. Thompson:
"James K. Thompson Golden Anniversary".... 1968 .... $15
Kenneth R. Thompson:
"The Mental Side of Golf" .... 1939 .... $225
      Second Edition .... 1947 .... $60
      Third Edition .... 1955 .... $30
M. B. Thompson:
"Miniature Golf: A Treatise On The Subject
      Containing Business Building Ideas" .... 1930 .... $300
P. M. Thompson:
"The Experience of A Dub Golfer" .... 1925 .... $275
Phillips B. Thompson:
"Simplifying The Golf Stroke"...................... 1929 .... $125
Robert Thompson:
The Chevy Chase Club 1882-1992".............. 1992 .... $30
W. J. Thompson:
"Commonsense Golf".................................. 1923 .... $95
Ben Thomson:
How To Play Golf" .... 1939 .... $45
Dave Thomson:
"Practical Golf" .... 1923 .... $115
George A. Thomson:
"The Story of The Yarra Yarra Golf Club" ...... 1972 .... $45

Thousands of color book illustrations visible at
www.rogeregilchrist.com

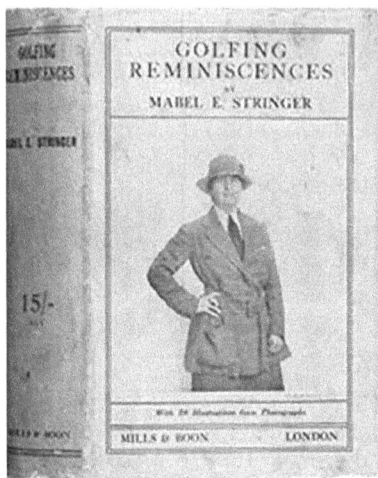

Stringer – Golfing Reminiscences
(Dust Jacket)

Surita – Royal Calcutta Golf Club
1829-1979

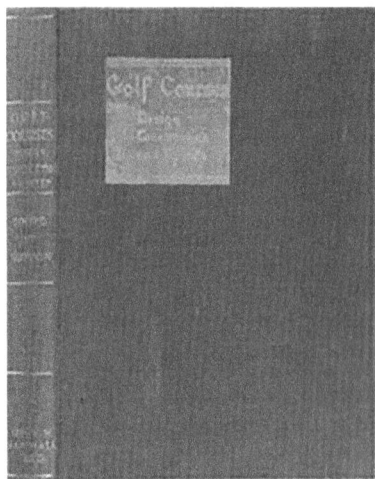

Sutton – Golf Courses
(1st Edition)

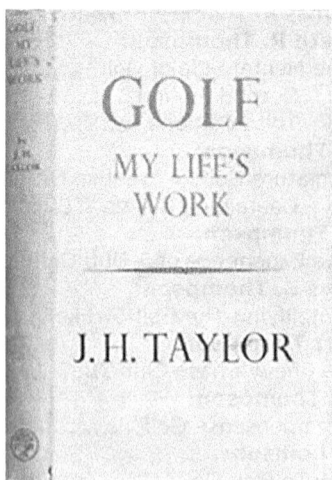

Taylor – Golf My Life's Work
(War Time Dust Jacket)

Thousands of color book illustrations visible at
www.rogeregilchrist.com

Jimmy Thomson:
"Hit Em A Mile! How To Drive A Golf Ball" ..... 1940 .... $50
John Thomson:
"Golfing And Other Poems And Songs" .... 1893 .... $925
  Limited Edition of 50 Copies .... 1893 .....$3,500
Peter Thomson:
"Players Golf" .... 1990 .... $10
Peter Thomson & Desmond Zwar:
"This Wonderful World of Golf" .... 1969 .... $30
Will J. A. Thomson:
"Golfing Memories, Including A Short History
  of The Titirangi Golf Club And Excerpts
  From Golf Lies And Otherwise" .... 1951 .... $135
Thormanby:
"Sporting Stories" .... 1912 .... $25
J. M. Thornburn:
"The Seeding and Preservation of Golf Links . 1899 ....$2350
Thorny Lea G. C:
"Thorny Lea Golf Club Centennial Edition
  1900-2000" .... 2000 .... $75
Bill Tidy:
"The World's Worst Golf Club" .... 1987 .... $10
Albert W. Tillinghast:
"Cobble Valley Golf Yarns And Other
  Sketches" .... 1915 ......$1,450
"The Mutt And Other Golf Yarns" .... 1925 .... $500
  Limited Edition of 250 .... 1925 .....$7,500
  USGA Reprint (1500 Copies) .... 1995 .... $125
"Planning A Golf Course" .... 1917 ......$9,500
"The Course Beautiful" .... 1995 .... $75
Bud Timbrook:
"Golf Mystic Solved" .... 1982 .... $15
W. A. Timpson:
"Hale Golf Club Seventy Five Years
  1903-1978" .... 1978 .... $15
Tippecanoe Lake C. C:
"Tippecanoe Lake Country Club" .... 1922 .... $150
E. R. Tipple:
"Testing Tee Shots And Their Value" .... 1937 .... $350
Andrew Hill:
"Crews Hill – The Story of a Golf Club
  1916-1991" .... 1992 .... $15
Sydney Todd:
"DB Sporting Records of New Zealand" .... 1976 .... $35

Desmond Tolhurst:
"Golf At Merion" (1500 Copies) .... 1989 .... $175
"Nassau Country Club, the Place to Be.
    1896-1996" .... 1995 .... $35
"St. Andrews Golf Club: The Birthplace
    of American Golf" .... 1989 .... $125
"The Wykagyl Country Club Centennial
    1898-1998" .... 1999 .... $75
Cyril J. H. Tolley:
"Drive And Iron" .... 1930 .... $175
"The Modern Golfer" .... 1924 .... $95
William G. Tonner Jr:
"Army Navy Country Club 1924-1989
    Historcal Review" .... 1989 .... $55
Edward Topham:
"Letters From Edinburgh" .... 1776 .... $450
    Reprint (500 Copies) .... 1971 .... $75
Toronto G. C:
"Fiftieth Anniversary of the Toronto Golf
    Club 1876-1926" .... 1926 .... $75
Torquay G. C:
"The Torquay Golf Club" .... 1932 .... $95
Bob Torrance:
"Room At The Top" .... 1989 .... $15
Bob Toski:
"12 Short Cuts To Better Golf" .... 1975 .... $15
"A Beginners Guide To Golf" .... 1955 .... $25
"Golf For A Lifetime" .... 1981 .... $15
"How To Cure Golf's Six Most
    Common Faults" .... 1974 .... $15
"Bob Toski's Complete Guide To Better Golf". 1977 .... $15
"Bob Toski's Guide To Better Golf" .... 1975 .... $15
"The Touch System For Better Golf" .... 1971 .... $20
Bob Toski & Jim Flick:
"How To Become A Complete Golfer" .... 1978 .... $20
Bob Toski & Davis Love Jr:
"How To Feel A Real Golf Swing" .... 1988 .... $20
Tournament Player Golf Annual:
"The Tournament Player Golf Annual 1978" .. 1977 .... $10
Tournament Player's Championship:
"Tournament Player's Championship 1982" ... 1982 .... $10
Kristen Tow:
"International Golf Directory: Resorts, Clubs,
    Courses Around The World" .... 1974 .... $20

Peter Townsend:
"Golf: 100 Ways To Improve Your Game" ..... 1977 .... $10
Richard B. Townshend:
"Inspired Golf" .... 1921 .... $125
Ann Trabue:
"History of the Los Angeles Country Club" .... 1936 .... $350
Laraine Tracy:
"Minnesota Valley Country Club 1923-1991" . 1991 .... $45
Tyler Trafford:
"The Calgary Golf and Country Club,
     1897-1997" .... 1997 .... $40
Don Trahan:
"Golf Plain And Simple" .... 1986 .... $10
Sandy Trapp:
"The Lighter Side of Golf" .... 1989 .... $10
Travellers Guide:
"Hotels And Golf Courses" .... 1991 .... $15
Jerome D. Travers:
"Travers Golf Book" .... 1913 .... $450
Jerome D. Travers & James R. Crowell:
"The Fifth Estate" .... 1926 .... $275
Jerome D. Travers & Grantland Rice:
"The Winning Shot" .... 1915 .... $165
Walter J. Travis:
"Practical Golf" .... 1901 .... $495
"Practical Hints on Golf – In Tennis and Golf
     of Every Description..." .... 1902 .... $850
Walter J. Travis and Jack White:
"The Art of Putting" .... 1904 .... $575
Archibald Treat:
"Golf and Lawyers" .... 1932 .... $650
Robert S Trebus & Richard C Wolffe:
"Baltusrol 100 Years" .... 1995 .... $95
Nicholas Tremayne:
"Golf How To Become A Champion" .... 1975 .... $10
Phil Tresidder:
"The Golfer Who Laughed" .... 1981 .... $15
Paul Trevillion:
"Dead Heat: The '69 Ryder Cup Classic" .... 1969 .... $30
"Tony Jacklin In Play" .... 1970 .... $20
"The Perfect Putting Method" .... 1971 .... $25
"Save Strokes Like The Stars" .... 1970 .... $20
Lee Trevino:
"Can I Help Your Game?" .... 1972 .... $15

"Groove Your Golf Swing My Way".............. 1976 .... $30
"I Can Help Your Game"............................. 1971 .... $15
"Lee's Secret: The Fascinating Success
      Story of Lee Trevino" .... 1969 .... $15
"Swing My Way" .... 1976 .... $10
Lee Trevino & Sam Blair:
"The Snake In The Sandtrap" .... 1985 .... $10
"They Call Me Super Mex" .... 1982 .... $30
George Trevor:
"A Blind Man Breaks 80" .... 1957 .... $10
Trevose G. C:
"Trevose Golf Club"................................. 1985 .... $15
Tri City Golf Association:
"Caddie Book" .... 1927 .... $100
Paul Triefus:
"The Most Excellent Historie of MacHamlet" .. 1922 .... $425
Eldon H. Trimingham:
"Golf In Bermuda".................................... 1952 .... $35
William A. Tripp:
"The Geometry of Golf"............................. 1960 .... $45
C. Pette Triscott:
"Golf In Six Lessons" .... 1924 .... $95
Troon G. C:
"Rules of the Troon Golf Club" .... 1889 .... $325
"List of Members, Rules And Winners
      of Competitions 1939"....................... 1939 .... $125
Troon Town Council:
"The Official Guide To Troon"..................... 1933 .... $45
John F. Trump:
"From A Hundred And Two To Eighty-Two
      In A Month Or Two" .... 1934 .... $65
Cecil F. Tucker:
"Nineteenth Hole Romances And The Devious
      Methods of Joseph Blotchford"............ 1927 .... $975
William H. Tucker:
"A Golf Course For Your Community" .... 1925 .... $70
Walter R. Tuckerman:
"The History of The Burning Tree Club" .... 1948 .... $85
Richard S. Tufts:
"The Principles Behind The Rules of Golf" ..... 1960 .... $550
      USGA reprint................................... 1989 .... $25
"The Scottish Invasion"............................. 1962 .... $120
W. W. Tulloch:
"The Life of Tom Morris, With Glimpses of St.

Andrews And Its Golfing Celebrities".... 1908 ...... $1,995
Reprint... 1982 .... $350
390 Memorial Tournament Edition .... 1987 .... $195
USGA Reprint (1500 Copies) .... 1992 .... $150
John Tullius & Joe Ortiz;
"Shakespeare On Golf" .... 1997 .... $15
John R. Tunis:
"Sport for the Fun of It" .... 1940 .... $15
Ruby Turberville:
"The Aberdeen Ladies Golf Club" .... 1992 .... $45
Turnberry Story:
"The Turnberry Story" .... 1985 .... $15
Charles Turner:
"The Official Year Book and Directory of
    Golf and Automobiling...." .... 1908 .... $550
Rupert Turner:
"Novelty Golf Match" .... 1942 .... $60
Jim Turnesa:
"12 Lessons To Better Golf" .... 1953 .... $20
"Driver: A Swing Analysis In Slow Motion".... 1950 .... $50
"Low Score Golf" .... 1953 .... $25
Turning Point:
"Turning Point-The 54th Amateur
    Championship of The United States
    Golf Association – 1954 Winner Arnold
    Palmer" .... 1983 .... $30
Gary Turnquist:
"Golf: Solving A Puzzle" .... 1985 .... $10
Tuthill:
"Annandale Golf Club, Pasadena California:
    75th Anniversary 1981" .... 1981 .... $40
Mex Tuthill:
"Golf Without Gall" .... 1938 .... $75
Thomas Tutko & Umberto Tosi:
"Sports Psyching" .... 1976 .... $45
Anthony Tuttle:
"Drive For The Green" .... 1969 .... $25
J. D. Tunicliffe:
A Century of Golf on the Gogs" .... 2001 .... $10
Tuxedo Club:
"Officers, Members, Constitution, and History
    Of the Tuxedo Club 1896-1986"` .... 1986 .... $75
"Tuxedo Club Golf Calendar" 1984 25

Thousands of color book illustrations visible at
www.rogeregilchrist.com

Richard Twiss:
"Miscellanies" .... 1805 .... $295
Two Counties Golf Guide:
"Two Counties Golf Guide: Being The
　　Itinerary of The Golf Courses In
　　Lancashire and Cheshire"................... 1939 .... $90
Martin Tyler:
"The Sportsman's World of Golf" .... 1976 .... $20
Ralph G. Tyler:
"The Golf Oracle, Or Golf Made Easy For
　　The Vest Pocket" .... 1913 .... $450
"A Handbook For Golf Beginners" .... 1914 .... $275
Roger & William Tyler:
"A 300-Year Land History of the
　　Country Club" .... 1982 .... $100
Frederick D. Tyner:
"The Golfer's Dream"............................... 1936 .... $95
Tyrrells Wood G. C:
"The Tyrrells Wood Golf Club"..................... 1951 .... $20
Uitenhage G. C:
"Uitenhage Golf Club 75th Anniversary
　　1891-1966" .... 1966 .... $15
UK & Eire 1983 Golf Guide:
"UK & Eire 1983 Golf Guide"....................... 1983 .... $15
John Uldrick:
"Golf Balls And Monkey Pods" .... 1996 .... $20
Ulen C. C:
"The Ulen Country Club Silver Anniversary
　　1924-1949" .... 1949 .... $20
Joe Ungvary:
"How To Be A Good Caddy" .... 1961 .... $10
Union League Golf & C. C:
"The Union League Golf and Country Club" ... 1930 .... $175
"Golden Jubilee: Union League Club,
　　Milbrae Golf & Country Club, Green
　　Hills Country Club"............................ 1980 .... $45
United Services G. C:
"United Services Golf Club" .... 1951 .... $15
United States Golf Association:
"Calkin System of Calculating Handicap" ...... 1927 .... $40
"Decisions On The Rules Of Golf"................. 1971 .... $25
"Facts About The Merion Course At
　　Ardmore PA"..................................... 1916 ....$9500
"Golf by Appointment" .... 1902 .... $300

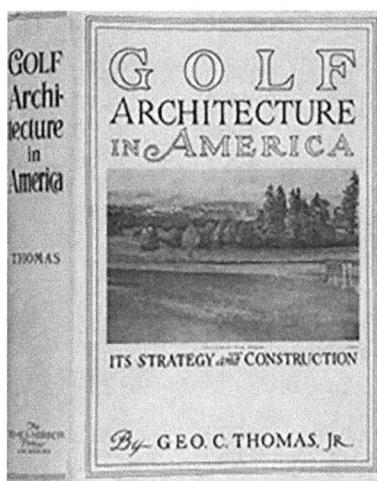

Thomas – Golf Architecture in America. (Dust Jacket)

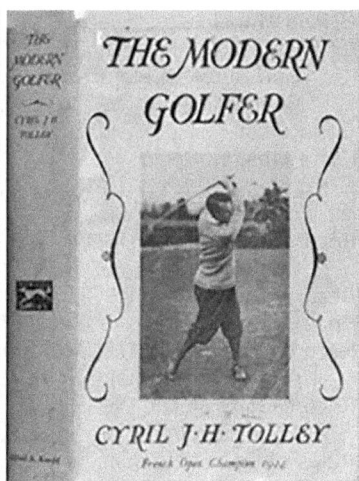

Tolley – The Modern Golfer (1st Edition Dust Jacket)

Travers – Travers Golf Book (Dust Jacket)

Tucker – 19th Hole Romances (Dust Jacket)

Thousands of color book illustrations visible at
www.rogeregilchrist.com

"Golf Is The Greatest Game" .... 1994 .... $45
"Golf Committee Manual And USGA
     Golf Rules In Pictures"....................... 1983 .... $20
     Revised edition................................. 1993 .... $10
"Golf Rules" .... 1900 .... $650
"Golf Rules" .... 1901 .... $750
"Grass"... 1942 .... $25
"Handicap Systems".................................. 1965 .... $35
"Record Book of The USGA
     Championships 1895-1953" .... 1953 .... $55
"Record Book of The USGA
     Championships 1895-1980" Two Vols. . 1980 .... $15
"Record Book of The USGA Championships
     And International Events" .... 1947 .... $75
"Record Book of The USGA
     Championships"............................... 1972 .... $15
"Rules of Golf ..."...................................... 1897 ......$3250
"The Rules of Golf..."................................. 1903 ......$2500
"Rules of The Game of Golf" .... 1909 .... $400
"The Club Makers" .... 1989 .... $45
"The Conduct Of Womens Golf".................. 1940 .... $80
"The Greatest Game" .... 1994 .... $35
"The United States Golf Association"............ 1940 .... $65
"United States Golf Association " .... 1903 .... $350
"United States Golf Association Yearbook" .... 1911 ......$1250
"USGA Course Rating System"..................... 1985 .... $10
"USGA GHIN: Golf Handicap And
     Information Operations Manual" .... 1984 .... $10
"USGA Handicap System With USGA Course
     Rating Systems For Men And Women
     And Golf Committe Manual" .... 1984 .... $15
"USGA Women's Golf Course Rating System" 1985 .... $10
USGA & The R&A:
"Decisions On The Rules of Golf". .... 1984 .... $35
United States Government Printing Office:
"Hickory Golf Shafts"................................ 1930 .... $60
United States Junior Chamber of Commerce:
"Jaycee Junior Golf Instructional Handbook" . 1962 .... $15
United States Senior's Golf Association:
"The First Seventy-FiveYears of USSGA
     1905-1980" .... 1980 .... $45
"A Record of Fifty Years USSGA 1904-1954". 1954 .... $65
"Senior Golf In The United States, Canada,
     And Great Britain" .... 1936 .... $75

Universal Golf Co:
"Universal Golf Dictionary" .... 1934 .... $175
John Updike:
"Golf Dreams" .... 1996 .... $35
Uplands G. C:
"Uplands Golf Club 1922-1997 75th
    Anniversary" .... 1997 .... $25
Upminster G. C:
"Upminster Golf Club"............................... 1961 .... $35
Robert Upton:
"Dead On The Stick"................................. 1986 .... $25
J. M. Urry:
"To St. Andrews For The Open
    Championship 1946" .... 1946 .... $65
Rich Ussak:
"Golfgames".. 1990 .... $15
Thomas H. Uzzell:
"Golf In The World's Oldest Mountains" .... 1926 .... $350
H. A. Vachell:
"The New Forest Golf Club" .... 1925 .... $45
Pembroke A. Vaile:
"Golf On The Green"................................. 1915 .... $200
"How To Approach" .... 1919 .... $60
"How To Drive".. 1919 .... $115
"How To Learn Golf: Spalding Primer
    Series"... 1919 .... $55
"How To Put And Training For Golf" .... 1919 .... $50
"Illustrated Rules Of Golf" .... 1919 .... $65
"Modern Golf"... 1909 .... $295
"The New Golf".. 1916 .... $295
"Putting Made Easy: The Mark Harris
    Method" .... 1935 .... $95
"Scientific Putting" .... 1927 .... $425
"The Short Game".................................... 1928 .... $95
"The Soul of Golf" .... 1912 .... $235
"Swerve Or Flight of The Ball"..................... 1905 .... $350
P.A. Vaille & H.B. Martin:
"The Illustrated Rules of Golf And The
    Etiquette of The Game" .... 1919 .... $395
Jessie Valentine:
"Better Golf Definitely" .... 1967 .... $10
Linda Valentine & Margie Hubbard:
"Golf Games Within The Game".................... 1992 .... $10

Jim Valli:
"Golf Guide: Central Otago-Southland" .... 1979 .... $35
Nicholas Van Daalen:
"International Golf Guide" .... 1976 .... $20
Jorge Vanden Berge:
"The Practice Book".................................. 1998 .... $20
John M. Vander Meulen:
"Getting Out of The Rough" .... 1926 .... $165
Maxine Van Evera:
"Building Your Swing For Better Golf
      With Amy Alcott" .... 1981 .... $10
Steven J. H. Van Hengel:
"Early Golf".. 1982 .... $85
"Early Golf: History And Development" .... 1972 .... $75
Kenneth Van Kampen:
"Visual Golf"... 1992 .... $10
Charles E. Van Loan:
"Fore!" .... 1918 .... $135
Guernsey Van Riper Jr.:
"Golfing Greats: Two Top Pros".................. 1975 .... $15
Cicely Van Straten:
"Caddie For A Crook"................................ 1985 .... $15
W. G. Van T. Sutphen:
"The Golfer's Alphabet"............................. 1899 ......$1,095
      Reprint.................................... 1969 .... $55
"The Golficide and Other Tales of The Fair
      Green" .... 1898 .... $565
"Harper's Official Golf Guide 1901" .... 1901 ......$1,595
"The Nineteenth Hole" .... 1901 ......$1,475
"The Official Golf Guide 1902".................... 1902 ......$1,000
"The Peripatetic Hazard" .... 1921 .... $200
Alfred Vardon & E. W .J. Wilson:
"Golfing Hints".. 1912 .... $275
      Reprint.................................... 1996 .... $25
Harry Vardon:
"The Complete Golfer" .... 1905 .... $775
      Reprint.................................... 1997 .... $20
"The Gist of Golf" .... 1922 .... $550
"Golf Club Selection" .... 1916 .... $550
"How To Play Golf" .... 1912 .... $600
"My Golfing Life" .... 1933 .... $750
      With Dust Jacket .... 1933 ......$2900
      300 Memorial Tournament Reprint ..... 1981 .... $400
      Reprint.................................... 1985 .... $250

Thousands of color book illustrations visible at
www.rogeregilchrist.com

Reprint.. 1992 .... $35
"Progressive Golf"..................................... 1920 .... $350
Harry Vardon & Others:
"Success At Golf"..................................... 1914 .... $135
E. C. Vare:
"Hip Pocket Golf Coach" .... 1983 .... $15
Bill Ventreska:
"Play Better Golf"..................................... 1966 .... $10
Michael E. Ventola:
"Fine Art of America's Fairways".................. 1998 .... $65
Ken Venturi:
"Comeback: The Ken Venturi Story" .... 1966 .... $45
"Let's Analyze Your Golf Swing" .... 1960 .... $10
"Venturi Analysis: Learning Better Golf
    From Champions" .... 1981 .... $15
"The Venturi System With Special Material
    On Shotmaking For The Advanced
    Golfer" .... 1983 .... $15
Frank VerBeck:
"A Handbook of Golf For Bears".................... 1900 ......$1,750
Verulam G. C:
"The Verulam Golf Club" .... 1934 .... $40
Victim:
"An ABC of Golf"...................................... 1898 .....$2,150
Al Victor:
"Arnie and His Army"................................. 1964 .... $15
Victoria Golf Association:
"Golf"... 1938 .... $125
Denis Vidler:
"Rye Golf Club, The First 90 Years".............. 1984 .... $35
Dean Vietor:
"Your Golf Game's In Big Trouble When" ...... 1984 .... $10
Carl Vigeland:
"Stalking The Shark" .... 1996 .... $10
Bosmand de Villiers:
"Gholf Saam Met Die Boere" .... 1959 .... $35
Lawrence Viney:
"Ashridge Golf Club 1932-1982".................. 1982 .... $25
"The Royal And Ancient Book of Golf
    Records" .... 1991 .... $25
"Old Rugbeian Golfing Society 1924-1994" ... 1995 .... $25
Nigel Viney & Neil Grant:
"An Illustrated History of Ball Games".......... 1978 .... $10

Thousands of color book illustrations visible at
www.rogeregilchrist.com

Garth Vipond:
"Maungakieke Golf Club. The First
Hundred Years" .... 2009 .... $25
Bill Vogeney:
"The Art of Putters: The Scotty Cameron
Story" .... 2001 .... $150
Viola & Volk:
"A Brief History of The Alliance Country
Club" .... (nd) $20
V. S. Viscellette:
"Golf Club Reconditioning" .... 1964 .... $10
Bill Vogeney & David Devine:
"The Art of Putters" .... 2001 .... $100
Mona Vold:
"Different Strokes" .... 1999 .... $10
Norman Von Nida:
"Golf Is My Business" .... 1956 .... $35
"Golf Isn't Hard" .... 1949 .... $45
Clifton L. Voorhies:
"The Mental Game of Golf" .... 1950 .... $15
Jerry Vroom:
"So You Want To Be A Golfer" .... 1973 .... $15
E. W.:
"The Yorkshire Union of Golf Clubs,
First County Championship" .... 1894 .... $375
G. B. W.:
"The Phraseology of Golf" .... 1893 ..... $1,200
Charles L. Wade:
"Blackwell Golf Club 1893-200" (550 Copies) 2001 .... $95
Collin Wade:
"Naracoorte G.C. 1928-1978 .... 1978 .... $45
"A Country Boy Including the History of the
Naracoorte G.C. 1928-1990 .... 1990 .... $25
Don Wade:
"And The Arnie Told Chi Chi..." .... 1993 .... $10
"And Then Chi Chi Told Fuzzy..." .... 1995 .... $10
"And Then Fuzzy Told Seve..." .... 1996 .... $10
"And The Jack Said To Arnie" .... 1991 .... $10
"And The Seve Told Freddie...." .... 1998 .... $10
James Wagenvoord:
"Golf Diary" .... 1981 .... $10
J. Parry Wagener:
"Keep the Ball a Rolling: A Pictorial History
of the Claremont Country Club.

Thousands of color book illustrations visible at
www.rogeregilchrist.com

1903-2003 .... 2003 .... $25
Glen Waggoner:
"Divots, Shanks, Gimmies, Mulligans, and
    Chilli Dips"...................................... 1993 .... $10
Corydon Wagner:
"Pacific Northwest Golf Comes of Age
    1892-1926" .... 1973 .... $10
"Tacoma Country And Golf Club 1894-1969
    Seventy-Fifth Anniversary" .... 1969 .... $50
Susan F. Wagner:
"History of Flossmoor Country Club
    1899-1979" .... 1979 .... $15
Arthur Wagstaff:
"Contra Costa Country Club Golden Jubilee
    1925-1975" .... 1975 .... $55
Waitikiri G. C:
"Waitikiri Golf Glub Golden Jubilee .... 1987 .... $45
Robert Walde-Grave:
"The Lawes and Actes of Parliament
    Maid de King James the First..."........... 1597 .... $900
Wales, A Golfing Guide:
"Wales: A Golfing Guide For The Business
    Traveller" .... 1980 .... $20
David G. Walker:
"Rick Tees Off" .... 1985 .... $10
Donald Walker:
"Games And Sports.."............................... 1837 .... $145
Edwin Walker:
"History of Golf At Fleetwood 1893-1993"..... 1993 .... $25
G. A. Walker:
"St Neots Golf Club: The First 100 Years" ..... 1990 .... $25
John Walker & Sons:
"The Rules of Golf"................................... 1911 .... $135
Oscar W. Walker:
"Practical Golf Lessons From a New Angle" ... 1949 .... $70
Robert Walker:
"Fairhaven Golf Glub" .... 1965 .... $10
"Ham Manor Residential Golf Club".............. 1951 .... $25
"The Newquay Golf Club" .... 1951 .... $20
"Parkstone Golf Club" .... 1953 .... $25
"Saltford Golf Club".................................. 1951 .... $25
"The Southerndown Golf Club".................... 1955 .... $15
"The Verulam Golf Club" .... 1957 .... $10

Thousands of color book illustrations visible at
www.rogeregilchrist.com

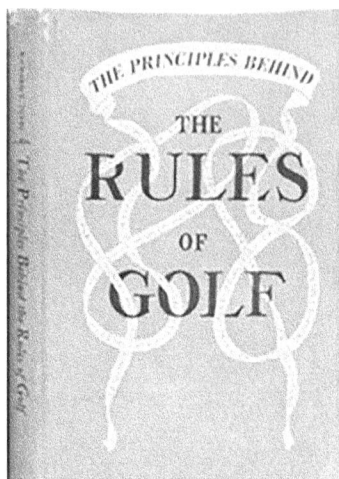

Tufts – The Rules of Golf
(Dust Jacket)

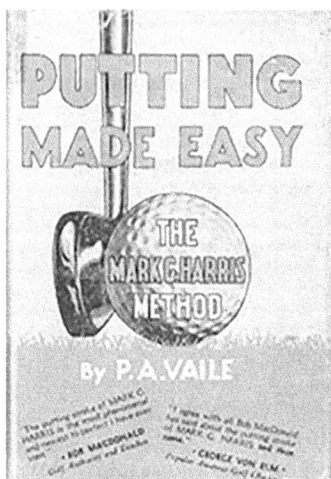

Vaille – Putting Made Easy
(Dust Jacket)

Van Loan – Fore!
(Dust Jacket)

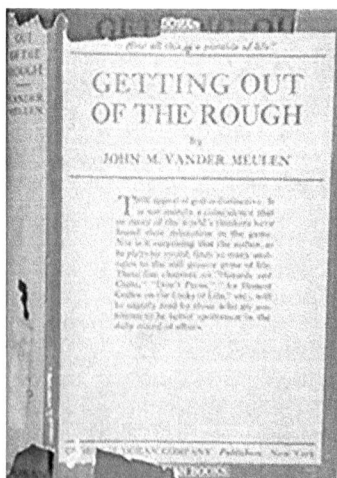

Vander Meulen – Getting Out
of the Rough (Dust Jacket)

Thousands of color book illustrations visible at
www.rogeregilchrist.com

Jim Wallace:
"DB Golfing Annual" .... 1974 .... $35
"Golf at the Links: Paraparaumu Beach
    Golf Club Inc. 1949-1999" .... 1999 .... $45
Wallach & Schwartz:
"Breaking 100: Eugene Country Club's First
    Century1899-1999" .... 1999 .... $25
Lillian Wallcock:
"With A Song In My Cart" .... 1970 .... $10
Brian Wallis:
"Echoes From An Old Fairway: A History of
    Horbury And District Golf Club
    1907-1965" .... 1965 .... $225
    Reprint of 350 copies .... 1986 .... $50
Walmer & Kingsdown G. C:
"Walmer And Kingsdown Golf Club" .... 1937 .... $75
Walsall G. C:
"Walsall Golf Club" .... 1938 .... $60
David Walsh:
"Mullingar Golf Club The First 100 Years" ...... 1994 .... $25
John H. Walsh:
"Seaford Golf Club: A History 1887-1986" .... 1986 .... $50
Leigh Walsh:
"How To Teach Yourself The Expert Golf
    Swing" .... 1956 .... $10
Tom Walsh:
"The Picture Way To Better Golf" .... 1956 .... $55
D. P. Walton:
"Golf at Alnmouth" .... 1992 .... $35
T. F. R. Waters:
"History of the Royal Hong Kong Golf Club" .. 1960 .... $125
Charles Ward:
"How To Play Little Aston Golf Course" .... 1965 .... $25
Hugh Ward:
"Effortless Golf" .... 1956 .... $10
Peter Ward:
"Came Down To Golf" .... 1984 .... $55
Pat Ward-Thomas:
"The Long Green Fairway" .... 1966 .... $35
"Masters of Golf" .... 1961 .... $25
"Not Only Golf: An Autobiography" .... 1981 .... $35
"The Royal And Ancient" .... 1980 .... $45
"The Royal North Devon Golf Club
    1864-1964" .... 1964 .... $135

Thousands of color book illustrations visible at
www.rogeregilchrist.com

"Shell Golfers' Atlas of England,
    Scotland And Wales" .... 1968 .... $35
"The Lay of The Land" .... 1990 .... $35
Pat Ward-Thomas & Others:
"The World Atlas of Golf"............................ 1976 .... $45
G. Waring:
"Golf: A Scientific Approach, The Mechanics
    of The Game"................................... 1958 .... $15
Warrington G. G:
"Warrington Golf Club Official Handbook" ..... 1963 .... $35
William Wartman:
"John Daly; Wild Thing" .... 1996 .... $15
"Playing Through" .... 1990 .... $20
Washington Golf & C. C:
"History of The Washington Golf And
    Country Club" .... 1947 .... $60
E. R. Wason:
"Golf Without Tears"................................. 1951 .... $35
T. F. R. Waters:
"A History of The Royal Hong Kong
    Golf Club".. 1960 .... $195
Ashley Watkins:
"History of The Bedfordshire Golf Club
    1891-1991" .... 1992 .... $45
Alick A. Watt:
"Collecting Old Golf Clubs" .... 1985 .... $65
A. Campbell Watson:
"Podson's Golfing Year"............................. 1930 .... $165
Alan S. Watson:
"The First 100 Years, A History of The Royal
    Belfast Golf Club 1881-1981" .... 1981 .... $90
Alfred E. T. Watson:
"The Badminton Magazine Of Sports
    And Pastimes"................................. 1895 .... $475
E. H. Lacon Watson:
"Notes and Memories of a Sports Reporter" .. 1930 .... $75
Gilbert Watson:
"A Caddie of St. Andrews"......................... 1907 .... $525
"Skipper".. 1906 .... $625
Gilbert Watson:
"A Short History of Craigmillar Park Golf
    Club 1895-1974" .... 1974 .... $50
John T. Watson:
"A History of New Galloway Golf Club..." .... 2002 .... $30

Limited Edition of 300

J. W. Watson:
"Little Lessons In Golf" .... 1921 .... $40
Tom Watson:
"Getting Back To Basics" .... 1992 .... $20
"Getting Up And Down" .... 1983 .... $15
"The New Rules of Golf" .... 1984 .... $15
"The Rules Of Golf" .... 1980 .... $10
"Tom Watson's Key Swing Thoughts" .... 1978 .... $20
Tom Watson & Sandy Tatum:
"The 25 Greatest Achievements of Golf" .... 1997 .... $25
Neil Watson Kerr:
"Golf: The Pros Don't Know It All" .... 1998 .... $15
Alick A. Watt:
"Collecting Old Golf Clubs" .... 1985 .... $75
"Collecting Old Golf Clubs" .... 1990 .... $25
R. Watts:
"How to Play Pennard Golf Course, Swansea" 1933 .... $195
Wyn Weaver:
"Golf Clubs, An Eccentric Sketch" .... 1925 .... $320
Clifford Webb:
"Stourbridge Golf Club Centenary
    1892-1992" .... 1992 .... $35
David Webb:
"Royal Perth Golf Club: Centenary Souvenir
    100 Years of Golf" .... 1995 .... $35
Marcus Webb & John Briggs:
"On Carrickmines Hill – The Story of
    Carrickmines Golf Club 1900-2000" ..... 2000 .... $45
Warren H. Webb:
"Lessons On Golf" .... 1907 .... $300
Harry C. Webber:
"Golf In Maine" .... 1930 .... $65
Louis Webber & Dennis Kennedy:
"Golf Manners" .... 1968 .... $15
Steve Webber:
"Bogey Blues" .... 1998 .... $10
Warren H. Webling:
"Lessons On Golf" .... 1907 .... $120
W. Hastings Webling:
"Fore: A Few More Golf Shots" .... 1908 .... $475
"Fore: The Call of The Links" .... 1909 .... $345
"Golf: In Verse And Reverse" .... 1924 .... $425
"An Interrupted Golf Match and Other

Thousands of color book illustrations visible at
www.rogeregilchrist.com

Stories".. 1910 .... $300
"Locker Room Ballards" .... 1925 .... $225
"On And Off The Links" .... 1921 .... $285
Wee Burn C. C:
"Wee Burn Country Club Inc"........................... 1949 .... $45
"Wee Burn Country Club, A History" .... 1979 .... $20
Weeder:
"The Doctors Golf Association of
Philadelphia 1915-1965".................... 1965 .... $75
"The Doctors Golf Association of
Philadelphia 1965-1990".................... 1990 .... $25
Bob Weeks:
"The World's Greatest Golf Courses" .... 1992 .... $20
Edward Weeks:
"Myopia, A Centennial Chronicle
1875-1975" .... 1975 .... $300
Harry Weetman:
"Add To Your Golf Power"........................... 1963 .... $25
"Golf Drive And 7-Iron Shot" .... 1960 .... $100
"The Way To Golf".................................. 1953 .... $15
Ralph Weidemnkopf:
"The Science Of Controlled Relaxation
In Golf" .... 1936 .... $35
Tom Weiskopf:
"Go For The Flag".................................. 1969 .... $15
Mike Weiss:
"100 Handy Hints On How To Break 100" ..... 1951 .... $20
Welch, Welch, & Radford:
"1000 Questions: The Golfer's Book of
Trivia".. 1985 .... $10
Stanley B. Weld:
"A History of The Great Chebeague Golf Club"
(250 Copies) .... 1962 .... $85
Oliver Weldon:
"Golf In Ireland" .... 1969 .... $75
Welsh Golfing Union:
"75th Anniversary Souvenir Report" .... 1970 .... $10
Charles W. Welsh:
"Seventy-Five Years of Golf At The Royal
Eastbourne Golf Club 1887-1962" .... 1962 .... $60
Lord Welwood:
"The Golfer at Home" .... 1898 .... $100
Clifford C. Wendehack:
"Golf And Country Clubs" .... 1929 .... $875

William P. Wendt:
"The Distance Builder" .... 1982 .... $10
Wentworth Club:
"Wentworth Club" .... 1959 .... $45
J. Wentworth Day:
"Best Sporting Stories" .... 1949 .... $25
D. N. Werner:
"Great Golfers of The Twentieth Century" ..... 1971 .... $20
"Lower Your Golf Score".............................. 1972 .... $10
Nick Weslock:
"Your Golf Bag Pro: Nick Westlock's Little
    Black Book of Key Golf Secrets".......... 1985 .... $10
Douglas B. Wesson:
"I'll Never Be Cured And I Don't Much Care" . 1928 .... $75
Henry L. West:
"The Columbia Country Club As It Was
    In The Beginning"............................. 1938 .... $75
"Lyrics of The Links"................................... 1921 .... $325
West Bradford G. C:
"West Bradford Golf Club: The Centenary
    1900-2000" .... 2000 .... $25
West Brookfield G. C:
"West Brookfield Golf Club Bi Laws"............. 1904 .... $125
Westchester C. C:
"Westchester Country Club Inc, Rye,
    New York" .... 1930 .... $125
Western Golf Association:
"Caddie Committee Manual" .... 1947 .... $20
"Caddie Master Manual"............................... 1955 .... $25
"Caddie Operations Manual" .... 1969 .... $10
"Camera Tour of Caddieville" .... 1955 .... $10
"Case For Caddies"...................................... 1965 .... $35
"New Caddie Committee Guide And
    Electric Cart Survey" .... 1955 .... $10
"Pin Pointers" .... 1948 .... $15
"Recruiting And Retaining Your Caddies" ...... 1951 .... $25
Westgate-On-Sea & Birchington G. C:
"The Westgate-On-Sea And Birchington
    Golf Club"....................................... 1926 .... $75
John W. Weston:
"A History Of Coombe Wood Golf Club
    1904-1970" .... 1985 .... $15
Weston-Super Mare G. C:
"The Weston-Super Mare Golf Club" .... 1955 .... $20

Thousands of color book illustrations visible at
www.rogeregilchrist.com

Dexter Westrum:
"Elegy For A Golf Pro"................................ 1994 .... $15
West Wilts G. C:
"The West Wilts Golf Club" .... 1938 .... $65
Richard W. Westwood:
"The History of the Washington Golf and
      Country Club" .... 1947 .... $75
H. Newton Wethered:
"The Perfect Golfer" .... 1931 .... $375
H. Newton Wethered & Tom Simpson:
"The Architectural Side of Golf"................... 1929 ......$2,995
      Signed Limited Edition...................... 1929 .... $12,500
      Reprint Limited edition of 565............. 1995 .... $95
"Design For Golf" .... 1952 .... $80
Joyce Wethered:
"Golfing Memories and Methods"................. 1933 .... $275
      Reprint.. 1954 .... $30
Joyce Wethered & Others:
"The Game of Golf, The Lonsdale Library"..... 1931 .... $575
Roger Wethered:
"The Temple Golf Club"............................. 1938 .... $55
Roger & Joyce Wethered:
"Golf From Two Sides"............................... 1925 .... $125
Weymouth G. C:
"The Weymouth Golf Club"......................... 1951 .... $20
Vera Wheatley:
"Mixed Foursomes: A Saga of Golf" .... 1936 .... $250
Where To Golf In Kansas City:
"Where To Golf In Kansas City".................. 1982 .... $10
Ernest D. Wichels & Robert W. Boardman:
"A History of the Green Valley Country
      Club 1949-1974" .... 1974 .... $35
H. J. Whigham:
"Athletic Sports The Outdoor Library" .... 1897 .... $185
"How To Play Golf".................................... 1897 .... $195
Winged Foot G. C:
The Winged Foot Golf Club Announcing the
      Opening of the New Courses" .... 1923 .... $750
Wilpshire G. C:
Wilpshire Golf Club Centenary 1890-1990" ... 1990 .... $25
Windwhistle G. C:
"Windwistle Golf Club 1932-1934"............... 1937 .... $450
Jack Whitaker:
"Prefered Lies And Other Tales" .... 1998 .... $10

Thousands of color book illustrations visible at
www.rogeregilchrist.com

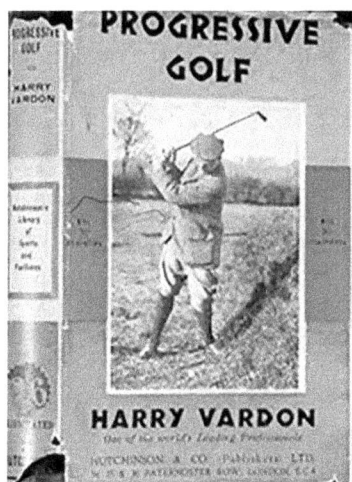

Vardon – Progressive Golf
(Dust Jacket)

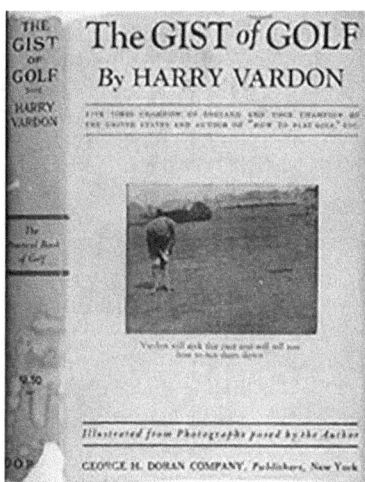

Vardon – The Gist of Golf
(1st American Edition Dust Jacket)

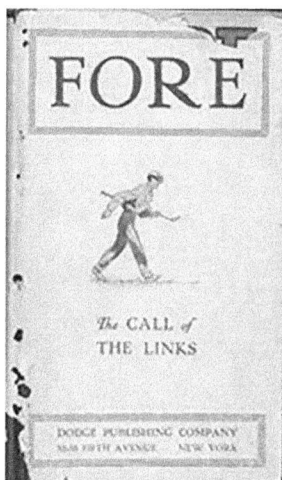

Webling – Fore
(Dust Jacket)

Wethered – Golf From Two Sides
(Dust Jacket)

Thousands of color book illustrations visible at
www.rogeregilchrist.com

Charles A. Whitcombe:
"Charles Whitcombe On Golf" .... 1931 .... $125
"Golf" .... 1949 .... $45
"Golf Shots: The Drive, Fairway Hazard
    Pocket Pro Series No 1" .... 1933 .... $50
"Golf Shots: The Iron, Fairway Hazard
    Pocket Pro Series No. 2" .... 1933 .... $45
"Golf Shots: The Mashie Niblick, Fairway
    Pocket Pro Series No. 3" .... 1933 .... $45
"Golf Shots: Niblick And Putter, Fairway &
    Hazard Pocket Pro Series No. 4" .... 1933 .... $45

Ernest R. Whitcombe:
"The Golf I Teach" .... 1947 .... $45
"How To Play Meyrick Park Golf Course" .... 1951 .... $15

Reginald A. Whitcombe:
"Golf's No Mystery" .... 1938 .... $95

Fairmount R. White:
"Golf In The Seventies For Those In
    The Sixties" .... 1962 .... $60

Graham White:
"The History of Lewes Golf Club 1896-1996". 1996 .... $50

Greg White:
"A Little Golf Guru" .... 1992 .... $35

Jack White:
"Easier Golf" .... 1924 .... $165
"Putting" .... 1921 .... $225

Randy White:
"70 Years at Rancho Santa Fe Golf Club
    1929-1999" .... 1999 .... $50

Ronald J. White:
"Golf As I Play It" .... 1953 .... $55

Stewart E. White:
"The Shepper-Newfounder" .... 1931 .... $65

James F. Whiteford:
"Tam At Golf Or The Nineteenth Hole" .... 1939 .... $60

Eric Whitehead:
"Hathstauwk: The Story of Capilano Golf
    and Country Club" (2000 Copies) .... 1981 .... $25

Whiteleaf G. C:
"Whiteleaf Golf Club" .... 1967 .... $20

Whitemarsh Valley C. C:
"Whitemarsh Valley Country Club 1908" .... 1908 .... $65

John Whitfield:
"Sunningdale Golf Club" .... 2000 .... $45

Marshall Whitlatch:
"Golf For Beginners And Others" .... 1910 .... $70
Caspar W. Whitney:
"A Sporting Pilgrimage" .... 1894 .... $225
Don E. Whitney:
"Golf From A-Z" .... 1982 .... $10
Howard F. Whitney:
"Decisions On The Rules of Golf" .... 1927 .... $40
Ron Whitten:
"Golf Has Never Failed Me" (400 Copies) ...... 1996 .... $295
Ivo H. Whitton:
"Golf" .... 1947 .... $45
Kathy Whitworth:
"Golf For Women" .... 1990 .... $15
Who's Who:
"Who's Who In Golf And Directory of
    Golf Clubs And Members" .... 1909 .... $795
Price Wickersham & Frank Lauder:
"The K.C.G.A. Caddie Book" .... 1921 .... $325
Verne Wickham:
"The Municipal Golf Course: Organizing
    And Operating Guide" .... 1955 .... $20
Lawrence A. Wien:
"The Golf Club At Astetuck" .... 1974 .... $15
H. J. Wigham:
"How To Play Golf" .... 1897 .... $275
K. G. Wilcock:
"Chorleywood Golf Club 1890-1990" .... 1989 .... $45
Morton Wild:
"Inwood Country Club Fiftieth Anniversary
    1901-1951" .... 1951 .... $40
Payson S. Wild & Bert L. Taylor:
"Brothers of The Book Miscellanea:
    The Links of Ancient Rome" .... 1912 .... $1050
    Second Edition .... 1935 .... $150
Roland Wild:
"Golf: The Loneliest Game" .... 1969 .... $45
Larry Wilde:
"The Official Golfer's Joke Book" .... 1977 .... $10
Wilderness C. C:
"Wilderness Country Club And Golf Course" .. 1930 .... $40
Elizabeth C. Wilkin:
"The Castle and the Club. Bald Peak Colony". 1964 .... $75

Elizabeth D. Wilkinson:
"History of The Toledo Women's
District Golf Association".................... 1931 .... $35
George Will:
"Golf The Modern Way".............................. 1968 .... $10
Ambrose Williams:
"The Principles of The Golf Swing" .... 1965 .... $10
Arthur C. Williams:
"Brooklawn Country Club 1895-1970
75th Anniversary"............................. 1970 .... $25
David Williams:
"How To Coach And Play Championship Golf" 1962 .... $10
"The Science of The Golf Swing" .... 1969 .... $15
Eddie Williams:
"How To Improve Your Golf With The
Developar" .... 1958 .... $10
Evan "Big Cat" Williams:
"You Can Hit The Golf Ball Farther".............. 1979 .... $15
Everall Williams:
"Wilmslow Golf Club1889-1989".................. 1989 .... $35
Gwen Williams:
"Unique Golf Resorts of the World" .... 1983 .... $20
Lewis Williams:
"Golf Without Tears"................................. 1940 .... $35
Michael Williams:
"Daily Telegraph Pocket Sports Facts: Golf" .. 1984 .... $10
"History of Golf"..................................... 1985 .... $20
"Grand Slam, Golf's Major Championships"... 1988 .... $20
"The Official History of The Ryder Cup" .... 1989 .... $35
Stewart Williams:
"The Cest of Time" .... 1981 .... $45
Tom Williams:
"Fairways of the Sea 100 Years of Golf
at Rosslare 1905-2005"...................... 2005 .... $45
Williams & MacMeeken:
"Sale Golf Course" .... 1954 .... $25
Lauren Williamson:
"Henly Golf Club: The First Eighty Years"...... 1986 .... $95
J. E. Willmott:
"Sutton Coldfield Golf Club Jubilee
1899-1939" .... 1939 .... $85
Ridley Wills:
"Belle Meade Country Club The First 100
Years"... 2001 .... $95

Thousands of color book illustrations visible at
www.rogeregilchrist.com

Wilmington C. C:
"Wilmington Country Club Certificate of
    Incorporation, By-Laws, Rules,
    Names of Members, 1913".................. 1913........ $275
"Wilmington Country Club Golf Schedule
    1921" .... 1921........ $150
Wimslow G. C:
"The Centenary Programme of Events:
    Wimslow Golf Club 1889-1989" .... 1989 .... $25
"Wimslow Golf Club 1889-1989: One Hundred
    Years of the Wimslow Golf Club" .... 1989 .... $25
Robert Windeler:
"Links With a Past: The First 100 Years of the
    Los Angeles Country Club Centennial... 1997 .... $225
Wilshire C. C:
"The Wilshire Country Club 1919-1989" .... 1989 .... $20
Enid Wilson:
"A Gallery of Women Golfers" .... 1961 .... $55
"Golf For Women" .... 1964 .... $20
Enid Wilson & Robert A. Lewis:
"So That's What I Do"............................... 1935 .... $95
Harry L. Wilson:
"So This Is Golf" .... 1923 .... $225
J. H. Wilson:
"The Golfers A Past Era" (1000 Copies) .... 1977 .... $175
Kenneth Wilson:
"It's All In The Swing" .... 1947 .... $35
"To Better Golf In Two Strides" .... 1938 .... $45
Mark Wilson:
"The Best Of Henry Longhurst" .... 1978 .... $15
"The PGA European Tour Guide To
    Better Golf" .... 1986 .... $10
"The Sunningdale Centenary 1900-2000" ..... 2000 .... $40
Wilson Sporting Goods:
"For The Esquire of The Golf Links".............. 1938 .... $45
"From Tee To Cup".................................. 1955 .... $20
"The Gateway To Golf"............................. 1932 ....$175
"The Gateway To Golf".............................. 1953 .... $65
"Harmonized With You And Your Game" .... 1952 .... $15
"Presenting The 7-Up Golf Tips By
    The Experts" .... 1957 .... $25
"Wilson Golf Clubs Are The Finest"............... 1949 .... $15
Wilson Staff:
"Where To Golf In Europe" .... 1961 .... $25

Thousands of color book illustrations visible at
www.rogeregilchrist.com

Winchester G.C:
    "Rules For Caddies" .... 1926 .... $40
Winchester C. C:
    "Breaking Ninety; 1897-1987 Winchester
        Country Club" .... 1987 .... $35
Herbert Warren Wind:
    "The Complete Golfer" .... 1954 .... $75
    "Following Through" .... 1985 .... $55
    "The Gilded Age of Sports" .... 1961 .... $50
    "Golf Quiz" .... 1980 .... $20
    "Golf Tips From The Top Professionals" .... 1958 .... $15
    "On The Tour With Harry Sprague" .... 1960 .... $95
    "The Open's Fourth Visit To Winged Foot" ..... 1984 .... $60
    "Shell's Wonderful World of Golf 1962" .... 1962 .... $90
    "The Lure of Golf" .... 1971 .... $40
    "The Story of American Golf: Its Champions
        And Its Championships" .... 1948 .... $500
        1956 Edition .... 1956 .... $75
        1976 Edition .... 1976 .... $75
    "Thorny Lea Golf Club 1900-1950 50th
        Anniversary" .... 1950 .... $60
    "The Realm of Sport" .... 1966 .... $35
    "Tips From The Top" .... 1955 .... $30
    "Tips From The Top Book 2" .... 1956 .... $20
    "Herbert Warren Wind's Golf Book" .... 1971 .... $65
Windemere G. C:
    "The Windemere Golf Club" .... 1949 .... $50
    "The Windemere Golf Club Centenary" .... 1991 .... $25
Robert Windeler:
    "Thunderbird Country Club: From Desert
        to Oasis 50th Anniversary History" .... 2002 .... $135
Frank Wing:
    "Fore! Eighty-Two Sketches Of The Same
        Number Of Minneapolis Golfers" .... 1929 .... $75
Roland Wingate:
    "12 Money Shots In Golf" .... 1935 .... $65
    "Saving Strokes" .... 1934 .... $250
Jack Winstanley:
    "The Wigan Century. A History of The Wigan
        Golf Club 1898-1998" .... 1998 .... $45
Ed Winter:
    "Simplified Golf Instructions" .... 1950 .... $30
Gary Wiren:
    "The PGA Manual of Golf" .... 1991 .... $25

Thousands of color book illustrations visible at
www.rogeregilchrist.com

"Golf" .... 1971 .... $20
"Planning And Conducting Jr Golf Programs" . 1973 .... $10
"Super Power Golf: Techniques For
    Increasing Distance" .... 1984 .... $10
"Picture Perfect Golf" .... 1998 .... $10
Gary Wiren & Dr. Richard Coop:
"The New Golf Mind" .... 1978 .... $20
Kris M. Wise:
"The Answers To Par Golf" .... 1978 .... $10
Sidney L. Wise:
"Carolina Golfer Directory 1976" .... 1976 .... $10
J.R. Wishart:
"Golf Course Guide To Southern Africa" .... 1983 .... $15
Tom W. Wishon:
"The Golf Club Identification And
    Price Guide" .... 1985 .... $20
Harry Woan:
"Swing Secrets Analysed, Explained and
    Simplified" .... 1934 .... $125
P. G. Wodehouse:
"The Clicking Of Cuthbert" (Dust Jacket)" ..... 1922 .... $1250
    Reprint .... 1986 .... $25
"Mr. Mulliner Speaking" .... 1929 .... $195
"Divots" .... 1927 .... $140
"Dr Sally" .... 1932 .... $75
"A Few Quick Ones" .... 1959 .... $125
"Love Among the Chickens" .... 1921 .... $95
"Fore: The Best of Wodehouse On Golf" .... 1983 .... $40
"The Golf Omnibus" .... 1973 .... $95
    Reprint .... 1991 .... $25
"Golf Without Tears" .... 1924 .... $95
"The Heart of A Goof" .... 1926 .... $125
"Wodehouse On Golf" .... 1940 .... $295
Maia Wojciechowska:
"Dreams of Golf" .... 1993 .... $15
Woking G. C:
Woking Golf Club" .... 1899 .... $250
William H. Wolford:
"Golfmasters: A Sure Way To Better Golf" .... 1940 .... $75
Wollaston Golf Club:
"Wollaston Golf Club: The Story of the Old
    Club, Fiftieth Anniversary 1895-1945" . 1945 .... $90
Wood, Pepper, Bennett, Miller Etc:
"The Boys Own Treasury of Sports and

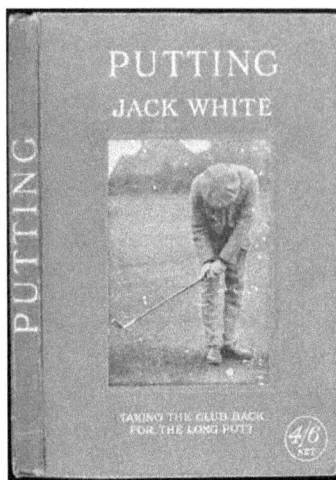

White – Putting (Dust Jacket)

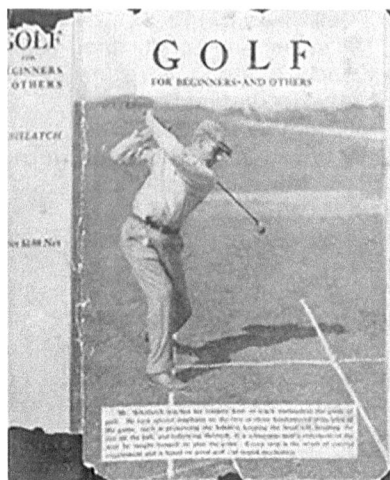

Whitlach – Golf for Beginner and Others (Dust Jacket)

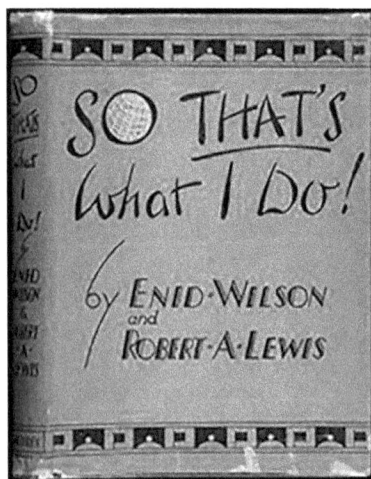

Wilson & Lewis – So That's What I Do! (1st Edition Dust Jacket)

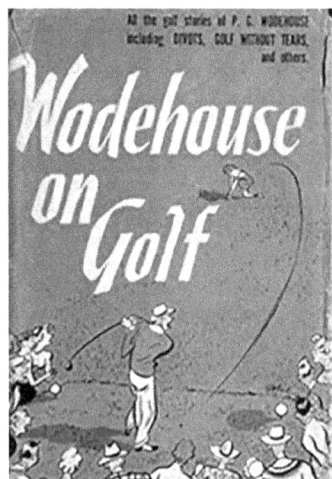

Wodehouse – Wodehouse on Golf (1st Edition)

Thousands of color book illustrations visible at
www.rogeregilchrist.com

Pastimes" 1871 150

A. G. Wood:
"Royal Jersey Golf Club"............................. 1965 .... $20

B. Britten Wood:
"Piqua Country Club History" .... 1975 .... $15

Craig Wood:
"Swinging Thru: How To Play Golf".............. 1935 .... $125
"How To Play Golf With The Rules of Golf" .... 1937 .... $75

Harry B. Wood:
"Golfing Curios And The Like" .... 1910 ......$1,500
    Subcribers edition (150 Copies) .... 1910 ......$3,650
    Reprint... 1980 .... $125

Woodbridge G. & C. C:
"Woodbridge Golf and Country Club.
    Seventy Five Years 1924-1999" .... 1999 .... $50

Woodbrook G. C:
"Woodbrook Golf Club" .... 1961 .... $25

Roy F. Woodbury & Charlotte I. Claflin:
"The Woodhall Spa Golf Club" .... 1951 .... $20

Arthur L. Woodhead:
"A History of Huddersfield Golf Club
    From 1891-1949" .... 1949 .... $400

Geoffrey Woodhead:
"The Story of Saddleworth Golf Club"........... 1998 .... $45

Alan Woodison:
"Ayershire Golf Guide" .... 1983 .... $15

Woodland G. C:
"Woodland Golf Club" .... 2002 .... $35

Tommy Woodrum:
"Golfing the Carolina Grandstrand" .... 1999 .... $30

Woods Hole G. C:
"1899-1999 Woods Hole Golf Club..." .... 1999 .... $20

E. J. Woodward:
"Golf Greens of England, Ireland And Wales" 1897 ......$1,700

Wooley & Yates:
"Rhos-On-Sea Golf Club, 1899-1999" .... 199 .... $45

Ian Woosnam:
"Ian Woosnam's Golf Masterpieces"............. 1988 .... $15
"Power Golf"... 1989 .... $15

Worthing G. C:
"Worthing Golf Club 1905-1980" .... 1980 .... $35

Gene Worthington:
"How To Acquire The Perfect Golf Swing"...... 1973 .... $10

Guy Worthington:
"The First Hundred Years Of Ganton
Golf Club 1891-1991"........................ 1992 .... $35
Bucky Woy:
"Sign 'Em Up Bucky: The Adventures of
A Sport Agent" .... 1975 .... $10
Wrexham G. C:
"The Wrexham Golf Club".......................... 1937 .... $60
Wright And Ditson:
"Wright and Ditson's Guide to American
Golf".. 1895 .... $51,000
"Wright and Ditson's Guide to American
Golf".. 1897 .... $7500
"Wright And Ditson Golf Guide" .... 1900 .... $675
Ben Wright:
"Good Bounces & Bad Lies" .... 1999 .... $10
Gordon Wright:
"The Golf Widow: A Comedy in One Act" ...... 1958 .... $200
Harry Wright:
"A Short History of Golf In Mexico And
The Mexico City Country Club"............. 1938 .... $475
Ian Wright:
"Summers With Seve" .... 1991 .... $20
Jack W. Wright:
"Guide To Vancouver Island Courses" .... 1977 .... $20
Mickey Wright:
"Play Golf The Wright Way" .... 1962 .... $25
Reprint.. 1990 .... $15
200 Memorial Tournament Reprint ..... 1994 .... $120
Joyce Wrinch-Schulz:
"The First Sixty Years, A History of The
Durban Country Club From
1922-1982" .... 1982 .... $125
Josephine Wunsch:
"Girl In The Rough" .... 1981 .... $10
Stevan Wygant:
"What's Your Golf I.Q.?"............................ 1962 .... $25
Wykagyl C. C:
"Constitution and By Laws; Officers And
Members of the Wykagyl County Club" 1904 .... $150
"Constitution and By Laws; Officers And
Members of the Wykagyl County Club" 1915 .... $75
Wyke Green G. C:
"Wyke Green Golf Club"............................ 1935 .... $60

Thousands of color book illustrations visible at
www.rogeregilchrist.com

Steve Wynn & Tom Fazio"
"Shadow Creek. From Barren Desert, to
Desert Oasis" .... 1995 .... $75
Anthony Wynne:
"Death of A Golfer" .... 1937 .... $135
Mr. X:
"Beginners Guide To Golf" .... 1972 .... $15
"Golf Lessons With Mr. X" .... 1968 .... $15
"Golf Monthly's Lessons" .... 1968 .... $15
"More Golf Lessons With Mr. X" .... 1971 .... $15
Yakima Country Club:
"Yakima Country Club, Dedication of The New
Club House" .... 1949 .... $10
Yardley C. C:
"Yardley Country Club: A Casual History
1928-1978" .... 1978 .... $65
George A. Yeager:
"The First Seventy-Five Years - Orange
County Club 1899-1974" .... 1974 .... $20
Yelverton G. C:
"The Yelverton Golf Club" .... 1938 .... $45
Count Yogi:
"Five Simple Steps To Perfect Golf" .... 1973 .... $30
G. Yeomans:
"The History of A Country Golf Club:
The First 100 Years of Didsley" .... 1989 .... $25
York Downs Golf:
"Celebrating the First Seventy Five Years" .... 1997 .... $50
Commodore William Yorgey:
"The Commodore Yorgey Scientific Stance
And Swing" .... 1972 .... $15
Yorkshire Union of Golf Clubs:
"Yorkshire Union of Golf Clubs
Yearbook 1899-1902" .... 1899 .... $200
"Yorkshire Union of Golf Clubs
Yearbook 1908-1909" .... 1908 .... $135
Yorktown C. C:
"Invitation for Life Membership in the Club" .. 1924 .... $200
You and Your Golf Course:
"You and Your Golf Course" .... 1955 .... $10
You Can Break 80:
"You Can Break 80" .... 1930 .... $150
Charley Young:
"Tips From Western New York Golf Pros" ...... 1955 .... $10

Thousands of color book illustrations visible at
www.rogeregilchrist.com

Douglas Young:
"St. Andrews: Town And Gown, Royal
And Ancient"................................... 1969 .... $35
Jerome A. Young:
"Documentary Proof That Insanity Is
Hereditary"...................................... 1951 .... $10
Tom McFarlane Young:
"The Open Championship In Scotland:
Prints And History"........................... 1985 .... $15
Your Golf Clubs:
"Your Golf Clubs And How To Care For
Them".. 1955 .... $10
Your Guide To The Open:
"Your Guide To The Open, St. Andrews" .... 1970 .... $15
Bertha D. Zadnik:
"The Connecticut Women's Golf
Association History 1919-1969" .... 1969 .... $10
Michael Zagst:
"The Greening of Thurmond Leaner" .... 1986 .... $20
Babe Didrickson Zaharias:
"Championship Golf" .... 1949 .... $95
"This Life I've Led" .... 1955 .... $75
200 Memorial Tournament Reprint ...... 1991 .... $175
Jack Zanger:
"Excersises For Better Golf"...................... 1965 .... $20
Donald Zec:
"Coombe Hill"... 2002 .... $55
"Bob Zender & Charles B. Cleveland:
"Winning Golf, The Professional Way" .... 1985 .... $20
Howard Ziehm:
"Golf In The Comic Strips"......................... 1997 .... $10
"Crimson Green" .... 1994 .... $10
Charles T. Zimmerman:
"Sixty Years Of Hartford Golf Club
1896-1955" .... 1955 .... $65
Russell H. Zimmerman:
"Westmoor Country Club, Sixty Years of
Family Fellowship and Sport".............. 1987 .... $45
Zodiac Home Golf Ball Booklet:
"Golf And How To Play It" .... 1910 .... $125
Joseph M. Zogbie:
"Golf Club Directory of 1947"..................... 1947 .... $30
Desond Zwar:
"Golf: The Dictionary".............................. 1984 .... $15

Thousands of color book illustrations visible at
www.rogeregilchrist.com

www.ingramcontent.com/pod-product-compliance
Lightning Source LLC
Chambersburg PA
CBHW060244100426
42742CB00011B/1640